JOHN TYLER

CHAMPION OF THE OLD SOUTH

Photograph by Mr. H. P. Cook, Richmond, Virginia, from a portrait by Hart in the Virginia State Library.

JOHN TYLER

JOHN TYLER

CHAMPION OF THE OLD SOUTH

BY

OLIVER PERRY CHITWOOD

NEW YORK

RUSSELL & RUSSELL · INC

1964

PRINTED IN THE UNITED STATES OF AMERICA

TO AGNES

FOREWORD

WHEN Professor Chitwood says in the course of this
biography that John Tyler "holds a unique place in
the history of misrepresentation," he piques curiosity; and
when he exposes the extent of that misrepresentation, he il-
lumines a dark chapter in American annals. He calls for a reversal of judgment as complete as that in the case of Andrew
Johnson. The fundamental ground for that reversal in the
high court of time is the fact that Tyler held to an ideal of
political consistency in an era of change. Earlier verdicts
against him were founded, so to say, on the testimony of
witnesses who were themselves subject to sudden and illogical
shifts of opinion. They could not credit Tyler with the formu-
lation of a political creed to which, disdainful of consequences,
he would unswervingly adhere to the last hours of his life.

I well remember when, as a young student, I first encountered close up the gaunt figure of Ex-President Tyler. At the
time I was investigating the secession of Virginia and, day by
day, was following in the newspapers the story of the turbu-
lent events of the later winter of 1860–61. The Richmond
journals reported the movements of the Ex-President and,
in respectful admiration, set the stage for his appearance in
the convention that was to decide the portentous issue of adherence to the Union or association with the Southern States.
So much importance seemed to be attached to the advice he
was expected to give the convention that I became curious
to know what he was to say. After more than thirty-five years,
I recall now the disappointment with which I read his vehement and unqualified plea for immediate secession. His
seemed the gloomiest of the "ancestral voices, prophesying
war." Had I been even a little acquainted at the time with his

political creed and code I would have realized that, after the
failure of the Peace Conference, his creed left him no alternative to secession and his code offered no honorable recourse
except to self-defence. His vote for secession was followed,
most significantly at Jamestown of all places, by his offer to
bear arms for Virginia, though he was then past seventy-one.
The two acts were the Q. E. D. of his theorem of government.

While it may be presumptuous to add to Dr. Chitwood's
judicial balancing of the evidence in Chapter XVII concerning Tyler's action on the bank bills, I believe a reminder of
the precise character of Tyler's political consistency may help
to clarify the evidence. He was a nexus between the revolu-
tionaries and the nationalists. Born just a year after the first
inauguration of Washington, and in attendance at Jefferson's
own Alma Mater while the political system of the third president was taking form, John Tyler was reared in the strictest
sect of Virginia Republicans. He was not a man to regard
himself as the custodian of a tradition, but he was a man to
adhere with singular tenacity to that tradition. If he was not
its missioner, he was its exemplar. The Mishnah and the Ge-
mara of the Talmud of strict construction alike were sacred
in his eyes. Clay and the other Whigs knew his record. It had
been expounded in scores of speeches. He felt that when they
had supported him, they had taken him for what he was.
He never thought for a moment that he should be—for he
could not be—what they wanted him to be in his construction
of the powers of the Federal government. In the critical clash
with the Whigs, the difference between the bill presented to
him and the bill transmitted for his signature, though slight,
well may have been, in his eyes, the difference between that
which was justified and that which was dangerous.

By portraying Tyler faithfully and clearly, Dr. Chitwood
has made all of us his debtors. He is to be congratulated on
his success in finding much material that had been lost. A
Federal soldier, upon whose report I happened to stumble,
wrote late in the War between the States of a visit to "Sher-

wood Forest," where, he said, the floor was ankle-deep in papers of the Ex-President that soldiers had plundered The beloved Lyon G. Tyler spent years of his life in studying the manuscripts that were saved and in collecting other memorials of his father. Since Dr. Lyon Tyler's death in 1935 his gracious widow has continued that family service. Dr. Chitwood has profited in his scholarly labors by what the devoted descendants of the misrepresented President have done to keep the faith.

DOUGLAS SOUTHALL FREEMAN

TABLE OF CONTENTS

PREFACE

JOHN TYLER'S place in history is still under dispute. Historians of today are not in agreement as to the reasons for his behavior in his quarrel with the Whig Party. Some think that in vetoing the bank bills he was acting from patriotic motives, while others consider that he was betraying his party in a selfish effort to win the succession. For example, a late historian of rank regarded Tyler as a prevaricator and his constitutional distinctions not worthy of refutation, "being of the flimsiest texture, cobwebs crossed by cobwebs." [1] On the other hand, another recent historian, with a reputation for scholarly fairness, expressed the view that Tyler "was actuated in the main by courage and consistency," and that "he acquitted himself in his quarrel with the Whigs only as might have been expected from a brave and determined man and a stanch believer in State rights." [2] Such divergence in opinion shows that the question as to whether he was a patriotic statesman or a disloyal politician has as yet never found a satisfactory answer. The problem should be solved or the impossibility of finding a solution should be demonstrated. The performance of this task is one of the major objectives of the present work.

In the preparation of this volume I have read all the letters to and from John Tyler in the Tyler collections of papers

---

[1] James Schouler, *History of the United States* (New York, 1894–1913), IV, 390.

[2] George P. Garrison, *Westward Extension, 1841–1850* (New York, 1906), 64–65.

Favorable views of Tyler are also presented by F. J. Turner in *The United States, 1830–1850* (New York, 1935); G. R. Poage in *Henry Clay and the Whig Party* (Chapel Hill, 1936); and H. R. Fraser in *Democracy in the Making* (Indianapolis, 1938). O. D. Lambert, in *Presidential Politics in the United States, 1841–1844* (Durham, N. C., 1936), upholds the unfavorable view.

and all of those that have been found in other collections. His record in the Virginia Assembly, both houses of Congress, the Virginia Convention of 1829–30, the Virginia Convention of 1861, and the Provisional Congress of the Confederacy have been carefully studied. Not only have all his speeches been read, in so far as they have been reported, but his vote on all important questions in these bodies has been noted wherever the yeas and nays are recorded. A careful analysis has also been made of all his messages to Congress while President. I have also read a number of addresses that he delivered and newspaper articles that he wrote while in retirement. For contemporary opinion regarding his public policies and sidelights on his private life, as well as his public career, I have perused a number of newspapers and the diaries of public men who were brought in contact with Tyler.

I feel, therefore, that there has been assembled virtually all the evidence now available which has any significant bearing on the public and private life of John Tyler. The destruction of his papers in the fire at Richmond during the War of Secession, of course, created a gap in the documents which it is difficult to bridge. From other sources of information, however, we are able to derive a correct, if not a full, narrative of his career.

I wish to express my appreciation of the courtesy shown and the obliging assistance given me by the officials and employees of the Library of Congress, where most of the material for the study was collected. I also acknowledge my indebtedness for valued assistance rendered in the preparation of this work by the following persons: Doctor Douglas S. Freeman, Editor of the Richmond *News-Leader*, who contributed the Foreword; Professor James S. Wilson, of the University of Virginia, for a useful constructive criticism of two chapters; Professor Thomas J. Wertenbaker, of Princeton University, and Doctor David D. Johnson, Head of the Department of English, West Virginia University, both of whom read the entire manuscript and made many helpful suggestions; the late Doctor Lyon G. Tyler, son of President Tyler, for information given in a personal interview and in answer to a questionnaire; Mrs. Pearl Tyler Ellis, only surviving daughter of the President, for interesting statements regarding the later career of her mother; Mrs. Lyon G. Tyler, for her gracious courtesy in allowing me a free use of the valuable manuscripts in her home ("Lion's Den") in Charles City County, Virginia; Mr. and Mrs. George P. Coleman, who kindly gave me access to the large and important collection of Tucker Papers in their home at Williamsburg; and Mr. J. Alfred Tyler, to whose hospitality I owed the opportunity of inspecting the house in which his grandfather, the ex-President, spent his last years. I wish also to thank Mrs. Helen Bullock, of Colonial Williamsburg, Incorporated, and Dr. Earl G. Swem, Librarian of the College of William and Mary, who aided me in gathering data from the archives in their custody. My thanks are also due to the following persons, by the assistance of whom I was able to procure transcripts and photostatic copies of letters not in the Tyler collections of papers: Professor Fletcher M. Green, of the University of North Carolina; the late Professor W. K. Boyd, of Duke University; Mr. Frederick S. Peck, of Providence, R. I.; Miss Norma Cuthbert, of the Henry E. Huntington Library; and Mr. K. D. Metcalf, of the New York Public Library.

The Committee on the Carnegie Revolving Fund of the American Historical Association has assumed financial responsibility for the publication of this work. For this generous aid the author wishes to express deep appreciation.

JOHN TYLER

CHAMPION OF THE OLD SOUTH

CHAPTER I

A REPUBLICAN JUDGE

ONE spring day in 1765 two law students with a flair for politics drifted into the Capitol in old Williamsburg to hear the discussions of the Burgesses. This happened to be the occasion on which Patrick Henry delivered his bold philippic against the Stamp Act. They were thrilled with the eloquence and glowing patriotism of the speech, especially that part of it in which George III was warned against incurring the fate of Caesar and Charles I.[1]

One of these young men was Thomas Jefferson and the other was his friend and roommate, John Tyler. The latter was so deeply impressed with this oration that from this time until his death he was an ardent republican. His opinions were embarrassing to his conservative father, who held office under the royal government and whose bread and butter, therefore, were tied up with loyalty to the crown. When the young hotspur would repeat with approval the heated effusions of the eloquent Henry, the elder Tyler would shake his head and warn his son of the danger of defying a government as powerful as that of the British empire. He is reported as having said: "Ah! John, they will hang you for a rebel. They will hang you yet." [2]

These forebodings were not realized, and John junior enjoyed a long public career under a new political regime which he had helped to establish. He became a successful lawyer and for many years had a comfortable seat on the

[1] William Wirt, *Sketches of the Life and Character of Patrick Henry* (Philadelphia, 1817), 60–61, 65.
[2] L. G. Tyler, *Letters and Times of the Tylers* (Richmond, 1884–96), I, 56. This work will afterwards be cited as *Letters and Times.*

3

bench. For this reason he is generally known as Judge Tyler.

At the beginning of the Revolution Williamsburg was the intellectual and social, as well as the political, capital of the Old Dominion. Though small of size and of no commercial importance, it was the center around which rotated the charming social life of the Virginia aristocracy. After the removal of the capital to Richmond, Williamsburg fell into obscurity and its former glory was largely forgotten by the outside world. But the beauty in which it was arrayed when it recently emerged from its chrysalis has impressively reminded us of its old-time splendor.

Williamsburg reached the zenith of its importance about the time Judge Tyler attained his majority. At this period a circle of fifty miles radius circumscribed about it would have enclosed as many patrician families as could have been found in any rural section of equal area in the western hemisphere. This favored region literally swarmed with "F.F.V's." Henry A. Wise lists no less than twenty prominent families in the Peninsula (the group of counties between the James and York Rivers). Recent scholarship has cast doubt on the claim that these old families were mainly descended from the English gentry, followers of Charles I, who had emigrated to the Old Dominion when that ill-fated monarch lost his throne and his head. But whether these families inherited or achieved their social eminence there is no doubt that by this time they possessed it. With them life had the charm and refinement of an old civilization without its pessimistic sophistication. The idealism of the Revolution had left traces of liberalism which imparted to the people a buoyant hopefulness. Besides, the frontier was still close enough to serve as a source of democratic ideas and an exuberant optimism.

High on the roll of the Virginia patriciate stood the name of the Tyler family, which had been closely identified with Williamsburg and the Peninsula since its emigration from England about the middle of the seventeenth century. Judge

Tyler could boast of a line of long descent, which, according to tradition, went back to an ancestor who had come to England with William the Conqueror and had aided him in depriving the Saxons of their liberty. His son, the President, was not proud of this progenitor, for he regarded the Norman Conquest as a "scurvy trick." [3] A reputed forbear of a different type was Wat Tyler, the blacksmith who headed a revolt against the poll tax in the reign of Richard II. There is no evidence to connect the Tylers of Virginia with this bold insurgent, but both the President and his father (though probably in jest) laid claim to descent from the courageous English rebel.[4] Certainly John Tyler, Sr., bold rebel and stern republican as he was, had a right to claim spiritual descent from Wat Tyler, even though the genealogical connection cannot be established.

The first of the Virginia Tylers was Henry, who came over from England about the middle of the seventeenth century. He obtained a grant of two hundred and fifty-four acres of land on January 7, 1653, and located at Middle Plantation, now Williamsburg.[5] According to Dr. Lyon G. Tyler, Henry Tyler was a Cavalier and had left England because the royalists had been defeated and England had been brought under Puritan control.[6] Henry Tyler had acquired by his death (1672) quite a landed estate and apparently was rated as a man of prominence in the community.[7] By his second wife, Ann Orchard, he had three sons, Henry, John, and Daniel.

Henry, the oldest of the three, was a man of comfortable estate and was able to play a useful part in the public life

---

[3] *John Tyler Papers* (Library of Congress), IV, 6761. Papers in the Library of Congress will hereafter be designated by the initials L.C.

[4] Tyler, *Letters and Times,* I, 38, note, 39–40; Tyler to John Ward Dean, Dec. 19, 1859; MS., Henry E. Huntington Library.

[5] *Virginia Land Register,* III, 165.

[6] There is, however, no evidence to support this claim except that Henry Tyler left the homeland shortly after the royalist cause had gone down in defeat both in England and Virginia. Tyler, *op. cit.,* I, 41–42.

[7] *York County Records,* Book I (Deeds, Orders, and Wills), 271; Book II, 122.

of the colony. A portion of the land that Henry Tyler II had inherited from his father was bought by the provincial government and on it was located the royal palace after the capital was moved from Jamestown to Williamsburg.[8] In 1699 he, Governor Nicholson, Benjamin Harrison, and others were chosen as a committee to superintend the settlement and building of the embryonic metropolis of Williamsburg.[9]

President John Tyler was fourth in descent from Henry Tyler II. The son, grandson, and great-grandson of the latter, who constituted the connecting links between Henry Tyler and his noted descendant, were all named John, and all of them lived in or near Williamsburg. Of these three Johns the most prominent was the third—the father of the President. He was a man of strong convictions and prejudices, both of which he expressed with utter fearlessness. In giving vent to his feelings regarding public questions he was not restrained by considerations of diplomacy to the same extent as was the younger Tyler. For this reason he leaves the impression of having had a more vigorous and picturesque personality than that possessed by his distinguished son.

The elder Tyler, like the younger, was educated at William and Mary College. While reading law in Williamsburg under Robert Carter Nicholas, he formed a warm attachment for Thomas Jefferson, who was prosecuting his legal studies under George Wythe. The fact that Jefferson was his senior by four years no doubt added a tinge of reverence to the affection in which Tyler held him. At all events this friendship endured throughout life, deriving strength from the virtual agreement of the two men on all important public questions.

After finishing his law studies, Tyler went to the adjoining county of Charles City to enter upon his profession. A few years later (1776) he married Mary, the only

[8] W. W. Hening, *Statutes at Large* (Va.), 13 vols. (1819–23), 285.
[9] *Ibid.*, 197, 285, 428, 431.

daughter of Robert Armistead, of Buck-Rowe, a prominent planter in Elizabeth City County. Soon after his marriage he took up his residence at "Greenway," near Charles City Courthouse, and here he spent the remainder of his life.

In the spring of 1778, he entered the Virginia House of Delegates, and served as a member of that body for eight years in succession (1778–86). His usefulness in the legislature is attested by the fact that during four of these years he held the position of Speaker of the House of Delegates. In one of the elections for the speakership he was nominated by Patrick Henry, and was able to win over so formidable an opponent as Richard Henry Lee.[10]

It was Tyler who offered (in the session of 1785–86) the resolution written by Madison calling the Annapolis Convention.[11] As it was at the suggestion of the Annapolis Convention that the Constitutional Convention met in Philadelphia in 1787, Tyler thus played an important part in inaugurating the movement which led to the adoption of the Federal Constitution. He was also a member of the Virginia Convention of 1788, and in this convention he took a decided stand against the ratification of the Federal Constitution.

For three years he served as a judge of the Virginia Court of Admiralty, and for twenty years as a member of the General Court, which was the highest criminal court in the State. Judges in this court were also *ex officio* members of the Supreme Court of Appeals, the highest civil tribunal in Virginia. In 1812 he was appointed judge of the United States District Court for Virginia, and he held this position until his death, a year or more later (1813).

Tyler's career as a judge was interrupted by his election to the governorship in 1808. He was chosen governor for three successive terms, as many as the constitution permitted

---

[10] *Journal of the Virginia House of Delegates*, 1778, 4.
[11] John Tyler to John C. Hamilton, July 14, 1855; *John Tyler Papers* (L.C.), IV, 6712–13.

without an interval of four years. He did not serve out his
last term, as he resigned to accept the Federal judgeship
mentioned above. When he resigned as governor his friend,
James Monroe, was selected in his place.

Judge Tyler was an ardent admirer of Patrick Henry
and named both a daughter (Maria Henry) and a son (Wat
Henry) in honor of the great Revolutionary leader. The
association of Tyler with Patrick Henry has been embel-
lished by tradition with an interesting story, which is strictly
historical in its setting even if it is not factual in all its
details. Tyler and Henry were in 1781 members of the
Virginia House of Delegates. Cornwallis was in control of
the territory around Richmond, the capital of the State,
and so the legislature convened at Charlottesville, a village
about eighty miles northwest of Richmond. Cornwallis com-
missioned Colonel Tarleton to advance to Charlottesville
and capture the members of the legislature and seize the
governor, Thomas Jefferson, at his home near Charlottesville.

Tarleton's plans were discovered and so both Jefferson
and the assembly were notified just in the nick of time. The
assembly hastily adjourned and the members, going in small
groups, betook themselves to precipitate flight. One of these
fleeing groups consisted of John Tyler, Patrick Henry, Colonel William Christian, and Benjamin Harrison. It thus included, besides the great orator of the Revolution, a signer
of the Declaration of Independence and a father and a
father-to-be of two future Presidents of the United States.
Harrison, who by signing the famous Declaration had de-
fied the scaffold, was now taking no chances with the halter,
and Henry, who on a former occasion had preferred death
to a loss of liberty, was now avoiding the risk of death with
an alacrity hardly in keeping with the unrestrained daring
of his utterances on a former occasion.

Greatness in retreat rarely presents an imposing appearance, and these noted statesmen in their undignified flight

apparently did not impress the people of the countryside with the respect and awe which under more favorable circumstances they would have had no difficulty in inspiring. At least, one patriotic but free-spoken woman of the hills, according to the traditional account, was not overawed by their presence, but on the contrary was strongly disposed to rebuke them for having acted, as she considered, in cowardly fashion. The story is as follows:

Late in the day, Messrs. Henry, Tyler, Harrison, and Christian, who had ridden together, fatigued and hungry, stopped their horses at the door of a small hut, in a gorge of the hills, and asked for refreshment. A woman, the sole occupant of the house, inquired of them who they were, and where from. "We are members of the Legislature," said Mr. Henry, "and have just been compelled to leave Charlottesville on account of the approach of the enemy." "Ride on, then, ye cowardly knaves," replied the old woman, in a tone of excessive indignation; "here have my husband and sons just gone to Charlottesville to fight for ye, and you running away with all your might. Clear out— ye shall have nothing here." "But," Mr. Henry rejoined, in an expostulating tone, "we were obliged to fly. It would not do for the Legislature to be broken up by the enemy. Here is Mr. Speaker Harrison; you don't think he would have fled had it not been necessary?" "I always thought a great deal of Mr. Harrison till now," the old woman answered; "but he'd no business to run from the enemy," and she was about to shut the door in their faces. "Wait a moment, my good woman," again interposed Mr. Henry; "you would hardly believe that Mr. Tyler or Colonel Christian would take to flight if there were not good cause for so doing?" "No, indeed, that I wouldn't," she replied. "But Mr. Tyler and Colonel Christian are here," said he. "They here! Well, I never would have thought it," and she stood a moment as if in doubt, but finally added, "no matter; we love those gentlemen, and I didn't suppose they would ever run away from the British; but since they have, they shall have nothing to eat in my house. You may ride along." As a last resort, Mr. Tyler then stepped forward and said, "What would you say, my good woman, if I were to tell you that Patrick Henry fled with the rest of us?" "Patrick Henry! I would tell ye there wasn't a word of truth in it," she answered angrily; "Patrick Henry would never do such a cowardly thing." "But this *is* Mr. Henry," rejoined Mr. Tyler, pointing him out. The old woman looked astonished. After a moment's consideration, and a convulsive twitch or two at her apron string, by way of recovering her scattered thoughts, she said, "Well, then, if that's Patrick Henry, *it must be all right*. Come in, and ye shall have the best I have in the house." [12]

Judge Tyler had an interesting and beautiful family life. He was fond of children and his home was generally alive with them. In addition to his three sons and five daughters, he reared twenty-one children for whom he was guardian. His wife died in April, 1797, and he never married again. He was in comfortable financial circumstances at the time he was rearing his numerous family. He owned plantations in James City and Charles City counties which aggregated more than nineteen hundred acres. He also had some mineral lands in Kentucky, which his son John afterwards sold for $20,000.00.[13] Patents were obtained for a large area of land in what is now West Virginia. This seems not to have been considered very valuable, however, as his heirs failed to pay the taxes on it and allowed it to revert to the commonwealth.[14] The home estate was located in Charles City County on the James River about midway between Richmond and Williamsburg. This estate included "Greenway," the main plantation, with two other farms adjoining it, with a total of 1200 acres of land.[15]

The mansion house at "Greenway" was a "genteel, well-furnished dwelling," a story and a half high, with six good-sized rooms. It was surrounded by a regular village of outbuildings, including a study, storehouse, kitchen, laundry, dairy, meathouse, icehouse, barn, two granaries, two carriage houses, twenty stalls for horses, an octagonal pigeon-house well stocked, a quarter for house servants, and several

[12] For this story, see [A. G. Abell], *Life of John Tyler* (New York, 1843), 10.
[13] See p. 417.
[14] Letter from John Tyler to Jonathan M. Bennett, Nov. 14, 1860; MS., Library of West Virginia University.
[15] Tyler, *Letters and Times*, I, 188–190, note.

other houses for slaves. The dwelling was located on a slight
eminence about a mile from the James River. An avenue
bordered on each side by cedars led up to the gate of the
front yard, which was adorned by a profusion of beautiful
flowers. Near the house there was a large willow tree, which
afforded an attractive area of shade in hot weather. This
spot was the favorite resort of the judge in the summertime.
Under this tree he entertained his children with tunes played
on his violin and with stories of the Revolutionary days.
Behind the house was a garden of shrubs and flowers, and
beyond it were broad level acres of land well suited to wheat,
corn, tobacco, and pasture. For the cultivation of these acres
and for attendance upon the personal wants of the inmates
of the mansion house and their guests there were on hand
more than forty obedient slaves.[16] This was the setting in
which the childhood and youth of a future President were
cast. For it was at "Greenway" that John, his sixth child and
second son, was born and reared.

[16] The above account of "Greenway" and surrounding lands was taken
from an advertisement which Judge Tyler had inserted in the Richmond
Enquirer, September 10, 1805. At that time he advertised his lands and slaves
for sale with the expectation of moving to Williamsburg, where two of his
sons were at college. He gives a minute description of these farms and their
buildings. This account has been supplemented with data obtained from Dr.
L. G. Tyler's *Letters and Times of the Tylers,* and from personal observations
made at "Greenway." The old mansion house and a few of the outbuildings
are still standing and are in a fair state of preservation.

CHAPTER II

HOME, SCHOOL AND OFFICE

THE childhood and youth of President John Tyler are largely veiled in obscurity. In extant letters and papers are very few references to his early life. There is almost an entire absence of the myths with which tradition usually fills in the gaps in the careers of noted men. It is more than likely, however, that his boyhood was not substantially different from that of other young scions of the Tidewater aristocracy of that day. Of one thing we may be sure—that he unconsciously imbibed many of the prejudices and convictions of a father whose personality was characterized by rugged individuality and whose patriotism was deeply tinged with localism. The greatest misfortune of his childhood was the death of his mother, which occurred when he was seven years old. But the lavish affection which Judge Tyler bestowed upon young John was in large measure a compensation for the loss of a mother's love and care.

During the early years of his life the future President exhibited few, if any, characteristics that gave promise of extraordinary eminence in the future. It is true that he was precocious and very good-looking, but these traits do not always augur exceptional success in later life. As a school boy he had "a slender frame, a very prominent thin Roman nose, silky brown hair, a bright blue eye, a merry mischievous smile and silvery laugh." [1] His personality apparently embodied more of the gentle virtues of his mother than the stern qualities of his father.

This smoothness and gentleness of character—the ability

[1] Tyler, *Letters and Times,* I, 198-199.

to make contacts with others with as little friction as possible —was a marked trait in Tyler's personality throughout his entire life. It was in some respects, however, a liability rather than an asset. As it covered up the sturdiness of his character, it at times hid from view a strength of will for which politicians and the general public failed to give him full credit.

So amiable and docile was he as a child that an overanxious parent might have feared a leaning toward effeminacy. This anxiety would have been groundless; for underneath the gentleness and softness was much of the granite which was conspicuous in the character of his father. That the bold spirit of the elder Tyler sometimes blazed out in his son is shown by an incident which occurred when the latter was about ten years old. Young Tyler and other boys in the neighborhood were attending a school kept by a Mr. Mc-Murdo, a Scotchman, who imposed a Spartan discipline. His rule over his pupils was so severe that, as President Tyler afterwards said, "it was a wonder that he did not whip all the sense out of his scholars." Finally his tyranny reached the point at which forbearance on the part of his pupils ceased to be a virtue, and they rose in revolt. Young Tyler headed this miniature rebellion.

The boys, after throwing McMurdo down, proceeded to tie his hands and feet. The victory having been won, the boys locked the door with their victim firmly bound within. He remained in this uncomfortable and humiliating position until late in the afternoon, when a passing traveler found and released him.

McMurdo was naturally very indignant and went at once to Judge Tyler and urged that he punish his son for the part he had played in this affair. But the Judge was too strong a hater of tyranny to take sides with an overbearing schoolmaster who had been manhandled by his students. Accordingly, he sent him away with this answer—"*Sic Semper Tyrannis!*"—the motto of Virginia. Judge Tyler must have been as surprised as he was gratified to learn that his mild-mannered son was proving himself a "chip off the old block." [2]

It is unfortunate that there are no apocryphal stories interwoven with the brief narrative of Tyler's youth, for no opportunity is afforded his biographers of exercising their skill in "debunking" the accepted account of his early life. He seems never to have sown any wild oats nor to have acquired in young manhood any habits that could hamper his career. The dim picture of Tyler as a boy that has come down to us—the outlines of which can be perceived only by a vigorous exercise of the imagination—represents him as a youth who accepted without question or protest the social ideals of his day. In this sketch appear no lineaments indicating that aggressive nonconformity and breezy individuality which made his father's personality so interesting.

Few men in American public life have been more fortunate both as to heredity and environment than was John Tyler. His mother, Mary Armistead, belonged to a family that has played a very worthy rôle in Virginia history. His father was the most eminent of a line of successful progenitors who had for several generations been leaders in the plantation life of the Peninsula. Though not a wealthy man according to modern standards, Judge Tyler was able to give his sons the best educational opportunities that the country afforded.

In 1802 young John entered the preparatory school of William and Mary College at the early age of twelve. A year or so later, probably in 1804, he entered the college proper and was graduated in 1807, a few months after his seventeenth birthday.[3] He delivered an address on Female Education at commencement time. To us it would seem almost like an impossible feat to compose an eloquent discourse on such a prosaic subject, and yet we are told that in the unanimous opinion of the faculty it was "the best com-

[2] Tyler, *Letters and Times,* I, 199–200.
[3] *John Tyler Papers* (L.C.), III, 6686.

mencement oration, both in style and matter, ever delivered at that institution within their recollection." [4]

We know almost nothing of Tyler's college life, as no letters written by him at this time are now extant. Even tradition relates no college pranks or thrilling violations of the rules of the institution. It is quite probable that he never disturbed the conventional decorum that had settled down upon the old college, for we are told that he was a great favorite of the president, Bishop James Madison.[5]

His father, however, did not view his progress at William and Mary with unqualified approval. Writing to his son while the latter was in his senior year, the elder Tyler took him seriously to task for his delinquency in one important particular. This rebuke was not for any misconduct or lack of application in his studies, but for his poor penmanship. In this letter, the Judge expressed his disapproval vigorously, as was his wont. He said: "I can't help telling you how much I am mortified to find no improvement in your handwriting, neither do you connect your lines straight, which makes your letters look so abominable. It is an easy thing to correct this fault, and unless you do so how can you be fit for law business of every description? Look at the handwriting of Mr. Jefferson, Wythe, Pendleton, Mercer, Nicholas, and all the old lawyers, and you will find how much care they took to write handsomely. Writing and

[4] Tyler, *Letters and Times,* I, 203.
According to tradition, this address was not entirely to the liking of Bishop Madison, the president of the college, who considered that it was overloaded with high-flown expressions. With the view to eliminating these the president, when the speech was delivered in old Bruton Parish Church, insisted on taking his stand at the end of the auditorium to indicate by signs what should be left out. But the young orator would not heed these suggestions, despite the wild gesticulations made by the bishop with hands and cane. This florid style was, however, acceptable to the audience, which greeted him at the close with a flattering ovation. *William and Mary College Quarterly Historical Magazine* (first series), III, 178, note.
[5] H. A. Wise, *Seven Decades of the Union,* 32–33.

cyphering well are absolutely necessary and cannot be dispensed with." [6]

This letter must have had the desired effect or else the paternal solicitude of the elder Tyler had exaggerated the badness of his son's penmanship. For in the letters that have come down to us from President Tyler the writing is very legible, more so than is the case with that of most of his contemporaries in public life.

John Tyler was closely associated with the College of William and Mary throughout his entire career, and he always had a strong affection for this venerable institution. The identification of the Tylers with William and Mary was a family tradition. Two of President Tyler's aunts had married professors in the college,[7] and his father and grandfather [8] had been students there. His father also served for a time as a member of the Board of Visitors. Two sons of President Tyler were students at William and Mary and another (Dr. Lyon G. Tyler) was for a number of years president of the institution.

To what extent Tyler's training at William and Mary influenced his education we cannot speak with positive assurance. In his student days the college was not in a very flourishing condition. It had an endowment of about $130,000, and was manned by a few instructors, who spent their time in teaching mathematics, the classics, and other subjects of a purely cultural nature. During the period between the Revolution and the War of Secession the number of matriculates never exceeded one hundred and forty, and the general average (exclusive of the grammar school) from the beginning to 1859 was not more than sixty. "Of the number of sands upon the shore of time, she boasts not, but of those rare and precious gems, which have been garnered from

[6] *John Tyler Papers* (L.C.), I, 8217.
[7] *William and Mary College Quarterly* (first series), III, 139–140.
[8] *Virginia Gazette,* September 2, 1773.

their midst, and which shine and will shine forever on her illumined brow." [9]

At first thought, it would seem that such an institution could not afford the proper preparation for life in any age. And yet this little college has had on its roster of students a list of names of which even the larger universities of to-day might well be proud. Tyler's college mates included William S. Archer, Chapman Johnson, Winfield Scott, Benjamin Watkins Leigh, John W. Jones, P. P. Barbour, William C. Rives, and John J. Crittenden.[10] This group, Tyler included, had to its credit in later life the following honors and achievements: One (Winfield Scott) became a distinguished general, the hero of two wars, and in 1852 was the nominee of the Whig Party for the Presidency; six served in the United States Senate; one sat on the bench as a justice of the Supreme Court of the United States; one (Crittenden) became a member of the President's Cabinet; and one was elevated to the Presidency of the United States.

The amount of information acquired by the students could not have been great. But somehow they learned from their professors, or imbibed from the atmosphere of the place, a taste for good reading and an ambition to learn, which ultimately brought them in contact with the cultural savings of the past. The college pointed out to her students the road to Athens and Rome, and impressed them with the fact that these ancient cities were centers of a culture that was worthy of their serious interest. Political economy was also taught at that time, and the text for the course was Adam Smith's *Wealth of Nations*. From the sentiments expressed by him in his speeches in Congress, we infer that Tyler's views on the economic questions of his day were

[9] This statement was made by John Tyler in an address delivered in 1859 over the charred ruins of the main building, which had been burnt a few months before. The text of this address is given in full in *DeBow's Review*, XXVII (July, 1859). See especially pages 145–146.

[10] Tyler, *Letters and Times*, I, 203–204; Richmond *Examiner*, Mar. 15, 1861.

greatly influenced by the concepts of this masterly treatise.

After leaving college the more ambitious of these young men continued to read and study along the lines chalked out for them by their instructors. In this way such men as Tyler became well acquainted with the history and literature of the Greeks and the Romans. They also acquired a fine appreciation of the masterpieces of English literature. Evidence of Tyler's familiarity with Greek and Roman history and the English classics is found in the numerous references to them in his public utterances and private letters.[11] He advised his daughter Mary to study Roman and Greek history and to read the works of Milton, Pope, Johnson, Gray, Goldsmith, and Addison. "Addison," he wrote, "is considered the best writer in the English language. . . . He paints virtue in her most lovely colors, and makes each sensitive mind her lover and admirer." [12]

He also read Hume's and Smollett's histories of England and Sidney's treatise on government. He regarded Hume and Swift, as well as Addison, as models of style.[13] He must have received a greater thrill from reading than does the average educated man of today, for he speaks of being so interested in Bulwer's new novel, *Eugene Aram,* that he sat up until twelve o'clock one night to read it. He considered it "deeply and painfully interesting." [14] If this rather commonplace novel could enlist his interest to the extent of causing him to keep such late hours, he must have been easy to please in the matter of reading.

Tyler was a youth of eighteen when his father went to Richmond to assume the duties of the governorship. The town did not present the appearance that one would expect from the capital of a proud commonwealth. The population was at that time only about nine thousand,[15] and in outward

---

[11] *John Tyler Papers* (L.C.), III, 6545, 6560, 6616.
[12] Tyler, *Letters and Times,* I, 546, 548–549, 550.
[13] *Ibid.,* 426–428.   [14] *Ibid.,* 555.
[15] The population as given by the census of 1810 was 9735. *Fifteenth Census of the United States:* 1930, I. Population, 19.

aspect the place was a small town rather than a city. "The surface on which the city stood was untamed and broken. Almost inaccessible heights and deep ravines everywhere prevailed. . . . The two now [1858] beautiful valleys were then unsightly gullies, which threatened, unless soon arrested, to extend themselves across the street north, so as to require a bridge to span them. . . . The street west of the [Capitol] Square was impassable much of the way, except by a foot-path. . . . The streets were unpaved, and sad was the fate of the unlucky wight who, otherwise than on horseback, undertook to pass through the lower part of the city."

The governor's mansion was called "the Palace," although it by no means merited this designation. It was a modest two-story frame building badly in need of repair. It "neither aspired to architectural taste in its construction or consulted the comforts of its occupant in its interior arrangements." [16] In a message to the legislature (December 3, 1810) Governor Tyler pointed out the inadequacy of the mansion as a place of residence for the governor's family and recommended the erection of a new building. "The present situation," he said, "is intolerable for a private family, there being not a foot of ground that is not exposed to three streets, besides a cluster of dirty tenements immediately in front of the house, with their windows opening into the enclosure." [17]

In this small unpainted house, despite its shabby appearance and cramped accommodations, the governor often entertained distinguished visitors. Some months after retiring from the Presidency (October, 1809), Jefferson accepted the invitation of his old friend to be a dinner guest at the executive mansion. It was the first time young Tyler

[16] The above description of Richmond in 1808 is based on a picture of the town of that date as given by Tyler in an address in Richmond in 1858. For excerpts of this address, see Tyler, *op. cit.*, I, 219–225.

[17] *Journal of the Senate of the Commonwealth of Virginia*, session 1810–11, 11.

had ever seen the great statesman whom he always regarded as his political master. He was acting as majordomo at the time and was determined that every proper courtesy should be shown the distinguished guest. Accordingly, two plum puddings were ordered for dessert. When the governor saw the puddings coming in he asked in surprise if this were not extraordinary. "Yes," replied his son, "but this is an extraordinary occasion." [18]

We have reason to believe that the social eminence of Richmond was greater than its size would indicate. For there were a number of prominent families residing in the town, and the interchange of hospitality among them must have been delightful. That John junior, with his handsome face and Chesterfieldian manners, cut a wide swath in this exclusive circle goes without saying. And yet we have no real knowledge of his social activities except that he belonged to a literary society which had been organized by the young men of the town as a means to cultivating their forensic abilities. One of the members of this group was Abel P. Upshur.[19] This association was the beginning of a friendship that later bound these two men into close personal and political affiliation. Little did they think at the time that one of them was to be called to the highest office in the land and the other to be associated with him as his premier.

After graduating from William and Mary, Tyler began to read law under the direction of his father. He also received valuable assistance in his studies from his cousin, Chancellor Samuel Tyler. When his father became governor, he continued his legal studies in Richmond under the guidance of Edmund Randolph, who had been Attorney General and Secretary of State under Washington.[20] The atmosphere of Richmond was conducive to the study of the law, as its bar was one of the most distinguished in the country. Among its lawyers the names of William Wirt,

---

[18] Tyler, *Letters and Times*, I, 229–230.
[19] *Ibid.*, II, 388.   [20] Tyler, *op. cit.*, 221.

Edmund Randolph, and John Marshall were particularly outstanding. Tyler seems to have been assiduous in his legal studies and to have taken full advantage of his good op-portunities. Being anxious to enter upon his profession, he applied for and received a license to practice before he had attained the age of twenty. This was, of course, below the minimum age required for admission to the bar. The disregard of the rule in this case was due to the fact that the examining judge made no inquiries as to the age of the applicant.[21]

It was not long before Tyler was able to build up a pay-ing practice. When elected to Congress in his twenty-seventh year he was deriving from his profession an annual income of $2000. Such an amount seems large when we consider that Daniel Webster at the same age was earning between $600 and $700.[22] Tyler was particularly successful in the defense of criminals. This was due mainly to his ability to speak fluently and effectively and to appeal to the emotions of the jurymen. Success in criminal practice in that day meant more than it does at present, for criminal cases then bulked largely in the practice of the ablest lawyers.

While Tyler was studying law in Richmond he took time enough from his books to cultivate a romance that had an important bearing on his career. Soon after his graduation from William and Mary he met at a party in the neighbor-hood of "Greenway" a beautiful young lady, slightly his junior in years. She was Letitia, daughter of Robert Chris-tian, of "Cedar Grove," in New Kent County. "Cedar Grove" was on or near the road between "Greenway" and Richmond and could be reached from either place by a few hours' drive.[23] As a member of the Virginia legislature

[21] *Ibid.*, 272.
[22] Tyler to Dr. Henry Curtis, Dec. 8, 1820; *John Tyler Papers* (L.C.), I, 6256; G. T. Curtis, *Life of Daniel Webster*, 2 vols. (New York, 1870), I, 74.
[23] "Cedar Grove" is about fourteen miles from "Greenway" and eighteen or twenty from Richmond. The main part of the mansion house is still standing and is in good repair. The graveyard enclosed with a square brick wall is near

Tyler spent a part of each year in Richmond after his
father resigned the governorship (1811). In all probability
he took advantage of the trips to and from the State capital
and other similar opportunities to make visits to the Christian home. Under such favorable circumstances the acquaintanceship grew into friendship and then into mutual love.
No difficulty arose from the fact that Robert Christian was
a Federalist and young Tyler and his father were both
ardent Republicans. These attractive young people were in
every way suited to each other, and they were married at
"Cedar Grove" on Tyler's twenty-third birthday (March
29, 1813).

Only one of Tyler's love letters to his fiancée has come
down to us. Apparently he did not write many, for this one
was the first he had ever sent to her and it was not written
until the courtship had been going on for about four years.[24]
The absence of correspondence, however, does not necessarily indicate a lack of ardor in his feeling, which was
doubtless shown during numerous calls at "Cedar Grove."
This letter, while expressing strong affection, has in it no
hint of that delightful silliness that should characterize the
relations of young lovers. It is dignified in style and in places
even philosophic in tone. In fact it sounds more like the
calm statement of a middle-aged husband than the impul-
sive effusions of a romantic lover.

Tyler even approached marriage without experiencing
the fears and thrills that are generally incident to the acceptance of new responsibility. In writing to his friend and
future brother-in-law, Dr. Curtis, on March 23, 1813, he
said, "On the 29th instant I lead my Letitia to the altar. I
had really calculated on experiencing a tremor on the near
approach of the day, but I believe I am so much of the *old*

the residence. In it tombstones mark the graves of Mrs. Tyler, two of her
daughters, and other members of her family.

[24] This letter was written Dec. 5, 1812. See *John Tyler Papers* (L.C.), I,
6224; VII, 528; and Mrs. Laura (Carter) Holloway Langford, *The Ladies
of the White House,* 2 vols. (New York, 1886), II, 25–28.

man already as to feel less dismay at a change of *situation* than the greater part of those of my age." We should greatly prefer that he had thrown off the weight of his twenty-three years and looked forward to this happy event with the enthusiasm of an irresponsible youth mingled with the apprehensions of prudent maturity.

Judged by these two letters, Tyler's love-making must have been conducted strictly in accordance with the conventional rules laid down by the planter aristocracy of the day. We are confirmed in this impression by a statement repeatedly made by him that until three weeks before the wedding he had never dared so much as to kiss Letitia's hand, "so perfectly reserved and modest had she always been." One way in which he gave expression to his romantic feelings was by writing a group of sonnets, most of which were addressed to the beloved Letitia.[25] While this courtship may not have been a very thrilling one according to modern ideas, the union was a real love-match and proved to be an ideally happy one.

Chance is generally thought to have played an unusual rôle in the public career of John Tyler. If this is true, bad as well as good luck had a hand in shaping his political record. While fortune sometimes looked upon his contests in the political arena with thumbs down, she acclaimed both his marriage ventures with generous applause. For few, if any, of our public men have been more happy in the choice of their helpmeets than was this hated and maligned President.

The first Mrs. Tyler did not have a good opportunity to display her talents, for she was an invalid during the entire period of her sojourn in the White House.[26] Prior to her husband's elevation to the Presidency her life—except for the short period when she presided over the execu-

[25] Mrs. Letitia Tyler Semple to Mrs. Laura Holloway Langford; Langford, *op. cit.,* II, 29.
Mrs. Tyler was unable to appear at public functions.
[26] Esther Singleton, *The Story of the White House* (New York, 1907), 283.

tive mansion at Richmond—was spent for the most part in the quiet seclusion of her home.[27] Her social activities were generally confined to a small group of friends and neighbors, although her personal qualities and the position of her husband would have given her *entrée* to the most exclusive society of the day. Such a mode of living does not, as a rule, stamp its impress on historical documents. Moreover, in the collections of papers now available there is not a single letter from her. Consequently, we do not know as much about her as we do of the second Mrs. Tyler.

We have enough evidence, however, to uphold the traditional opinion that she was a lady of exquisite taste, strong mind and character, exceptional physical and spiritual beauty, and unusual charm of manner. Her portraits remove all doubt as to her personal attractiveness.

The high esteem in which her character was held by Tyler is revealed in a letter which he wrote to his oldest daughter Mary (1830). In giving advice as to how to improve her mind and conform to the best models of conduct, he said: "I could not hold up to you a better pattern for your imitation than is constantly presented to you by your dear mother. You never see her course marked with precipitation; but on the contrary everything is brought before the tribunal of her judgment, and her actions are all founded in prudence." [28]

Tyler's marriage was also a means of promoting his professional and political ambitions, as it strengthened his connections with the influential families of the Peninsula. For the Christians were a numerous tribe and many of them were prominent in the social and political life of the Old Dominion. Robert Christian was a man of considerable property [29] and influence. As Mrs. Tyler's parents both died

[27] For the impression she made in Washington while her husband was in the Senate, see p. 144.

[28] Tyler, *Letters and Times,* I, 546.

[29] Robert Christian's estate at "Cedar Grove" was one of 1449 acres. *Land Book of New Kent County* for 1813 (Va. State Library Archives).

soon after her marriage, the legacy received by her must
have proved a valuable aid to a young lawyer just getting
on his feet.

Tyler and his bride took up their residence at "Mons
Sacer," a plantation adjoining "Greenway," which he had
inherited from his father. Two years later he sold "Mons
Sacer" and moved to a neighboring tract. Here he erected
a comfortable residence, which he called "Woodburn."
After living at "Woodburn" for six years he purchased
"Greenway" (1821) and moved to the home of his child-
hood.[30]

The management of a Virginia plantation placed a large
measure of responsibility upon the mistress of the home. She
had to supervise not only the housekeeping and cooking,
but the making of clothes for the slaves, the nursing of the
sick, and the caring for the needs of all the inmates of the
mansion house and the dwellers on the plantation. Every
large estate was at that time not only a farming community
but to some extent an industrial plant as well. The lady in
the "big house" could make ends meet in the farm economy
only when she was an efficient entrepreneur. The success
with which Mrs. Tyler discharged this responsibility enabled her husband to support his large family on an income
which, prior to his accession to the Presidency, was never
very large. These duties and those incident to the rearing
of her seven children [31] made such demands upon her as
to leave little time for social activities other than those related to her home and neighborhood.

[30] Tyler, *op. cit.*, I, 307–308.
[31] She was the mother of nine children, two of whom died in infancy.

CHAPTER III

A YOUNG SOLON

TYLER began his long career as a statesman in the service of his beloved Virginia. In 1811, shortly after he had attained his majority, he was elected by the citizens of Charles City County as their representative in the House of Delegates, the lower house of the Virginia Assembly. His record in this body must have been quite satisfactory to his constituents, for he was chosen for five successive terms. In one of his campaigns, although he had seven opponents, he is said to have received every vote but five cast in Charles City County.[1]

Tyler served in the House of Delegates for three periods (1811–15, 1823–26, 1839). During this time the Virginia Assembly included in its membership a number of able men, and in the first two periods the House of Delegates was the more important of the two branches. This body, therefore, afforded a good arena for effective public service. This was especially the case during the first period of Tyler's incumbency, as the War of 1812 was going on during the greater portion of the time and difficult and important questions were arising.

In the journals of the House of Delegates for these years the speeches of members are not reported and only a brief outline of the proceedings is given. For this reason detailed information is not obtainable as to the part played by Tyler. The meager sources now extant clearly indicate, however, that he exerted considerable influence even from the beginning. Despite his youth and inexperience, he was put on the important Committee for Courts and Justice at the begin-

[1] [Abell], *Life of John Tyler*, 13.

ning of his first session,[2] and he retained his place on this
committee throughout the entire first period. He was also
placed on the committee that was charged with the duty of
arranging the counties into Congressional districts.[3]

To the Committee for Courts and Justice were referred a
number of petitions from freed Negroes asking permission
to remain in Virginia. In a few instances these requests were
granted, but often they were denied.[4] The manner in which
these petitions were disposed of shows that the committee
shared the opinion generally held in the South that free
Negroes were an undesirable element in any community.
Not only were they liable to become dependent upon the
public for their sustenance, but their presence in considerable
numbers was considered a menace to the peace and security
of the community. This difficulty of disposing of the freedmen was one of the great obstacles to the emancipation of
the slaves in the South, and the desire to meet this difficulty
gave rise to the unsuccessful effort to colonize free Negroes
in Africa.

Tyler had not been a member of the legislature long before he was able to commit himself very definitely on two
related political issues which played the leading part in his
public career. These were the doctrine of States' rights and
the theory as to the power of Congress to establish a national bank. The position taken by him on these two questions on this occasion were rigidly adhered to during his
entire life.

The assembly had in the session of 1810–11 instructed
the Virginia Senators in Congress to vote against a recharter
of the Bank of the United States.[5] Contrary to these instructions, the Senators, William B. Giles and Richard
Brent, had voted for a renewal of the charter. Tyler not

---

[2] *Journal of the House of Delegates of the Commonwealth of Virginia,*
session 1811–12, 5.
[3] *Ibid.,* 50.
[4] *Ibid.,* session 1811–12, 55, 56, 60–61; session 1812–13, 39, 40.
[5] *Journal, Virginia House of Delegates,* session 1810–11, 70.

only regarded the bank bill as unconstitutional, but he also
considered that the Senators in disregarding their instructions had been guilty of an unwarranted defiance of the
authority of the State. In keeping with these sentiments he
offered (January 14, 1812) three resolutions censuring the
Senators for their refusal to obey these instructions—Brent
for voting for a renewal of the charter and Giles for deny-
ing the obligatory effect of instructions emanating from the
legislature. The third resolution declared, "That the said
Richard Brent and William B. Giles did, on that occasion,
cease to be the true and legitimate representatives of this
State." [6]

Later (February 19) B. W. Leigh offered a substitute
for Tyler's resolutions, which was adopted both by the
House and the Senate. Leigh's motion contained three resolutions, which expressed disapproval of the conduct of Giles
and Brent in voting for a bank; declared in favor of the
right and duty of State legislatures to instruct Senators in
Congress on important questions; and affirmed the solemn
opinion that "no man ought henceforth to accept the appointment of a Senator of the United States from Virginia
who doth not hold himself bound to obey such instructions."
The instructions to be given and obeyed were not, however,
to require "the Senator to commit a violation of the Constitution, or an act of moral turpitude." [7] This was certainly
pushing the doctrine of States' rights to the extreme limit.
Indeed, it was reducing it to absurdity.

These unwise resolutions, by a strange irony of fate, were
at a later date a source of great embarrassment to their
authors. The principle behind them was invoked by their
enemies when Tyler and Leigh were themselves United
States Senators, and resolutions intended to instruct them
out of their seats were passed by the legislature.[8]

Early in the next session (December 8, 1812) an address
to the Senate and House of Delegates from Senator Giles

[6] *Journal, Virginia House of Delegates*, session 1811–12, 77.
[7] *Ibid.*, 155–161.   [8] See pp. 136–137.

was being read when Leigh moved that the reading be suspended and the address laid on the table. Fortunately this
unfair motion was defeated by a large majority (38 ayes
to 128 noes), but Tyler voted aye.[9] This action on the part
of Leigh and Tyler would indicate that they were not willing to give the Senators a hearing. Such an unsportsmanlike
attitude was not in keeping with Tyler's general record,
for, as a rule, he was inclined to deal with opponents in a
spirit of fair play.

The States' rights feeling in Virginia did not in the least
hamper the legislature in its efforts to uphold the Union in
the struggle with England. In this hour of danger the Old
Dominion stood firmly behind her Republican President
and ably sustained his war measures. Among those members of the legislature who advocated a vigorous war policy
Tyler held a pre-eminent place. Every resolution looking to
the support of the Federal government by Virginia received
his hearty endorsement.

When word was brought to America of the hard proposals made by the British commissioners at Ghent, a wave
of indignation swept over the Virginia legislature, which
found expression in forceful resolutions. On November 9,
1814, the House of Delegates passed a resolution declaring
that it regarded the terms proposed by the commissioners
of Great Britain at Ghent "with the liveliest emotions of
indignation, as arrogant on the part of Great Britain, and
insulting to the United States, meriting instantaneous rejection, and demanding the united exertions of every citizen
of these States, in the vigorous and efficient prosecution of
the war, until it shall be terminated by a just and honorable
peace." [10]

This motion was passed by a vote of 121 ayes to 22 noes,
Tyler voting aye. Not only did Tyler support this measure,
but he also voted against the amendments that were offered

[9] *Ibid.*, session 1812–13, 38.
[10] *Ibid.*, 54.

to soften down its harshness.[11] When this resolution went
before the Senate it was modified slightly and prefaced by
a preamble. In this amended form it passed both houses,
being unanimously adopted by the House of Delegates.[12]

Tyler's efforts in defense of Virginia against British attack were not confined to his activities as a legislator. In
the summer of 1813, after the English forces had captured
Hampton, plundered the town, and subjected the inhabitants
to outrage, the people in east Virginia were aroused to a
feeling of horror and indignation. Tyler put himself at the
head of a company raised in Charles City County for the
defense of Richmond and the region along the James. This
company was in service for only a short time, and no opportunity was offered for encountering the enemy, as the threatened attack on Richmond did not take place. By this brief
military service of two months Tyler won the title of "Captain" and a claim to western lands.[13] It was this title rather
than that of President by which some of his Whig enemies
chose to designate him while he was holding the office of
Chief Magistrate.

Tyler was elected to the House of Delegates for a fifth
term in 1815, but shortly after the legislature convened he
resigned his seat to accept membership in the Council of
State, to which position he had been chosen by the assembly.[14] The Council held an important place in the government of the commonwealth. It was made up of eight
members, who constituted the cabinet or advisers of the
governor. His election to this body was a token of the high
esteem in which he was held by his colleagues in both houses
of the assembly. He served on the Council of State until
November, 1816, when he was elected to the United States
House of Representatives.

[11] *Journal, Virginia House of Delegates,* 59–61.   [12] *Ibid.,* 75–76.
[13] *Pennsylvania Magazine of History and Biography,* XXV, 533; *John Tyler
Papers* (L.C.), III, 6703–04.
[14] *Journal of the Senate and House of Delegates of the Commonwealth of
Virginia,* session 1815–16, 10.

In the fall of 1816, there was a vacancy in the Virginia delegation in the lower branch of Congress, occasioned by the death of Representative John Clopton. Tyler was a candidate for this place. He and his opponent, Andrew Stevenson, who was then Speaker of the Virginia House of Delegates, belonged to the same political party and were personal friends. He had been elected speaker on the nomination of Tyler. Both candidates stumped the district, but the canvass was kept on a high plane and never degenerated into mudslinging and demagoguery. The race, however, was hotly contested, and Tyler won the election, but only by a majority of thirty or forty votes. Tyler owed his success over his able opponent partly to his influential family connections but mainly to his fluent speaking and good campaign methods.[15]

When Tyler entered the House of Representatives on December 17, 1816,[16] he had not yet reached his twenty-seventh birthday and was one of the youngest members of that body. He assumed the honor and responsibility of his new position with becoming modesty, although it could have been overlooked if he had allowed his head to be turned by attaining this distinction at such an early age.

At this time the House of Representatives had in its membership an unusually large number of men of ability. It was presided over by Henry Clay, who had already entered upon a career of brilliant oratory and bold statesmanship. Among the other outstanding members were William Lowndes, John Randolph of Roanoke, Daniel Webster, and John C. Calhoun, who was soon to leave for a seat in the Cabinet. Tyler was impressed with the ability of the leading Representatives and the decorum with which the sessions of the House were conducted.[17]

Owing to the character of its personnel the House at this

[15] Tyler, *Letters and Times*, I, 282; Richmond *Enquirer*, Nov. 30, 1816.
[16] *Annals of Congress*, 14th Cong., 2nd sess., 297.
[17] Tyler, *op. cit.*, I, 289–291.

time was exerting an influence in the government greater
than that of the Senate. Congress was still grappling with the
problems of reconstruction which the War of 1812 had left
in its wake, and the occasion called for real statesmanship
in both houses. Tyler, therefore, had a good opportunity to
employ his gifts as a public speaker and his training as a
legislator.

The Republican Party, to which he belonged, had by this
time gone far from its original doctrines of States' rights.
It had sponsored nationalistic legislation which would have
given even Hamilton pause. But Tyler had not fallen in
line with these nationalistic tendencies. He had been elected
as a States' rights Republican and in the House of Representatives he showed himself still a believer in the old Jeffersonian doctrine of strict construction of the Constitution.
Every speech made and every vote cast by him while he was
a member of the House were in harmony with his theory of
States' rights. He, therefore, opposed Calhoun's policy of
internal improvements by the Federal government, though
he "ably supported all the great measures necessary to repair the breaches of the war." [18]

The first measure to engage the serious attention of the
young Representative from Virginia was the one that would
determine the compensation to be received by Congressmen.
This same Congress in its first session had passed a compensation act raising the pay of members of Congress from six
dollars a day to fifteen hundred dollars a year.[19] This law,
generally known as the "Salary Grab Act," had been greeted
with a storm of adverse criticism throughout the country,
and Tyler's constituents joined in the general chorus of
protest against it. So vehement was the opposition that
Clay's support of the measure came near causing his defeat
when he came up for re-election.[20]

[18] H. A. Wise, *Seven Decades of the Union* (Philadelphia, 1876), 70-71.
[19] *Annals of Congress,* 14th Cong., 1st sess., 189, 203–204, 1188.
[20] Carl Schurz, *Henry Clay* (Boston, 1887), I, 138–140.

Tyler had been a member of the House only about a month when the question of repealing the Compensation Act came up for consideration. He acted in accordance with the wishes of his constituents and so favored the repeal of the objectionable measure. Not only did he vote against every proposal to fix the pay of Congressmen above the rate of six dollars a day, but he also made two speeches in support of his position. One of these, delivered on January 18, 1817, was, so far as the records show, the first speech ever made by him in Congress. This maiden attempt, though in no sense extraordinary, was worthy of a young man whose success in the Virginia Assembly had raised hopeful expectations as to his future career.[21]

Shortly after he took his seat the young Representative from Virginia was able to register a protest against the trend toward nationalism. A bill sponsored by Calhoun was before the House which provided for the setting aside as a permanent fund for internal improvements the bonus paid by the National Bank and the annual profits received on the stock owned by the government. Tyler voted against this measure [22] and a number of bills and resolutions which were later offered with a view to committing Congress to the policy of constructing internal improvements out of Federal funds.[23]

True to his old Republican instincts, Tyler usually favored a lowering of taxes wherever possible and, therefore, supported every motion looking to a repeal of the internal duties.[24]

The short term for which Tyler was at first chosen expired in June, 1817, and he came up for re-election in the spring of that year. In his campaign he issued a statement

[21] *Annals of Congress,* 14th Cong., 2nd sess., 619–621.
[22] *Ibid.,* 186, 191, 211–213, 296–297, 361, 934, 1052.
[23] *Annals of Congress,* 15th Cong., 1st sess., 451–460, 1114, 1381, 1384–89, 1657, 1678–79; *Niles' Register,* XIV, 62–63, 65–66.
[24] *Annals of Congress,* 14th Cong., 2nd sess., 954–955, 989–990, 1015–16; 15th Cong., 1st sess., 443.

to his constituents, published in the Richmond *Enquirer*, in which he reviewed his record in the House and gave reasons for the stand he had taken on important questions. He justified his opposition to Calhoun's policy of internal improvements on the ground that the Federal government had no authority under the Constitution to construct roads and canals. He was also "not disposed to represent the State of Virginia in so poor a condition as to require a *charitable* donation from Congress." Besides, he thought that the surplus should all go to pay off the national debt. "The day, it is to be hoped, has passed, in which a national debt was esteemed a national blessing." [25]

The issue of the *Enquirer* in which appeared Tyler's address to his constituents also carried an announcement of Andrew Stevenson's candidacy for the House of Representatives. Again the friendly rivals stumped the district together and observed the utmost courtesy toward each other. Their adherents, however, seem to have carried on quite a warm fight for their respective candidates. One of Tyler's supporters took his horses and wagon and drove for three days in Charles City County bringing men to the polls. He brought "the maimed, the halt, the blind, and those who had never voted for anyone." [26] The result was that Tyler's majority in that county was greater than the total vote had ever been before. Of the 200 votes cast Tyler is said to have received all but one.

In the Fifteenth Congress Tyler voted and spoke against the Uniform Bankruptcy Bill. His speech on this occasion was a sensible, straightforward one and was not marred by frills, tiresome homilies on loyalty to honor, or fulsome praise of Virginia, as was sometimes the case with his addresses. [27]

Tyler had not been in Congress long before he had an opportunity to enter upon his long fight against a national

[25] Richmond *Enquirer*, Mar. 17, 1817.   [26] Tyler, *op. cit.*, I, 296–297.
[27] *Annals of Congress*, 15th Cong., 1st sess., 444, 896, 907–913, 1027.

bank. The Second Bank of the United States had fallen into disfavor with a large portion of the people, especially in the South and West. There arose such a clamor against it that an investigation of its affairs was ordered by the House of Representatives. A committee was appointed (November 30, 1818) to inspect the books and examine the proceedings of the Bank and report whether the provisions of its charter had been violated. This committee of five included Spencer, of New York, as chairman, and Lowndes, McLane, Bryan, and Tyler as members.[28]

The committee went at once to Philadelphia and entered upon its task with commendable energy. It was in session regularly from ten in the morning until four or five in the afternoon. It wrestled with the seeming mysteries of bank terms, exchanges, etc., waded through numerous large folios, and made many calculations. In writing of his work on the committee to Dr. Curtis, Tyler said: "I certainly in the same time never encountered more labor." [29] The president, cashier, some of the directors, and some minor officials were interrogated under oath. "Finishing their investigation at the parent bank in Philadelphia towards the close of December, they separated, the more easily and expeditiously to examine into the affairs of some of its branches, and while Messrs. Spencer, Burwell, and McLane visited Baltimore, Messrs. Lowndes and Tyler repaired respectively to Washington and Richmond." [30]

The members of the committee were tempted to interrupt their arduous labors by participating in the social diversions which were offered them by the aristocracy of Philadelphia. Frequent invitations to dine were received from the wealthy families of the city but only those for Sundays were accepted. One of these Sunday dinner parties was at the home of Nicholas Biddle, who in after years figured

[28] *Ibid.,* 15th Cong., 2nd sess., 317, 325–335.
[29] *John Tyler Papers* (L.C.), I, 6237.
[30] Quoted in Tyler, *Letters and Times,* I, 303–304.

so prominently as president of the Bank. A noted guest on
this occasion was the exiled ex-King of Spain, Joseph Bona-
parte.[31]

Thanks to its industrious activity, the committee was able
in a few weeks to make a long report (January 16, 1819)
—one that covers twenty-seven pages in the *Annals of
Congress*.[32] This report, according to a high authority on
the Bank (Catterall), "was exceedingly weak, being contradictory in its charges, and in places incomprehensible. The
author of it [Spencer] had too feeble a grasp on the com-
plicated questions before him, and consequently failed to
make the most of his advantages."[33] The majority report
charged the Bank with speculation, mismanagement, and
violations of the charter. There was, however, no accusation of criminality, as the frauds of the Baltimore branch
were not known until later.

The influences favorable to the Bank were so strong that
nothing could be done except to pass a law making it impossible for individual stockholders to cast more votes than
they were allowed by the charter.[34] Motions to sue out a
scire facias and to repeal the charter, as well as others less
stringent, were voted down by large majorities.[35]

Tyler was convinced from the revelations growing out
of the findings of this committee that the Bank was not
worthy of a longer lease of life. Writing to Dr. Curtis, he
said: "What think you of our banking gentry? Did you
dream that we had been visited by so much corruption? I
shall vote a *scire facias* and am almost willing to vote a
positive repeal of the charter without awaiting a judicial
decision."[36] He favored a *scire facias,* as by that method

[31] Tyler to Dr. Curtis, *John Tyler Papers* (L.C.), I, 6237–38.
[32] *Annals of Congress,* 15th Cong., 2nd sess., 552–579.
[33] R. C. H. Catterall, *The Second Bank of the United States* (University
of Chicago Press, 1903), 58.
[34] *Annals of Congress,* 15th Cong., 2nd sess., 2521–22.
[35] *Ibid.,* 593, 600, 921–926, 1407–09.
[36] *John Tyler Papers* (L.C.), I, 6239.

the charges against the Bank would be brought up for judicial determination.

He was satisfied that the charter had been "most shamefully perverted to the purposes of stock-jobbing and speculation," and that if these violations were investigated by a court of justice the charter would be declared null and void. To support this contention he made a long speech before the Committee of the Whole in connection with the report of the Banking Committee. He began on Saturday (February 20) and had not finished when the committee rose. Beginning again on Monday morning, he spoke on this second day for nearly two hours.[37]

In his long address, Tyler took a vigorous stand against the Bank. He contended that the granting of the charter had been unconstitutional and since it had been violated the charter should be annulled.[38]

Although Tyler had a great admiration for Clay, he could not be classed as one of his regular followers in the House. Not only did he oppose the nationalistic policies advocated by the brilliant Kentuckian, but he also voted against some measures that did not touch the doctrine of States' rights. One of the latter sort was a resolution offered by Clay which provided for an appropriation to cover an outfit and salary for a minister to the United Provinces of the River Plata whenever the President should deem it expedient to send a minister to the government of said Provinces. This motion was defeated (March 30, 1818) with Tyler voting against it.[39]

Clay did not cease his efforts in behalf of the South American republics, and two years later (February 10, 1821) he was able to secure the adoption by the House of a resolution in their favor. This resolution expressed sympathy for these republics and interest in the success of their

[37] *Annals of Congress,* 15th Cong., 2nd sess., 1309–16, 1316–28.
[38] *Ibid.,* 1309–28.
[39] *Ibid.,* 15th Cong., 1st sess., 1652–55; *Niles,* XIV, 102.

efforts toward independence, and pledged to the President the support of the House whenever he might deem it necessary to recognize the independence of any of the said republics. Tyler regarded this motion as quite different in character from the one formerly offered and so voted for it and made a speech in its defense.[40]

It was while Tyler was serving his second term in the House of Representatives that he had his first clash with Andrew Jackson. The occasion of this encounter was an attempt made in the House to censure the General for his alleged highhandedness in Florida. Jackson had been sent into southern Georgia (1818) to chastise the Seminole Indians. In pursuit of this aim he had invaded Florida, captured two Spanish forts, and ordered the execution of two British subjects, Alexander Arbuthnot and Robert Ambrister, who had been found guilty by court martial of having incited the Indians to revolt.[41] In carrying out this bold policy Jackson was exceeding his instructions, though he had received the impression (so he said) from his instructions and his correspondence with a friend that the authorities at Washington would welcome the occupation of Florida. Despite the international complications that might arise from British and Spanish protests, the Cabinet decided to sustain Jackson.[42]

Unfortunately the controversy did not end here. In the session of 1818–19 resolutions were offered in the House of Representatives condemning Jackson's conduct in Florida.[43] These were debated before galleries crowded to suffocation. It "was one of the ablest and one of the most animated discussions that ever took place in that body [the House

[40] T. H. Benton, *Abridgment of the Debates of Congress*, 16 vols. (New York, 1857–61), VII, 95, 96.

[41] *American State Papers, Military Affairs, 1789–1838*, 7 vols., I, 701–734; *Niles' Register*, XV, 270–281.

[42] J. Q. Adams, *Memoirs* (Philadelphia, 1874–77), IV, 107–115.

[43] *Annals of Congress*, 15th Cong., 2nd sess., 583, 588.

of Representatives]." [44] Tyler spoke at length (February
1, 1819) against the execution of Arbuthnot and Ambrister
and the seizure of Pensacola and St. Marks. His arguments
were able and convincing and were delivered with due courtesy and without any objectionable personal allusions.

He contended that the enactment of the resolutions
would not be a vote of censure, as "censure implies bad
motives and bad acts." Jackson's motives were not ar-
raigned but were conceded to be correct. "We do nothing
here but combat the opinions and actions of the General,
and if gentlemen will have it so, of the Executive." This
criticism of their acts did not involve a lack of respect and
admiration for either the General or the President [Mon-
roe], for both of whom he had the highest regard. He
referred to Jackson as "this gallant hero" and to Monroe's
record as one of "unshaken patriotism" and "of the greatest
devotion to the public weal." The previous service of the
General should not be regarded as giving him exemption
from disapproval. "However great," he continued, "may
have been the services of General Jackson, I cannot consent
to weigh those services against the Constitution of the
land." "Your liberties cannot be preserved by the fame of
any man." [45]

This speech was considered by Henry A. Wise as one of
the ablest and most eloquent ever made by Tyler.[46]

In taking this aggressive stand against the country's idol,
Tyler was exhibiting a courage and disinterestedness that
have been only too rare in the history of American statesmanship. Nor can we explain his action on any other ground
than that of patriotism and loyalty to principle. It is hardly
believable that he was prompted by partisanship in his opposition to Jackson. This young doctrinaire, who was trying

[44] James Parton, *Life of Andrew Jackson*, 3 vols. (Boston, 1883), II, 533;
Annals of Congress, loc. cit., 1132–33, 1135–36, 1138.
[45] *Ibid.*, 926–935.   [46] H. A. Wise, *Seven Decades of the Union*, 72.

to carry the ideals of youth into politics, was too guileless
to be motivated by anything less high than loyalty to conviction, though he might have been used for less worthy
purposes by practical politicians. He did not fail, however,
to pay for this extravagant indulgence in virtue. By this
speech he incurred the ill will of Jackson,[47] and the Old
Hero was not inclined to regard lightly a criticism which
he considered a personal affront.

Tyler's opposition to Jackson appears especially courageous when we remember that the speech against him was
delivered on the eve of the Congressional election. Besides,
he had been so busy with his duties in the House that he
had had no time to devote toward the mending of his political fences. He had not even been able to prepare a circular
for distribution among his constituents. His speech on the
National Bank, however, had been printed and this was
distributed among the voters. But he had made a fine record for a beginner, having spoken on two of the most important questions that had come up during the last session.
Besides, there was no need of his carrying on an active
campaign, as he had no opposition.[48]

[47] H. A. Wise, *Seven Decades of the Union, 73.*
[48] *John Tyler Papers* (L.C.), I, 6245; Tyler, *Letters and Times,* I, 308.

CHAPTER IV

THE DEATH WARRANT OF SLAVERY

WHEN Tyler first arrived at Washington to take up his duties as Representative he must have been disappointed in the appearance of the ragged little town of about twelve thousand inhabitants.[1] For there were few if any indications that it would ever become one of the most beautiful cities in the world.

The streets were unpaved and sometimes carriage wheels would sink down to their hubs in mud. Broad Pennsylvania Avenue, lined as it was with Lombardy poplars, presented a rather imposing appearance;[2] but in dry and rainy seasons the dust and mud made travel on it quite difficult and uncomfortable. So much was this the case that Senator Eaton once said (1822), probably with exaggeration, that travel was "impossible for horse or foot." There were sidewalks in front of private homes, but none across the wide unoccupied spaces still held by the government. The street lamps along the Avenue were kept lighted at night in 1817; but next year the city treasury could not afford to buy oil for the lamps, and so for this year Washington's main thoroughfare was shrouded in darkness.[3]

Away from Pennsylvania Avenue there were scattered here and there isolated houses and clusters of residences. English travelers as late as the 'thirties were impressed with the lack of compactness of the little city. Thomas

[1] The population of Washington in 1820 was 13,247. *Fifteenth Census of the United States, 1930. Population,* I, 19.
[2] Moore, J. W., *Picturesque Washington* (Providence, 1884, 1887), 26.
[3] Proctor, John C., ed., *Washington, Past and Present* (New York, 1930), I, 95–97.

Hamilton, who was in Washington in 1831 or 1832, spoke of the houses as being "scattered in straggling groups, three in one quarter, and half a dozen in another," with occasionally a desolate building standing alone in a square.[4] Miss Harriet Martineau (1835) said that in making calls she "had to cross ditches and stiles, and walk alternately on grass and pavements, and strike across a field to reach a street." [5]

A large part of the town area was given over to malaria-infested swamps and green cow pastures. The cows, however, were not confined to the pastures, but were allowed to wander about the town, and at times John Marshall, Henry Clay, and Daniel Webster probably had to contest with them the right to the sidewalk.[6]

The Capitol and the Executive Mansion, which had been burned by the British (August, 1814), were being rebuilt, but neither was yet ready for occupancy. Congress met in a privately-owned two-story building near the Capitol,[7] which was known as the "Brick Capitol." It was on the upper floor of this modest structure that Tyler made the acquaintance of statesmen whose names have become household words with the American people. By December, 1819, the Capitol was sufficiently restored to house Congress, and its sessions were held there after that time.[8]

Like most Congressmen, Tyler did not move his family to Washington. Mrs. Tyler's duties as a mother and mistress of the plantation, her attachment to her home, and

---

[4] [Thomas Hamilton], *Men and Manners in America* (Edinburgh, 1833), II, 30.

[5] Harriet Martineau, *Retrospect of Western Travel* (New York, 1838), I, 144.

[6] Claude G. Bowers, *Party Battles of the Jackson Period* (Boston and New York, 1928), Ch. I.

[7] The "Brick Capitol" was located on the lot now occupied by the Supreme Court Building.

[8] *Washington, City and Capital,* Federal Writers' Project (1937), 49, 50; Proctor, *op. cit.,* I, 92.

the expense of maintaining an establishment in town made it desirable for the family to remain in Charles City.[9]

Travel between Charles City and Washington was generally by boat via the Potomac River. When this route was closed by ice the journey was made by stagecoach or partly by boat and partly by stage. The monotony of these long fatiguing trips was often relieved by a lively interchange of ideas with fellow travelers; for Tyler was a good listener as well as an interesting talker. On one occasion (in the winter of 1819–20) he had to go home at a time when the steamers were tied up on the icy Potomac. On taking his place in the stagecoach he had the good fortune to be seated by an unusually attractive fellow passenger. During the entire journey to Richmond he was entertained with conversation so delightful that he was hardly conscious of the jolts of the coach. His seat mate was a young man who had recently returned from a trip abroad and was describing with ardent enthusiasm his experiences and observations on the grand tour. This interesting traveler was Hugh S. Legaré, a promising lawyer from South Carolina, who later held the post of Attorney General in President Tyler's Cabinet.[10]

There were a number of very good hotels in Washington, which offered reasonable rates. At the best of them one could get a comfortable room, with board and a generous supply of drinks, at prices that would seem ridiculously low at present. But a young husband with a rapidly-increasing family could hardly be expected to indulge in the extravagance of living at a hotel on the salary then paid a member of Congress. Tyler, therefore, lived at a boardinghouse (probably during the entire period of his membership in the House), as did most of his fellow Congressmen. One of the boardinghouses at which he lodged must have been

---

[9] Only once or twice during his entire Congressional career was Tyler able to persuade Mrs. Tyler to spend a winter with him in Washington. She was with him while he was in the Senate, in the winter of 1828–29. (See page 144).

[10] Tyler, *Letters and Times,* II, 384–386.

a very poor one; for while there he ate some stale fish which brought on a serious illness. It was to this illness that he traced a stomach trouble from which he suffered periodically the remainder of his life.[11]

To what extent Tyler participated in the brilliant social life of the capital we are not positively assured. That a young Representative of his easy and polished manners and conversational powers had *entrée* to the most exclusive circles cannot be doubted. This supposition is confirmed by the fact that before he had been in Washington two months he had received three invitations to the home of President and Mrs. Madison. The President's family was at this time domiciled in a residence not far from the Executive Mansion, which was known as the "Seven Buildings." [12] Here "Dolly" Madison dispensed hospitality in "superb style," for she had no superior in America as a hostess. Tyler fully appreciated the fine quality of her entertainment, but did not particularly relish the food. It was prepared in the French way and was not to his liking—less so than that served by his colored cook at home. The drinks, however, were excellent, especially the champagne, "of which, you know (so he wrote Mrs. Tyler), I am very fond." [13]

The fact that Tyler was re-elected to the House of Representatives in 1819 without opposition shows that the people of his district were pleased with his record in that body. In the next session of Congress he was able fully to justify the confidence which his constituents had imposed in him, for he waged a vigorous opposition to two measures that were particularly inimical to Southern interests. These were an unsuccessful effort to raise the tariff and a successful attempt to restrict slavery in the territories.

Early in the year 1820 a tariff bill was introduced in the House, which, as finally framed, raised the duties on a large

[11] Tyler, *Letters and Times,* I, 316–317, 334.
[12] H. P. Caemmerer, *Washington, the National Capital* (Washington, 1932), 45.
[13] Tyler, *op. cit.,* I, 288–289.

number of commodities. This increase applied to some articles that did and others that did not compete with American manufactures.[14] On April 22, Tyler moved to strike out the enacting clause of this bill, and two days later he spoke for about an hour in favor of this motion. In this speech he made a good argument against protection and advanced some very sensible ideas. He contended that manufacturing was no worse off than other industries, but was only sharing in the general depression of the time. He attributed this condition of depression to the fact that Europe, the war now being over, was supplying her own needs and was no longer buying heavily from the United States. Another cause of hard times was the disordered state of the finances occasioned by a hotbed banking system.

The friends of protection contended that a high tariff by stimulating manufacturing would cause workers to leave the farm and go to the factory. In this way cities would be built up and there would be an increase in consumers not raising farm products. A home market for food supplies would thereby be created. This increase in the ratio of consumers to producers of farm commodities would raise the price of these commodities and thus improve the condition of the farmer.

Another argument much used at the time in favor of the protective system was that it would tend to make the country economically independent. By the aid of a protective tariff industries would be developed to such an extent that in time of war they could supply our people with clothing, munitions of war, and other necessary articles even if we should be cut off from communication with the outside world.

There was nothing, Tyler maintained, in either of these arguments. It was not necessary to encourage domestic manufactures in order to make our country economically independent; for manufacturing nations are the most dependent

[14] *Annals of Congress*, 16th Cong., 1st sess., 924, 1663-69, 1913-16; *Niles' Register*, XVIII, 164-165.

and agricultural countries the most independent. Nor does
the policy of protection favor the expansion of the home
market for the farmer, though it does lead to the contrac-
tion of his foreign market. While manufacturing may con-
centrate in cities the purchasers of farm products, it does
not increase their number. On the other hand, it discourages
exportation by imposing restrictions on imports, since we
cannot expect foreign nations to buy of us for any length of
time unless we buy of them. By curtailing exports we limit
the market for our farm products and thus discourage agriculture. The protective system rests on a desire to engross
all wealth to ourselves and to beggar others, whereas the
wisest policy would be to promote the wealth of foreign purchasers of our commodities and thereby strengthen their
buying power.[15]

This speech is an important milestone in the career of
Tyler, as it shows that his intellectual development was near-
ing its zenith. It is characterized not only by sound logic,
clearness, and forcible expression, but also by a breadth of
view that is indicative of high statesmanship. In the broad
charity expressed toward other countries he revealed an international attitude considerably in advance of his time. At
no other period in his entire career was he more effective in
his advocacy of Jeffersonian agrarianism. The importance
of this speech is not to be unduly discounted by the fact that
most of its ideas were not new but had been brilliantly set
forth by Adam Smith and the other economists of the classical school. That he was greatly indebted to these economists for his views is quite probable. For although no
reference to Adam Smith is made in this address, some of
the strongest arguments sound like those of the great Scotch
economist. Wise statesmanship consists not so much in the
initiation of original theories as in the adoption and effective presentation of sound doctrine.

Tyler was joined by a large majority of the other Repre-

[15] *Annals of Congress, loc. cit.,* 1950, 1952–63.

sentatives from Virginia in opposing this tariff measure. When the vote was taken in the House (April 28, 1820) on the proposal that the bill be engrossed and read a third time, the motion was carried, but there was only one vote from Virginia for the bill, while there were fifteen against it.[16]

The all but unanimous opposition of the Virginia delegation in the House to the tariff bill was a reflection of the sentiment of the people of the State. During the recess of Congress it was discovered that there was a good deal of uneasiness in Virginia about this protective measure. The merchants of Richmond drafted a very able memorial against the tariff and sent it to Tyler to be presented to the House. Accordingly, he offered it early in the next session. Henry Baldwin, of Pennsylvania, afterwards justice of the Supreme Court of the United States, made a speech (November 30, 1820) severely arraigning the memorial for the language used. Tyler defended the merchants with great warmth. His defense was so good that Baldwin came over to his desk and complimented him on the spirit he had shown. Baldwin prophesied for Tyler on this occasion a bright political future, and whenever in after years the latter received a political promotion he was reminded by Baldwin of this prophecy.[17]

The most important question that came before Congress during the period in which Tyler was a member of the House was that of the admission of Missouri into the Union. In 1819 a bill providing for the admission of Missouri as a State was offered in the House of Representatives in response to petitions from the people and a memorial of the legislature of the Territory of Missouri. To this bill James Tallmadge, of New York, offered an amendment providing that no more slaves should be brought into Missouri

---

[16] *Ibid.*, 2139–40. This tariff bill was defeated in the Senate by the narrow majority of one vote.
[17] Tyler, *Letters and Times*, I, 334.

and "that all children born within the said State, after the admission thereof into the Union, shall be free at the age of twenty-five years." [18]

This resolution precipitated a debate in Congress which lasted a year. During this time that body was keyed up to a high pitch of excitement, and into the controversy all the prominent members of both houses were ultimately drawn.

The Missouri Bill, as amended by the Tallmadge proposal, passed the House in February, 1819. Tyler, of course, voted against both clauses of the amendment.[19] In the Senate the amendment was rejected but the original bill was accepted. The House would not recede from its position and so the measure was lost.[20]

The issue was now before the people, and Congressmen on returning home soon saw how their constituents felt on the burning question. Resolutions adopted by mass meetings and State legislatures showed that the North was virtually a unit in favor of restriction and the South was equally strong against it.[21]

When the next session of Congress convened in December, 1819, the members were in a more belligerent mood than before. The intensity of their convictions had been increased by contact with the heated feelings of their constituents, and so the session gave promise of being a stormy one. Tyler in writing to Dr. Curtis on February 5, 1820, said: "Missouri is the only word ever repeated here by the politicians. You can have no possible idea of the excitement that prevails here. Men talk of a dissolution of the Union with perfect nonchalance and indifference." [22]

The Missouri Bill came up again early in the session, but it was not until late in January that the discussion was resumed. After the debate had warmed up Tyler entered the

18 *Annals of Congress,* 15th Cong., 2nd sess., 418, 1166, 1170.
19 *Ibid.,* 15th Cong., 2nd sess., 1214-15.
20 *Ibid.,* 272-273, 279, 1433-38.
21 *Niles,* XVII, 199-201, 241-242, 287, 342, 343, 544.
22 *John Tyler Papers* (L.C.), I, 6247.

lists, and for more than an hour spoke against restriction (February 17, 1820).

Beginning his address, as was his wont, with modest-seeming protestations, he said that his state of health had kept him from speaking on the bill until that time. Even then his health was not yet restored, but he felt impelled by a sense of duty to take part in the discussion. He made an earnest plea in favor of extending to the people of Missouri the same rights as those enjoyed by the citizens of other States. "Place them," he said, "upon a footing with the people of New York, Connecticut, and of the other States. What are the rights of the people of Connecticut and the other States? They have the right to alter, to amend, to abolish their constitutions. Connecticut has lately done so. Will you deny to the people of Missouri this right?"

But even if Congress had a constitutional right to place this limitation on Missouri it would be unwise and impolitic to do so. This Territory was purchased out of the common purse and the North and the South were joint tenants of it. To oust one section to the advantage of the other would be an act of gross injustice.

The most brilliant part of his speech was his argument in favor of the diffusion of slavery as an advantage both to the slave and his master. He contended that the opening of Missouri to slavery would not encourage the importation of more slaves into the country from Africa, but would alleviate the condition of those already here by preventing the overconcentration of them in the old States. The expansion of the market for slaves would increase their value, and the more valuable the slave became the more it would be to the interest of his owner to treat him kindly. By such a policy, the cause of abolition would also be furthered. For by lessening the number of slaves in the South the economic cost of general emancipation there would be reduced and abolition would be brought within the range of possibility.

"Slavery has been represented on all hands," he continued, "as a dark cloud, and the candor of the gentleman from Massachusetts [Mr. Whitman] drove him to the admission that it would be well to disperse this cloud. In this sentiment, I entirely concur with him. How can you otherwise disarm it? Will you suffer it to increase in its darkness over a particular portion of this land until its horrors shall burst upon it? Will you permit the lightnings of its wrath to break upon the South, when by the interposition of a wise system of legislation, you may reduce it to a summer's cloud?" [23]

The House and the Senate could not agree upon terms for the admission of Missouri, and a conference committee was appointed to break the deadlock. This committee accepted an amendment, offered by Senator Thomas, of Illinois, which provided for the admission of Missouri to the Union without the slavery restriction and for the exclusion of slavery from the remainder of the Louisiana Territory north of the parallel of 36° 30'. These proposals were adopted by both houses as a settlement of the controversy.

Of the forty-two votes cast against the Missouri Bill all but five were from the South, seventeen of them being from Virginia. Tyler not only voted against the measure as finally passed but also against every proposal to restrict slavery in Missouri or in any other part of the Louisiana Purchase. [24]

As the President signed the bill, the controversy was now apparently settled, but the agreement proved to be only a truce, not a permanent peace. About the middle of the year 1820 Missouri adopted her constitution, which contained a clause prohibiting the immigration into Missouri of any free Negroes and mulattoes. [25] When this constitution was presented to Congress in November as a basis for the admission of Missouri as a State, objection to it was raised on the ground that this paragraph was in violation of the Con-

23 *Annals of Congress,* 16th Cong., 1st sess., 1382–94.
24 *Niles,* XVII, 455; XVIII, 14, 15.   25 *Ibid.,* XIX, 52.

stitution of the United States. In some States, it was contended, Negroes were citizens and to exclude them from
Missouri would be to violate that clause in the Federal Constitution which says that "the citizens of each State shall be
entitled to all the privileges and immunities of citizens in the
several States."

The controversy was now reopened and a long and acri-
monious debate followed. Tyler was drawn into the discussion and made another speech on the Missouri question
(February 2, 1821). He had maintained a "profound silence" during the session and had, he said, been induced to
break that silence by the position which Sergeant, of Pennsylvania, had taken with reference to the contest for power
between the two sections. He strongly deprecated the raising of the sectional issue, which he regarded as a dangerous
and fiendish one. Such a struggle ought not to be thought of
between people of the same country. He urged a speedy
settlement of the question by the admission of Missouri into
the Union.[26]

Meanwhile Clay had assumed the management of the
case. He suggested a formula which, after slight modification and considerable discussion, was finally agreed upon by
both sides. By the second Missouri Compromise, as it was
called, Missouri was to be admitted to the Union with the
understanding that the legislature of the State should declare
by a solemn public act that the objectionable clause in her
constitution would never be so construed as to deprive a
citizen of any other State of the rights guaranteed to such
citizen by the Constitution of the United States.[27]

Tyler felt that the Missouri convention had acted unwisely in putting this trouble-breeding clause in her constitution, although he did not regard Negroes as citizens. However, he favored the admission of Missouri into the Union

[26] *Annals of Congress*, 16th Cong., 2nd sess., 1022–24.
[27] *Niles*, XIX, 398–399, 409–410, 412, 431; XX, 12, 14.

with the prescribed condition and so voted for Clay's formula.[28]

The settlement of the controversy over the Missouri question has been termed a compromise. It was, however, less of a compromise than a surrender of the South to the North. The antislavery party had gained much and conceded little. That part of the Louisiana Territory from which slavery was to be excluded was the lion's share of the division and out of it numerous States could be carved in the future, while that part of the territory south of the parallel of 36° 30′ furnished but one slave State. As slavery was already legal by custom in all the settled portions of the Louisiana Purchase, and without further legislation would be legal in the rest of it whenever it should be settled, this restriction was a great concession to the antislavery cause. By voting for the compromise, Southern Congressmen were also admitting that Congress had the constitutional right to restrict slavery in the territories.

Nor did the South receive much, if anything, to offset this loss. The admission of Missouri as a slave State was not a concession. Congress could not have refused admission to Missouri with its proslavery constitution without violating the spirit of the Federal Constitution. In contending that Congress could not impose upon new States conditions not provided for in the Constitution, the South was on firm legal ground. Its position was so strong that there was no need of yielding. If the Northern Representatives had persisted in their refusal to admit the new State without restrictions, the Southern leaders could have placed the responsibility of the deadlock upon them.

This defeat for the cause of slavery was a knockout blow. The Thomas Amendment was the death warrant of American slavery, and the existence of the institution after that was due only to a reprieve of the sentence. By excluding slavery from that vast empire north of the fateful line it

[28] Tyler, *Letters and Times*, I, 331; also *Annals of Cong., loc. cit.,* 1239–40.

turned over to the North a vast area that would in the future insure its preponderance in the Union. As soon as this region should be settled and carved up into free States it would give the North a voice in the Federal government which the South could never hope to equal.

While this preponderance might not be strong enough to change the Constitution so as to abolish slavery in the Southern States, it would give the North such control of Federal legislation as to make the South's place in the Union a very undesirable one. Therefore, those Congressmen from the South who stubbornly fought the Thomas Amendment to the bitter end were acting in strict accord with the interests of their section, provided it were assumed that slavery should not be abolished in the South.

In the light of subsequent developments it seems strange that the South on this occasion should have surrendered so completely to the North. The former section had control of the executive branch of the government and had equal strength with the North in the Senate. It could, therefore, by united and persistent action have prevented the enactment of the Thomas Amendment.

The loss of this decisive battle in the fight for slavery is to be explained partly by the blindness of the Southern leaders as to the real significance of the bill and partly by that shortsightedness which is disposed to balance a present gain of small value against future losses of greater importance. For the gain to slavery as a result of the defeat of the restriction on Missouri was as nothing compared to the loss growing out of the restriction on that extensive region north of the thirty-six-thirty parallel. The patriotic desire to save the Union from a serious menace also figured as an important motive for this great sacrifice on the part of proslavery Congressmen. Tyler was one of the Southern leaders who realized the significance of this defeat. In speaking of it in 1861, at a time when the Union was dissolving, he said that he regarded the passage of the Thomas Amendment as "the opening of Pandora's Box, which would let out upon us all the present evils which have gathered over the land. . . ." "I would have died in my shoes," he continued, "suffered any sort of punishment you could have inflicted upon me, before I would have done it [yielded to the Missouri Compromise]." [29]

But Tyler was not farsighted enough to read aright the signs of the times or he would have seen that slavery was doomed and the most that statesmanship could do was to postpone its demise. Instead of trying to avert the inevitable he and his Southern colleagues should have striven for such an adjustment to the new order as would have been favorable to their section. Instead of wasting their efforts in lamenting that new wine was being poured into old bottles, they should have been busy in the hunt for new bottles.

The Tallmadge Amendment pointed the way to a proper solution of the slavery question. The Southern leaders should have accepted the principle of gradual emancipation suggested by it and have insisted that it be *offered* to all the States and not *imposed* on Missouri. The proposal should also have been made attractive to the slave States by coupling with it a clause pledging the Federal government to a policy of liberal compensation to any State that by constitutional changes should provide for the gradual extinction of slavery. In this way slavery could have been abolished without imposing a crushing burden on the slaveowners. The fear of the Southerners of the social evils that would result from the removal of the disciplinary restraints of slavery could have been met by the setting aside of ample portions of the public lands in the West for the colonization of the freedmen. With the vast area of unoccupied lands at the disposal of the government, the creation of a Negro territory would have raised no serious difficulty.

The neglect of this opportunity by Tyler and the other ardent supporters of Southern interests revealed a serious

[29] Tyler, *op. cit.*, 329.

defect in their statesmanship. It is true that the Northern Congressmen would have objected to such a solution on the ground that the cost would have been beyond the financial ability of the government. They were probably too short-sighted to realize at what a terrible price in blood and treasure abolition would be purchased in the future.

The deep South also would doubtless have offered strong resistance to such a policy, as gradual abolition, even if coupled with compensation, would have brought about a revolution in its social and economic order. But if the leaders in this section had had the vision which always characterizes sound statesmanship, they would have seen that the whole trend of the age was against slavery and that it could not last many decades. They should have recognized this disagreeable fact and persuaded their people to adjust themselves to it. With such foresight they would readily have preferred a gradual revolution with the protection of vested interests to a sudden revolution with a disregard of property rights.

Furthermore, it would have been good tactics for the Southern Congressmen to make this attempt even if there were no chance of success. It would have enabled them to pose as champions of freedom and to brand their Northern opponents as protagonists of slavery. In this way the South could have wrested the offensive from the North. In the long contest between the sections over slavery the South was generally handicapped by being on the defensive. If the Southern Congressmen had grasped the opportunity afforded by the Missouri question the rôles would have been reversed.

A wise solution of the slavery problem was precluded by the ultraconservatism of the political leaders of that day and of the succeeding generation. The country was launched upon a hazardous policy because American statesmanship during the third, fourth, and fifth decades of the nineteenth century was not illumined by a sane radicalism. The Northern leaders were somewhat radical, in that they were willing to stretch the Constitution in their support of a protective tariff and in their opposition to slavery. The Southern leaders, on the other hand, instead of opposing the mild radicalism of the North by an aggressive radicalism of their own, urged an extreme conservatism that ignored the tendencies of the age. Instead of boldly advocating a change in the Federal Constitution that would adapt it to the conditions of their time, they persistently fought for a rigid interpretation of it, apparently thinking that the problems of their day could be solved by the political philosophy of the eighteenth century. It was this conservatism that proved the undoing of the South. It caused the statesmanship of that section to take the position of a man who tries to keep one foot on a stationary platform while the other is on a moving train.

In apportioning responsibility for this serious mistake, a large share must be laid at the door of John Tyler. He failed to realize what a great opportunity for settling the slavery issue was afforded by the Missouri controversy. It was his conservatism that kept him from rising on this occasion above the level of opportunism to that of farseeing statesmanship. This conservatism made Tyler an attractive and effective mouthpiece of the Southern cause but rendered him unequal to that bold and original leadership of which his section stood in such dire need. As a Southerner he was a hundred percenter, and hundred percenters never attain to the higher reaches of greatness. They do not mold public sentiment, but are generally molded by it. When honest, they develop into mild-mannered, respectable politicians like Aristides; when dishonest, they become loud-mouthed demagogues like Cleon; but never do they assume the rôle of bold leaders like Pericles.

In fairness to Tyler it ought to be added that he was no more shortsighted than other Congressmen. Indeed he saw farther into the future than most of them by forecasting to some extent the effect on the South of the Missouri Compromise. None of the Southern leaders, not even the very ablest, seemed to appreciate and understand the strength of the forces that were working against the South's peculiar institution. They did not realize that the stars in their courses were fighting against Sisera.

CHAPTER V

GOVERNOR OF VIRGINIA

TYLER had made an enviable record in the House of Representatives. His every vote and utterance had been in strict harmony with the doctrine of States' rights, and the Old Dominion could feel that he had ably championed her cause. His speeches had been sensible and logical and he had not weakened his influence by appearing on the floor too often. Soon after entering Congress he wrote to Dr. Curtis not to expect much of him in the way of speechmaking. So much time, he said, was wasted by useless talking on the part of members that he thought it best to refrain from the practice as far as possible.[1] He could not, however, be classed as one of the silent members of the House, as he spoke often during the latter period of his service. Not all of these speeches are recorded in the *Annals of Congress,* owing to the poor reporting system then in use.

Despite his success in Congress, Tyler decided early in 1821 that he would not run for re-election, and in January of that year he published in the Richmond *Enquirer* a statement to that effect.[2] Ill-health was given as the reason for this decision. In an undated letter to Governor Floyd he said that he was "tired of Congress and nothing but a strong sense of duty would keep me [him] there." [3] The condition of his health was not, however, the only cause of his giving up his seat. Writing to his friend and brother-in-law, Dr. Curtis (December 8, 1820), he gave other reasons for wishing to return to the practice of his profession. These were as follows:

[1] Tyler, *Letters and Times,* I, 299.
[2] Richmond *Enquirer,* Jan. 18, 1821.
[3] *John Floyd Papers* (L.C., abbreviation for Library of Congress).

He could not, he felt, realize his hope of increasing human happiness by remaining at this post, for he was in such a decided minority that he could do no good in the House. With party conditions as they were at that time, he could exert no influence except by his vote and a mere automaton could perform that function. He spoke of the "daring usurpations of this government—usurpations of a more alarming character than have ever before taken place even during the fearful period of '98–'99."

There was also little to look forward to in the way of furthering the aims of ambition. He would probably never rise to a higher station than that which he had already attained, as not one in a thousand did. Moreover, his private interests, and especially his financial affairs, demanded more of his attention than they had been receiving. "My children will soon be treading on my heels and it will require no common exertions to enable me to educate them." To do this he had to rely on his profession and he could not carry it on successfully while in Congress. His legal practice before he went to Congress was yielding an income of $2000 a year and was growing, whereas it then amounted to $1200 or less. "Independent of this, I should promote my peace of mind and with it my health, as I fain would hope, which now is very precarious." [4]

Tyler's friend and former opponent, Andrew Stevenson, now entered the race for Congress. Tyler supported him and he was elected. Stevenson remained in the House for fourteen years and was Speaker for a number of terms.

When Tyler refused to become a candidate for reelection to the House of Representatives, he was probably looking forward to a long vacation from public life. He would now be free to devote all his energies to his professional and business interests. If such were his hopes, he was doomed to disappointment. For in little more than two years

[4] *John Tyler Papers* (L.C.), I, 6255–56.

he was again drafted into the public service by the people of his home county. At their earnest solicitation he agreed to become a candidate for the House of Delegates and was again elected.[5]

He was a member of the lower house from December, 1823, to December, 1825, at which time he resigned to accept the governorship.[6] Thanks to his previous experience as a member of the House of Delegates and the prestige he had won as a member of the Federal House of Representatives, he was able to play a prominent part in the deliberations of the legislature. He was given his old place on the Committee for Courts and Justice, and was appointed to other important committees, both special and permanent.[7]

During this second period of Tyler's service in the legislature no problems of outstanding importance or dramatic interest were brought forward for solution. He seems to have taken a sensible attitude toward the questions that came up in the ordinary routine of legislation and to have voted on them as one would expect of a competent, educated, and experienced legislator.[8]

When the session of 1823–24 opened, the Presidential campaign was engaging the attention of ambitious politicians. Tyler was in favor of Crawford, who was expected to receive the support of the Congressional caucus. But a majority of the Republican members of Congress were opposed to the caucus as a method of nominating Presidential candidates, and the legislature of Tennessee had adopted some resolutions strongly condemning the practice. Tyler

[5] Richmond *Enquirer*, April 22, 1823; Tyler, *Letters and Times*, I, 335–337, 339–341.

[6] Richmond *Enquirer*, Dec. 13, 1825.

[7] *Journal, Virginia House of Delegates*, session 1823–24, 12, 13, 29, 41, 42, 55; session 1824–25, 9, 10, 48, 125; session 1825–26, 10, 111.

[8] He voted (February 15, 1825) in favor of the bill for improving the navigation of the James River and for connecting the waters of that stream by canal with the Great Kanawha (*Jour.*, session 1824–25, 175–176). He voted (February 7, 1825) for the bill forbidding the sale of foreign lottery tickets in Virginia. (*Ibid.*, 154–155.)

put up a vigorous fight to have the Virginia Assembly adopt resolutions offered by him as an answer to those of Tennessee. The opposition was able, however, to defeat his proposals by the close vote of 76 yeas to 77 nays.[9] He was sorely disappointed at this action, and in a letter to James S. Barbour said that he was "covered in sackcloth and ashes." About forty Republicans had voted against Tyler's measure, although nearly all of them were for Crawford. They had opposed it because of their dissatisfaction with the caucus as a plan for choosing candidates for the Presidency. Tyler's chagrin over this apparent setback to the prospects of his favorite did not last long, as the Republican members a week later held a meeting and by an almost unanimous vote adopted resolutions in favor of Crawford.[10]

One of the ablest speeches made by Tyler in this second period of service in the House of Delegates was on the question of moving the College of William and Mary from Williamsburg to Richmond. The president and faculty were petitioning the legislature in favor of the change. The institution was on the decline and there were at that time only twenty-two students in attendance. President Smith had likened it to a person in a deep consumption, and the regular physician, having exhausted all efforts to cure, had recommended a change of place. Richmond, it was said, was a better site for a college than Williamsburg because of its greater size and better climate.[11] Without a change in location William and Mary could not successfully compete with Hampden-Sydney, the University of North Carolina, and the University of Virginia.

Tyler spoke earnestly and ably against this contention and succeeded in defeating the effort at removal. The bad plight of the college, he maintained, was due not to its location but

[9] *Ibid.*, session 1823–24, 55, 74–76, 77, 95; Tyler, *Letters and Times*, I, 341–342; Richmond *Enquirer*, Jan. 1, 1824.

[10] Tyler to James S. Barbour, Jan. 5, 1824; N. Y. Public Library MSS.

[11] *Journal, Virginia House of Delegates*, session 1824–25, 91, 113, 133, 135-136, 141, 146, 147.

to administrative mismanagement and the high prices students were required to pay for board—hindrances which
could easily be removed. He did not fear the crippling of
his *alma mater* from the growth of rival institutions; she
could hold her own in the face of all this competition. A
small town or rural community is the proper place for a
school because it offers fewer temptations to youth and more
of the quietude necessary for study than does a city or large
town. He had always thought that "Philosophy loved the
shade and delighted in the stillness of solitude," and was
surprised at hearing "that the sciences are more successfully to be courted in Bedlam; that Philosophy delights in
noise and uproar."

This was a fine speech. The reasoning was good, and in
some places there were flashes of oratory. It deserves to be
considered as a service for old William and Mary compa-
rable to that performed for Dartmouth by Daniel Webster
in his famous argument in her defense before the Supreme
Court of the United States.[12] For the removal of the college
to a new site would have weakened to a great extent the
sentimental ties that bound it to its glorious past.

Tyler realized, however, that reforms were badly needed
at the college and so recommended some important changes
in administration. These were adopted,[13] and it was probably due to this policy that the institution entered upon a
new career of success with a gradual increase in student attendance. By 1840 the matriculates numbered 140, said to
be the largest enrollment for any year since the founding of
the college.[14]

After serving for two years in the legislature Tyler was
advanced to the most honored position in the State. On December 10, 1825, he was nominated for the governorship by
his friend, Robert Douthat. The name of John Floyd, who

---

[12] The text of this speech is given in the Richmond *Enquirer*, Feb. 8, 10, 1825.
[13] Tyler to Robert Tyler, Nov. 28, 1836; Tyler, *op. cit.*, I, 564.
[14] *Niles*, LVIII, 199.

was then a member of the Federal House of Representatives, was also placed before the assembly. There seems to have been some misunderstanding as to Floyd's candidacy, as two of his friends who were members of the legislature were surprised at his nomination. This would indicate that Floyd's claims were not vigorously pressed, and this lack of energetic support on the part of his friends was doubtless an important reason for the smallness of the vote cast for him. At any rate, Tyler received 131 votes to 81 for Floyd, two votes being scattered.[15]

At that time it was the custom for the governors to be installed without any elaborate ceremony and without an inaugural address. In keeping with this tradition Tyler received (December 10), in writing, a brief notification of his election from a committee of the legislature, and he replied to it with like brevity. In his letter of acceptance, he said:

SIR—The General Assembly has conferred on me a great honour. In accepting it I shall make no professions of patriotism. Public agents should be judged by their acts, and my constant exertions shall be directed to the fulfillment of the obligations imposed by the constitution and laws. I trust that neither the rights nor the interests of Virginia will suffer disparagement at my hands.

I tender to you, sir, and the committee of the House of Delegates, and through you to the General Assembly, assurances of the highest respect.

John Tyler.[16]

The position to which Tyler had been chosen was one of considerable dignity but of little power. Virginia was still living under her first constitution, the one adopted (June, 1776) in the heat of the rebellion against the mother country. Her last royal governor, Dunmore, had recently left her shores bearing with him the maledictions of the people

---

[15] Richmond *Enquirer*, Dec. 13, 1825; *Journal, Virginia House of Delegates*, session 1825–26, 17.

[16] *Journal, Virginia House of Delegates*, session 1825–26, 20.

because of his alleged highhandedness in dealing with the revolt. Owing to their experiences with Dunmore, the framers of the constitution were obsessed with a fear of the executive and determined to hedge about the authority of their governor with such limitations as would render him incapable of tyranny. But in making him impotent for evil they also left him almost powerless for good.

The governor was elected for a term of one year by both houses of the legislature voting separately. He could recommend legislation to the assembly but had no power of veto. Many of the administrative and appointive powers that we now associate with the chief executive of a State were conferred upon him, but in the exercise of this authority he was limited by the advice of the Council of State, a body of eight men chosen by the legislature.[17]

The governor did not have behind him in the legislature a dominant and well-disciplined party which looked to him for leadership. He thus had no political whip with which to chastise into regularity recalcitrant members who might vote without regard to his wishes. His influence over legislation was, therefore, very slight as compared with that exercised by the governor of any commonwealth today. And yet his position was one of sufficient prominence to place him on an elevated platform from which he could make his voice heard not only in the legislature but also throughout the State. The executive mansion was thus a sort of broadcasting station, and messages sent out from it were listened to attentively by both the people and their leaders.

Nothing of importance occurred during the first half of Tyler's first term as governor, and his duties were almost entirely of a routine character. Indeed, this whole term would have passed without any event of dramatic interest had not Thomas Jefferson's death occurred on July 4, 1826. Before his death Jefferson had fallen into financial straits

---

[17] F. N. Thorpe, comp. and ed., *Federal and State Constitutions, Colonial Charters, etc.,* 7 vols. (Washington, 1909), 3816–18.

and felt unable to meet his personal obligations. The Virginia legislature had passed an act allowing him to dispose of his land by lottery to pay his debts. There was a feeling, however, that an ex-President should not be forced to such a pass, and the citizens of Richmond made plans for raising a fund for him by private subscription. In June a meeting was held at the Capitol, which was presided over by Governor Tyler. At this meeting a committee, of which John Marshall was chairman, was appointed to receive donations. On the day that the subscriptions were to be taken the great commoner passed away.[18]

Appropriate ceremonies were held in Richmond (July 11) in honor of the noted statesman who had done so much for Virginia and the country. It was eminently appropriate that the funeral oration on this occasion should have been delivered by Governor Tyler, who was probably at that time the most ardent admirer of Jefferson to be found in America. It must have afforded him keen satisfaction to have this fine opportunity of lauding one to whom both he and his father had always looked as the mentor of their political careers. The governor was equal to the occasion and delivered a speech worthy of the great apostle of political and religious liberty.[19]

In this address he gave in outline the public record of Jefferson, with an appraisal of his outstanding achievements. He spoke at some length of the great contributions that Jefferson had made to thought and of the lasting benefits that he had conferred upon his country and the world. It is needless to say that of these achievements there was expressed the warmest appreciation and the most favorable opinion. He was loud in his praise of the Declaration of Independence and the reforms that Jefferson had initiated in Virginia. In the closing sentences of an encomium on his

---

[18] *Jour., Va. House of Delegates,* session 1825–26, 159, 176–178; W. A. Christian, *Richmond, Her Past and Present* (Richmond, 1912), 106–107.

[19] Richmond *Enquirer,* July 14, 1826.

work for freedom of conscience as embodied in the statute for religious freedom in Virginia, he rose to real oratory as follows:

"Let it, then, be henceforth proclaimed to the world, that man's conscience was created free; that he is no longer accountable to his fellowman for his religious opinions, being responsible therefor only to his God; that it is impious in mortal man, whether clothed in purple or in lawn, to assume the judgment-seat; and that the connection between church and state is an unholy alliance, and the fruitful source of slavery and oppression; and let it be dissolved."

While Tyler was putting the finishing touches to his oration on Jefferson, word was received in Richmond that John Adams had died on that same Fourth of July. He then added a paragraph in which he linked the name of Adams with that of Jefferson in a beautiful tribute to the former. His speech ended in the following words:

"Scarcely has the funeral knell of our Jefferson been sounded in our ears, when we are startled by the death-bell of another patriot, his zealous coadjutor in the holy cause of the Revolution—one among the foremost of those who sought his country's disenthrallment—of Adams, the compeer of his early fame, the opposing orb of his meridian, the friend of his old age, and his companion to the realm of bliss. They have sunk together in death, and have fallen on the same glorious day into that sleep that knows no waking. Let not party spirit break the rest of their slumbers, but let us hallow their memory for the good deeds they have done, and implore that God who rules the universe to smile on our country." [20]

Tyler's reverence for Jefferson must have added an emotional quality to his elocution that imparted to it exceptional fervor. The Richmond *Enquirer* reported that the speech had been received with the warmest acclamations in every quarter. After quoting the *National Intelligencer* as pro-

[20] For the text of this address, see Tyler, *Letters and Times*, I, 346–354.

nouncing it a "brilliant and impressive oration," the *Enquirer* added, "But what if the editor of the *National Intelligencer* had heard it delivered." [21] This address was not a mere eulogy on admired greatness; it was a confession of faith. In it may be found much of the doctrine that constituted Tyler's political creed.

It was not until the opening of the next session of the legislature (December 4, 1826) that the governor sent in his first long, formal message. This message is a paper worthy of the pen of the chief executive of a great commonwealth. The proposals were sane and wise, the arguments in their favor able, and the method of presentation clear and convincing. It proclaimed an abiding belief in the doctrine of States' rights and a strong disapproval of the centralizing tendencies of the Federal government. Except for its undue length it is almost a model as a state paper.

The prosperity and happiness of the country were alluded to in the usual conventional way. As a means to the perpetuation of these blessings a plan of education for the masses was suggested. For "if the mind be set free from the bonds in which ignorance would bind it, the body will sooner or later partake of its condition; and the most effectual mode of enslaving the one is by benighting the other." The educational system outlined was to be built on the slender foundations that had already been laid.

The first step toward the establishment of a public school system in Virginia was made in 1810, when a bill was passed by the legislature providing for the creation of the Literary Fund. The act ordered that "all escheats, confiscations, fines, penalties and forfeitures, and all rights accruing to the State as derelict, shall be set aside for the encouragement of learning." Tyler's father was governor of the commonwealth at this time, and it was probably in response to his recommendation that this law had been enacted. An act was passed the next year by which the Literary Fund was set

[21] *Ibid.*, 354.

apart for the purpose of "providing schools for the poor in any county of the State." [22]

The fund had grown continually from the beginning, and on Tyler's accession had reached an amount little less than $1,400,000. The annual income from this fund was about $70,000, more than two-thirds of which ($45,000) was used for the education of indigent children.[23] In this way 9,779 children were given a little schooling as a public charity.

The governor indicated great dissatisfaction with this plan of public instruction. He maintained that only a small number of the youth were reached by it and that it was of little benefit to them because of the irregularity and uncertainty of the system. In some instances a school would be open for a few months, and in others a year. But it often happened that after the children had made a good start in the primary branches, the school would be discontinued and the pupils would be returned to their parents to forget what they had already learned. He might also have added that the aid given indigent children caused them to be looked down upon as paupers by their fellow pupils. It is quite likely that in many instances the intellectual gain under such a system was offset by a spiritual loss resulting from the development of a sense of inferiority in the beneficiaries of these charity schools.

Moreover, this method of instruction was more expensive than it should have been. By drawing a comparison between the educational system of New York and that of Virginia he showed that the people of the former commonwealth were getting a great deal more for their money than were those of the latter. Virginia needed a public school system (the message went on to state) not for poor children alone, as was then the case, but for all classes. And it was particularly desirable that the children of the great middle class should be given the means of education.

[22] C. J. Heatwole, *History of Education in Virginia* (New York, 1916), 104.
[23] *Jour., Va. House of Delegates,* session 1826–27, 147–150.

As a remedy for these unsatisfactory conditions he proposed that the counties be divided into school districts and in each a permanent school be established, under the management of trustees elected by the people. This school should be directed by a competent instructor. Attendance should be absolutely free or else the tuition charge should be low enough to afford all the children an opportunity for an education.[24]

This was a well-meant gesture in favor of a public school system, but it proved to be an empty one. There was one fatal defect in the plan—it did not carry an adequate system for financing the scheme. The governor recommended that expenditures from the Literary Fund be suspended until the accumulations had increased to the point at which the interest would be sufficient to finance the schools. Just what should be done during this period of waiting he did not suggest. Schooling for the poor during the interim would either have to be suspended or provided for out of county levies.

A public school system worthy the name could not have been established in Virginia at that time without supplementing the income derived from the Literary Fund by a substantial revenue raised by taxation. Tyler did not have the boldness to recommend such a plan.

At one time it looked as if the governor's scheme of public education, with certain modifications, would be put into effect promptly. Resolutions favorable to the idea were adopted and a bill embodying the principles laid down in them was reported to the House of Delegates. This bill, however, was laid on the table, and no further action on it was taken during this session of the legislature (or at least no mention of it can be found in the *Journal*). Apparently, nothing was later done to carry out the governor's suggestions.[25]

[24] *Ibid.*, session 1826–27, 6–13.
[25] *Ibid.*, 147–150, 200.

A good deal of space in the governor's message was devoted to internal improvements. He made specific recommendations as to improvements in the means of communication by the construction of roads, and locks and dams on the James River and other streams, with a view to connecting the east more closely with the west. He pointed out that a considerable portion of the State lying west of the Alleghany Mountains, though rich in soil, was in certain regions almost in a state of nature. The citizens there could not reach the capital without going out of the State and using transportation facilities furnished by other States. It was not a matter of surprise, therefore, that the tide of emigration had passed around this area and gone farther west. Two roads should be opened up from the western borders of the State to the Valley region. There was also considerable ill feeling between the eastern and western sections of the commonwealth, and this sectionalism could be destroyed by the proper means of communication.

Another reason given for the State's speeding up its improvements in land and water transportation was that in so doing it would take away the excuse of the Federal government for expending money on internal improvements in the States. In this way a great political menace would be averted. For, as he considered, "more danger is to be apprehended to the State authorities by the exertion of the assumed power over roads and canals by the general government than from almost any other source. It holds out the tender of the strongest bribe which can be offered to a people inhabiting a country yet in its infancy, and which invites the exertions of man to its improvement in almost every direction." Let the State meet these demands and accustom the people to look to the State instead of the United States government for these improvements.[26]

Tyler's administration must have been generally regarded

[26] For text of this message, see *ibid.*, 6–13.

as successful, as no one appeared against him when he came up for re-election December 10, 1827. He received all the votes cast but two, which were scattered.[27]

One of the last of Tyler's recommendations (made on February 1, 1827) was in regard to the journals of the legislature. These records had been carelessly looked after, and the proceedings of three important sessions had been lost. Some of the journals were in manuscript and others were out of print. He suggested the reprinting of those that were out of print and of placing complete sets in the public offices and among the chief literary institutions.[28]

So far as the social and ceremonial functions of the office were concerned, Tyler performed them admirably. He was especially well fitted by education, training, and culture to play the rôle of social leader. George Wythe Munford, who, by virtue of his position as clerk of the House of Delegates, was in close touch with official life in Richmond, considered Governor Tyler exceptionally happy in the performance of his duties at the executive mansion. ". . . such was his ease and familiarity," he said, "that everybody could approach him without the least restraint, and he transacted business with such promptness that it was a pleasure to have official intercourse with him. He was so frank and generous, so social and cordial, so genial and kind, and withal so manly and high-toned, and so familiar with the duties of his station that you were ready to give him your hand and heart in return for his, which he seemed ever ready to proffer." [29]

The governor was ably assisted by his charming wife. She was perfectly at home with the exclusive society of Richmond, and the social life at the executive mansion set a high standard for simplicity and naturalness. The one and only drawback to complete success in this line of activity was a lean purse. The governor's salary was small, and Tyler—so

<hr>

[27] *Ibid.*, 22. [28] *Jour., Va. House of Delegates, loc. cit.*, 131.
[29] Tyler, *Letters and Times*, I, 356.

he afterwards asserted—was too poor to meet the social demands of the office.[30]

Richmond at this time was not out at the elbows as it
had been when his father was governor. It was now a well-
appointed little city with a population of about fifteen thousand.[31] The ugly and uncomfortable structure that housed his
father's family had been replaced by a new executive mansion. This was a plain building but was adequately furnished
and well adapted to social functions. In the inventory of the
furnishings at the time it was occupied by the second Governor Tyler, mention is made of considerable silverware and
mahogany furniture. Champagne glasses and seventy-seven
wine glasses are listed. Candlesticks are mentioned but no
lamps. The four bedrooms were furnished with mattresses
and feather beds.[32]

Tyler served only a small part of his second term. He
was elected United States Senator and so sent in his resignation as governor to take effect March 4, 1827. When he retired from the governorship he was honored with a dinner
given by members of the legislature and citizens of Richmond. The following toast was offered: "John Tyler—our
friend and guest—a Republican too firm to be driven from
his principles—too upright to be swerved by the laws of
ambition or power." Tyler replied by a speech of some
length, which he concluded by offering this sentiment: "The
Federative system: In its simplicity there is grandeur; in its
preservation there is liberty; in its destruction, tyranny." [33]

[30] At the time of his inauguration as governor he invited the members of the
legislature to a banquet. He had for them a plentiful supply of Virginia ham
and a huge mass of well-cooked corn bread, together with a copious supply
of Monongahela whisky. With this plain fare he hoped to show the law-
makers how much in need the governor was of a higher salary. Foote, H. S.,
Casket of Reminiscences (Washington, 1874), 58.
[31] In 1820, the population was 12,060; in 1830, 16,060. *Census Reports,
Eleventh Census, 1930. Population*, I, 18.
[32] *Jour., Va. House of Delegates, loc. cit.*, 99–101.
[33] Tyler, *op. cit.*, I, 371–373.

CHAPTER VI

THE FASCES EXCHANGED FOR
THE TOGA

IT IS one of the strange anomalies of history that John Tyler, whose long public career was one persistent fight against nationalism, owed his election to the two highest positions ever held by him to the support of political groups which were strong protagonists of nationalism. He could not have been elected to the United States Senate in 1827 nor to the Vice-Presidency in 1840 had he not been supported by political factions that were opposed to the doctrine of States' rights and favored a broad and loose construction of the Constitution. Moreover, his election to the Senate was secured at the cost of defeating the most brilliant champion of the States' rights cause of his day and generation.

John Randolph had been chosen by the Virginia Assembly in December, 1825, to fill out the unexpired term of James Barbour, who had resigned his seat.[1] As this term would end in 1827, the Virginia legislature proceeded at the beginning of this year to choose his successor. The States' rights wing of the Republican Party had a majority in the assembly, and since Randolph had always been an ardent advocate of the States' rights doctrine, it was expected that he would be chosen to succeed himself. The influential Richmond *Enquirer* was supporting him and predicting his reelection without opposition.

The friends of Adams and Clay were bitterly opposed to him, whom they rightfully considered the archenemy of the

---

[1] Richmond *Enquirer*, Dec. 10, 1825.

73

Administration. Thomas Ritchie, the able editor of the *Enquirer*, thought that the Administration would move heaven and earth to compass his defeat. "This is no time," he continued, "for Virginia to sacrifice John Randolph at the shrine of an Administration which she dislikes." [2]

John Randolph had early in his Congressional career been in opposition to the elder Adams because he was a Federalist and he had attacked John Quincy Adams's policy with still greater vehemence. "I bore some humble part," he said, "in putting down the dynasty of John the First, and, by the Grace of God, I hope to aid in putting down the dynasty of John the Second." [3] With his brilliant and biting sarcasm, his apt use of illustrations, his numerous literary references, he proved a most formidable opponent of the administration of John Quincy Adams. Randolph, as he says, put his hand, like Hannibal, on the altar and swore "eternal enmity against him and his, politically." [4] The ill will he displayed toward Adams was not without provocation, for the latter was also an adept in venting spleen. Adams characterized Randolph as "the image and superscription of a great man, stamped upon base metal." [5]

Henry Clay, the Secretary of State, also came in for a large share of the vitriolic abuse that Randolph was hurling against public men. On one occasion Clay was likened to a rotten mackerel lying in the sun, which keeps on shining and stinking. Finally, throwing discretion to the winds, he spoke of the association of Clay and Adams as "the coalition of Blifil and Black George," a combination "of the Puritan with the blackleg." [6] Clay felt that this insult demanded a challenge and he promptly sent one to Randolph. The courage and generosity displayed by Randolph in the duel which

---

[2] *Richmond Enquirer*, Dec. 14, 1826.

[3] W. C. Bruce, *John Randolph of Roanoke* (New York and London, 1922), I, 543.

[4] *Ibid.*, I, 511.   [5] Tyler, *Letters and Times of the Tylers*, I, 395.

[6] Bruce, *op. cit.*, I, 513; *Register of Debates in Congress*, 19th Cong., 1st sess., 401.

followed went far toward expiating the inexcusable impetu-
ousness that had provoked it. For he refused to return
Clay's fire after the latter had missed him.

The Adams-Clay faction of the Republican Party, therefore, determined to prevent the re-election of Randolph if
there were any possibility of doing so. But as their followers
in the Virginia Assembly did not exceed thirty in number,[7]
they could hope to accomplish their aim only by winning support from the States' rights men. This was not an unreasonable expectation, however, as some of the latter group
strongly disapproved of the antics that Randolph had performed in Congress. They felt that by his unconventional
behavior he was weakening their cause and exposing himself
as their spokesman to ridicule. One of the anti-Administration members of the assembly said that he wanted someone
in the Senate who would represent the ideas of Virginia
"with temperance and moderation, without inflaming his
enemies and mortifying his friends." [8] Randolph's opponents exploited this feeling as far as possible and related
with due exaggeration every instance of his violation of Senatorial decorum.

When the question of choosing a successor to Randolph
came up, Tyler was in favor of his re-election and expressed
the hope that Judge Barbour would not appear as a candidate against him. He admitted, however (in a confidential
letter to his brother-in-law, Judge Christian), that his enthusiasm for him had been shaken by the "most extraordinary excitement" exhibited by Randolph in the previous
spring at the race track in Richmond. He still preferred him
to anyone else, although he deplored his course, believing
that it was due to the influence of high political fervor,
which "would give way to rest and the summer's repose."
Before the meeting of the assembly Tyler thought that
Randolph would certainly be re-elected.[9]

[7] Richmond *Enquirer,* Aug. 21, 1827.   [8] *Ibid.,* Dec. 21, 1826.
[9] Tyler, *op. cit.,* I, 343–344.

The opponents of Randolph approached Tyler and assured him that they could and would elect him if he would allow them to use his name. Tyler had made a creditable showing in 1824 in the race for the Senate against Littleton W. Tazewell, although the latter was his senior by fifteen years. Since that time his prestige had been increased by a successful record as governor, and he would, therefore, be a strong candidate if he could be induced to run. To this overture Governor Tyler replied through his friends that he was not a candidate and did not want the office. On the contrary, he still urged the re-election of Randolph. The opposition then apparently veered toward Barbour; but he declined the offer, and again it seemed that Randolph would have no difficulty in winning the election.

On the day before the vote was taken Mr. Caperton, a member of the legislature, had an interview with Tyler, and stated that the opposition was going to run him. Tyler protested and gave both political and personal reasons against the proceeding. "But he declared the fixed purpose of the majority to run me at all events. I declared it to be against my decided wishes and that I would not yield my consent to be nominated. On the same morning I supplicated and entreated Mr. Caperton to turn aside the purpose of the supposed majority, but he declared himself fixed in his views and pronounced the election certain. He returned to me at night. My opposition continued undiminished."

This sounds like the statement of a man who says no but would like to be understood as meaning yes. It looked as if he were wavering between two opinions, being pulled away from the office by a feeling of friendship for Randolph and toward it by his political ambition. Caperton probably sensed this feeling and asked him the point-blank question whether he would accept the office if it were tendered him. Hitherto his position had been that of not choosing to run, but now he had to be more definite. His answer was that he "claimed to myself [himself] the right to decide that question as I [he] thought proper." [10]

There was nothing dishonorable in his entering the race for the Senate. Few public men in that or any other day would have declined so great a distinction, even though the acceptance of it had placed him in rivalry with a political friend. The personal relations between Tyler and Randolph were not close enough to justify the sacrifice on the part of either of high political preferment out of deference to the interests of the other. Certainly Randolph, who had obtained his seat through the defeat of his own half-brother, could not expect such sacrificial altruism from one who had never been intimately associated with him.

Soon after Caperton had left, William O. Goode appeared to present to the governor a letter signed by Banks, Smith, and three other prominent members of the assembly. This letter was as follows: "We understand that the friends of the Administration and others will support you for the Senate in opposition to Mr. Randolph. We desire to understand distinctly whether they have your consent or not; and if not, will you be pleased to say explicitly that you will not abandon the Chair of State at this time to accept a seat in the Senate?" [11] Some of Tyler's friends regarded this letter as having been prompted by a dictatorial spirit and the intention to force him into an abandonment of those persons who were leading the opposition to Randolph.[12]

To this abrupt, if not rude, request Tyler made a dignified and proper reply. It was in substance as follows: He was not acquainted with the political preferences of those who were disposed to sustain him for the Senate; his views on the fundamental principles of the government were the same as those held by Randolph; and he had a high admira-

---

[10] John Tyler to Dr. Curtis, Apr. 13, 1827; *John Tyler Papers* (L.C.), I, 6271–73.

[11] Richmond *Enquirer*, Jan. 16, 1827.   [12] *Ibid.*, Feb. 27, 1827.

tion for him because of "his undeviating attachment to the
Constitution, manifested . . . through all the events of a
long political life." He had also opposed all solicitations
from his friends that he should become a candidate against
Randolph, and had uniformly declared to everyone with
whom he conversed everywhere that there was no consideration, either political or private, which could lead him to desire the office. "Should the office in opposition to his wishes
(a result which he could not anticipate), be conferred upon
him, he would then give to the expression of the legislative
will such reflection and pronounce such decision, as his sense
of what was due to it might seem to require." [13]

On Saturday, January 13, 1827, the assembly took up the
question of the election of a Senator. Randolph and Tyler
were both put in nomination and speeches were made in behalf of each candidate. One speaker in supporting Tyler said
that Tyler and Randolph had the same principles and that
"the only difference was that Mr. Tyler had not the same
personal antipathies." He also contended that Randolph
had no influence in the Senate and that he had abused Jefferson, Madison, and Monroe. "Wit and sarcasm could do no
good."

Samuel McD. Moore, of Rockbridge County, was especially severe in his criticism of Randolph's erratic behavior.
"The Senate of the United States," he said, "had been the
most august and dignified body in the world until Mr. Randolph was elected to it. . . . But, if the accounts of Mr.
Randolph's conduct in that body are to be believed, it no
longer possessed that dignity and elevation of character.
On one occasion, it was said, he strewed his papers all over
the floor, and prohibited anybody from touching them; on
another, he undressed and dressed himself in the Senate
Chamber." He also charged that Randolph drank to excess
and cut the capers of a Merry Andrew.[14]

It is needless to say that these accusations were based

[13] *Richmond Enquirer,* Jan. 16, 1827.   [14] *Ibid.,* Jan. 16, 1827.

largely on rumor, and many of them were slanderous, but it is quite likely that Randolph could have served his State to much greater advantage had he not given too free a rein to his idiosyncrasies.

The claims of Randolph were also ably upheld. One of his adherents said: "No man ever loved a country more than John Randolph loves Virginia. He loves your institutions, your policy, your usages, your manners." He appealed to the members to vote for Randolph as a protest against the Administration and contended that his defeat would be construed outside the State as an endorsement of the Administration by Virginia. Outsiders will think that "she is like the sheep in the fable, who sacrificed their dogs to conciliate the wolves."

Wilson, another friend of Randolph, answered the charges made by Moore, asserting that they rested on hearsay evidence. He had, he said, no objection to Tyler from a moral or political point of view, but did not think he "could sustain the principles of Virginia with the same ability." Moreover, if Tyler were chosen he would be placed in an unpleasant position. He would be supported by all the Administration forces and by only a small minority of his own party. If he should represent this minority he would not be representing the majority that elected him. On the other hand, if he should represent the Administration party "he would misrepresent the State." He was satisfied, however, that Tyler would act in accordance with his convictions.[15]

At this juncture, Christian, a brother-in-law of Governor Tyler, rose and said that reports regarding the latter's view and wishes had been circulated which were calculated to injure him. He understood that a member of the House had a letter from Tyler and he desired that it be read. Gordon rose and said that he was in possession of this letter. It was the one which the governor had written in answer to the communication received from Banks, Smyth, and other

[15] *Ibid.*

members of the assembly. These papers were handed to the clerk and both were read by him.

When the vote was taken Tyler was elected by a very small majority on the first ballot. The vote was as follows: Tyler, 115; Randolph, 110; scattering, 2; and blank, 1.[16]

The causes and significance of Tyler's victory were discussed by Thomas Ritchie in an able editorial in the *Enquirer*. He expressed surprise and regret over the defeat of Randolph. "Whatever were the errors," he continued, "into which the excess of his sensibility betrayed him, he had defended the ramparts of the Constitution with a zeal which never wavered, and an eloquence which none could equal. He seemed in some respects the very man who was called for by the occasion. Corruption had cowered beneath him and the panders of public abuses were shrinking under the matchless powers of the modern Chatham." Ritchie was not, however, discouraged over the choice of Tyler, whom he regarded as an ardent States' rights man and a strong opponent of the Administration. "John Tyler is bound by every consideration of uniform principle and of generous interest to go with the doctrines of Virginia. He will carry into the Senate of the United States that love for the school of '98 and '99, which he has so loudly and so often proclaimed. The friends of the Coalition will be deceived, if they count upon him." This statement proved to be a true prophecy as to Tyler's record in the Senate.[17]

Ritchie thought that Randolph's defeat was due to a combination of several causes. Those who voted for Tyler included all those who had once belonged to the Federalist Party, with perhaps one or two exceptions; all of the friends of Adams and Clay; some of those who favored internal improvements at the expense of the national government; and some anti-Administration men of the States' rights school, who had turned against Randolph because of his al-

---

[16] *Journal, Va. House of Delegates,* session 1826–27, 97.
[17] Richmond *Enquirer,* Jan. 16, 1827.

leged sayings and actions in the Senate during the preceding winter. Tyler's opponents had also used bad tactics in sending a curt inquiry to the governor. Ritchie was of the opinion that the reading of this letter and Tyler's reply to it won for him four or five votes.

Randolph's defeat was also due in part to the fact that he refused to use even the legitimate arts of a politician. He made no effort to win a personal following among the members of the legislature. But all of these circumstances combined would not have defeated Randolph had not Tyler received the support of some personal friends in the assembly. The result was, therefore, to a considerable extent a personal victory for Tyler, and he had a right to be proud of the outcome.

This defeat was a terrible blow to Randolph's pride; for not only did he value above everything else the good opinion of his fellow Virginians, but he preferred the place of Senator to that of any other in the government. How deeply he was hurt was shown by the following letter to his friend, Dr. Brockenbrough:

My first impression was to resign. There were, notwithstanding, obvious and strong objections to this course; my duty to my friends, the giving of a handle to the charges of my enemies that I was the slave of spleen and passion, and many more that I need not specify. There was but one other course left, and that I have taken, not without the decided approbation of my colleague, and many other friends here. I find, too, that it was heartily desired by my enemies that I should throw up my seat. . . . Nothing then remains but a calm and dignified submission to the disgrace that has been put upon me. It is the best evidence that I can give my friends of the sense which I feel, and will forever cherish, of their kind and generous support.[18]

No sign of his disappointment did he allow to appear to the curious and unsympathetic public in Washington. On the contrary, he accepted his defeat with an outward calm

[18] Bruce, *op. cit.*, 539–540.

that was worthy of the great man he was. While the newspaper boys were crying on the streets of the city the news of his defeat and while a number of his enemies were seated in the Senate Chamber, who had come over from the House to gloat over his downfall, he delivered a speech which was one of the most remarkable of his entire career. A correspondent of the *Enquirer* said of it that he spoke "with a dignity of manner, beauty of expression, and force and propriety of argument, which charmed and delighted all his friends." [19]

This contest and its aftermath brought to Tyler also a good deal of heartburning. In a personal letter to Dr. Henry Curtis, written nearly three months later, he complained feelingly of "the gall and venom of personal rancor and political disappointment" that had been poured upon him. He referred particularly to a speech made by R. Morris in Hanover County, in which Morris had "assailed me [Tyler] with great asperity and charged me with having purposely lulled Mr. Randolph's friends into a state of security, thereby deadening their exertions with the intent of consummating my own election. That my preference was expressed for Mr. Randolph over Judge Barbour with the view of forcing Judge Barbour from the field and thereby of concentrating the whole vote of the discontents on myself." [20]

Strange to say, Randolph seemed to harbor no ill will toward Tyler nor to blame him for his defeat. When they met at the races in Richmond, Randolph advanced toward Tyler with outstretched hand and said: "And how is your Excellency? and when I say your Excellency I mean *your excellency*." [21] When Tyler went to Washington to take his seat in the Senate, Randolph called on him.[22] Ten days later Tyler wrote to his daughter Mary: "Tell your mother that

[19] Richmond *Enquirer*, Jan. 20, 1827.
[20] *John Tyler Papers* (L.C.), I, 6271-73.
[21] *Tyler's Quarterly Historical and Genealogical Magazine,* II, 140.
[22] Tyler, *Letters and Times,* I, 380.

I returned Mr. Randolph's visit, and was received in a style somewhat stately, but entirely respectful; since when I have received another card from him. He conversed in a low whisper, and said that he labored under pulmonary consumption." [23]

The first important problem that confronted Tyler after his election to the Senate was that of deciding which of the aspirants for the Presidency he would support. Although the election would not be held for nearly two years, the campaign was on and prominent politicians were expected to line up behind one or the other of the candidates. The contest was between Jackson and President Adams and had been going on since the accession of the latter.

It was well-nigh impossible for anyone to remain neutral in a fight to which Jackson was a party. And yet for a while Tyler tried to act this difficult rôle. For some months he would not make any statement as to his attitude in the coming election. This silence was caused partly by the feeling that his opponents in the Senatorial contest were trying to force him into an endorsement of Jackson, and he was determined not to be pushed into a commitment by them.[24] Besides, he was not entirely satisfied with either of the candidates. His preference was for DeWitt Clinton, of New York, whose success in constructing the Erie Canal had demonstrated the feasibility of making internal improvements by the States. He, therefore, regarded Clinton as the proper exponent of the States' rights doctrine.[25]

By December 8, 1827, however, he had come out definitely for Jackson. But he was supporting him then largely as a choice of evils, and not with the enthusiasm that a politician usually exhibits for an admired leader. In letters to John Rutherford and Dr. Curtis (December, 1827) he

---

[23] *Ibid.*, 390.
[24] Tyler to Dr. Curtis, Mar. 18, 1828; Tyler, *Letters and Times,* I, 384.
[25] *Ibid.*, I, 375.

stated his position quite clearly. He was by that time "most earnestly solicitous for Jackson's success" and believed that it was "loudly called for by the present state of things." He admitted that he had entertained the strongest objections to General Jackson, and even then there were many whom he would prefer to him. "But every day that passes inspires me with the strong hope that this administration will be characterized by simplicity—I mean Republican simplicity." He was of the opinion that Jackson would not be inclined to raise the protective duties and would be against internal improvements at Federal expense, although he had voted for roads and canals.[26]

Even if Jackson were not an ideal candidate he was the only available alternative, now that Clinton was not a possibility. Adams he would not consider at all because the principles laid down by him in his first message were "entirely ultra." "That message I have ever regarded as a direct insult upon Virginia. It mocked at her principles, and was intended to make her the laughingstock of the rest of the Union." "The mere fact that Daniel Webster (a Hartford Conventionist) had been his mouthpiece from the beginning, had always been with me enough to damn him." [27] "Turning to him [Jackson] I may at least indulge in hope; looking on Adams I must despair." [28]

[26] Tyler to Dr. Curtis, Mar. 18, 1828; Tyler, *Letters and Times*, I, 376–380.
[27] *Ibid.*, 379.
Tyler was mistaken in thinking that Webster had been a member of the Hartford Convention.
[28] *Ibid.*, 383–386.

CHAPTER VII

LAWMAKING IN STATE AND NATION

THE rapid advance in Tyler's political fortunes was accompanied by a corresponding increase in his domestic responsibilities; for he was rearing a large family which had to be maintained according to the high standard set by the landed aristocracy of Virginia. To meet these requirements he was often forced into uncomfortable financial straits. So much time had been devoted to public affairs that very little had been left for developing a legal practice which when attended to had promised a remuneration sufficient for the proper support of his family. Moreover, his devotion to public life had not been rewarded with a large income, for the emoluments of the offices which he had held were all small.

One of these seasons of financial embarrassment came at the time he was preparing to go to Washington to assume the duties of Senator. On September 4, 1827, he wrote to his brother-in-law, Dr. Curtis, saying: "My monied affairs are all out of sorts—so much so that I scarcely know how I shall reach Washington." To meet these pressing needs he asked Dr. Curtis to buy one of his slaves, Eliza Ann, or if he did not wish to do this to sell her for him.

Dr. Curtis declined to buy her and Tyler again wrote to him to sell her as speedily as possible as he had to dispose of her in order to get to Washington. "I have to request," he said, "that if you cannot meet with a *ready sale* in your neighborhood, which I would prefer, you will hand her over to the Hubbard's for public auction." A little later (November 16) as he was starting to Richmond to arrange for his trip, he again referred to his financial straits and the necessity of selling Eliza Ann. He spoke of his needs as being "very pressing, more so than at any previous period." He thought that if Dr. Curtis had not already sold her "the better way would be to put her in the wagon and send her directly to the Hubbard's. Her sale has become indispensably necessary to meet the demands of my trip to Richmond." [1]

Whether the obliging doctor succeeded in finding a buyer for Eliza Ann the records do not disclose. This sale must either have been effected or some other financial arrangement made, for Tyler was able to go to Washington and take his seat in the Senate at the opening of the term in December, 1827.[2] He seems, however, to have been absent during the greater part of January, as his vote is not given in the yeas and nays prior to the twenty-second of that month. At this time he made his first appearance on the floor of the Senate in a speech on the Cumberland Road Bill. His absence had doubtless been due to illness, for in a speech on February 4 he referred to the fact that he was not yet restored to his normal health.

In his first speech he entered upon a renewal in the Senate of his lifelong fight against nationalism, which he had begun in the House a few years before. He strongly opposed the policy of making internal improvements at the expense of the Federal government. In this initial battle for the doctrine of States' rights he took a stand on the strict construction of the Constitution that must have received the entire approval of the straitest sect of the Virginia school.

By this time the Cumberland Road had been built as far as Bridgeport, Ohio. A bill was now before the Senate providing for the extension of this turnpike from Bridgeport to Zanesville, Ohio, and for surveying a route from Zanesville to Columbia, Missouri. Tyler opposed the measure on the

[1] *John Tyler Papers* (L.C., abbreviation for Library of Congress), I, 6275, 6277-79.
[2] *Register of Debates in Congress,* 20th Cong., 1st sess., 1.

ground that it was both inexpedient and unconstitutional. One objection he raised was that it would increase the patronage of the executive, an evil which should be carefully guarded against. "What an electioneering weapon dc gentlemen thus place in the hands of this government." [3]

The position taken by Tyler on internal improvements in his first speech was persistently maintained throughout his entire career as Senator. From time to time bills were offered and passed providing for the extension of the Cumberland Road farther and farther west. All of these measures were opposed by him.[4]

Tyler made a second speech in the Senate on February 1. Despite the handicap of ill-health, he felt called upon to raise his voice in opposition to a measure for appropriating $1,200,000 to the surviving officers of the Revolutionary War. This appropriation would, so he contended, be a bonus, as the government had already fully met its pledges to these officers. This was one of the ablest speeches that he ever made. His arguments were virtually unanswerable and were presented in a straightforward, logical manner.[5]

Tyler was able again to voice his opposition to protection when the tariff of 1828 came up for consideration. This bill, which provided for high duties on hemp, wool, iron, and molasses, was proposed by the friends of Jackson to strengthen his chances for the Presidency rather than to promote the economic interests of the country. Because of its objectionable features it was known as the "Tariff of Abominations." [6] It is needless to say that Tyler voted against this bill.[7] He regarded the rates of the act of 1824 as oppressively high, and was strenuously opposed to increasing them. The one redeeming feature of the proposed

[3] Ibid., loc. cit., 107–109.
[4] Ibid., 20th Cong., 1st sess., 470, 608, 675; 2nd sess., 43–44, 74; 21st Cong., 1st sess., 340, 343.
[5] Ibid., loc. cit., 228–234.
[6] Massachusetts Historical Society Proceedings, February, 1916, 212.
[7] Register of Debates, loc. cit., 785, 786.

measure, he thought, was the provision for a tax on molasses, wool, iron, and hemp, because it would impose burdens on the North corresponding to those borne by the
South.[8] Later (April 23) when he became convinced that
the bill would be passed, he was somewhat consoled by the
fact that it included a high duty on these commodities. "We
shall be able," he said, "to hold on to molasses, hemp, iron,
and wool, and if it passes we may hope for reaction in the
North which may ultimately enable us to get back to safe
principles." [9]

He thus considered the most attractive feature of the bill
to be those provisions that the New Englanders regarded as
its abominations. His anxiety to keep them in the bill arose
from the hope that their inclusion would cause the defeat of
the whole proposal. This idea is expressed in a letter to Dr.
Curtis, May 1, 1828. He said: "The hated tariff bill—that
curse to the whole South—is reported to the Senate with sundry villainous amendments. Its fate rests upon our ability
to preserve the bill in its present shape. If we can do so it
will be rejected." [10]

Tyler's career in the Senate was interrupted for a few
months by a call to Richmond to aid in changing the fundamental law of the Old Dominion. For more than half a
century the government of Virginia had been based on the
constitution written by George Mason and adopted in 1776.
The Declaration of Rights that prefaced this constitution
was conceived in the spirit of the times and, therefore, proclaimed the equalitarian philosophy soon afterwards em-

[8] Tyler to Dr. Curtis, Mar. 18, 1828; Tyler, *Letters and Times,* I, 385.
[9] Tyler to Dr. Curtis, Apr. 23, 1828; *John Tyler Papers* (L.C.), I, 6287.
[10] *Ibid.,* I, 6290.
In the short session of the Twentieth Congress (the second, lasting from
December 1, 1828 to March 3, 1829) Tyler took no important part. His name
is not given at all in the list of speakers. This was a "lame-duck" Congress and
nothing of prime importance came up. Moreover, for a month or more of this
time he was confined to his room by illness. Tyler to John Rutherford, Feb. 23,
1829; MS. in Duke University Library.

bodied in the Declaration of Independence. With such a profession of faith one would expect a democratic scheme of government; but this was not the case. That distrust of the masses which was characteristic of the ruling classes of the Revolutionary and post-Revolutionary periods found expression in this the first constitution of the Old Dominion. It is true that the government of Virginia under this constitution was more liberal than it had been under royal rule, but it was still strongly tinged with aristocratic practices. That this constitution should have lasted as long as it did, without modification, is both a high tribute to the statesmanship that framed it and an indictment against the conservatism that sustained it.

The first quarter of the nineteenth century had not ended before the spirit of democracy, which was growing up so vigorously in the West, had taken deep root in the western portion of Virginia. And just as the West was clamoring for a louder voice in the management of national affairs, so the western Virginians were demanding a larger share in the government of their State. They were asking for a democratic system of representation—one in which membership in the legislature would be based on white population and chosen by universal suffrage. They were dissatisfied with the constitution, largely because under it suffrage was limited to freeholders, and each county, regardless of size, was accorded two representatives in the lower house of the assembly. Under this method of apportionment the east with its small counties could outvote the west with its large counties. Such a system gave property a stronger voice in the State and local government than the malcontents were willing to grant. Moreover, certain abuses had arisen in connection with the administration of local affairs. These conditions called for change, and accordingly a reform movement was in due time set on foot. All parts of the State were represented in the call for reform, but the demand was most insistent in the region west of the Blue Ridge

Mountains. This agitation led to the calling of a State constitutional convention.

The calling of this Convention was a cause of embarrassment to Tyler. His prominence in public affairs imposed upon him the obligation to serve the State as a member of the Convention provided his services were desired. And yet active participation in the work of this body would involve commitments which would lessen his popularity in certain portions of the State. To take a stand on any of the important questions that were at issue between east and west would be to antagonize one or the other of these sections. A politician whose constituency was the entire State would naturally wish to avoid such a risk if he could do so without seeming to shirk his duty. It was just such an attitude that Tyler showed in a letter (February 23, 1829) to his friend John Rutherford.[11] There is no doubt that Tyler's reluctance to take part in the Convention, as indicated in this confidential letter, was based on a real desire to avoid an embarrassing responsibility rather than on the indifference

[11] The original of this letter is in the collection of manuscripts belonging to Duke University. It was printed by Dr. Lyon G. Tyler in the *William and Mary College Quarterly* (first series), I, 128–130.

In this letter Tyler asked that his friend Rutherford contrive some way by which he could escape from the dilemma in which circumstances had placed him. "What then," he said, "can be done to keep me out? It can only be done, it appears to me, through the instrumentality of some of my particular friends, among whom I rank yourself. Might not arguments be urg[e]d to the members from the District by yourself and Christian calculated to satisfy them, without my being seen in it? Nay, might not a ticket be agreed on by you, from which my name should be excluded? I rely upon your friendship, which has so repeatedly been manifested to me. Converse with Christian and write me shortly. I have said that I did not desire my own wishes or views to be made known. The reasons are obvious. I do not wish to manifest an indifference or repugnance to the public will—which if once *openly declar[e]d* I must and will obey. This is the principle which has always govern[e]d me and to which I have always submitted. To manifest openly, however, a disinclination to be in the Convention might be tortur[e]d by my enemies into a fear of responsibility, etc., etc. If this thing be not arrested before I reach home, I fear it will be too late to move in it. My friends must manage it in my absence, otherwise if there be a settled design to run me, I fear it will be too late to arrest it. Yourself and Christian are the only persons to whom I have communicated these views, and whatever you decide upon will be satisfactory to me."

to honors which politicians are fond of simulating. That he was opposed to calling a convention is shown by the fact that on February 5, 1825, he voted in the House of Delegates against a bill to take the voice of the people as to whether a convention should be called to revise the constitution.[12]

An additional reason for Tyler's not accepting membership in the State Convention was an important change which was made (1829) in his private affairs. At this time he moved from the home of his boyhood to "Gloucester Place," in Gloucester County, on the northern side of York River. This property had been taken over in payment of a debt owed him by a friend.[13] As he did not feel able to hold both places, he had in the meantime sold "Greenway." The proper adjustment of his family to the new arrangement would doubtless call for all the time he could spare from his Senatorial duties.

He remained in Gloucester for eight years, and during this period devoted as much time to his law practice as his political duties would permit. He must also have carried on rather extensive farming operations for his plantation consisted of 631 ½ acres of land [14] and was manned with from twenty-three to twenty-six slaves over twelve years of age.[15]

Tyler's objections to serving in the Convention were overcome and he became a candidate to represent his home district, which included the Peninsular counties and the cities of Williamsburg and Richmond.[16] In a delegation of four he received the second highest vote, which was exceeded only by that cast for John Marshall, the Chief Justice.[17]

The Convention met at the time appointed and was in session three and a half months (October 5, 1829-January

---

[12] *Journal, Va. House of Delegates*, session 1824–25, 148–149, 149–150; Richmond *Enquirer*, Feb. 8, 1825.

[13] Tyler, *Letters and Times*, I, 415.

[14] *Ibid.*, 415–416; *Gloucester County Land Book*, 1833–34 (Archives, Va. State Library).

[15] *Property Book for Gloucester County*, 1834–37, *ibid.*

[16] *Proceedings and Debates of the Virginia State Convention* of 1829–30, 3.

[17] Tyler, *op. cit.*, I, 397.

15, 1830).[18] Its membership of ninety-six comprised many of the most noted men in the Old Dominion. The roster of names included two ex-Presidents of the United States (Madison and Monroe) ; one future President (John Tyler) ; the Chief Justice of the United States (John Marshall) ; one governor (William B. Giles) ; two United States Senators (Tyler and Tazewell) ; twelve members of the Federal House of Representatives (prominent among whom was Philip Doddridge) ; several State judges (including A. P. Upshur) ; and a number of eminent lawyers (in which group B. W. Leigh was particularly prominent).[19]

On motion of ex-President Madison, James Monroe was unanimously chosen president of the Convention.[20] Four committees were promptly appointed to present measures for the deliberation and action of the Convention.[21] The most important of these four committees was the one on the legislative branch of the government. The chairman of this committee of twenty-four was B. W. Leigh, of Chesterfield, a county overlapping the boundary between the Tidewater and Piedmont sections. He was the dean of the conservatives. Other prominent members of the committee were Madison, Tazewell, Tyler, Randolph, and Doddridge.[22] The report of this committee furnished the basis of a great part of the debates of the Convention.

The western reformers, led by Doddridge, at first asked that representation in both houses of the assembly be apportioned according to population. Later they were willing to compromise on the basis of white population for the lower house and Federal numbers for the Senate. By this

---

[18] *Proceedings*, I, 883, 895.

[19] Hugh B. Grigsby, *The Virginia Convention of 1829-30* (*Virginia Historical Collections*, Richmond, 1854) ; *Niles' Register*, XXXVI, 285, 410; *Southern Literary Messenger*, XVII, 297-304.

[20] Monroe's health was poor, and later in the session (December 12) he resigned the presidency of and membership in the Convention. Thereupon, Philip B. Barbour, who had been acting as president, *pro tempore*, was chosen as the presiding officer. *Proceedings*, 620.

[21] *Ibid.*, 9-10, 20, 21.   [22] *Ibid.*, 22.

plan three fifths of the slaves would be counted in apportioning representatives in the Senate.[23] The conservatives, led by Leigh, Upshur, and other easterners, contended for Federal numbers for both houses.[24]

For a while the Convention was deadlocked on these issues. Finally, after a great deal of speechmaking, an agreement was reached on the questions of suffrage, representation, and the minor issues. The knotty problem of apportionment was settled by an arbitrary distribution between east and west of representatives in both houses. This distribution was practically on the basis of white population according to the census of 1820.[25]

As a method of distributing seats in the future could not be agreed upon, it was decided that apportionments could be made at intervals of not less than ten years by a two-thirds vote of both houses of the legislature. In making these distributions of seats, the assembly was free to follow any principle that might seem wise to a two-thirds majority of both houses.[26] Suffrage was broadened so as to include all adult male taxpayers who were heads of families or owned leasehold estates with a rental value of twenty dollars.[27]

In the settlement of the minor disputes, the conservatives won over the reformers. The term of the governor was extended to three years and his powers were enlarged. He was, however, still to be chosen as formerly by a joint ballot of the two houses of assembly.

The new constitution was very unsatisfactory to the trans-Alleghany region. When it was submitted to the voters for acceptance or rejection, every county but three in that section gave majorities against ratification. In Doddridge's county the vote was unanimous in favor of rejection.[28]

---

[23] *Ibid.,* 571.
[24] C. H. Ambler, *Sectionalism in Virginia from 1776–1861* (Chicago, 1910), 158.
[25] *Proceedings,* 667, 897–898.   [26] *Ibid.,* 849, 854.   [27] *Ibid.,* 900.
[28] Richmond *Enquirer,* Feb. 23, 1830; *Proceedings,* 3–5, 882, 903. See Ambler, *op. cit.,* 172, for map showing the vote by sections on the constitution.

Tyler did not play a conspicuous rôle in the Convention. He offered no important resolutions and took only a minor part in the discussions. He spoke several times, but these speeches were mostly short statements or explanations. So far as the recorded proceedings show, he did not address the Convention until December 3. In this talk he made an appeal for agreement between east and west based on compromise. He had come to the Convention, he said, "prepared to bind up in one common bond all the people of Virginia— to preserve the integrity of the State." A plan that would effect such a result would be gladly accepted by him even if it "visited the counties of his district with extensive disfranchisement." "His district paid an amount of revenue, equal within a very small fraction, to the amount paid by all the trans-Alleghany country." Under the plan which he was advocating Charles City, the county of his birth and residence, was to lose much of its political power. But he was willing to make this sacrifice "sooner than be instrumental in destroying those sentiments of brotherly feeling which had heretofore bound the State together." In his loyalty to Virginia he acknowledged no discrimination between those of the new blood and those of the old. In all his public course he had "acted in reference to all Virginia" and he "should continue to do so." Others, he felt, should be willing to go as far in the interest of harmony.[29]

Tyler's willingness to make concessions to the west was more apparent than real. In actual practice he proved himself a conservative, supporting the claims of the east. It is true that in a few instances he voted with Doddridge and the reformers,[30] but in the main on questions at issue between east and west he supported the measures championed by Leigh, Upshur, and the other eastern leaders. He admitted that under the old constitution there was not a fair distribution of seats in the assembly,[31] but he was not willing to

[29] *Proceedings*, 548–549.   [30] *Ibid.*, 636, 638, 689.
[31] In a letter to his daughter (April 30, 1828), Tyler declared that it was

make white population the basis for a new apportionment. According to a statement made in later life, he was in favor of white population as the basis of the lower house and a mixed ratio for the upper house of the assembly. In this way property would act as a check on numbers. Such an arrangement was quite in accord with his firm belief in the doctrine of checks and balances. He spoke of this plan privately to Judge Upshur and Chief Justice Marshall, but made no public utterance on the subject because of the uselessness of doing so, as the current of opinion was so strong the other way.[32]

Tyler's action in the Convention was not in harmony with the view thus expressed, for his votes, as recorded in the proceedings, were consistently against making white population the basis of representation in the lower house.[33] He also opposed every proposal to have future seats distributed according to white population.[34] One of these plans, offered by Doddridge, provided for future representation in the House of Delegates on the basis of white population and that of the Senate on Federal numbers. Tyler voted against it.[35] On the other hand he voted in favor of a proposal to

---

unjust for Charles City County with 180 voters to have the same number of representatives in the House of Delegates as Shenandoah County with 1200 voters. Tyler, *Letters and Times*, I, 399.

[32] Tyler to Col. Robert McCandlish, Feb. 22, 1851; *ibid.*, 402.

[33] As a member of the Legislative Committee he voted (October 16) against the resolution to put representation in the House of Delegates on a white basis. When this resolution was considered by the Convention, he voted with Leigh and against Doddridge in favor of tabling it. Another motion was offered the same day which declared for white population as the basis of apportionment in the lower house. Tyler voted no on this proposal. A month earlier (November 16) he had voted in the Committee of the Whole for Federal numbers as the basis for apportionment in the lower house. He went along with the other easterners in supporting the proposal finally adopted which provided for an arbitrary distribution of seats in both houses. He favored, however, a modification of this plan so as to give the smaller counties one representative each and the larger counties more than one in the lower house of the assembly. A plan to this effect was prepared by him, which on the advice of his colleagues he refrained from presenting to the Convention. A. C. Gordon, *William Fitzhugh Gordon* (New York and Washington, 1909), 160; *Proceedings*, 322, 341–342, 548, 667–668, 837, 838, 842.

[34] *Ibid.*, 835, 850, 851.   [35] *Ibid.*, 680, 681, 690.

put representation in the lower house on a combined basis of property and numbers.[36]

Not only did Tyler oppose the westerners in their efforts to secure a larger representation in the assembly, but he also voted against the attempts of the reformers to broaden the right of suffrage so as to include all adult male taxpayers who were householders or heads of families.[37] His aristocratic leanings were still further shown by his opposition to the popular election of the governor and sheriff.[38] In a short statement (December 21) he objected to any increase in the power of the governor provided he were to be chosen by the people. He also warned against the danger from the slightest infusion into the executive office of "a spice of monarchy." [39]

From this check on Tyler's record it is evident that he did not participate actively and aggressively in the proceedings of the Convention. This lukewarm attitude is accounted for by his son and biographer on the ground of ill-health.[40] In support of this theory it should be said that he was undoubtedly suffering during a part or all of the session from a stomach trouble that attacked him periodically throughout the greater part of his career.[41] It is probable that his views (as statements made by him in the campaign of 1840 [42] would indicate) were not so conservative as those of the voters of his district. If this were the case a strenuous op-

---

[36] *Proceedings*, 690.   [37] *Ibid.*, 640, 641, 642, 647, 650, 654, 827.
[38] *Ibid.*, 709, 710, 821, 822, 712–713.   [39] *Ibid.*, 711.
[40] Tyler, *op. cit.*, I, 399.   [41] See page 44.

[42] While Tyler was on his western tour in the campaign of 1840 (page 189), he was asked a number of questions by the Democratic Club of St. Clairsville, Ohio. In one of the queries he was requested to state whether in the Convention of 1829 he had favored a property qualification for voting and had opposed the election of the governor and the sheriffs by the people. His reply was that he had voted in that body as he had been instructed and had gone along with Chief Justice Marshall. St. Clairsville *Gazette*, Oct. 3, 1840.

A similar question was asked him at Steubenville, Ohio, to which he made a like reply. The Steubenville *Herald*, quoted in the Pittsburgh *Daily Advocate and Advertiser* for October 10, 1840.

position to reform would be prevented by conviction and an enthusiastic advocacy of it would be discouraged by prudence.

He was also forced into the embarrassing position of having to serve two masters. Good politics demanded that he please the conservatives of his district without antagonizing the liberals of the west, to whose support he would have to look if he kept his place in the United States Senate. Such a policy would require that his opposition to the demands of the west attract as little attention as possible and that it be softened by declarations of good intentions, in the use of which he was a past master. This might account for his protestations of love for the whole State without regard to sections.

Illness cannot fairly be urged as an excuse for his failure to assume responsibility in the Convention. If his health were poor enough to hamper his usefulness, he should have resigned his membership, as did ex-President Monroe. Whatever were the motives that prompted his comparative inactivity, Tyler's record in this body was not equal to the expectations raised by his previous career. In scanning the proceedings of the Convention one receives the impression that he played the part of a politician rather than that of a statesman. He did not add anything to his prestige by his connection with this body. Indeed, it would have been better for his reputation if he had yielded to his preferences and refused to become a candidate for the place.

The achievements of the Convention were pitiably small in comparison with the opportunity offered and the efforts put forth. When we contrast the ability and character of the men who sat in the Convention with the meager result of their deliberations, we feel that the reformers had ground for the complaint that the mountain had once more labored and given birth to a mouse. While some faltering steps toward democracy had been taken and some of the inequal-

ities as to representation had been remedied, virtually nothing had been done to remove the fundamental cause of the
breach between east and west.

The failure of Virginia to set her house in order and to
inaugurate a policy at this opportune time that would ce-
ment the two sections together, as South Carolina had done,
proved to be a grave sin of omission and one that led to
tragic results in later years. This failure to placate the west
was one of a series of events that ultimately led to the
separation of West Virginia from the mother State. The
disruption of Virginia in the 'sixties was a most important
factor in tipping the scales in favor of victory for the North.
If the Old Dominion in 1861 could have presented a united
front against the enemy the outcome of the war might have
been less disastrous to the cause which was so close to the
heart of Tyler and his conservative colleagues in the Convention. For the dissatisfaction of the trans-Alleghany region over the new constitution was great enough to warrant
the assumption that there was a vital connection between the
action, or rather nonaction, of this Convention and the
disruption of Virginia and the collapse of the Confederacy.[43]

If this view is correct, Leigh, Tyler, and the other conservatives, in upholding the immediate interests of their section, were advocating a policy which in the long run proved
inimical to the institution which they were so anxious to protect.

[43] It is true that the Constitution of 1850 met many of the demands of the
west and thus removed the outstanding causes of complaint under the Constitution of 1830. But this tardy recognition of rights did not entirely heal a
breach which a feeling of dissatisfaction had kept open for decades.

CHAPTER VIII
AN INDEPENDENT DEMOCRAT

IF Tyler and Tazewell, his colleague, had hurried to Washington immediately after the close of the Virginia Constitutional Convention they would have been in time to hear the great debate between Daniel Webster and Robert Y. Hayne. It is quite likely that they witnessed this display of oratorical fireworks, though of this we are not positively certain.[1] Tyler, however, was there in time to put up a vigorous fight against internal improvements by the Federal government.

In May, 1830, there was under consideration in the Senate a bill authorizing a subscription of stock in the Maysville, Washington, Paris, and Lexington Turnpike. In the course of the debate an uncomplimentary reference was made by Clay to the poor roads of Virginia and the prejudices of her people. Tyler considered these references as a slur on the old State and was provoked by them into making a reply. His speech on this occasion was a very good one, although, as he said, it was "as unpremeditated as that attack was unexpected." It was adorned with Biblical references and was in good literary form. While some of the statements were somewhat exaggerated, the address as a whole was characterized by clear thinking and sound argument.

[1] In George P. A. Healy's painting, "Webster Replying to Hayne," now in Faneuil Hall, John Tyler is portrayed as one of the Senators who were listening to the speech with rapt attention. This is not proof, however, that Tyler was really present, for Healy has in this picture faces of persons who were undoubtedly not present on this noted occasion. See Claude M. Fuess, *Daniel Webster* (Boston, 1930), I, 375-376, also footnotes. For a copy of this picture see op. p. 374.

A good portion of his speech was directed against the dangers of nationalism, of which, as he considered, this bill was a specimen. He showed a strong antipathy to the term "national." "I have," he said, "no such word in my political vocabulary. A nation of twenty-four nations is an idea which I cannot realize. A confederacy may embrace many nations; but by what process twenty-four can be converted into one, I am still to learn."

He also pointed out that this road, of sixty miles in length, was not of interest to the whole country. The advocates of the bill contended that the road was to be linked up with other roads and thus form a part of a great country-wide system. By such a line of reasoning any road could be declared of national character, for every road is connected directly or indirectly with some thoroughfare. The county road "passing by my door intersects the principal road leading from this city to Richmond, and from thence to Huntsville, in Alabama." "It is a part of a national road, and is mediately or immediately connected with every other road in the United States." [2]

In opposing the Maysville Road Bill, Tyler was pursuing a policy that was quite acceptable to President Jackson. Despite the opposition of the States' rights advocates, the bill was passed by both houses of Congress and sent to the President. After due deliberation, Jackson decided to veto the measure. His objections to it were based both on practical and constitutional grounds.[3]

Tyler and Tazewell were close personal friends, as is shown by the fact that Tyler had named a son after Tazewell. On all important issues the two were in hearty accord, as both were ardent champions of old-school Republicanism. Both had supported Jackson in the campaign of 1828, and both sustained the President in his fight over the Mays-

---

[2] *Register of Debates in Congress*, 21st Cong., 1st sess., 433–435.
[3] J. B. Richardson, *Messages and Papers of the Presidents* (Washington, 1900), II, 483–493.

ville Road Bill. They were, therefore, Democrats in good and regular standing. But these two champions of the rights of the States were too independent in their thinking to be amenable to party discipline. So it was not to be expected that they would conform for any length of time to the precepts of political orthodoxy and party regularity.

Their first clash with the Administration came over a matter of comparative unimportance. Jackson had nominated for various positions a number of newspaper editors who had supported him. When they came before the Senate for confirmation all but one, Amos Kendall, were voted down, and Kendall was saved only by the casting vote of Calhoun, the Vice-President. Jackson, however, was not to be outdone by this opposition, and so he sent up these names a second time. Some of them were now confirmed and the rest were consoled with other positions. Tyler and Tazewell both voted against the confirmation of these appointees on the ground, as stated by Tyler, that "the press, the great instrument of enlightenment of the people, should not be subjected, through its conductors, to rewards and punishments; and that the Sedition Law was not more obnoxious than a system of rewards to be doled out from the public Treasury by means of the public offices." [4]

To practical politicians who see the need of yielding on lesser issues in order that they may win on greater ones, this question must have seemed of too little importance to warrant a disturbance of party harmony. Owing to their stand on this question Tazewell and Tyler were declared to be in opposition to the Administration. Hard names were applied to them, and their motives were maligned.[5] Even Tyler himself at a later period (1853) expressed the opinion that they had probably been "too Utopian." [6] While the wisdom of their course on this occasion may properly be questioned,

[4] Tyler, *Letters and Times*, I, 408–409.
[5] *Register. of Debates*, 21st Cong., 2nd sess., 270.
[6] Tyler, *op. cit.*, I, 410.

there is no doubt as to the honesty of their intentions and the sincerity of their motives.

In voting against one of these nominees, Tyler found his duty an exceptionally unpleasant one. In the list of names presented to the Senate was that of Major Henry Lee, who had been nominated for the consulship at Algiers. He was a son of General Henry Lee ("Light Horse Harry"), of Revolutionary fame, and a half-brother of Robert E. Lee. Major Lee was a writer of no mean ability, and is said to have written Jackson's inaugural address. A serious charge of immorality was brought against him, the truth of which he virtually admitted. Though deeply penitent, he contended that he should not be deprived of a minor office for a misdeed no worse than that of which Jefferson had been guilty. But this act of "Black Horse Harry" (as he is sometimes called) was considered by the Senate as a serious offense, and he was unanimously rejected.

Lee, it seems, was inclined to blame Tyler for this action of the Senate.[7] In defense of himself against this false impression Tyler wrote a letter of explanation to Richard T. Brown, although in doing so he was breaking his rule never to allow himself to be questioned concerning his act as a Senator by any individual on whose case he had passed. He explained in this letter that he had not tried to influence the vote of any other Senator and had expressed no opinion in the Senate regarding Lee except as to "his innocence of certain more aggravated additions to the charge under which he labored." His vote against him had been cast very re-

[7] Henry Lee to Richard T. Brown, Aug. 24, 1833; *Personal MSS*. (L.C.). The letter in which Lee excused himself for having seduced his sister-in-law was written to Richard T. Brown to be sent by him to Tyler. He argued at great length to show how inconsistent it was for Tyler to judge harshly a sin of the same character as one alleged to have been committed by Jefferson, whom Tyler looked up to as a political paragon. See also B. J. Hendrick, *The Lees of Virginia* (Boston, 1935), 382, 400–403; and *John Tyler Papers* (L.C.), I, between 6319 and 6320.

luctantly, he added, because Lee and he had been in college together.[8]

By voting against the confirmation of the President's appointees, the Virginia Senators had committed an act of insurgency. Although in so doing they had been motivated by a high sense of duty, they had to some extent compromised their regularity. They were, however, still regarded as Democrats and supporters of the Administration. But it was not long before they were guilty of another breach of party discipline which seriously jeopardized their party standing. This second offense was their criticism of the action of the President regarding the Turkish Mission.

In September, 1829, Jackson appointed a commission to go to Turkey and carry on negotiations with that government.[9] These commissioners were chosen during a recess of Congress, but their names were not submitted to the Senate for confirmation at any time during the next session. This was considered by some members of the Senate as an infringement of the rights of that body; for it was clearly stated in the Constitution that appointments of this character could be made only with the advice and consent of the Senate.

Such an assumption of authority on the part of the executive, unwarranted, in their opinion, by the Constitution, could not be condoned by such sticklers for strict construction as the doctrinaire 'Senators from Virginia. Tyler and Tazewell were thus running true to form when they voiced a strong protest against this act of the President. Their opportunity for attacking this policy came in February, 1831, when the general appropriation bill was before the Senate; for in this bill there was an item covering the salaries and other expenses connected with the mission to Constantinople. Tazewell moved to strike out the items relating to

[8] Tyler, *Letters and Times*, I, 409–410.
[9] *Ibid.*, I, 417.

compensation for the commissioners and spoke at length in support of his motion.[10]

Tyler (on February 24) made a speech in which he sustained Tazewell in the position he had taken and charged the President with having exceeded his authority. He said: "Let us meet this question boldly and fearlessly. Let us tell the President he has erred. Let us be true to ourselves, to our constituents, but, above all, to the Constitution." His criticism of the President was, however, restrained and did not degenerate into objectionable personalities. He contended that Jackson had no right to take exception to his opposition, because he was impelled to this course by a sense of duty.

Tyler did not object to paying these commissioners if he could at the same time save the principle for which he contended. To do this he offered an amendment providing that the appropriation of money in payment of the commissioners should not be construed as in any way approving their appointment by the President alone during the recess of the Senate and without its advice and consent.[11]

Tyler realized that in making this speech he was hazarding his good standing with the President, for the latter was not the type of man that could easily brook opposition. He usually considered that disapproval of his measures was based on ill will toward him rather than on loyalty to principle. So he generally regarded a political opponent as a personal enemy. The night after Tazewell made his speech on the Turkish Mission the flow of ice on the Potomac broke down a part of the bridge that connected Washington with Virginia. Immediately afterwards an observant gentleman remarked to Tyler with archness that "the connexion between Virginia and the President's mansion is now severed." [12]

In taking this independent stand Tyler had weakened

[10] *Register of Debates*, 21st Cong., 2nd sess., 215–241.
[11] *Ibid.*, 260–270.   [12] *Ibid.*, 261.

his position with some of Jackson's adherents in Virginia. Thomas Ritchie, a strong pro-Administration man, in an editorial in the Richmond *Enquirer* expressed disapproval of his action on this occasion. He endorsed the principle of Tyler's motion but thought that his manner had not been as friendly to the Administration as it might have been.[13]

Tyler had no thought at this time of leaving the Democratic Party. Nor was he inclined to oppose Jackson's policies unless his convictions forced him to do so. Indeed, before this year ended he cast a vote in the Senate that must have pleased Jackson as much as his action on the Turkish Mission displeased him.

Van Buren had been appointed minister to England during the interim of Congress and had gone to London to assume his duties. When his name came before the Senate his political opponents made a fight against his confirmation. The accusation brought against him was that while Secretary of State he had issued improper instructions to McLane, the American minister to England. McLane had been directed to say that the election of Jackson and the incoming of the Democratic Party would mean a change in our attitude in regard to our relations with England. This, it was charged, was bringing partisan politics into foreign affairs.

Van Buren's enemies were able to muster sufficient strength to bring about a tie in the vote of the Senate. Calhoun, the Vice-President, cast the deciding vote against his opponent, feeling that his rejection by the Senate would mean the political death of Van Buren. But in all these calculations Andrew Jackson was not taken sufficiently into account. The Old Hero resented this slight to his protégé and determined to leave no stone unturned to promote the fortunes of the "Little Giant." As a result of this determination on the part of Jackson, Van Buren soon became Vice-President and thus president of the body that had tried to disgrace him. Thomas H. Benton was one of the Senators

[13] Richmond *Enquirer,* Mar. 10, 1831.

who foresaw that the effort to discredit Van Buren would
lead to his advancement. "You have broken a minister," he
said to one of the Senators who had voted against confirmation, "and elected a Vice-President." [14]

Tyler had exerted himself from the beginning of the session to procure Van Buren's confirmation. He did this not
because "he liked the man over much," but because he did
not want to identify himself with the factious opposition of
the National Republicans and also because he did not think
the charge against him had been proved. In a letter to his
son Robert (February 2, 1832) he said that he considered Van Buren qualified for the place and therefore he
voted for him. He admitted that there were some suspicions
against him, but he did not feel that he should be rejected on
the mere ground of suspicion. [15]

Tyler also supported Jackson for re-election in the campaign of 1832. [16] Evidently he had no desire to break with
the Administration when he made his speech on the Turkish
Mission. More than a year later (April, 1832) he showed a
very friendly attitude toward the President. At that time a
motion had been made in the Senate by Clay to strike out
the proposed appropriation for the salary and outfit of the
chargé to Guatemala, who had been duly appointed and confirmed. Tyler voted against Clay's motion and thus sustained
the position of Benton, the Administration leader. [17] A few
days later he voted against a motion to strike out the appropriation for a minister to Columbia. [18]

Early in the session of 1831–32 the tariff again loomed
up as an important issue in Congress. Clay offered a resolution in the Senate (January 10, 1832) providing for a lessening of the revenue from the tariff and (as he said) for a
more equitable adjustment of the burdens of taxation. The

[14] E. M. Shepard, *Martin Van Buren* (Boston and New York, 1888), 234;
T. H. Benton, *Thirty Years' View* (New York, 1864), I, 214–220.
[15] Tyler, *op. cit.*, I, 427.
[16] Tyler to his daughter Mary, Apr. 20, 1832; *ibid.*, 429.
[17] *Register of Debates*, 22nd Cong., 1st sess., 768, 774.   [18] *Ibid.*, 794.

duties on tea, coffee, wine, and other articles not competing with American products were to be lowered, but the principle of protection was to be left unimpaired. It was anent this resolution that John Tyler had the temerity to oppose the brilliant Kentuckian. He made a speech against Clay's resolution the delivery of which occupied portions of three days (February 9, 10, and 14). He had but recently recovered from an illness and would have remained silent, he declared, if his sense of duty had allowed him to consult his own feelings.

The friends of protection were still repeating the economic-independence and home-market arguments (page 45) in favor of a protective tariff. Tyler's speech on this occasion was an effort to refute these arguments and to point out the positive objections to a protective tariff. As on a former occasion in the House of Representatives, he wielded some lusty strokes against the claim that protection would make the United States independent of foreign countries and would provide a home market for agricultural products.

A considerable portion of the speech was devoted to showing the evils of a protective tariff. Under the protectionist system, it was maintained, a heavy and unnecessary tax was imposed upon the consumers in the form of high prices. The tariff system was not only unfair, but its benefits and burdens were unequally distributed as between individuals and sections. It encouraged manufacturing and the businesses allied with it whereas it penalized farming. By raising the prices of farm implements and the clothing and other commodities needed by farm hands it enhanced the cost of producing agricultural commodities.

To offset the burdens imposed upon the farmer as a consumer there were no compensating advantages in marketing conditions. On the contrary, protection tended to restrict rather than enlarge the market for agricultural commodities. For if the exports from other countries were admitted freely

into the United States these foreign countries would buy
more of our products. Thus a duty which discourages importation automatically discourages exportation. Spain would,
he thought, concede much in the way of trade favors if her
sugar were admitted free into this country. France had already indicated a willingness to trade with the United States
on the most favorable terms provided our ports should
prove hospitable to her silks and wines. Other nations would
do likewise. A protective tariff by reason of the exactions
which it levies on the commodities of foreign countries com-
pels them to produce the foodstuffs which otherwise they
would buy from us; "and thus, while it cripples the farming
interest of the Union, operates as a direct premium to that
same interest in other countries."

This discrimination in favor of one industry and against
another results in bestowing favors on certain sections of
the country and imposing burdens on others. At that time
manufacturing was very backward in the Southern States,
whereas it was making rapid progress in a number of the
Northern States. Therefore, the special privileges granted
to manufacturers by the protective tariff had the effect of
favoring the industrialized sections at the expense of the
rural communities. In short, it favored the North at the expense of the South and the West. A policy that would drop
the hailstones of destruction on one group of States while
raining benefits on another was manifestly unjust and was
calculated to accentuate the feeling of sectionalism that was
already developing too rapidly.

He contended that manufactures without any governmental aid would come to America just as rapidly as the
growth of the country would warrant. To encourage by
artificial stimulation the premature development of industry
in this country, especially in the newer States, would be to
run counter to the decrees of nature. For nature had ordained that the people of all frontier regions should devote
their energies to the clearing of the wilderness and to the

producing of raw materials rather than to the developing of manufactures on a large scale in competition with old and established societies. To attempt in the frontier States of America manufacturing on any large scale was to duplicate the effort made in 1661 to establish the silk industry in Virginia. In speaking of this futile experiment and its failure he used the following eloquent language: "Many of the mulberry trees, then planted, still exist in the neighborhood of Williamsburg, and the wind, as it sighs through their decayed branches, speaks, in plain and intelligible language, of the impotence and folly of all human policy which is attempted to be set up in opposition to the decrees of nature." [19]

Tyler had reason to be proud of this speech, as it was worthy of the important question with which it dealt. Some of the statements, to be sure, rest on hearsay evidence, but there runs through the arguments a spirit of fairness and judicial-mindedness. His discussion of the subject was so able that it won the commendation of both John Marshall and James Madison.[20] The dignity of the address is not marred by an improper display of emotion, and there is an utter absence of disagreeable personal allusions. The style is clear and in places ornate—even to the degree of eloquence.

In this long address Tyler formulated once for all his views on the tariff and the arguments with which he upheld them. These convictions were never changed, apparently, during the entire period of his life. It is true that when President he signed a tariff bill in which the rates were as high as those of the bill against which he was now speaking. But when he supported a high tariff as President he did so because the necessities of the Federal treasury demanded it as a revenue measure. The opinions herewith set forth are precisely those to be expected from an ardent believer in States'

[19] *Register of Debates*, 22nd Cong., 1st sess., 335–367.
[20] *John Tyler Papers* (L.C.), I, 6312.

rights, a lover of the Southland, and a warm advocate of
Jeffersonian agrarianism. It was a doctrine in strict harmony
with the philosophy of Adam Smith and the other economists of the classical school.

If the policy advocated by Tyler had been adopted by the
government and adhered to during the century that has in-
tervened between the date of this speech and the present
time, the economic history of our country might have been
quite different from what it has been. Manufacturing would
not have developed as rapidly as it has, and agriculture
would have enjoyed its economic predominance longer than
has actually been the case. But the United States was destined to become a great industrial region and would have
been such today even if the government had not lent its aid
in hastening the result. For nature had dedicated our country to industry when she stored rich deposits of iron, coal,
and other minerals in our hills and placed the waterfalls in
our streams. Workers in increasing numbers would gradually
have been called from the field to the factory to aid in ex-
ploiting the great natural resources at our command. Industries, however, would not have sprung up so rapidly and
would have rooted themselves more deeply in the economic
life of the country.

Despite the opposition of the advocates of low tariff this
bill passed both houses of Congress (July, 1832) and was
duly signed by the President.[21] The position taken by Tyler
on the tariff question has been repudiated by the country,
for the policy of the government since 1865 has been directly opposite to that advocated by him. We have been inclined to think, therefore, that his views were erroneous.

Public opinion today is not so positive in its condemnation
of the antiprotectionist position as it was a few decades
earlier. When we consider the international friction which
has been caused by the feverish activity in industry in all of
the great countries of the world, we wonder if industrializa-

[21] *Register of Debates, loc. cit.,* 335–367.

tion has not been too rapid. Moreover, if our country had been industrialized more slowly and gradually, a more efficient technique might have evolved for grappling with and wisely solving the problems which have grown out of the industrial revolution. If the log had been fed a little more slowly the saw might have taken it without the breaking of teeth. Then, too, if our industries had not been pampered by government aid and had been forced to rely more on self-help there might have developed in our business leaders an initiative and sturdy self-reliance that were badly needed but woefully lacking in the recent period of economic stress. For if American industry had not been inflated into abnormal dimensions by governmental pumping and had kept within natural limits and thus adapted itself to the climate, resources, and economic needs of the country, it might have had sufficient stability to withstand the forces of panic which have lately been beating against it. It yet remains to be determined, therefore, whether John Tyler in his tariff policy was behind or ahead of his day.

CHAPTER IX

NULLIFICATION AND THE
COMPROMISE OF 1833

TYLER was often late in arriving at the capital for the opening of the sessions of Congress, but in the fall of 1832 he was ahead of time. He went to Washington earlier than usual to serve on the Committee for the District of Columbia, which was preparing a code to take the place of the ill-digested laws of the District.[1] It was fortunate for him that he was on the ground when the Senate convened. For when the question of choosing a president *pro tempore* came up, his name was presented for the place by the opponents of the Administration. He made a very good showing in the race for this honor, and was not defeated until the fifth ballot, when Judge Hugh L. White was elected by the close vote of seventeen to fourteen. Before Tyler was placed in nomination he had already voted for Judge White and refused to change, as he felt committed in favor of his rival. Tyler's refusal to endorse his own candidacy insured the election of White, who was also supported by the Administration forces.[2]

Shortly after the election of 1832 Tyler definitely broke with the Administration. The occasion of the breach was the nullification crisis. He had never been a strict party man, as

[1] Tyler, *Letters and Times*, I, 442-443.
[2] Tyler to John Floyd, Dec. 4, 1832; *John Floyd Papers* (L.C., abbreviation for Library of Congress).
Tyler's action on this occasion involved no small degree of self-sacrifice. For Calhoun was expected to resign the Vice-Presidency (as he did) and with the presidency of the Senate would go the possibility of the succession to the Presidency.

he had more than once opposed a measure that was dear to the President. But up to this time he was regarded as a Democrat in good if not regular standing. Jackson's policy toward South Carolina was so objectionable to him that he aligned himself with the anti-Administration forces, and finally left the Democratic Party. To support or even acquiesce in the President's measures would be, as he considered, to sacrifice his States' rights principles—a sacrifice which at no time in his entire career was he willing to make.

That his disagreement with Jackson's policy arose from deep conviction and not from a spirit of factious opposition is clearly proved by his letters to two of his most intimate personal and political friends. In writing to Governor John Floyd, of Virginia (January 16, 1833), he declared that "if South Carolina be put down, then may each of the States yield all pretentions to sovereignty. We have a consolidated government, and a master will soon arise. This is inevitable. How idle to talk of preserving a republic for any length of time with an uncontrolled power over the military, exercised at pleasure by the President." [3]

The clash between South Carolina and the Federal government came when the former, acting through a State convention, declared the tariff laws of 1828 and 1832 unconstitutional and therefore null and void. These acts were not to be carried out within her limits and secession was to be resorted to if force were used by the Federal executive to compel the obedience of the State.

In response to this action Jackson issued a proclamation (December 10, 1832) in which he took a strong stand against nullification, which, he declared, was against both the letter and the spirit of the Constitution. He made it clear that the tariff act would be enforced and the doughty little State would be severely disciplined if she attempted the use

[3] John Tyler to Governor John Floyd, Jan. 16, 1833; *Personal MSS.* (L.C.). Shortly afterwards (February 2, 1833) in a letter to Tazewell he voiced his fears regarding the Proclamation in similar strain.

of force in support of nullification.⁴ The position of the President was sustained by Congress, which passed the "Force Bill," authorizing him to employ the army and navy in carrying out the laws.

The dire threats of the Proclamation were accompanied by acts that were just as menacing. Seven revenue cutters and a ship of war were sent to Charleston with orders to be ready for instant action. Soldiers were also despatched there from Fortress Monroe to strengthen the garrison, and General Scott was put in command of the defenses.

Along with the sword the President bore the olive branch. In his annual message to Congress (December 4, 1832) he referred to the early extinction of the national debt and recommended a gradual reduction of the tariff.⁵ After an unsuccessful attempt of the Democrats to carry out this suggestion, Clay offered in the Senate a compromise tariff measure. By this bill there was to be a gradual reduction of the tariff until 1842, at which time the rate should not exceed twenty per cent on any article. This compromise was the result of an agreement between Clay and Calhoun, who had resigned the Vice-Presidency to take his seat in the Senate. With such backing the measure was easily put through Congress and was accepted by South Carolina. The crisis thus passed with both sides claiming the victory.

John Tyler's attitude and reactions to this crisis were precisely those which one would expect of a firm believer in States' rights who was at the same time strongly loyal to the Union. He thought that the country was threatened with civil war, and he was willing to do all he could to avert so great a calamity.⁶ His friend, Henry A. Wise, writing two-score years after the event, represents him as favoring nullification. Wise considered this the greatest mistake ever made by Tyler,⁷ but he was entirely wrong in his opinion.

⁴ Richardson, *Messages and Papers of the Presidents*, II, 640–656.
⁵ *Ibid.*, 597–599.
⁶ *Register of Debates*, 22nd Congress, 2nd sess., 20–21.
⁷ Wise, *Seven Decades of the Union*, 121–122.

For although Tyler believed that a State had a constitutional right to secede from the Union, he did not approve of South Carolina's action. In a speech against the "Force Bill" made in the Senate (February 6, 1833) he said: "I disclaim the policy adopted by her; all here know that I did not approve of her course. [But] I will not join in the denunciations which have been so loudly thundered against her, nor will I deny that she has much cause of complaint." [8]

He waged a most strenuous opposition to the policy of coercion recommended by Jackson in his Proclamation and adopted by Congress in the "Force Bill." He considered that Jackson's Proclamation had "swept away the barriers of the Constitution and given us in place of the Federal government, under which we had fondly believed we were living, a consolidated military despotism." He was sick of the double-dealing and would like to retire from public life. It was, therefore, a matter of indifference to him whether the Virginia legislature would or would not re-elect him.[9]

When the "Force Bill" was up for passage in the Senate all the opponents of the measure except Tyler had withdrawn, and so he cast the only vote against it.[10] By so doing Tyler was able to pose as a man of courage who could not be induced to compromise his principles by acquiescing in so iniquitous a law. And yet it is by no means certain that his protest might not have been stronger had he co-operated with his Southern colleagues in a policy of passive resistance.

Tyler's opposition in the Senate to the policy of coercion was not confined to his vote against the "Force Bill," but he also felt impelled to speak against this measure. On Febru-

---

[8] *Register of Debates, loc. cit.,* 371.
[9] Tyler to Tazewell, February 2, 1833; *John Tyler Papers* (L.C.), I, 6318.
[10] *Niles' Register,* XLIII, 430.
When the "Force Bill" was voted on, some of its opponents were absent from the Senate Chamber. After vainly trying to have action on the measure postponed, Calhoun and his friends walked out, contending that their adverse votes would not represent the full strength of the opposition. Tyler was requested to go along with them but he refused to do so. Charles W. March, *Reminiscences of Congress* (N. Y., 1850), 247–248.

ary 6, 1833, he made a long and able speech against this (to him) iniquitous bill. He realized, he explained, that in taking this action he was jeopardizing his interests and was running counter to the warnings of many of his friends, who advised him to keep quiet. But he could not remain silent while an imperative sense of duty was constantly urging him to speak out without regard to personal considerations.

This introduction was not merely a self-laudatory exordium, like those with which politicians often preface their speeches, but it was rather a true statement as to his feelings and the risks he incurred by giving expression to them. His re-election to the Senate was still hanging fire in the legislature of Virginia. A speech boldly attacking a major policy of the President might cool the ardor or arouse the opposition of Democratic legislators who otherwise might be inclined to support him. Most politicians, if similarly circumstanced, would have considered that passive resistance would meet the demands of conviction and so would have maintained a discreet silence. It is very much to the credit of Tyler that he was able and willing to jeopardize his immediate political future in the active championship of a just but dangerous cause. His action can be explained only by assuming that it was inspired by disinterested patriotism and sustained by a sacrificial courage that is exceptional in politicians.

This was on the whole a good speech and portions of it were eloquent. It reiterated the stock arguments in favor of the federal as against the national character of the Union, and stated in unmistakable terms his belief in the theory that sovereignty resided in the States and not in the Union. The Constitution was ratified not by the people in mass but by the people acting as States. It was a revision of the Articles of Confederation and had created a league of States, not a consolidated national government.

While few if any original arguments were advanced in favor of State sovereignty, that doctrine was presented with a straightforward candor that was truly refreshing. The theory was stripped of the qualifying explanations with which it was often clothed and made to stand out in unblushing nudity. The following excerpts from this speech show that his acceptance of this theory was without reservations: "The government was created by the States, is amenable by [to] the States, is preserved by the States, and may be destroyed by the States." The Federal government holds its "existence at the pleasure of these States." "They may strike you [the Federal government] out of existence by a word; demolish the Constitution, and scatter its fragments to the winds." "The true state of the case is this: It is because I owe allegiance to the State of Virginia that I owe obedience to the laws of this [Federal] government. My State requires me to render such obedience. She has entered into a compact, which, while it continues, is binding on all her people. So would it be if she had formed a treaty with a foreign power. I should be bound to obey the stipulations of such treaty, because she willed it. . . . It is because I owe allegiance there, that I owe obedience here. . . ." "I owe no responsibility, politically speaking, elsewhere than to my State."

"A redress of grievances and not force is the proper remedy in this crisis. It is an argument of pride to say that the government should not yield while South Carolina is showing a spirit of revolt. It was just such an argument that was used against the American colonies by the British government—an argument spoken against by Burke and Pitt. Civil war is imminent, and to prevent it a resort to force should be deprecated." "We can never be too tardy to begin the work of blood." "But it is a bad mode of settling disputes to make soldiers your ambassadors, and to point to the halter and the gallows as your ultimatum." [11]

Tyler's activity in meeting the nullification crisis was not confined to his attempt to prevent coercion but also included a strenous effort to remove the grievance complained

[11] For the full text of this speech see *Register of Debates, loc. cit.,* 360–377.

of by South Carolina. To this end he threw himself with enthusiasm into the movement for tariff reform. He was a member of the Finance Committee and was thus in a position to make his voice heard.

Tyler was a strong supporter of Clay's Compromise Tariff Act of 1833, and, in the opinion of his son, Doctor Lyon G. Tyler, suggested the proposal that resulted in this agreement. Our sources are not full enough to confirm Doctor Tyler's claim in its entirety, but we do have sufficient evidence to show that Senator Tyler had an important part in initiating the movement for compromise.

Soon after Jackson's Proclamation appeared the Virginia Senator spoke to Clay urging him to sponsor a compromise measure, pointing out the great opportunity he now had for settling the controversy. Tyler's account of his interview with Clay as given by him years later was as follows: South Carolina was ready to defy the Federal government and thousands of her citizens were eager to take part in what seemed to be an approaching conflict. "Under this state of things, I waited on Mr. Clay. I had voted against him in the election just passed. I had differed radically from him in his course of domestic policy. I belonged, in short, to the old Jeffersonian party, from whose principles of constitutional construction I have never, in one single instance, departed. He well knew my personal admiration of him, and he received me cordially. We conversed about the times. He saw the danger. I appealed to his patriotism. No man ever did so in vain." [12]

"For a moment Mr. Clay paused in his course; he adverted to the feeling manifested in the House, and expressed his preference to permit others to lead in the matter, but yielded to an earnest remonstrance against inertness on his part." [13] "The difficulties in the way were immense. He re-

[12] Address by Tyler at the Clay banquet in Richmond, April, 1860; Tyler, *Letters and Times*, I, 466–467.
[13] Address by Tyler in Baltimore, Mar. 20, 1855; *ibid.*, 458, note.

sponded as a patriot. I referred him to another man as the only person necessary to consult, and that man was John C. Calhoun. He had to reconcile his own party—he had to satisfy an opposite party by large concessions. They met, consulted, agreed. The Compromise Tariff was the result." When Clay rose in the Senate to offer the Compromise Tariff—that "great measure of peace and reconciliation—I [Tyler] occupied the extreme seat on the left, he a similar one on the right of the Senate Chamber. We advanced to meet each other, and grasped each other's hands midway in the chamber." [14]

As these statements by Tyler were made quite a while after the event (one in 1855 and the other in 1860) there would be room for doubt as to their accuracy were they not confirmed by other and contemporary evidence. In a letter of January 10, 1833, to John Floyd, Tyler referred to this meeting with Clay and expressed the belief that his suggestion had not been entirely disregarded. He also outlined a plan for the gradual reduction of the tariff which was quite similar to the one afterwards proposed by Clay. As this letter was written a little more than a month before Clay offered his resolution, it affords some basis for the contention that the plan of compromise adopted was proposed by Tyler.

Tyler must have been on the "inside" as to the plans for compromise, as he was quite hopeful at this time (January 10, 1833) that the crisis would be passed, and one of the "old 13" would not be stricken out of existence by military force. "I may almost say to you that the battle is fought and won. My fears for the Union are speedily disappearing." [15]

In his speech on the "Force Bill" (February 6) Tyler made a statement that would indicate a knowledge of Clay's purpose regarding the tariff. He said that while he favored a

[14] *Ibid.*, 467.
[15] Tyler to John Floyd, Jan. 10, 1833; *John Floyd Papers* (L.C.).

reduction of the tariff he was opposed to a sudden change that would be unfair to the manufacturing interests.

The evidence thus cited goes far toward establishing the claim that the first steps toward the compromise were taken by Tyler, and that his suggestions were an important influence in deciding Clay to take up the measure. On the other hand, Clay in a letter to Francis Brooke (February 14, 1833) stated that although the details of the tariff bill had been determined upon just a few days earlier, the principles of the measure had long since been settled in his mind. It may be, however, that Clay in this letter was referring to another compromise—quite different from the one finally offered and adopted—which he had shown to Webster in December, 1832.[16]

Tyler never appeared to better advantage in his entire career than he did in the part he played in the nullification crisis. While the soundness of his views as an ultra-States' rights advocate may be a question for debate, there can be no disagreement as to the courage, patriotism, and sincerity of conviction that he displayed on this occasion. Besides, his speech on the "Force Bill" showed him to be an orator of no mean ability. The Compromise of 1833 was easily the finest piece of legislation enacted by Congress in the two decades of the 'thirties and 'forties, and Tyler was justly proud of the part he played in this achievement. Even if the claim of his biographer that to him belongs the credit of having initiated the Compromise of 1833 cannot be fully established, it is incontestably true that he put up a noble fight for the rights of the South and for a peaceable settlement of the controversy.

Tyler had to come up for re-election at a time when the nullification controversy was at white heat. His vigorous opposition to Jackson's policy toward South Carolina had estranged some of the Democrats who gave unqualified support to the Administration. This opposition had begun to

[16] Tyler, *op. cit.*, I, 460; G. T. Curtis, *Life of Daniel Webster*, I, 434–435.

manifest itself before the end of the year 1832. An anonymous correspondent of the Richmond *Enquirer* said: "As a man I respect Mr. Tyler, but as a politician I cannot." [17]

The Virginia Assembly had at first decided upon January 30, 1833, as the time for the Senatorial election. Tyler's opponents were able, however, to secure a postponement on the alleged ground that he should be given an opportunity to speak on the "Force Bill." [18] Tyler accepted the challenge and delivered the able address against it referred to above. He was followed by his colleague, Rives, who spoke in favor of it.

Nine days after Tyler made his speech in the Senate, the Virginia legislature entered upon the election. The opposition had united on James McDowell, who had made "a glittering and imposing speech" in favor of the Proclamation. Tyler was nominated by William H. Roy, of Mathews County, who reviewed his career and defended his action in those instances in which he had opposed Jackson. [19] Clay favored Tyler's re-election and wrote a letter in his behalf (January 23, 1833) to Francis Brooke, a prominent Virginian. [20] Tyler was elected on the first joint ballot by a majority of only one vote, though he had a plurality of twelve over his nearest competitor. [21]

He had thus had a narrow escape from defeat. Evidently, he had alienated some of his former supporters in the Virginia legislature by his opposition to the President's policy with reference to South Carolina. The Virginia Democracy was, apparently, inclined to forgive his irregularity in voting against the confirmation of the editors nominated to office by Jackson and in criticizing the Administration on the Turkish Mission. If, therefore, the nullification question had not arisen he would not in all probability have encountered any serious opposition. But the bold defiance of the

[17] Richmond *Enquirer,* December 4, 1832.
[18] *Jour., Va. House of Delegates,* session 1832–33, 136, 137, 138, 183–184.
[19] Tyler, *op. cit.,* I, 453.   [20] *Ibid.,* 459–460.
[21] *Jour., Va. House of Delegates,* session 1832–33, 183–184.

President as shown in his speech on the "Force Bill" was too much for some of the Democratic legislators, who regarded party loyalty as one of the highest virtues.

This was shown by the fact that on January 28 several of the leading friends of both McDowell and Tyler had met and decided to drop the former and unite on the latter. There were no less than seven members of the legislature who had entered into this agreement, and all of them voted for McDowell. This change in their attitude had been caused by Tyler's speech on the Proclamation.[22] Governor Floyd thought that seventeen of the States' rights party had thrown away their votes.[23] On the other hand, there is some evidence to indicate that Tyler had strengthened his position with the Virginia legislature by this speech, for apparently a majority of its members were opposed to the "Force Bill." [24]

At any rate his course seems to have been warmly endorsed by the people of Gloucester, the county in which he was then living. On returning home after Congress had adjourned he was given a banquet at Gloucester Courthouse to which a large number of guests were invited. In response to a toast in honor of his single vote against the "Force Bill," he made a speech explaining his attitude toward nullification and coercion. While he disapproved of the action of South Carolina, he strongly objected to the policy of force.[25]

Tyler was not eager to retain his place in the Senate, for he was holding it at a financial sacrifice. "I am," he said, "almost resolved to abandon public life." "My numerous

[22] Tyler, op. cit., I, 454–455.

[23] C. H. Ambler, ed., Diary of John Floyd (Richmond, 1918), 211.

[24] Benton was informed by his brother-in-law, James McDowell, that Tyler had pleased the majority of the Virginia assemblymen by his speech against the "Force Bill." He was also of the opinion that there had been quite a change in sentiment since the opening of the legislature. At that time no one who was opposed to the Administration could have been elected, but now he thought that Tyler would be chosen. Benton to Van Buren, Feb. 16, 1833; Van Buren Papers, XVIII, 4041. See also C. H. Ambler, Thomas Ritchie (Richmond, 1913), 152.

[25] Tyler, op. cit., I, 462.

family makes calls upon me that I can hardly resist." [26] But having entered the race he wanted to be spared the humiliation of defeat, and so was gratified when the news reached him of his final victory.[27]

[26] Tyler, *op. cit.*, I, 449.
[27] Tyler to Governor Floyd, Jan. 16, 1833; *Personal MSS.* (L.C.).

CHAPTER X

THE HIGH COST OF CONSISTENCY

BEFORE Tyler entered upon his second term in the United States Senate the breach between him and the President had become irreparable. The chief cause of the continuance of this disagreement was the Bank of the United States. When it is remembered that Tyler and Jackson were in entire accord as to the unconstitutionality of a national bank, it is surprising that they should have clashed so violently as to the ways and means of giving expression to this belief.

Jackson's first term had not ended before the Bank was again brought into politics. The National Republican leaders were looking for an issue in the coming Presidential election and thought the Bank would be a good one. Accordingly, they advised Nicholas Biddle, its president, to apply for a re-charter before the election. This was done and a bill providing for the extension of the charter for fifteen years was passed by both houses of Congress.[1] Jackson vetoed the measure and gave a number of reasons for so doing. Certain provisions were considered by him as unconstitutional, and others were objected to on practical grounds.[2]

When the question of granting a continuation of the charter came up in the Senate, Tyler was still a Democrat and willing to support the policies of the Administration whenever he could do so without hurting a conscience which was supersensitive as to States' rights. Moreover, Virginia and the greater part of the South were opposed to a re-charter of the Bank. Tyler was, therefore, obeying the dictates of both

[1] *Register of Debates,* 22nd Cong., 1st sess., 1073, 3852.
[2] Richardson, *Messages and Papers of the Presidents,* II, 576–591.

124

principle and policy when he persistently opposed the Bank bill from the beginning until the President's veto was sustained. He not only voted against the measure on its final passage, but was also against most of the amendments that were offered.[3]

As the Bank was the leading issue in the campaign of 1832, Jackson naturally interpreted his great victory as a plebiscite in favor of his opposition to it. He was, therefore, resolved that its career should end in 1836. To ensure such a result he decided that no more government funds should be deposited with the Bank or its branches and that the money then held by them (approximately $9,000,000) should be drawn out gradually to meet the current expenses of the government. The government deposits were to be placed in certain State banks. To carry out this policy he transferred Roger B. Taney from the office of Attorney General to that of Secretary of the Treasury. Taney was an ardent supporter of the President's bank policy, and at once (September 26, 1833) ordered his subordinates to cease making deposits in the Bank and its branches.

By this time the breach between Tyler and the Administration was complete and he was hand-in-glove with the anti-Jackson men. His support of the President's bank policy ended with his vote sustaining the veto of the bill for recharter. Up to that time his attitude toward "the monster" had been all that the most ardent Jacksonian could wish. But when Jackson continued his war on the Bank, with the apparent purpose of destroying it, Tyler refused to follow him, and was henceforth aligned with Clay and the other friends of the Bank.

When Congress assembled in December, 1833, Secretary Taney reported to both houses his action in withholding deposits from the Bank of the United States and its branches with the reasons that prompted his action. By this time the banking question had become the main issue between the

---

[3] *Register of Debates, loc. cit.,* 1025-27.

political parties. The regular Democrats had lined up behind Jackson in opposition to the Bank, while the National
Republicans were virtually a unit in its support. Working
with the latter were some former Democrats, who had been
read out of the party. For party leaders were plainly told by
Benton that support of the Bank would be construed as hostility to Jackson." [4]

Clay opened the attack on Jackson's bank policy. On
December 26, 1833, he offered two resolutions which censured the President and Secretary Taney for their action in
the removal of the government deposits.[5]

Clay made a two days' speech in support of his resolutions,
thus starting a debate which occupied most of the time of
the Senate for three months.[6] Tyler held a prominent place
in the list of the anti-Jackson leaders, though at the beginning of the session he seems to have been undecided as to
whether it would be wise to restore the deposits to the Bank.
In a letter to Tazewell written Christmas Day, 1833, he
showed uncertainty as to whether he would vote for restoration of the deposits and apparently wanted Tazewell's advice. If the Bank expected to make no further fight for a
charter, a restoration of the deposits might enable it to
withdraw its loans gradually and thus wind up its affairs
without causing any shock to business. On the other hand, if
it were bent on a fight for a re-charter a restoration of deposits might "increase its ability and render its spasms more
disturbing and hurtful to the country." [7]

This hesitation was soon ended, however, and in about two
weeks his mind was fully made up.[8] On February 24 he made
a speech in the Senate in which he argued at length and with
considerable vehemence against the act of the Secretary of
the Treasury, charging that he had been "guilty of a flagrant

[4] Theodore Roosevelt, *Thomas Hart Benton* (Boston and New York, 1886,
1914), 115.
[5] *Register of Debates,* 23rd Cong., 1st sess., 58–59.
[6] *Ibid.,* 58–94.   [7] Tyler, *Letters and Times,* I, 481–482.
[8] Tyler to Tazewell, Jan. 9, 1834; *ibid.,* 483.

assumption of power." The removal of the deposits was a breach of faith with the Bank and a violation of a contract. It was conceded on all sides, he contended, that the government's moneys were safe in the Bank; that the Bank had fulfilled all its engagements to the Treasury; and that the currency was in the soundest possible state.[9]

After nearly six weeks of debate, Clay's second motion was referred to the Finance Committee, of which Webster was chairman and Tyler a member. The order for referring it to the committee was voted at four o'clock one day (February 4, 1834) and the report was made at noon the next day. The recommendations of this committee were the center of a heated controversy which culminated in the adoption by the Senate (March 25) of two resolutions of censure. These declared that the reasons assigned by the Secretary of the Treasury for the removal of the government funds from the Bank and its branches were unsatisfactory and insufficient, and that the President in his action regarding the public revenue had "assumed upon himself authority and power not conferred by the Constitution and laws, but in derogation of both." [10]

These resolutions were adopted and sent to the House of Representatives, but in this body they were not even taken up for consideration.[11] Tyler and Leigh voted aye on both of these unwise measures. In so doing they were acting in obedience to instructions from the Virginia legislature. Virginia had supported Jackson until the time of the removal of the deposits from the Bank; but this policy was so unpopular in the Old Dominion that in the spring elections of 1834 the Jackson party was badly defeated.[12]

The anti-Jackson party signalized its victory by having the legislature issue instructions to the Senators in Congress, Tyler and Rives, to vote in favor of the resolutions of cen-

[9] *Register of Debates, loc. cit.,* 663–679.
[10] *Ibid.,* 145–156; Benton, *Thirty Years' View,* I, 394–396.
[11] Benton, *op. cit.,* I, 397–399.
[12] Tyler to Tazewell, May 9, 1834; Tyler, *op. cit.,* I, 496.

sure.[13] Tyler obeyed these instructions with alacrity, as they were right in line with the decision he had already made. Rives felt that he could not obey them and resigned his seat. The vacancy was promptly filled by the selection of Benjamin Watkins Leigh, who was in favor of the resolutions.

As the session of 1833–34 advanced, Tyler's opposition to Jackson became more and more pronounced. By February, 1834, he felt that the Administration was sinking and he did not "doubt that in six months it will be almost flat." Shortly thereafter he spoke of "the mad course of this Administration," [14] and still later in this same year he regarded Jackson as a "man who in all his proceedings appears to be more the creature of passion than of judgment." [15]

When Taney's name was presented to the Senate for Secretary of the Treasury (June 24, 1834), Tyler voted against his confirmation. He did this because he thought that Taney in removing the deposits had been serving as the tool of Jackson. He was mistaken in this opinion as Taney was carrying out his own views. Tyler afterwards realized his mistake and became a friend and admirer of the rejected Secretary, now Chief Justice of the United States. When Tyler was President, Taney was a frequent and welcome visitor at the White House. Later in an address in Baltimore (1855) Tyler expressed regret for his vote of disapproval and declared that had he known Taney as well in 1834 as he then knew his record as Chief Justice, he would have supported him for any office in the gift of the American people.[16]

---

[13] *Journal, Va. House of Delegates*, session 1833–34, 169.
[14] Tyler to Dr. Curtis, Feb. 17, Apr. 5, 1834; Tyler, *op. cit.*, 485, 491.
[15] *Ibid.*, 499.
In a letter to a friend (June 20, 1834) Tyler referred to the recent abuse in the Post Office Department and predicted other exposures. He spoke of "the rottenness and corruption that exists" and likened conditions in the Federal government to an Augean Stable which he and the other reformers should clean out. MS. in the Huntington Library.
[16] Tyler, *op. cit.*, 497–498, note; C. B. Swisher, *Roger B. Taney* (N. Y., 1935), 449.

At first sight it might appear that Tyler's opposition to Jackson's later bank policy was inspired by a spirit of partisanship rather than by principle. It is true that it was easier for him to oppose the President, now that he had been alienated from him, and yet it would not be fair to say that the break with Jackson was the cause of the stand he took. His action in voting against a re-charter of the Bank was in no way inconsistent with his opposition to removal, as he considered this an unwise and unjust policy toward an institution whose days were already numbered.

On the last day of the session (June 30, 1834) a motion was carried in the Senate through the efforts of the supporters of the Bank providing for an investigation of the Bank by the Finance Committee. The Committee was to sit during the recess of the Senate and was to inquire as to whether the Bank had violated its charter; whether it was a safe depository of the public funds; and "what had been its conduct since 1832 in regard to extension and curtailment of loans, and its general management since that time." The members of the Finance Committee were Webster, Tyler, Ewing, Mangum, and Wilkins. All of them except Wilkins were friendly to the Bank and in opposition to the Administration. Wilkins refused to serve, and King, of Alabama, who was proposed in his stead, would not accept the appointment. As the remaining members were all considered favorable to the Bank, Benton looked upon the investigation as an effort to clear the institution of the charges that had been brought against it. He spoke of this body as "a committee to proceed to the city of Philadelphia to wash out its foul linen." [17]

Webster was chairman of the Finance Committee, but he declined to serve, and so Tyler, who was next in rank, acted as chairman of the investigating board. Webster's refusal to sit with his colleagues was based on the feeling that owing to his long record in support of the Bank his presence on the

[17] Benton, *op. cit.*, I, 470–471.

Committee might subject its findings to the charge of partiality. Tyler would impress the country as being fairer.

Immediately after the adjournment of Congress, the Committee repaired to Philadelphia and entered upon its difficult task. The members were courteously received by Biddle, who promised full access to all the papers of the institution. The Committee soon separated and to each member was assigned the duty of examining the branches that were most easily accessible from his place of residence. Tyler devoted most of the summer to this work. He examined the branch bank at Norfolk, and while there was given a banquet by the Whigs. He then went to Richmond, and was so busy with the investigation there that he could not find time to visit his friend and brother-in-law, Dr. Curtis, who lived a short distance away in Hanover County. He also had to make a trip to Boston in connection with this work.[18]

After these investigations of the branches, a majority of the Committee returned to Philadelphia to conduct a thorough examination of the parent Bank. The data thus assembled had to be organized and presented to Congress in proper form. Tyler took a prominent part in this work. On December 15, 1834, he wrote to his son Robert as follows: "Since I have been here, I have encountered heavy labor in preparation of the Bank report. It is now finished, and will be passed on by the Committee tomorrow." [19]

Tyler, as acting chairman of the Committee, made his report to the Senate on December 18, 1834. According to Benton, the report was written by Tyler, and was so long that it took two and a half hours to read it.[20] The Committee had not attempted to go back of the year 1820, as an investigation by the House of Representatives had been made at that time. The management of the Bank had afforded the committeemen (so ran the report) every facility that was desired for their investigation.

[18] Tyler, op. cit., I, 503.   [19] Ibid., 503–504.
[20] Benton, op. cit., I, 481.

The report was on the whole quite favorable to the Bank, though there was some adverse criticism. Some of the charges that had been made against the institution were answered and much was said in its behalf. The report pointed out that despite the difficulties recently encountered, the removal of the government deposits, the hostile action of the government, etc., the people still had a deeply rooted confidence in the solvency of the Bank. This was shown by the fact that its notes were as much sought after as ever. For these reasons the Committee felt "that the public moneys deposited in the Bank are abundantly safe." No evidence was found to prove that the Bank had been intermeddling with politics.[21]

As soon as the report was read Benton rose and made a speech against it. He expressed opposition to the Bank and defended President Jackson, Van Buren, Secretary Taney, Senator Grundy, and himself, all of whom, he considered, had been attacked by the report.[22]

Benton's criticisms of the Bank report were characterized by rude severity and were not softened by the amenities customary in dignified controversy. On one occasion Tyler, in a short statement anent the report, spoke of having learned at his mother's knee that "honesty is the best policy." Benton in reply said that he had never heard Tyler terminate a speech without some asseveration of the kind. "Every speech he had read commenced and ended with a high-wrought encomium upon his own integrity, disinterestedness, his impartiality, and regard for truth."

In answer to Benton's furious attack on the work of the Committee, Tyler made on the same day a speech in its defense. The report, he declared, was based in its entirety on documentary evidence. "There is not an assertion in it which is not sustained by proof." If Benton had heeded more care-

---

[21] The text of this lengthy report, but not the accompanying documents, is given in *Register of Debates,* 23rd Cong., 2nd sess., Appendix, 185–208.
[22] Benton, *op. cit.,* I, 481–486.

fully the reading or had waited to see the report in print he
would not have hazarded the statement that it was "an elaborate defence of the Bank." Tyler maintained that the Committee had not attempted to defend the Bank but to give the
facts, both favorable and unfavorable, and leave it to the
Senate to decide. A part of the report condemned by Benton
was in the very language of Taney, whom Benton wished to
defend. The speech ended with a strong denial of Benton's
charge that the Committee had been used as an instrument
in its favor by the Bank. Tyler declared that he would be
highly pleased if the report of the Committee were referred
to another committee for the most rigid examination and he
would like to see Senator Benton on this committee.

In closing he summed up his position as follows: "I am
opposed to the Bank. In its creation I regard the Constitution as having been violated; I desire to see it expire. But the
Senate have appointed me, with others, to inquire whether
it be guilty of certain charges; and I should regard myself
as the basest of mankind, if I could consent to charge it
falsely. The report is founded on unquestionable documentary evidence." [23]

At the end of the session Tyler received a signal honor at
the hands of his colleagues. In the evening of March 3 he
was elected president *pro tempore* of the Senate, and for the
few hours between six o'clock and midnight he presided over
that body.[24]

Tyler was no more amenable to discipline after he joined
the Whig ranks than he had been when he was a Democrat.
Both now and then he did not hesitate to oppose pet measures of his party if he did not approve of them. This is
shown by his attitude toward two questions of lesser importance that came up in 1834. One was his vote for the
confirmation of Andrew Stevenson as minister to Great

[23] *Register of Debates,* 23rd Cong., 2nd sess., 30–33.
[24] Benton, *op. cit.,* I, 599–600; Benton, *Abridgment of the Debates of Congress,* XII, 639.

Britain. The other was his refusal to sustain two resolutions offered by Webster providing for the suspension of the appropriation for the British Mission until a minister had been appointed with the consent of the Senate. Tyler felt that Stevenson was well suited to the place and saw no real reason for not confirming his appointment. He voted against Webster's resolutions because he regarded them as a reflection upon and a threat to the executive.[25]

The vote in favor of Stevenson's confirmation required more courage than at first appears. The Whig Representatives considered that Stevenson in the exercise of his powers as Speaker of the House had been narrowly partisan and, therefore, unfair to them. They were bitter in their opposition to him and were determined to bring pressure to bear on Tyler to whip him into line. In the following session of Congress he received a letter from James H. Pleasants, editor of the Richmond *Whig,* warning him that his nomination for the Vice-Presidency would be "resentfully opposed" if he voted for Stevenson again.[26] Just what Tyler's answer to this letter was we are unable to say, and we can only conjecture what he would have done in 1836 when Stevenson's name was again presented to the Senate by Jackson. For in the meantime Tyler had been instructed out of his Senatorial seat and so did not have to face this responsibility. Stevenson was, however, confirmed, and so Jackson won at last.

Clay's resolutions of censure proved to be a dangerous stumbling block in Tyler's Senatorial career and were indirectly the cause of his laying aside the toga. Immediately after the resolutions were passed Benton announced that he would commence a series of motions for the purpose of expunging them from the journal. On the last day of the session, he had a motion which he had made to this effect laid on the table "in order to keep the matter alive."[27] He

25 Tyler, *op. cit.,* I, 499–501.   26 *Ibid.,* 502.
27 Benton, *Thirty Years' View,* I, 529.

brought it up at the opening of each session of Congress with the determination to keep the question before the Senate and the country until the measure was passed.

Jackson's vigorous policy with reference to France had strengthened him in Virginia. The Democrats had a strong organization in the State, and so were able to defeat their opponents in the spring elections of 1835. They resolved to use their victory as a means of instructing the two Whig Senators out of their seats and filling their places with Democrats. The editor of the Richmond *Enquirer* saw the advantage that this situation gave his party, and for months before the meeting of the legislature rang the changes upon the subject.

On December 14, 1835, the threatened resolutions were introduced in the House of Delegates. Tyler had some personal friends who did not want to see him sacrificed to party policy. To lighten the blow, therefore, a plan was suggested whereby Tyler would be ensconced in another office. James Semple, who had been judge of the circuit centering at Williamsburg, had died and his place had been filled temporarily by John B. Christian, a brother of Mrs. Tyler. It was known that Christian and Tyler were good friends and that the former would be willing if necessary to stand aside and allow Tyler to be appointed to the judgeship. So Tyler was offered this place if he would voluntarily resign from the Senatorship. This offer was made to him through the Rev. William S. Morgan, a member of Congress from Virginia. Tyler very properly replied that he would not allow his name to be considered for the office. His reasons were that "to accept any retreat from my present station would be dishonorable." Besides, Mr. Christian will make an able judge, "and is better qualified for the station than myself or any man who will be opposed to him." [28]

The resolutions in favor of instructions lingered for several weeks in the Virginia House of Delegates. In the mean-

[28] Tyler to Col. Thomas Smith, Dec. 16, 1835; Tyler, *op. cit.*, I, 525.

time Tyler tried to keep his own counsel and make no statement as to what he would do in case the instructions passed. When asked, "Will you abandon the Constitution?" his reply was, "Of what avail is the effort on my part to sustain the Constitution if the people be opposed to me?" [29]

While the Virginia Assembly was considering the motion for instructions, Tyler was trying to get the advice of the Whig leaders in Virginia as to whether he should resign in case he could not obey the instructions. Prominent in the list of those whose opinions he asked were General William F. Gordon and ex-Governor James Barbour. It seems, however, that he had made up his mind to resign before replies to his inquiries were received. In a letter to General Gordon (January 8, 1836) he referred to the expected action of the Virginia legislature as a perversion of the important power of instruction. As the assembly was using its authority as a party weapon, he did not feel under any moral obligation to comply with its request. But to disobey the instructions would be to put his party and himself on the defensive and thus to play into the hand of his opponents.[30]

His political friends were not in agreement as to what course he should pursue. Both ex-Governor Barbour and General Gordon thought that he should retain his seat. The former was of the opinion "that however sacred instructions may be held when honestly and properly given, yet if this great power is abused to factious and fatal purposes to break down the Senate by requiring its own degradation, and for the purpose of obtaining a servile body to the executive, and thus give him absolute power, then I would not yield to such a movement, but, standing on the Constitution, I would boldly appeal to the people, and disclose the means and the ends of the party." [31]

General Gordon was decidedly of the opinion that he

[29] Tyler to Robert Tyler, Jan. 16, 1836; *ibid.*, 529.
[30] John Tyler to William F. Gordon, Jan. 8, 1836; MS. Library of Duke University.
[31] Tyler, *Letters and Times*, I, 527.

ought not to resign. "That would be to do precisely what your adversaries desire you should do." He said that if he were in Tyler's place he would obey the instructions and dissipate the hopes of his political opponents, who wanted both Senators to relinquish their seats in order that they might get their places. Tyler had suggested the propriety of resigning and appealing to the people. General Gordon was strongly opposed to this procedure. He said: *"Discard the idea, power can only be controlled by power.* In your place you have power. You have a point from which you can defend yourself. If you resign, you sink into the great mass of citizens, without a shield to ward off the attacks of the press and the office power of the Administration." [32]

The Whig leaders felt that Tyler and Leigh should act in concert on whatever decision was made,[33] and quite a number of them advised that both give up their places. John Hampden Pleasants, editor of the Richmond *Whig,* was among those who held firmly to this view. He thought that if the Virginia Senators disregarded these instructions and refused to resign they would be charged with dishonorable motives, love of office, and the determination to thwart the will of the people. "A great clamor will be got up, with design to influence the elections in April," and the results for the Whig Party will be disastrous. "If you *disobey,* and retain your seats I do not hesitate a moment to say, that our hopes of carrying the State, spring and fall, will be annihilated at once." [34]

By the middle of February, Tyler had definitely decided that he would not obey the instructions and would resign. In a letter to his son Robert (February 15, 1836) he referred to the fact that the "villainous instructions" had at last passed the House of Delegates and would probably be passed by the Senate in the course of a week, as there was in that body "also a majority of suppliant instruments." "My

32 Tyler, *op. cit.,* I, 527–529.   33 *Ibid.,* 527, 533.
34 J. H. Pleasants to Tyler, Jan. 13, 1836; *ibid.,* 525–527.

resolution," he continued, "is fixed, and I shall resign. Such, too, seems to be the wish of my friends in Richmond. I cannot look to consequences, but perhaps I am doomed to perpetual exile from the public councils. If so, I am content, nor should I repine at it." [35]

A compromise plan was proposed to Tyler by his friends. The suggestion was that Tyler and Leigh hold on but issue a statement declaring their willingness to resign in the spring if the elections then should indicate a wish on the part of their constituents that this be done. Tyler did not approve of the proposal. The old cry, he said, would be raised of "Leigh or no Leigh." Leigh was unpopular with the masses, especially the westerners. The latter were opposed to him because he had spoken and voted against their interests in the Constitutional Convention of 1829–30. Therefore, if Tyler's name were linked with that of Leigh and an appeal should be made to the people the cause would go down in defeat.[36]

When the resolution of the Virginia Assembly reached him [37] Tyler sent a dignified letter to the Vice-President (February 29, 1836) stating that he had on that day resigned into the hands of the legislature of Virginia his seat in the Senate. He spoke of the Senate as "the representative of those federative principles of our system to preserve which unimpaired has been the unceasing object of my public life." [38] Evidently, it was with great reluctance that he gave up his high position and with it the prospects of a further career as a national figure. Reference was made to his leaving friends, pleasant associations, etc. as "sacrifices which it gives me pain to make." His letter of resignation ended as follows: "I shall carry with me into retirement the principles

[35] *Personal MSS.* (L.C.).   [36] Tyler, *op. cit.,* I, 514, 529.
[37] Governor Tazewell refused to transmit the expunging instructions on the ground that they were unconstitutional. *Niles' Register,* L, 92, cited by H. H. Simms, *The Rise of the Whigs in Virginia, 1824–1840* (Richmond, 1929), 100.
[38] *Register of Debates,* 24th Cong., 1st sess., 636. See also the *John Tyler Papers* (L.C.), II, 6355.

which I brought with me into public life, and by the surrender of the high station to which I was called by the voice of the people of Virginia, I shall set an example to my children which shall teach them to regard as nothing place and office, when either is to be attained or held at the sacrifice of honor."

Tyler's action in this case was quite in keeping with his behavior in general. In refusing to endorse a foolish effort to mutilate the record of the Senate he displayed sound sense and statesmanship; in resigning he showed himself a victim of a dilettante doctrinairism that often marred his record as a statesman. In thus surrendering an unexpired two-thirds of his term he not only made a needless personal sacrifice but also gave aid and comfort to his political opponents. And yet in so doing he was acting with perfect consistency. He had voted for the resolution of censure in obedience to an instruction from the legislature, and when a member of the Virginia Assembly he had offered a resolution censuring Senators for not doing what he was now doing.[39] But to purchase consistency at such a price was hardly to be expected of a practical politician. The great mistake made by him was in championing the doctrine of instructions. He might have repudiated this unwise doctrine and excused his lack of consistency in so doing on the ground that when he enunciated it he was only an inexperienced youth.

The Whig leaders strongly advised Tyler against this sacrifice to idealism, and Calhoun and Clay were deputed by them to persuade him not to resign. This was his reply: "Gentlemen, the first act of my political life was a censure on Messrs. Giles and Brent for opposition to instructions. The chalice presented to their lips is now presented to mine and I will drink it even to the dregs." [40] This answer and the act that he suited to these high words show that Tyler was a man who put loyalty to principle above every other consideration. The circumstances which called for this sacrifice would, however,

[39] See p. 28.   [40] *John Tyler Papers* (L.C.), III, 6694.

never have arisen had his record in the Virginia Assembly been characterized from the beginning by sound judgment in political affairs. And so while he was displaying an integrity equal to that of the admired Jefferson he was at the same time exhibiting a marked inferiority to him as a practical politician.

Leigh declined to resign, though he indicated that he would in all probability give up his seat at the end of the session. In a long statement addressed to the Speaker of the House of Delegates and the President of the Senate of the Virginia Assembly he announced his intention to vote against the expunging resolution and gave his reasons for so doing and for refusing to resign.[41]

Tyler was severely condemned by the Northern press, and even the Richmond *Whig*, whose editor had advised both of the Virginia Senators to resign, censured him for not going along with Leigh after the latter had decided to hold on. In fact, the Whig Party was placed in an awkward position by this divergence in policy of the two Senators. It had to defend Leigh for retaining his seat, and Tyler's action made that difficult. So strong was the feeling against Tyler that threats loud and strong rose in the Maryland legislature, which was still in session, to cancel its nomination of him for the Vice-Presidency unless he stood with Leigh and voted against the expunging resolution.[42]

Soon after Tyler had returned home after resigning his seat a dinner was given to him and Leigh by their Whig friends. The Whigs were very enthusiastic at this meeting, and toasts were given in honor of both Senators. Two of these in honor of Tyler were as follows:

> More true joy Marcellus exiled feels,
> Than Caesar with a Senate at his heels.

[41] Leigh's letter to the Virginia legislature (dated March 2, 1836) was published in pamphlet form.
[42] Tyler, *Letters and Times*, I, 537, note.

"Our honored guest, John Tyler, 'Expunged' from a post that he adorned, and the functions of which he ever faithfully and ably discharged, by the complying tools of an unprincipled aspirant, he is but the more endeared to the hearts of his countrymen."

It must have been an embarrassing situation to be called on to praise two Senators—one for having resigned and the other for having refused to resign. The anomaly of this situation did not escape the observation of Ritchie, of the Richmond *Enquirer*. He spoke of a waggish friend as having described the toasts as follows:

"John Tyler: His obedience to the requisitions of the Legislature, by resigning, does honor to his principles.

"Benjamin Watkins Leigh: His firmness in resisting the instructions of the Legislature does honor to his principles.

"Mr. Tyler: Honor to him! because he could not with honor retain his seat.

"Mr. Leigh: Honor to him! because he could not with honor relinquish his seat." [43]

The vacancy caused by Tyler's resignation was immediately filled by the selection of William C. Rives, who was in favor of the expunging resolution. Benton's perseverance was finally rewarded, and his measure was passed (January 16, 1837). The Whigs regarded this action of the Senate not only as a defeat and humiliation for their party but also as a dishonor to that dignified body.

In the last years of his Senatorial career Tyler had an opportunity to take a stand on those phases of the slavery question that were agitating the public mind. In 1832 the legislature of Virginia was seriously considering a plan looking to the emancipation of the slaves of the commonwealth. At that time the Congressional Committee on the District of Columbia, of which he was a member, was working on a new code for the District. He tried to get inserted in this

[43] Quoted by Tyler in *Letters and Times*, I, 542.

code provisions that would put an end to the slave trade in the District of Columbia.[44] In a speech in the Senate (February 16, 1835) in support of this restriction he contended that it would abolish some unjustifiable punishments that had been inflicted upon the blacks, and would prevent the District of Columbia from being used as "a depot for the slaves brought from the neighboring States." [45] On this occasion he was proving himself a worthy son of a father who had opposed the ratification of the Federal Constitution partly because it allowed the importation of slaves for twenty years.

He also took a more sensible view than did Calhoun and other prominent Southern leaders with reference to the petitions that were sent to Congress asking the abolition of slavery in the District of Columbia. Two petitions of this character were presented to the Senate (January 7, 1836) by Senator Morris, of Ohio. The usual procedure was to refer these petitions to the Committee on the District of Columbia. But Calhoun proposed to reject them *in limine* on the ground that they contained a gross, false, and malicious slander on eleven States. Tyler saw that Calhoun's proposal, if adopted, would link up the right of petition with the cause of the Abolitionists and greatly strengthen their position. He took issue, therefore, with the great Carolinian and advocated a reference to the District Committee, of which he was at the time chairman. He said Calhoun's plan would give *"these petitions too much consequence.* Let them go to the lion's den, and there will be no footprints to show their return." He thought, however, that the Senate ought to adopt a distinct and positive resolution disclaiming any power in Congress to legislate on this subject. Such action on the part of the Senate would put to rest the agitation of the question.[46]

[44] Sen. Doc., 22nd Cong., 2nd sess., no. 85, 267–268.
[45] *Register of Debates in Congress,* 23rd Cong., 2nd sess., 456–457.
[46] *Ibid.,* 24th Cong., 1st sess., 72, 90.

Tyler's willingness to receive petitions in favor of abolishing slavery in the District of Columbia was not due in any degree whatever to sympathy or agreement with the opinions of the petitioners. On the contrary, he was as strongly opposed to the interference by Congress of slavery in the District (except as to the slave trade) as was Calhoun or other proslavery Southerners. He felt that if Congress should abolish slavery in the District of Columbia without the consent of Virginia and Maryland, such an act "would be a gross violation of good faith, which could not fail to lessen our confidence in the Government, and in no small degree our attachment to the Union." [47]

While the numerous antislavery petitions that were sent to Congress were annoying to the Southerners, they did not constitute so serious a menace to slavery as the propagandist efforts of the Abolitionists carried on through numerous pamphlets distributed throughout the South. In these pamphlets slaveholders were held up as brutal tyrants and the slaves as innocent victims of the most cruel barbarities. This agitation was calculated to create dissatisfaction among the slaves and arouse in their masters the fear of insurrection. It goes without saying that such a course stirred up great excitement in the South and a violent feeling against Abolitionism.

Virginia shared in the general feeling of opposition aroused by the circulation of the Abolitionist pamphlets, and meetings were held in various parts of the State to denounce the libelous propaganda. Tyler addressed one of these meetings held in James City County and another at Gloucester Courthouse. At the latter place he spoke (August 22, 1835) in the plainest terms against the Abolitionists and the campaign that they were waging against slavery. He contended

[47] Tyler's views as to the abolition of slavery in the District of Columbia were given in a speech delivered at Gloucester Courthouse (August 22, 1835), an article published in the Richmond *Whig* (September, 1836), and a letter to Henry Clay (January 28, 1838). See Tyler, *Letters and Times,* I, 581-582; *Niles,* LI, 44-46; *Clay Papers* (L.C.), XXI, 3695.

that the Abolitionist newspapers and pamphlets were misrepresenting conditions in the South and were thus agencies of slander. This Abolitionist propaganda "has invaded our firesides, and under our own roofs is sharpening the dagger for midnight assassination, and exciting cruelty and bloodshed. The post-office department, which was established for the purpose of commercial interchange or to transport from remote places the friendly greetings of those of kindred blood, has been converted into a vehicle for distributing incendiary pamphlets, with which our land is at this moment deluged." [48]

He did not attempt to justify slavery or contend that it was a blessing either to the whites or the blacks. He considered slavery as an evil that had been inflicted upon his people, and felt that the only course open to the South was to bear this thorn in its side with as little discomfort and as much patience as possible. It seems never to have occurred to him and his *confrères* of like faith that to have made a strenuous effort to remove the thorn would have been more sensible and Christian than to have borne it with stoic fortitude.

We have rather meager information regarding Tyler's treatment of his slaves. But from the few sources that are available and the inferences that may properly be drawn from them we can safely assume that he was a just and kind master. To a man of his good sense and refined feelings, wanton cruelty to a helpless Negro would have jarred upon his instincts as a gentleman and his judgment as a man of business. For understanding the nature of the blacks, as his long and close association with them enabled him to do, he fully realized that an unhappy Negro was an unprofitable servant. So in his directions to his overseers we find him advising such a management of the "hands" as will keep them happy. For, as he said, encouragement is a better incentive to work than fear.[49]

---

[48] Tyler, *op. cit.*, I, 573–579.   [49] Tyler, *op. cit.*, I, 437, 562.

CHAPTER XI

STRANGE BEDFELLOWS

THE nine years spent by Tyler in Washington as Senator were doubtless the most enjoyable season of his long public career. He was in the prime of life and his intellectual gifts and personal charm appeared to their best advantage in this dignified and formal body. He seems to have had sufficient leisure for a good deal of reading, and his letters show that his interests included the books of the day as well as the English classics. He was able, therefore, to bring out of the storehouse of his mind ideas both new and old.

While Tyler was serving in the Senate his family (except for the first two years, when it was at "Greenway") was living on his plantation in Gloucester County. Mrs. Tyler spent only one or two winters in Washington during this entire period.[1] While there she evidently made a most favorable impression on her husband's friends and associates. Among the prominent people whom she met was Mrs. Anne Royall, who spoke of her and her oldest daughter, Mary, in the following extravagant terms: "If I was pleased with the appearance of Mr. Tyler, I was charmed with that of Mrs. and Miss Tyler, particularly the latter. The little sylph, she stood behind me when taking notes, the last day of the session, and in her own smooth fascinating way, fairly beguiled me of my senses. Besides her and Mrs. Tyler, there were one or two other ladies in the party, all of whom for beauty of person and eloquence of manner greatly exceed any females I met in Washington." [2]

[1] Mrs. Laura Carter Holloway Langford, *The Ladies of the White House* (New York, 1886), II, 45.
Mrs. Tyler was apparently in Washington during the session of 1828–29.
[2] Anne Royall, *Letters from Alabama* (Washington, 1830), I, 550, note.

Such a compliment was calculated to make a young lady conceited, and to guard against this danger Tyler wrote to his daughter stating that "Mrs. Royall's praise is of very little value; and, therefore, you are not to be rendered vain by it." [3] Later (1835) Mary returned to visit her father, and was received very cordially by Washington society. "Visitors have come in numbers, and invitations have thickened upon her." [4]

It was unfortunate that Tyler had to be away from his family at this period, for it was a time when it needed him most. His letters reveal an ardent affection for his children and a pathetic longing to be with them. As a partial substitute for direct contacts, he wrote rather formal letters to them in which he gave much good advice. He seemed especially anxious that they should maintain proper relations with their associates and impressed upon them the value of courtesy, kindness, modesty, and good temper. More than once did he quote to them Cardinal Wolsey's injunction to Cromwell:

> Still in your right hand carry gentle peace,
> To silence envious tongues.

To Mary he pointed out the value of education to young women, stating that "without intellectual improvement the most beautiful of the sex is but a figure of wax work." John, the second son, was given this counsel: "Have *hours* for reading and *minutes* for playing, and you will be a clever fellow." Sometimes his advice to his daughter took a philosophical or semireligious turn. In these letters mild reproof for shortcomings sometimes found a place, but more often praise for good conduct.

To Robert, the oldest son, were directed inquiries as to how he was getting on with his studies and how often his teacher had whipped him, along with admonitions to study diligently and behave properly. He was urged to read Lord Chesterfield, as "half the success in life depends on man-

---

[3] Tyler, *Letters and Times*, I, 550.   [4] *Ibid.*, 510–511.

ners." During the last years, Robert was at William and
Mary and, of course, was given good advice as to how to
spend his time. He was told to go into genteel society as
much as his studies would permit. Robert had refused a foolish challenge to a duel by a fellow student and was commended by his father for his good sense. Professor Dew was
to be promised early payment of the balance due on fees for
the previous year.[5]

Most of Tyler's letters to his children measure up both
in style and content to a high standard of epistolary excellence. Especially fine in sentiment was a communication to
his son John, written on the occasion of the illness of the latter's fiancée which caused a postponement of their marriage.
Parental solicitude and affection for his son and his future
daughter-in-law are expressed in a manner well worthy of a
disciple of Addison.[6]

In the counsel given to his daughters he showed himself in
complete agreement with the straitest sect of the early Vic-
torians as to the rules that should govern the relations of
young people of opposite sexes. Indeed, to the present post-
war generation the code imposed upon his daughters would
seem to be based on a senseless prudery. Apparently he would
not permit them to deviate in the slightest from the rigid
conventions which restricted the freedom of womanhood in
that man-governed age.

The following incident affords an illustration of this sub-
servience to an unreasonable convention. On one occasion
he enclosed with one of his own a letter written to his daughter by his nephew, John Waggaman. She was cautioned
against answering it. If she were to write to him—although
he was her first cousin—the gossips would, he feared, con-
strue it as an indelicacy unbecoming a young woman of her
standing. But to avoid offending the young man, she should

[5] For these letters, see Tyler, *Letters and Times*, I, 484–485, 508–511, 514,
529–531, 534–535, 546–565.
[6] The original of this letter, which was written November 4, 1838, is in
the collection of Tyler papers at Duke University.

write to his mother, her aunt, and have her report to him how she was getting along in music, French, etc.[7]

With such strict views as to the proper behavior of young men and women, it is no wonder that he was shocked the first time he witnessed the waltz. In writing to his thirteen-year-old daughter (December 26, 1827), he spoke of having dined at Cary Selden's, where he witnessed, apparently for the first time, the disgusting performance of the waltz. He described it as "a dance which you have never seen, and which I do not desire to see you dance. It is rather vulgar I think."[8] Later in life, however, he seems to have held a more liberal view toward waltzing, as this form of amusement was indulged in at the White House while the second Mrs. Tyler was reigning as First Lady. It might be added that on this occasion some of Tyler's opponents experienced a shock similar to that felt by Tyler himself at an earlier time.

When Tyler resigned from the Senate and returned to his home in Gloucester he found his private affairs in such disorder as to require his "unremitted and undivided attention." The marriage of his daughter shortly before this time had made extraordinary demands on a slender purse, and he was burdened with financial obligations, some of which were urgent. Accordingly, he was detained at home during the summer and fall devoting his energies to putting his house in order.[9] He had not, however, withdrawn from the arena of politics. On the contrary, he had entered the race for the Vice-Presidency in the campaign of 1836.

By the spring of 1834 there had grown up a new party, which had assumed the name of "Whig." It was a coalition composed of anti-Masons, National Republicans, and anti-Administration Democrats. Jackson's vigorous policies, notably his attitude toward the nullification of South Carolina and his removal of the Bank deposits, had given serious jolts

---

[7] Tyler, *Letters and Times*, I, 553.   [8] *Ibid.*, I, 390.
[9] *John Tyler Papers* (L.C.), II, 6355, 6359; Tyler, *Letters and Times*, I, 530; III, 67.

to the Democratic Party and had shaken out quite a number
of dissenters, who had joined the ranks of the opposition.
The list of seceders included Nullifiers, moderate States'
rights men, and others who had broken with the President
for various reasons.

The Southern members of the new party who adhered to
the doctrine of States' rights looked to Calhoun for leadership. Prominent among those who belonged to this group in
Virginia were Tyler, Abel P. Upshur, William F. Gordon,
Littleton W. Tazewell, and Henry A. Wise. The alliance
between the States' rights men of the South and the nationalists of the North was not a love match but a marriage of
convenience.[10] By uniting with a party that had all along
advocated measures to which they were fundamentally opposed, the insurgent Democrats of the South had thrown
consistency to the winds.

The formation of the Whig Party was one of the most
important events in the career of John Tyler, for to it he
owed his elevation to the Presidency. And yet his mind was
in all probability disturbed (or should have been) with
strong misgivings when he joined hands with the National
Republicans of the North. For not only did he abhor the
principles advocated by them, but he also distrusted some
of their outstanding leaders. Of these leaders Webster was
particularly offensive to him. Webster's nomination for the
Presidency by the Whigs, he thought, would be a great
blunder. It would revive the tariff issue and the question of
slavery in the District of Columbia.[11]

The coalition of groups known as the Whig Party first
tried out its national strength in the Presidential campaign
of 1836. With so many diverse elements, agreement as to
a platform or even a candidate was not possible and so no

[10] A. C. Cole, *The Whig Party in the South* (Washington, 1913), 30; *Niles*, XLVI, 101, 131.

[11] Tyler to W. F. Gordon, Nov. 9, 1834; A. C. Gordon, *William Fitzhugh Gordon* (N. Y. and Washington, 1909), 293-295. The original manuscript of this letter is in the collection of Tyler papers at Duke University.

national convention was held. The strongest faction in the coalition was the National Republican element, and in the main it endorsed William Henry Harrison, a reputed hero of the War of 1812. In Massachusetts, however, the National Republicans supported Webster, and he received the vote of that State.

The States' rights Whigs of the South (except the Nullifiers of South Carolina) supported as their candidate Judge Hugh L. White, of Tennessee, who "was a strict constructionist of the purest type." [12]

Tyler was the favored Whig candidate in the South for the Vice-Presidency, though little interest was taken in this phase of the campaign. By the beginning of the year 1835 his name had been suggested by the *Virginia Free Press*. In December of the same year the Washington *Sun* followed suit, and about the same time the Richmond *Whig* spoke favorably of his candidacy. He was also endorsed for the second place on the ticket by the Whigs of Maryland, Virginia, North Carolina, and Georgia.[13] Of all the endorsements received, the one given by the Old Dominion was doubtless the most gratifying. A convention of the Virginia States' rights Whigs was held in Richmond (February 10, 1836) to nominate the standard-bearers of their party. White and Tyler were unanimously chosen—White for the first place and Tyler for the second. A friend of Tyler's, in writing to him about the action of the convention, expressed himself as "highly delighted with the unexampled unanimity and sincere cordiality with which your nomination was received."

White and Tyler made good running mates, for the latter had come out for the former as early as May of the preceding year.[14] The people of western Virginia, however, preferred Harrison to White, and a State convention was held

---

[12] Cole, *op. cit.,* 41–43.

[13] Tyler, *Letters and Times,* I, 518–519, 532–534; Richmond *Whig,* Dec. 19, 1835.

[14] W. Crump to Tyler, Feb. 14, 1836; Tyler, *op. cit.,* I, 517, 533; Richmond *Enquirer,* Feb. 13, 1836.

later which named Harrison and Tyler. The White electors were accepted by this convention on the understanding that if elected they would vote for Harrison or White depending on which one received the larger popular vote. This "double-shotted" ticket was, in the opinion of Tyler, the cause of the Whigs' losing the State.[15]

The very day on which the States' rights Whigs in Richmond nominated Tyler for the Vice-Presidency the Democratic lower house of the legislature passed the resolution which instructed him out of his seat in the Senate.[16] His political friends and opponents in the home State were thus respectively attempting to honor and discredit him—the former by assisting him in the effort to don the Vice-Presidential mantle and the latter by trying to strip him of his senatorial toga.

Tyler had a strong following in Ohio. A convention of more than a thousand Whigs met at Columbus (February 22, 1836), and, of course, nominated Harrison for the Presidency. Tyler was supported by the States' rights wing of the party for the Vice-Presidency. This group, in the opinion of two of his friends, had a majority in the convention. One of his adherents felt that three-fourths of the delegates to the meeting and a like proportion of the Whigs of the State favored Tyler's nomination. Despite all this, however, the anti-Masons were able to control the body and nominate Francis Granger. Letters from Washington came to leaders of the convention urging that Granger be named. Pennsylvania had already endorsed Harrison and Granger, and it was contended that Harrison might not be sustained by the Keystone State if Ohio refused to endorse its nominees.[17]

The Democrats nominated Van Buren for the Presidency, and Colonel Richard M. Johnson for the Vice-Presidency. The Whigs did not expect that any one of their three candi-

[15] Ambler, *Thomas Ritchie*, 179.   [16] Tyler, *op. cit.*, I, 532.
[17] *Ibid.*, 520–522.

dates would receive a majority in the Electoral College, but they hoped that enough votes would be drawn away from Van Buren to prevent his receiving a majority. The election would then be thrown into the House, where a Whig would have a good chance to be chosen.

In all probability Tyler did not take a prominent part in this campaign, but he always comported himself with the proper decorum and dignity. He refused to allow the excitement of the contest to upset his serenity, nor did he arouse unnecessary antagonisms by heedless words and tactless acts. One of his fortunate traits was the ability to conciliate opponents and inspire them with a feeling of sympathetic friendliness. This quality was shown in marked degree in the first meeting he had with Henry S. Foote, afterwards Senator from Mississippi. It was during the Presidential campaign of 1836, when they happened to be passengers on a steamboat going up the James River to Richmond. Foote, who was for Van Buren, had just been engaged in a heated debate with two Whig leaders. Under the influence of Tyler's calm and genial manner he cooled off quickly and was at once brought under the spell of his fine conversational ability and magnetic personality. "He was (declared Foote in later years) really one of the most genial and captivating men I ever encountered; there was not a particle of hauteur or assumption in his aspect or demeanor; he seemed to be eminently frank and unconstrained in his conversation; had a clear and ringing voice, possessed a ready and insinuating smile, and, in fact, few could hold converse with him for ten or fifteen minutes even without feeling strongly impressed with his many high qualities, nor without feeling more or less inclined to sympathize with his fortunes." [18]

Van Buren was elected President. Tyler received forty-seven electoral votes, having carried the States of Maryland, Tennessee, South Carolina, and Georgia. He was thus third in the race for the Vice-Presidency. Johnson received a plu-

[18] Henry S. Foote, *Casket of Reminiscences* (Washington, 1874), 55–58.

rality but not a majority of the electoral votes. The Senate was, therefore, called upon to make a choice between him and Granger, his closest competitor. Johnson was chosen on the first ballot.[19]

The campaign being over, Tyler was now in a position to devote all his time to his profession. As "Gloucester Place" was not a good situation for a lawyer, he began to make plans for taking up his residence in Williamsburg. In the fall of 1837 he was able to purchase from his old friend, Judge N. Beverley Tucker, a large and comfortable residence with a number of lots adjoining it.[20] He sold his farm in Gloucester and settled down in the town of his ancestors, where, in all probability, he expected to spend the remainder of his days. He was living here at the time of his election to the Vice-Presidency.

He was allowed to remain in private life for only a short time, however, as he was again elected (1838) to the Virginia House of Delegates. This time he went as the representative of a district of which Williamsburg was the center. As he had bought his house in the fall of the previous year and had, therefore, not resided or owned property in the district quite six months prior to the election, the question was raised as to whether he was eligible to take his seat in the House of Delegates.[21] Tyler was very much chagrined that this question should have been raised and announced his intention of resigning on reaching Richmond if he should find doubt in the mind of anyone whom he esteemed. He must have been reassured by his colleagues, for he took his seat and was elected Speaker of the House with great unanimity.[22]

---

[19] T. H. Benton, *Thirty Years' View*, I, 683; Edward Stanwood, *A History of the Presidency* (Boston, 1898), 183, 185.

[20] *John Tyler Papers* (L.C.), II, 6370.

[21] See deposition (December 24, 1838) of Judge N. Beverley Tucker in *James City County Petitions* (Archives, Va. State Library). Also petition of Robert Henderson, December, 1838; *ibid*.

[22] *John Tyler Papers* (L.C.), II, 6370.

When Tyler became a member of the House of Delegates for this his third period of service, he was a national figure and any opinions expressed by him in the legislature might be of interest to the country as a whole. Of such national significance was his attitude toward the disposal of the public lands. As chairman of the Select Committee on Public Lands he made a long report to the House on January 17, 1839. It was an able argument in favor of distribution among the States of the proceeds of the sales of the public lands.

A series of resolutions was then proposed declaring in favor of distribution and requesting the Virginia Senators and Representatives in Congress to lay them before the two houses of Congress.[23] These resolutions gave rise to a long debate. Tyler, although unwell, spoke for two hours (January 28) in favor of them. In the course of his speech he referred to Henry Clay [24] in a most complimentary way. The resolutions were passed by the Whig House of Delegates and laid on the table by the Democratic Senate.[25]

The position taken by Tyler on distribution at this time was later used against him by his enemies who were trying to convict him of disloyalty to Whig principles. When President he would not accept without modification Clay's plan of distribution. According to Clay's supporters, Tyler, in refusing to sign this measure, was acting inconsistently with his record in the Virginia Assembly. There was, however, a difference in the policy of distribution as advocated by Tyler in the Virginia House of Delegates and that afterwards sponsored by Clay in the United States Senate.

It was while Tyler was serving his last period in the House of Delegates that he figured prominently in a long-drawn-out fight with the friends of William C. Rives for a seat in the United States Senate (pp. 145 ff.). By this contest he aroused

---

[23] Richmond *Whig and Public Advertiser* (daily and semi-weekly), Jan. 22, 1839; Richmond *Enquirer*, Feb. 19, 1842.

[24] Richmond *Enquirer*, Jan. 29, 1839.   [25] *Ibid.*, Jan. 31, Feb. 2, 1839.

the enmity of some of the prominent Whigs, and lessened his influence as a party leader in Virginia.

In the interval between his withdrawal from the Senate and his return to the House of Delegates, Tyler was accorded an honor by his fellow Virginians which was doubtless highly prized by him. This was his election to the presidency of the Virginia Colonization Society. The desire of Southern leaders to remove from their midst the menace of the free Negro led to the formation of the American Colonization Society. The purpose of this organization was to promote emancipation by encouraging the emigration of free Negroes from this country to a colony on the west coast of Africa.

For a number of years Tyler was vice-president of the Virginia Colonization Society and in January, 1838, was elected president. In his speech accepting this honor, he alluded to the fact that he was present when the parent society was organized in Washington. At that time he regarded this plan for removing free Negroes from the United States as a Utopian scheme—"a dream of philanthropy, visiting men's pillows in their sleep, to cheat them on their waking." Now, however, he was enthusiastic as to its possibilities both as a missionary and colonizing venture. He predicted that the colony already established in Liberia would prove the starting point from which settlers would rapidly spread over Africa, "and Monrovia will be to Africa what Jamestown and Plymouth have been to America." [26]

The election of 1836 convinced Calhoun that he could not hope to mold the new Whig Party to his views. The Northern wing had shown decided nationalistic tendencies, and even in the South some of the Whigs had followed the nationalist lead, while the others had voted for a Proclamation man. Besides, he and Clay encountered difficulties in their newly formed alliance. Clay saw that Calhoun was an

[26] Tyler, *Letters and Times*, I, 567–570.

obstacle to that union and concert of action which he was trying to effect in Congress among the Whigs. Calhoun felt that if the coalition were kept up the party would be dominated by the nationalist element and he would lose his own following. Both political and personal considerations, therefore, prompted him to break away from the Whig Party.

At this juncture, too, the Democratic leaders acted with rare wisdom. They entered upon a systematic campaign to show that the differences between themselves and the States' rights Whigs were of degree and not of kind and that nullification was now only a memory and should not figure as an issue. They invited these former friends to return to their first love, and received with marked cordiality those who did return.

The fight over the Subtreasury gave Calhoun his opportunity. He supported this Administration measure and thus got back into the Democratic Party. There went along with him some other prominent leaders, not only in South Carolina but also in other Southern States. Among these were R. M. T. Hunter, W. F. Gordon, and Littleton W. Tazewell, of Virginia, and John A. Quitman, of Mississippi.

Tyler, unfortunately, did not accompany his warm personal friend, Tazewell, back into the Democratic fold. Nor did Wise. The decision to continue in the Whig ranks was probably the greatest mistake ever made by Tyler. It was only natural that he should have opposed Jackson's measures at the time of the nullification trouble, for an honest man of courage with his convictions could hardly have done otherwise. In opposing the Administration, therefore, he was acting in entire consistency with his whole previous career. Nor was he seriously open to the charge of inconsistency when he supported Judge White for the Presidency. By so doing he could protest against the objectionable measures that had been carried out by the Democratic Administration and at the same time endorse a leader whose views were in the main in accord with his own. He was, however, aiding and abetting a movement which if successful would have meant victory for a party the dominant element of which stood for policies which his whole public career had been spent in combating. But even if we excuse him for leaving the Democratic Party in 1836, no such excuse can be urged for his remaining in the Whig Party after this election had clearly shown that the Nationalist wing of that party was in the ascendency.

At that time few, if any, of the principles of the Democratic Party were fundamentally different from the views that he had all along so ably championed. On the other hand, the dominant faction of the Whig Party was still in favor of such measures as a protective tariff, internal improvements, and a national bank—policies that he had always opposed. If he had been as consistent at this time as he had hitherto been he would have been spared the humiliation to which he was afterwards subjected while President. He doubtless would never have attained the Presidency, but in all probability would have pursued a career of usefulness and happiness without the attendant notoriety which was invoked by his elevation to the Chief Magistracy.

By continuing his membership in a political party dominated by National Republicans he was certainly sojourning in a land whose people worshiped strange gods. For a man of his pronounced States' rights views it must have been a sort of Babylonian exile. To be consistent with his past career he would have to continue his ardent professions in favor of States' rights and his unswerving opposition to the nationalistic measures lately championed by his erstwhile opponents but present political friends. It was truly an embarrassing position. A regular politician would have hung his harp on the willows and remained silent. But circumstances would not let Tyler remain quiet, and so he tried to sing the Lord's song in a strange land.

CHAPTER XII

REJECTED AND HONORED BY
THE WHIGS

TYLER'S political aspirations may have been dampened, but certainly they were not suppressed, by his defeat in the Vice-Presidential campaign of 1836. On the contrary, he still hoped to return to the United States Senate. The term of Rives, who had succeeded him, would expire on March 3, 1839, and both Rives and Tyler were candidates for the place. At this time conditions in the assembly were most favorable for a deadlock, as neither the Whigs nor the Democrats could control a majority on a joint vote of the two houses.[1] The Democrats had a narrow majority, but in their number were included about sixteen insurgents, who were known as Conservatives. This name was applied to the last group of seceders from the Democratic Party. They had remained loyal to Jackson throughout both his terms but had become dissatisfied with Van Buren's financial policy. They were opposed to the Subtreasury plan, feeling that the use of State banks as repositories for Federal funds should receive a longer trial.[2] The Conservatives were scattered through several States, but most of them were in New York and Virginia.[3] At first, they were in accord with the Administration except as to the Subtreasury plan; but the breach

---

[1] The total membership of both houses was 166. As Tyler did not vote as long as his name was being considered, it required 83 to make a majority. According to the estimate of a Whig member of the assembly, the strength of each of the parties was as follows: Whigs, 81 (less Tyler 80); Administration Democrats, 69, including one vacancy; Conservatives, 16. The Richmond *Enquirer,* January 29, 1839.

[2] The Charlottesville *Jeffersonian Republican,* quoted by the Richmond *Enquirer,* Jan. 17, 1839.

[3] Richmond *Enquirer,* Feb. 14, 1839.

once made kept widening, and the *Madisonian,* their organ, advocated a separate political organization.

In the election of a Senator the Conservatives held the balance of power between the Whigs and the regular Democrats, and were courted by both. If these insurgents could be induced to return to the reservation, Van Buren would be able to carry Virginia in the next election. The orthodox Democrats were thus ready to make large concessions to their dissatisfied brethren if by so doing they could win them back to regularity. As Rives was the most outstanding Conservative in Virginia, the Administration forces seemed disposed to overlook his opposition to the Subtreasury plan and favor his re-election provided they could count on his loyalty and support on other points.[4] But Rives maintained a noncommittal attitude toward the opposing groups and succeeded in balancing himself skillfully on the fence. Such a position was construed as a leaning toward the Whigs, and his persistent silence left no ground for hope to the Democrats. When they met in caucus, therefore, Rives's name was not presented and John Y. Mason, a judge of the General Court, was named as the candidate of the party.

The Whigs were willing to make a strong bid for the support of Rives and the group of Conservatives led by him. If they could be detached from the Democratic Party and incorporated into the Whig Party, the latter would have a good chance to carry Virginia in the spring elections and in the next Presidential campaign. As Virginia had a large representation in the Electoral College, her vote might determine the outcome of the contest in 1840. If the Conservatives were driven back into the arms of the Administration the Whig Party would be defeated the following April and would have no hope of carrying the State in the fall election. "We shall no more be able to retire to Elba," said the Richmond *Whig;* "we shall find ourselves shut up in St. Helena." "If we drive the Conservatives back into the

---

[4] Richmond *Enquirer,* Jan. 26, Feb. 7, 1839.

Democratic Party, it is the last time we shall be able to strengthen our party from the enemy's ranks." [5]

Tyler was the logical candidate of the Whigs, and in all fairness should have been endorsed. As he had lost his seat three years earlier because of his loyalty to Whig policies, his friends felt that he should be rewarded for his fidelity to the party. Under ordinary circumstances this view would have prevailed and Tyler would have received the unanimous support of his Whig colleagues in the legislature. This is shown by the fact that when a successor to Leigh was elected in December, 1836, the Whigs (who were then in the minority in the Virginia Assembly) complimented Tyler with their vote.[6] But now gratitude for past favors from Tyler did not move the Whig leaders so much as the hope of future aid from Rives. They were, therefore, willing to sacrifice Tyler on the altar of party expediency. It was charged by his friends (and there is good ground for the accusation) that the Whigs had agreed to vote for Tyler at first and then go to Rives. In this way they could make it appear that the former could not be elected and they would be justified in dropping him.[7]

On the appointed day (February 15) the legislature received nominations for United States Senator with the view to an immediate election. As a warm political contest was in sight, considerable interest and even excitement were aroused. "The public anxiety is highly wrought up. The City is thronged with visitors. The Capitol was crowded with persons of all descriptions, all ages, and of both sexes. The scene was graced with the presence of a great number of ladies." Mason, Tyler, and Rives were all presented as candidates and each was strongly commended by one or more of his spellbinding advocates. One of Tyler's friends in sustaining his nomination made a speech of two hours' length.[8]

[5] Quoted in the Richmond *Enquirer*, Feb. 14, 1839.
[6] *Journal, Va. House of Delegates*, session 1836–37, 18, 29.
[7] Richmond *Enquirer*, January 29, February 16, 1839.
[8] *Ibid.*, Feb. 16, Mar. 2, 5, 7, 1839.

The debate on the candidates was carried on in each house separately and then the vote was taken in joint session. At first a majority of the Whigs voted for Tyler, and he kept his lead over Rives for the first five ballots. On the sixth ballot Rives ran ahead of Tyler. The latter then asked that his name be withdrawn, declaring "that if his Whig brethren would present a thoroughgoing Whig to the House, he would vote for him with great cheerfulness." [9]

Up to this time Tyler had abstained from voting and had taken no part in the contest. He now entered the fray and determined to prevent the election of Rives. The persistent opponents of Rives—about a baker's dozen in number—were known as "impractical and impracticable Whigs." The "Forlorn Hope," as the "Impracticables" termed themselves, stood firm in its opposition and thus prevented the election of Rives. The last attempt to break the deadlock was made on Saturday, February 23, when six ballots were taken. The Spartan Band of Conservatives, about fourteen strong, joined with the majority of the Whigs in support of Rives, but the combined groups lacked four votes of the number necessary for a choice. There was no prospect of the different factions coming to an agreement, and a resolution was passed in the House (February 25) in favor of an indefinite postponement of the election. For some unaccountable reason Tyler voted against this sensible motion. As the Senate promptly agreed to the House resolution, the contest was adjourned and Virginia was left with only one representative in the United States Senate.

It was unfortunate that so much time had been wasted on this abortive attempt at an election when other important measures were demanding the attention of the legislature. The blame for this was rightfully placed by the *Enquirer*, not on the Democratic Party, but on the coalition between the Conservatives and the Whigs. Ritchie's impressions of the futile contest were stated as follows:

[9] Richmond *Enquirer*, Feb. 21, 23, 1839.

"The struggle has been the most arduous one which was ever witnessed in Virginia. The roll was called twenty-eight different times." Eight days were wasted and sometimes night sessions were held. The only redeeming feature of the situation was that the debate, though intensely animated, was carried on without rancor and with the utmost decorum. "We heard not a violent word used—not a passionate gesture—no jostling—no quarrelling—but the whole crowded assembly seemed actuated by all the refinements of gentlemen." [10]

All indications pointed to the fact that Tyler's failure to secure the Senatorial seat at this time was due largely, if not mainly, to the influence of Henry Clay. Clay was kindly disposed toward Tyler, and, political considerations apart, preferred him to Rives. But he felt that if Rives were elected by the Whigs, the Conservatives would be detached from the regular Democrats and Virginia would be thrown into the Whig column in the Presidential election of 1840. Clay was anxious to win in the Old Dominion, the State of his birth, partly for sentimental reasons but mainly because of the strong vote that it cast in the Electoral College. He is reported as having said that he would rather carry Virginia and be defeated than to lose it and be elected. [11]

That influences emanating from Washington were affecting the situation in Richmond became apparent when it was observed that all the Clay papers from Boston to Richmond were advocating the election of Rives. Noting this, Judge John B. Christian, a brother-in-law of Tyler, wrote to Henry A. Wise to see Clay and get from him an explanation of his support of Rives. Wise, who was then representing an eastern Virginia district in the House of Representatives, was a fiery young Whig and a loyal adherent of Tyler. He saw Clay and warned him of the unwisdom of intriguing

[10] *Ibid.*, Feb. 26, 1839.
[11] Clay to Judge Brooke, Dec. 26, 1838; Tyler, *Letters and Times,* I, 591–592, note.

against his friend. He pointed out to Clay that he was opposing a Whig who had lost his seat for refusing to vote for
the expunging resolution and was endorsing a Democrat
who had voted and fought for this objectionable measure.
The Whig Party, he declared, would lose more votes in Virginia by such a procedure than it would gain. Clay admitted
that he knew of the attempt to elect Rives. He expressed,
however, a preference for Tyler if he could be elected, but
said that if Tyler could not win it would be best for the party
"to take Mr. Rives, or any other weapon with which to
bruise the head of the serpent of Van Burenism." Wise replied that if the effort to elect Rives were persisted in, it
would cause Clay to lose Virginia in the nominating convention.

Wise was approached twice after this by the supporters
of Clay, who urged him to use his influence with his friends
in Richmond in favor of breaking the deadlock by electing
Rives. For quite a while Wise was unmovable in his opposition to Rives, but finally the appeals from Clay became so
urgent that he yielded to the point of making terms. He
suggested that the Whig leaders promise to endorse Tyler
for the nomination for the Vice-Presidency and that Tyler's
friends in the Virginia legislature agree to give up their opposition. If we can trust this account, the accuracy of which
is questionable, this promise was given.[12]

Whether the terms of this agreement were ever reported
to Tyler we have no means of knowing, as there are now
available no source materials which bear upon this point.
But if he did know of it, he must (as his son, Dr. L. G. Tyler,

[12] This account is based on Wise's *Seven Decades of the Union*. When it is
remembered that this work was prepared about a third of a century after
the event described, it can readily be seen that Wise's interesting story is open
to doubt. It sounds as if some links which could not be furnished from memory
had been supplied by a vivid imagination. Moreover, we know that a part
of the account is incorrect. It is probably true that Wise, as he claims, wrote
a letter in Clay's presence to Judge Christian giving the results of his interview with the Whig leader. But, unfortunately, this letter is not extant, or at
least has not been found. See pp. 157–161.

says he did) have spurned the proposal; for he and the other "Impracticables" continued to vote against Rives and thus protracted the deadlock to the end of the session. When Rives was finally elected Tyler had been nominated for and elected to the Vice-Presidency.[13] In the meantime Rives had supported Harrison and Tyler in the Presidential election of 1840 [14] and had been accepted as a Whig in good standing by most of the party leaders in Virginia. But a few of Tyler's old friends in the legislature (the "Impracticables") could not shut their eyes to Rives's past record, and three of them still stubbornly refused to vote for him. By their unyielding opposition they were able to deadlock the assembly and prevent the election of Rives until January, 1841.[15]

This long fight over the Senatorship aroused some bitterness of feeling toward Tyler which weakened his hold on the Whig Party in the Old Dominion. It was doubtless due in large measure to this feeling that the Virginia delegates to the Whig national convention declined to give their enthusiastic support to Tyler for the Vice-Presidency. And yet Rives, who had the most reason for taking offense, seems to have harbored no grudge against his opponent. When Tyler became President, Rives was his chief supporter in the Senate and remained loyal to him after all his Whig colleagues had repudiated him. The Whig Party also reversed its action and made ample amends for the slight which had been given to Tyler. For the national Whigs chose him to preside over

[13] Wise incorrectly intimates that Tyler accepted the terms of the agreement. He says that his friends did not vote at all on the last ballot, and in this way Rives got a bare majority. But he failed to state that this happened two years after the agreement was alleged to have been made.

[14] In February, 1840, Rives published a letter in which was announced his intention to support the Whig ticket for President and Vice-President. Richmond *Enquirer,* Feb. 25, 1840.

[15] Richmond *Enquirer,* Dec. 7, 1839; Jan. 11, 18, 21, 23, 30, Feb. 1, Mar. 5, 1840; Jan. 19, 1841.

the very body to which the State Whigs had denied him admission.

This high honor was conferred upon Tyler by the national convention of the Whig Party. This body met on December 4, 1839, at Harrisburg, Pennsylvania, to select their candidates for President and Vice-President. The convention was organized by making Governor James Barbour, of Virginia, permanent chairman, or president, and Tyler one of the thirteen vice-presidents.[16]

The convention did not proceed in the usual way in making its nominations, but adopted a plan similar to that of the unit rule of present-day political assemblies. The responsibility of choosing candidates for President and Vice-President was intrusted to a general committee composed of representatives from the State delegations. In the general committee the vote of each State (determined by a majority of the delegation) was to be the same as its vote in the Electoral College. After the general committee had made a selection its decision would be ratified by the convention as a whole.[17]

The general committee entered upon its work with a due sense of the importance of the task that had been assigned to it. For the Whig leaders felt that victory or defeat for their party at the polls would depend largely upon the action of this convention in selecting a standard-bearer. They had to consider not only ability but also availability. The names of Clay, Scott, and Harrison were all presented to the committee. Clay was easily the best known of the three and was doubtless the ablest of them all. But during his long career in Congress he had taken a decided stand on some public questions about which there was marked disagreement among the Whigs. For this reason it would be difficult for the diverse elements in the party to unite on him. On the

[16] H. W. Hilliard, *Politics and Pen Pictures at Home and Abroad* (N. Y., G. P. Putnam's Sons, 1892), 4–5.
[17] *Tyler's Quarterly Historical and Genealogical Magazine*, IX, 90–95.

score of availability, therefore, he was thought by some to be the weakest of the three candidates.[18]

Strange to relate, a majority of the delegates from the South, the stronghold of the States' rights doctrine, favored the nomination of Clay, despite his past record in support of a nationalistic policy. Since his championship of the Compromise Tariff of 1833, he had been regarded by them as the "Great Pacificator," "who was willing to sacrifice personal ambition to patriotic ends." As he was a slaveowner and a Southerner, he was also supposed to be right on the slavery question. His acceptance of the Compromise eliminated the tariff as an issue in the campaign. Moreover, in a recent letter to a prominent Southerner (Judge N. Beverley Tucker) he had declared that in view of what the States had done for internal improvements, Congress should not begin any new work. All he now insisted upon was that Congress provide for the distribution among the States of the proceeds from the sale of public lands.[19]

For these reasons Tyler, White, Wise, Barbour, and other leaders of the strict constructionist school felt justified in supporting him for the Presidency in 1840. White declared that Clay was preferable to Van Buren "in regard to financial policy, attitude toward executive power and patronage, and general motives." Preston urged the expulsion of "the Stuarts, whoever may replace them." Wise declared: "I would choose any decent *white* man in the nation to be President in preference to Martin Van Buren." [20]

Unfortunately for Clay there were in line for the Whig nomination two military "heroes"—Generals Winfield Scott and William Henry Harrison. Each of these leaders had had a creditable record in the War of 1812, and might properly be classed as heroes of the moderate type. Moreover, Harrison had won the soubriquet of "Tippecanoe" by having

[18] Horace Greeley, *Recollections of a Busy Life* (N. Y. and Boston, 1868), 129–133.
[19] Clay to N. B. Tucker, Oct. 10, 1839; Tyler, *Letters and Times*, I, 601–602.
[20] Cole, *The Whig Party in the South*, 55 and note on p. 55.

led in a battle with the Indians at a place by that name, and this word would sound well in a campaign slogan. Scott's public career had been confined to military affairs, and Harrison's record as a Congressman and territorial governor had been an inconspicuous one. To the great mass of the voters, therefore, the attitude of both of these candidates on public questions was unknown, and neither was associated in the public mind with any policy that would arouse violent antagonisms.

During the first day and the greater part of the second the committee was deadlocked and could report no name to the convention, for no one of the three had a majority. Clay had a plurality of the delegates, but they came mainly from States which were not expected to go for any Whig candidate.[21]

In the ranks of those who were opposed to Clay was Thurlow Weed, an astute politician from New York. He professed great admiration for Clay and preferred him, he said, to all others for the Presidency. His opposition to his nomination was based on the conviction that the "Great Pacificator" could not carry New York and Pennsylvania and could not be elected without the vote of these two States. Weed at first supported Scott, but later he and the entire New York delegation went over to Harrison and the latter received the nomination.[22]

Although the nomination of Harrison was accepted by the convention with the outward semblance of unanimity there lurked a feeling of bitter disappointment in the hearts and minds of the supporters of Clay. This disappointment was especially keen among the Southern leaders.[23] Among Clay's adherents none experienced more disappointment than John Tyler. Horace Greely, who was present at the convention, though not a delegate, said that Tyler voted for Clay

---

[21] Hilliard, op. cit., 7; Greeley, op. cit., 130–131.
[22] T. W. Barnes, Memoirs of Thurlow Weed (Boston & N. Y., 1884), I, 480–482; II, 75–77; Hilliard, op. cit., 8.
[23] Hilliard, op. cit., 9–10; Niles, LVII, 248–252. According to Weed, "that unanimity was anything but cordial." Memoirs, I, 482.

first, last, and all the time, and was for him whether he could be elected or not. "When it was announced that Mr. Clay was defeated, he [Tyler] *cried* (so it was reported); and that report (I think) gave him the nomination for Vice-President. . . ." [24]

The general committee met Saturday morning to select a running mate for General Harrison.[25] Some votes for Vice-President had been cast while the previous balloting was going on, but the contest for the Presidential nomination had enlisted the interests of the delegates to such an extent that little attention was given to the race for the Vice-Presidency. The first vote cast for Tyler for this place was that of H. W. Hilliard, a delegate from Alabama. On every ballot from the very beginning he had voted for both Clay and Tyler. Hilliard had made the journey from Washington to Harrisburg in company with Tyler,[26] and his steady support was probably due to the good impression made on the young Alabaman by the pleasing personality of the Virginia statesman.

While the general committee was considering the Presidency, it was unanimously agreed that if Clay were selected, the Vice-Presidential nominee must come from a free State; whereas if Scott or Harrison were chosen to head the ticket, the second place would go to a candidate from a slaveholding State. In the latter event Tyler would be the logical man for the Vice-Presidential nomination. He was a strong States' rights man and was an ardent supporter of Clay. Having been on the ticket with Judge White in the previous campaign, he was well known to the Whig voters of the

---

[24] Greeley, *op. cit.,* 131. This story about Tyler's weeping over the defeat of Clay is a legend which has no basis in fact. In later years Tyler laughed it off as ridiculous. And yet it may have had some influence on uncritical Clay supporters in the convention.

[25] *Tyler's Quarterly Historical and Genealogical Magazine,* IX, 90–95.

[26] Hilliard, *op. cit.,* 4.

Hilliard said: "I have traveled to Harrisburg in company with Mr. Tyler, and I was honored by his attentions to me. There was an indescribable charm in his manners, and his conversation was fascinating."

South. His nomination would be a recognition of the Southern element of the party and a peace offering to Clay's followers. Benjamin Watkins Leigh, who was the sole representative of Virginia on the general committee, received the impression from private conversations with his colleagues of this committee that a majority of them would favor Tyler for Vice-President if either Scott or Harrison were selected for the first place. This impression was reported by Leigh to his fellow members of the Virginia delegation, doubtless to the embarrassment of Tyler. "Mr. Tyler," he says, "was present and disclaimed *all* wish upon the subject." [27]

In supporting Clay Tyler was thus apparently jeopardizing his own chances for the high honor which he coveted. He was placed in the dangerous position of having to choose between self-interest and loyalty to an admired leader. To a man of Tyler's sense of honor there was only one alternative —that of remaining true to a political friend without regard to the possible effect on his own political aspirations. This sacrificial devotion, however, was destined not to be repaid in kind. For it was due mainly to Clay's opposition to his quondam friend that Tyler in less than two years from that time was expelled from his party and branded as a traitor to its principles.

When the general committee met to name a candidate for the Vice-Presidency, the States were called in the same order in which they were accustomed to vote in the House of Representatives. Massachusetts, the third on the list, cast her ballot for Leigh. Leigh thereupon explained that as he was the single representative from Virginia on the committee and as no member of the Virginia delegation had suggested his candidacy, it would be indelicate for him to allow his name to be voted on. For this reason and others, he stated he would not accept and he advised the Massachusetts committee to retire and make another selection. This it did. The result of the balloting showed that Tyler had received a

[27] *Tyler's Quarterly*, IX, 92.

large majority of the votes of the committee. The State committees that had not voted for him now retired and returning cast their ballots also for Tyler. In this way the chairman of the general committee was able to report to the convention that Tyler had been recommended by the unanimous vote of the delegations except that of Virginia, which had not voted at all.[28] The recommendation of the general committee for Vice-President was accepted by the convention without a dissenting voice.

The refusal of his own State to endorse Tyler called for an explanation. Leigh accordingly stated to the convention that the Virginia delegation was unanimous for Tyler but had refrained from voting at the latter's request. Tyler, he said, had asked his colleagues to take no part in the balloting for Vice-President, inasmuch as he was a member of the Virginia delegation. Later, in a letter to the Richmond *Whig*, Leigh explained his action as follows:

"As Mr. Tyler was a member of the Virginia delegation, I thought that delegation would best consult his feelings and his dignity by withholding their vote altogether, so that the nomination would be entirely the act of the other delegations. I did not take this course because I thought the Virginia delegation would hesitate to concur in the nomination, and that willingly and promptly. My real and my declared purpose was, now that Mr. Tyler had received the nomination, to place him before the country on the most elevated ground on which he could stand." [29]

The statement made by Leigh is one of those explanations that do not explain. This overscrupulous delicacy went even beyond the most exacting demands of doctrinairism. Whether it left the impression at the time that this was only an excuse to cover up the opposition of the Virginia delegation to their colleague does not appear in the documents now available. But to the fair-minded student of today there peeps out from behind this squeamishness as to the propri-

[28] *Ibid.*, IX, 93–94.   [29] *Ibid.*, 90–95; Richmond *Whig*, Dec. 1, 4, 1841.

eties a disinclination on the part of the delegates from the
Old Dominion to bestow this high honor on their fellow
Virginian. This view is borne out by the fact that the Whig
State convention which met at Staunton in September, 1839,
and chose delegates to the Harrisburg Convention had expressed a preference, not for Tyler but for Tallmadge, for
the Vice-Presidency.[30]

This impression is also confirmed by the further explanations given out by Leigh. According to his own admission,
Leigh was at the time of the convention opposed to the
nomination of Tyler. His first choice was that of Willie P.
Mangum, of North Carolina, or if a Virginian were to be
chosen he would favor Governor Barbour. Besides, the other
delegates from Virginia could not have been strongly in
favor of Tyler's nomination. For the delegation decided not
to instruct its representative on the general committee
further than to direct him to vote on the second ballot for
someone whose name had been presented on the first ballot.
If, however, a candidate should get a majority on the first
ballot, he was to concur in this vote. Leigh also said that so
far as he could remember, only one member of the Virginia
delegation spoke to him about Tyler's nomination and he expressed strong disapproval of it.[31] As Virginia in the election
cast her vote against Tyler, it appears that his home State
did not esteem him as highly as did other sections of the
country. Indeed, it looked as if this prophet of the States'
rights doctrine was not without honor save among his own
people.

At this distance it seems strange that the delegation from
the Old Dominion was the only one to throw cold water on
Tyler's high aspirations. This indifference or even hostility
to his nomination is not satisfactorily explained by contemporary writers. The Richmond *Whig* afterwards declared that
the Virginia delegates were unwilling to vote for Tyler. He
was entirely obnoxious to them because of his conduct in the

[30] Richmond *Enquirer,* Oct. 1, 4, 1839.   [31] *Tyler's Quarterly,* IX, 93.

Senatorial contest of January, 1839. No body of Whigs in Virginia "would have trusted him for any place." He was the jest of his own political friends.[32] John Minor Botts also afterwards said that at the time of his nomination Tyler could not have been elected in Virginia to the lowest of county offices.[33] Neither of these statements, however, can be accepted at face value, for both were made after Tyler had been repudiated by his party, and were inspired by the bitterest partisan feeling. If he was in such marked disfavor with the Whigs of Virginia it is hard to explain why his enemies at the time were so silent and permitted him to represent their party as a delegate to the national convention.

A partial explanation might lie in the assumption that Leigh had not yet forgiven Tyler for breaking away from him and resigning his seat in the Senate in 1836. By so doing Tyler had left his colleague in a difficult position, and the failure of the two Senators to act in unison had involved the Whig Party in Virginia in considerable embarrassment. For this embarrassment Tyler was more at fault than Leigh, in the opinion of a number of prominent Whigs, both in Virginia and elsewhere. To this offense Tyler had added a more recent breach of party discipline; for it was due to the stubborn opposition waged by him and a handful of supporters that the Whigs had failed in their effort to elect Rives to the Senate. As this fight had been made in the first part of this same year and the seat in the Virginia representation was still conspicuously vacant, there was in all probability a good deal of ill feeling toward Tyler among Whig leaders in the Old Dominion, though not so much as was indicated by the statements of Botts and the editor of the Richmond *Whig*.

We have no reliable information as to the other names,

---

[32] Richmond *Daily Whig*, Dec. 1, 1841.
[33] See Botts's speech in the House of Representatives, Sept. 10, 1841; *Niles' Register*, LXI, 79.

if there were such, that were voted on for the Vice-Presidency by the general committee. There are a number, however, in the list of those who were approached for the office if accounts, alleged to be contemporary, can be credited. But these statements are too contradictory to be accepted as reliable historical evidence.[34] As it turned out, the selection of a candidate for the Vice-Presidency was by far the most important act of the Harrisburg Convention. And yet it seems to have been done with very little if any serious thought and attention. Thurlow Weed afterwards said that the office went a-begging and was given to Tyler because no one else would have it.[35] To none of the delegates did it seem highly probable that in naming a man for the second place the convention was really choosing a President of the United States.

It seems, from the meager sources we have, that Tyler was given the second place on the ticket mainly because he was from the South and had been a strong advocate of States' rights. And yet later on, after he had incurred the ill will of most of his fellow Whigs, he was accused of having secured his nomination by a profession of belief in a national bank. That Tyler had announced such a change of heart in favor of a national bank at the Harrisburg Convention and in the previous summer was charged by a number of his enemies. Prominent among these accusers was John Minor Botts, a member of the House of Representatives from Virginia. Botts had been a warm political friend of Tyler but was now one of his chief enemies.

[34] An example of these contradictions is afforded by two editorials in the Richmond *Daily Whig* for December 1 and 3, 1841. In the first of these accounts it is said that Mr. Tallmadge, of New York, was offered the nomination. Leigh was the next choice. After his refusal, Tyler was suggested by Governor Owen of North Carolina. In the second editorial Crittenden, Bell, and Willie P. Mangum were represented as having been offered the nomination in the order named.

[35] According to him, the place was offered to Clayton, Leigh, and Governor Dudley, of North Carolina, no one of whom would accept it. The accuracy of this statement is open to question, as it is contradicted in part by the statement of Leigh given above. Barnes, *Memoirs of Thurlow Weed*, I, 482; II, 77.

A careful examination of the evidence produced (see Appendix B) shows that these charges cannot be sustained and, therefore, should be dismissed. This view is supported by a fair, unprejudiced statement made by Webster in July, 1841, before the controversy had been raised to white heat by the Presidential vetoes. He said: "When Harrison and Tyler were nominated, their opinions on public questions were generally known. And especially was Tyler's attitude toward the bank question well known—known as well as any public man's position on any subject whatever. From 1819 to the day of the nomination, those sentiments had been expressed and repeated in all forms, both in and out of Congress. The convention nominated both these gentlemen without asking or receiving pledges and solely on the ground of their known characters and opinions; and on this ground the canvass was commenced and carried on." [36]

A correct appraisal of all the evidence now available justifies the acceptance of the following statement made by Tyler in July, 1842: "I have no recollection of having opened my lips in that body [the Harrisburg Convention] on any subject whatever. In short, I do state, resting upon my memory, which is not apt to deceive me, that I was perfectly and entirely silent in that Convention. I was . . . wholly unquestioned about my opinions and was selected, as I firmly believe, because of my uniform opposition to a broad construction of the Constitution, and my known advocacy of the principles of a good, old, honest, Republican Party." [37] Nor is there any reliable evidence to show that Tyler made any effort to secure the nomination. At a Whig dinner in Washington in 1840 he said: "I do declare, in the presence of my Heavenly Judge, that the nomination given to me was neither solicited nor expected." [38]

[36] Webster to Hiram Ketchum, July 16, 1841; *The Writings and Speeches of Daniel Webster* (Nat. Ed.), XVI, 345.
[37] Richmond *Enquirer,* July 2, 1842.
[38] *National Intelligencer,* Aug. 27, 1844.

CHAPTER XIII

"TIPPECANOE AND TYLER TOO"

IT is needless to say that the action of the convention brought sore disappointment to Clay, no whit of which he was able to conceal behind a poker face. On the contrary, he lost control of his feelings and in an emotional outburst charged his friends with disloyalty. Upon Henry A. Wise, of Virginia, devolved the unpleasant task of notifying Clay of his defeat. In writing of this interview a third of a century later Wise gave the following account:

"Such an exhibition we never witnessed before, and we pray never again to witness such an ebullition of passion, such a storm of desperation and curses. He rose from his chair, and, walking backwards and forwards rapidly, lifting his feet like a horse stringhalted in both legs, stamped his steps upon the floor, exclaiming, 'My friends are not worth the powder and shot it would take to kill them. . . .' 'If there were two Henry Clays, one of them would make the other President of the United States.' . . . 'It is a diabolical intrigue, I now know, which has betrayed me for a nomination when I, or any one, would be sure of an election.' " [1]

In this account Wise indulged in that love of dramatics which is so characteristic of his writings. To appraise these statements correctly we must remember that they were written from a memory that had been dimmed by a lapse of more than thirty years and the accuracy of which had in the meantime been subjected to the strain of strong partisan feeling. Even if Clay's emotional exhibition was as undignified as Wise represents it to have been, we are inclined to overlook

[1] Wise, *Seven Decades of the Union,* 171.

his lack of self-control on this occasion; for he was missing his only real opportunity to secure a prize for which he had been striving for a lifetime.

No effort was made in the convention to adopt a platform. The coalition which went by the name of the Whig Party was composed of groups of such diversified views that there was no possibility of an agreement on the important issues of the day. A straightforward statement of principles would have destroyed the unity of the party and invited defeat.

Harrison and Tyler were both promptly notified by letter of their selection as standard-bearers of the Whig Party, and each made a brief reply accepting the honor. Harrison expressed his gratitude for the nomination and modestly alluded to himself as "a retired and unpretending individual" not equal to other leaders of "most distinguished talents." He did not attempt to state the principles by which he would be guided if elected, for the reason that they had already been announced in two letters. He, however, renewed the promise already made that if elected he would "under no circumstances consent to be a candidate for a second term."

Tyler's reply contained only one paragraph. He expressed himself as being greatly honored in being associated with the "eminent patriot" nominated for the first place, and most of his letter was devoted to praise of Harrison.[2]

The Democratic Party held its national convention early in May in the city of Baltimore. The meetings were characterized by exceptional harmony, and Van Buren was renominated unanimously. No agreement, however, could be reached as to a candidate for the Vice-Presidency. There were several aspirants for the second place, and the convention decided to make no choice between them, hoping that as the campaign advanced some one of the number would develop sufficient strength to cause the others to withdraw from the race. This expectation was realized, for Colonel Richard M. Johnson, the incumbent of the office, showed

[2] *Niles' Register*, LVII, 379.

signs of running ahead of his competitors and they, one after the other, retired from the contest.[3]

The Democrats were hopeful of victory, as they were presenting a united front to the enemy. For twelve years this party had controlled the Federal patronage and also that of most of the States. Another valuable asset was the prestige and popularity of Andrew Jackson. There was, however, one dark cloud on the horizon. Times were still hard, and, of course, the Administration received the blame for this unfortunate state of affairs.[4] Moreover, they allowed their opponents to outplay them in the game of dealing out buncombe to the voters. By a mistake in tactics they gave the Whigs an opportunity to create a great wave of popular enthusiasm and harness it to their cause.

Soon after the Harrisburg Convention the Baltimore *Republican*, a Democratic paper, published an unwise statement made by its Washington correspondent. The latter, in talking with a Whig who was disgruntled at the nomination of Harrison over Clay, suggested casually that the Whigs set aside Harrison and take up Clay. To the query as to how this could be done this correspondent replied "that upon condition of his receiving a pension of two thousand dollars and a barrel of cider, General Harrison would no doubt consent to withdraw his pretensions, and spend his days in a log cabin on the banks of the Ohio." [5] The Whigs seized upon this indiscreet remark and used it to the very best account. It enabled them to represent their candidate as being a simple farmer belonging to the class that drank cider and lived in log cabins. As a great many of the farmers at that time especially in the West, lived in log cabins, it made a very favorable impression on the masses.

[3] *Niles' Register*, LVIII, 147–152, 397.
The three candidates who withdrew were Messrs. Forsyth, of Georgia; King, of Alabama; and James K. Polk, of Tennessee.
[4] J. S. Buckingham, *The Eastern and Western States of America* (London, 1842), III, 431.
[5] See Baltimore *Republican*, March 23, 1840.

The Whigs already had one good slogan—"Tippecanoe and Tyler too"—and this gave them another—"Log Cabin and Hard Cider." The log cabin and the cider barrel also lent themselves very appropriately to the dramatics of the campaign. At every great political rally a log cabin with a cider barrel in front and a coonskin tacked on the door—the latchstring of which was always on the outside—served as headquarters for the various delegations. Log cabins were also transported long distances to these meetings and were borne in the processions. At the meeting held at Columbus, Ohio, some of the delegations carried in the procession life-sized pictures of General Harrison following the plow. One represented "the Farmer of North Bend, with his plow and team halted midway in the furrow, regaling himself with a cup of his favorite *hard cider.*" Harrison's house at North Bend, on the Ohio River, was quite a comfortable one according to the standards of that day; but, as part of it was made of logs covered with weatherboarding, he could maintain that he lived in a log cabin.

In using the log cabin as an emblem of democracy and in attempting to identify their candidate with the plain people, the Whigs went to the extreme limits of an unscrupulous demagoguery. Webster, in a speech at Saratoga, New York, expressed regret that he had not been born in a log cabin and satisfaction over the fact that his older brothers had been so honored.[6] Even Harrison so far forgot the dignity of his position as to become a party to this ridiculous mode of deception. In a speech at Fort Greenville (August, 1840) he referred to his love of the simple life and his desire to continue with his family in *"the peace and quiet of our log cabin at the Bend."* [7]

In contrast to the plebeian farmer of North Bend, Van Buren was represented as an aristocratic epicurean living in

[6] *The Works of Daniel Webster,* 4th ed., 6 vols. (Boston, 1851), II, 30.
[7] A. B. Norton, *Reminiscences of the Log Cabin and Hard Cider Campaign* (Cleveland, 1888), 245.

the greatest luxury and extravagance in "the Palace," as the White House was termed. This soft and self-indulgent monarch walked across royal Brussels and Wilton carpets "deep enough for a good locofoco Democrat to bury his foot in," reclined on costly Turkish divans; and ate in the "court banqueting room," where gold spoons, gold and silver plate, and silver tureens were used. This contrast was well brought out in one of the songs used in the campaign, the title of which was "Gold Spoons and Hard Cider." [8]

Of course, there was no foundation in fact for the charge that Van Buren was living in extravagance and luxury. He was not responsible for the furnishings of the White House, which had been bought by the Committee of Public Buildings. Nor were these furnishings beyond the requirements of such a pretentious building. A competent observer (J. S.

---

[8] The words of this song were as follows:
"In a cabin made of logs,
  By the river side,
There the Honest Farmer lives,
  Free from sloth and pride.
To the gorgeous palace turn,
  And his rival see,
In his robes of regal state,
  Tinsell'd finery.

At the early morning light,
  Starting with the sun—
See the farmer hold the plow
  'Till the day is done.
In his silken bed of down
  Martin still must be;
Menial servants waiting round,
  Dress'd in livery.

See the farmer to his meal
  Gayfully repair;
Crackers, cheese, and cider too,
  A hard but homely fare.
Martin to his breakfast comes
  At the hour of noon;
Sipping from a china cup,
  With a golden spoon."
    A. B. Norton, *Tippecanoe Songs of the Log Cabin Boys and Girls of 1840*
(Cleveland, 1888), 73.

Buckingham), who was present at a public levee at the White House in 1838, "was struck with the moderation and simplicity of everything connected with the House, its furniture, attendants, and accompaniments. We have since seen the private dwellings of many merchants in Boston, New York, Philadelphia, and Baltimore, the fitting up of which must have cost a much larger sum." [9] Moreover, Van Buren was a self-made man of middle-class parentage, whereas Harrison and Tyler were both scions of old and aristocratic families and could boast of the proudest patrician blood.

In this campaign of vituperation and misrepresentation, the Whigs were not the only offenders. The Democratic leaders saw to it that Harrison, as well as Van Buren, should receive the full measure of abuse. Harrison's military record was attacked and he was accused of cowardice in the War of 1812. His refusal to take an unequivocal stand on controversial questions laid him open to the charge of trying to be all things to all men.

Enthusiastic meetings were held throughout the country. Prominent among the political gatherings was the one assembled on the site of the battle of Tippecanoe.[10] A very large one was also held at Dayton, Ohio, on September 10. The crowd that listened to General Harrison speak on that occasion covered ten acres of ground by actual measurement, and was estimated at 75,000 or 80,000. Others in the town, it was thought, brought the total number present up to nearly 100,000.[11] At the Erie meeting a bystander asked the marshal how long the procession was. His answer was: "Indeed, sir, I cannot tell; the other end of it is forming somewhere in the State of New York." [12]

---

[9] J. S. Buckingham, op. cit., III, 431–438. See also Jessie Frémont, Souvenirs of My Time (Boston, 1887), 29–30.
[10] Allan Nevins, ed., The Diary of Philip Hone (New York, 1927), I. 493–494.
[11] Niles, LIX, 56–57.
[12] F. W. Seward, ed., Autobiography of William H. Seward (N. Y., 1877), 498.

The American people have in all periods of their history been excessively fond of political rallies, and such meetings have always had a peculiar fascination for the rural portion of the population. It is a time when farmers from all parts of the county can get together and exchange views on crop tillage, politics, and other questions of mutual interest. Politics is a great leveler of social barriers, and at political gatherings patrician candidates and their henchmen meet plebeian voters as social equals. On such occasions the latter are not made uncomfortable by the condescension or patronage of their rich or prominent neighbors. These meetings also furnish exceptional opportunity for amusement. If the assemblage is a large one it attracts patent-medicine quacks, who intersperse their sales talk with jokes and clever repartee; and cheap-John peddlers, who in recommending their wares display a fluency of speech and a cleverness at sleight of hand that are wonderfully interesting. Then, too, there is the ubiquitous lemonade vender, who offers at a low price to the thirsty and perspiring youth a marvelous drink with a nectarine flavor and sweetness.

These attractions, however, furnish only the minor and preliminary thrills while the crowd is awaiting the more exciting events of the day. In the campaign of 1840 the procession was the outstanding feature on every occasion. Callous-handed farmers, with their tired wives and timid children, while looking at or taking part in these processions, would throw off their embarrassment and self-consciousness, despite the stiffness and discomfort imparted by their "Sunday clothes," and would join in the enthusiasm aroused by the stirring band music and the loud hurrahs of the crowd. They would observe with keen enjoyment local leaders prancing back and forth on white horses and visiting statesmen seated in moving carriages, constantly raising their silk hats in response to cheers.

The political speeches also afforded great amusement. In them the merits of the Whigs and the shortcomings of the

Democrats were forcibly depicted in language clearly under-standable to all. They were also usually enlivened with a homely imagery and numerous jokes, some of which, though old, had not yet circulated throughout the countryside. But the crowning event of the day was the barbecue. Long tables loaded down with barbecued meat and other kinds of food invited the hungry crowd to appease an appetite that had been sharpened by long waiting and ardent expectation.

Singing played a very important part in this campaign. One prominent Whig said that "General Harrison was sung into the Presidency." [13] Of the numerous songs used some were long and not adapted to campaign purposes. Others had a jingle and quick rhythm that made them easy to sing. Well-known airs were generally used.[14] One of the most popular of the campaign songs was entitled *What Has Caused This Great Commotion?* sung to the tune of *Little Pig's Tail*. It had an easy swing and a jingle that lent itself readily to mass singing. It went as follows:

What has caused this great commotion, motion, motion,
     Our country through?
   It is the ball a rolling on, on,

           Chorus:

For Tippecanoe and Tyler too—Tippecanoe and Tyler too,
  And with them we'll beat little Van, Van, Van,
     Van is a used up man,
    And with them we'll beat little Van.

Like the rushing of mighty waters, waters, waters,
     On it will go,
   And in its course will clear the way
For Tippecanoe, etc.[15]

[13] *Hone's Diary*, II, 652.
[14] Among the most popular tunes used were the *Marseillaise Hymn; Not a Drum Was Heard; Bonnets O' Blue; Old Oaken Bucket; Little Pig's Tail; Auld Lang Syne; Yankee Doodle; Rosin the Bow; Star-Spangled Banner; Hail Columbia;* and *The Campbells are Coming.* For a list of these songs, see Norton, *Tippecanoe Songs of the Log Cabin Boys and Girls of 1840,* 2–102.
[15] Norton, *Tippecanoe Songs,* 18.

It is certainly not to the credit of the American people that they allowed themselves to be swept off their feet by this long-continued exhibition of political clownishness. But it must not be overlooked that at this time a great many voters were illiterate and uncritical in their mental attitudes and could be easily reached by an emotional appeal. They were more receptive to dramatic displays and enthusiastic demonstrations than to enlightening discussions on the issues of the day. Besides, there was a marked scarcity of amusements, and "a political meeting that combined the dramatic quality of the theatre with the charms of a circus and a tavern could not fail to be popular." [16]

As the campaign was a succession of holidays, it afforded numerous opportunities for escape from the drabness of daily routine. The women could get away for a day from the wearing cares of the home and the men from the dull drudgery of the farm. In thus furnishing the masses with such a fine opportunity for recreation the Whigs were atoning in some degree for the sin of deception practiced upon the people in such wholesale fashion. This aspect of this frolicsome campaign was well described by a contemporary as follows: "If one could imagine a whole nation declaring a holiday or season of rollicking for a period of six or eight months, and giving themselves up during the whole time to the wildest freaks of fun and frolic, caring nothing for business, singing, dancing, and carousing night and day, he might have some faint notion of the extraordinary scenes of 1840." [17]

As the Whigs had no platform and the component factions of the party were not in agreement on most of the major issues of the day, their speakers in the campaign generally took a noncommittal attitude on important questions. When they touched upon controversial subjects they usually confined themselves to pleasing generalities or they

[16] Dorothy B. Goebel, *William Henry Harrison* (Indianapolis, 1926), 352.
[17] Nathan Sargent, *Public Men and Events,* 2 vols. (Philadelphia, 1875), II, 107–108.

hedged their statements about with so many exceptions, qualifications, or explanations as to satisfy the unwary on both sides. Probably at no other time in the history of our country have politicians been more successful in the use of language to obscure thought. Most of their efforts were directed toward the laudation of the Whig candidates, the criticism of the Administration, the disapproval of certain policies advocated by the Democrats, and the praise of that simplicity and frugality in living that was symbolized by the log cabin.[18] If it is true that the American people like to be humbugged, they had abundant reason to be pleased with the methods of this rollicking campaign. Carl Schurz was of the opinion that in no Presidential election had there been "more enthusiasm and less thought." [19]

Harrison's vague and noncommittal attitude on the main issues gave ground for the charge that he too engaged in these disingenuous practices. While he denied these accusations and declared that his position with reference to certain measures had been misrepresented, he did little or nothing to enlighten the people as to where he stood on important public questions. In his campaign utterances he dwelt on the necessity of curbing the executive and preventing its encroachments upon the legislative branch of the government. He deplored the use of the patronage for partisan purposes and repeatedly declared in favor of limiting the tenure of the Presidency to one term. Aside from this he confined himself largely to reminiscences of the War of 1812.[20]

He did not altogether refuse to mention public questions, however, but usually discussed them in such a way as to leave his hearers in uncertainty as to his convictions regarding them. For example, in his speech at Dayton, Ohio, September 10, he declared that he was not a bank man and yet ex-

[18] *Niles' Register*, LIX, 45–47.
[19] Carl Schurz, *Henry Clay*, 2 vols. (Boston, 1899), II, 187.
[20] Goebel, *op. cit.*, 364; *Western Pennsylvania Histor. Mag.*, I, 145–151; Norton, *Reminiscences*, 178–187, 288–301; *Nat. Intel.*, Aug. 10, 1840; *Niles*, LV, 360–361.

pressed himself in favor of a correct banking system because there was not enough of the precious metals to enable the country to get along with hard money alone. "A properly devised banking system alone possesses the capability of bringing the poor to the level of the rich." [21]

The Whigs did not take a great deal of interest in the contest for the Vice-Presidency. What little attention was paid to Tyler's rôle in the campaign was due mainly to the fact that "Tyler too" rhymed with "Tippecanoe." "Ty" also proved a good syllable in the slogan "Tip and Ty." Dogs were frequently named "Tip," and often a span of horses was called "Tip" and "Ty." [22] This disposition to disregard the Vice-Presidential contest was not due to opposition to Tyler, but rather to the feeling that the place which he was seeking was one of comparative unimportance. Apparently few if any of the leaders expected that Tyler would be the real occupant of the Executive Mansion, for Harrison to all outward seeming was in good health and gave every promise of living long after he had finished the single term to which he aspired. [23]

Tyler was not, however, entirely overlooked. Occasionally resolutions in praise of the head of the ticket would also commend the distinguished gentleman from Virginia. Among

[21] Norton, *Reminiscences*, 295–296.

In an address made in the campaign in North Carolina, George E. Badger, who later resigned from Tyler's Cabinet because of his veto of the second bank bill, defended Harrison against the charge of being for a bank. He said: "The charge is false. His opinions, on the contrary, are against a Bank. He has declared it an institution which if President, he would not recommend." Quoted by Tyler, *Letters and Times*, I, 614. See also *Madisonian*, Aug. 26, 1841.

The Richmond *Whig*, which later took a leading part in the savage attack on Tyler because of his bank vetoes, declared (January 13, 1840) that the Whigs "want no Federal Bank." A month later (February 13, 1840) it attempted to refute the charge that Harrison was for a national bank. A year later (February 24, 1841) it declared that Virginia was opposed to a Bank of the United States and reaffirmed its belief that it was "unconstitutional and of most doubtful political expediency." Tyler, *op. cit.*, I, 612–613.

[22] F. W. Seward, *Autobiography of William H. Seward*, 497; A. B. Norton, *Reminiscences of the Log Cabin and Hard Cider Campaign*, 357.

[23] *Niles*, LVIII, 282–283.

the earliest of these were the resolutions passed by the Whig members of the Maryland legislature and those adopted by the opponents of the Administration in the District of Columbia (February 15, 1840).[24]

He did not take a very important part in the canvass, and apparently he remained quietly at home most of the time. His opponent, Colonel Johnson, however, made a vigorous campaign in the West, and was very cordially received. The reception accorded Johnson in Ohio caused Tyler, late in the contest, to bestir himself and engage in a speaking campaign in western Virginia, eastern Ohio, and southwestern Pennsylvania.[25]

The occasion of this trip was a convention held at Columbus, Ohio, by Whigs who had formerly been supporters of Jackson or Van Buren. When Tyler was invited to address this body he promptly accepted, although he had hardly recovered from an illness when he started on the long and tiresome journey.[26] Passing through St. Clairsville, Ohio, he drew the fire of the *Gazette,* a Democratic paper published in that town. "John Tyler, the aristocrat," it announced, "who voted in the Virginia legislature [convention] against poor men voting for county or state officers, unless they have a property qualification," passed through St. Clairsville on Wednesday, September 23, en route for the Columbus fandango.[27] The hurt to his pride caused by this bitter taunt was soothed by the cordial welcome given him by the Whigs when he reached Columbus. Arriving at the State capital at sunset, he was escorted to the National Hotel by a procession of gentlemen in carriages and on horseback.

At the hotel speeches of welcome were made by the mayor of the city and the editor of *The Ohio Confederate and Old School Republican.* To these Tyler replied in happy vein and

[24] *Ibid.,* 5, 19–21.
[25] *Niles,* LIX, 88–89; LX, 115–116; *Time Book of Thomas P. Ray,* Oct. 6, 8, 10; MS., W. Va. University Library.
[26] *The Ohio Confederate and Old School Republican,* Oct. 1, 1840.
[27] The St. Clairsville *Gazette,* Sept. 26, 1840.

good taste.[28] Next day (September 25) he addressed the convention in a speech of more than two hours' length.[29]

After leaving Columbus Tyler made a number of speeches in Ohio and Pennsylvania. Of these the most noted was the one delivered at Pittsburgh (October 6) before the Whig convention which had assembled to commemorate the battle of the Thames. The meeting was presided over by Walter Forward, later Secretary of the Treasury under President Tyler. According to the Whig newspapers, this convention was a great success. The estimates as to the number of people present varied from 27,000 to 60,000. Tyler declared that it was the largest audience before which he had ever appeared, and his voice, weakened by overexertion in recent speaking, could not reach the outskirts of the crowd.[30] The Democratic papers, on the other hand, maintained that the meeting, despite the great preparations that had been made, was a failure and that the number in attendance by actual count was less than 4300.[31]

From the newspaper accounts it is evident that the Vice-Presidential candidate in this swing around the circle fell in with the methods usually employed by the Whigs in this campaign. He was ardent in his praise of the head of the ticket and tried to tie in with the "log-cabin" demagoguery. At Grave Creek, Virginia, attention was called to the fact that the Whig candidates were both born in Charles City County, Virginia, and their fathers had stood shoulder to shoulder in their fight for freedom in the Revolutionary period. ". . . side by side they battled in maintaining the rights of that country in the days of the Revolution; and now it is not a little singular their sons have been placed on

[28] *The Straight-out Harrisonian* (Columbus, O.), Oct. 2, 1840.
[29] *The Ohio Confederate and Old School Republican*, Oct. 1, 1840; *Ohio State Journal*, Sept. 29, 1840.
[30] *Daily Pittsburgh Gazette*, Oct. 7, 1840; *Daily Advocate and Advertiser* (Pittsburgh), Oct. 10, 1840.
[31] *Daily Pittsburgher*, Oct. 7, 1840; *The Pittsburgh Mercury*, Oct. 7, 1840.

the same ticket to run side by side in rescuing that country from the misrule of designing and ambitious men." [32]

Just how his audiences were impressed with his efforts, it is difficult to say. The Democratic *Gazette* considered that his speech at St. Clairsville "was of the lowest declamation possible" and "beneath criticism," while two Whig papers of Columbus were unstinted in their praise of his speeches in that city.[33] Of his address at Pittsburgh a hostile editor had this to say: "Mr. Tyler is a graceful, easy speaker, with all that blandness of manner which belongs to the Virginia character. But there was nothing forcible or striking in his speech; no bright thoughts, no well-turned expressions; nothing that left an impression on the mind from its strength and beauty—*nothing that marked the great man.*" [34]

Another Democratic editor thought that Tyler by taking a stand in favor of the Compromise of 1833 had caused Harrison to lose hundreds if not thousands of votes in Pennsylvania.[35] On the other hand, Tyler's speech at Pittsburgh was thought by some of his friends to have been an important factor in the winning of the Whig victory in Pennsylvania. This opinion was quite consoling to him as a counterbalance to the loss of Virginia, which in some quarters out of the State had been ascribed to his unpopularity.[36]

Although the Vice-Presidential candidate, like the other Whig leaders, tried to avoid commitments on controversial questions, he declared at both Steubenville, Ohio,[37] and

[32] *Marshall* (Va.) *Beacon,* quoted in *The Old Confederate and Old School Republican* for Oct. 22, 1840.
[33] St. Clairsville *Gazette,* Oct. 3, 1840; *The Ohio Confederate and Old School Republican,* Oct. 1, 1840; *The Straight-out Harrisonian* (Columbus, O.), Oct. 2, 1840.
[34] *Daily Pittsburgher,* Oct. 8, 1840.
[35] *The Pittsburgh Mercury,* Oct. 7, 1840.
[36] Tyler to James Lyons, Dec. 16, 1840; Huntington Library MSS.
[37] Steubenville *Herald,* quoted in *Daily Advocate and Advertiser* (Pittsburgh), Oct. 10, 1840.

Pittsburgh his adherence to the Compromise of 1833. At
Pittsburgh this admission was forced upon him by hecklers,
much to his embarrassment. A cry arose in the audience asking for his position on the tariff. Over his head and all
around him were banners bearing the inscription, A PRO-
TECTIVE TARIFF, and by his side stood Walter Forward, a great champion of protection. Besides, the Whigs
of this city had in a recent meeting denounced the Compromise and declared for its repeal. No wonder that the speaker
hesitated to answer this question. But the demand was so insistent that he came out with a straight-from-the-shoulder
statement. "I am," he said, "in favor of what General Harrison and Mr. Clay are in favor of; I am in favor of preserving the compromise bill as it now stands; between General Harrison, Mr. Clay, and myself, there is no difference
of opinion on this subject." [38]

On the bank question he was not so explicit, but tried to
go along with his fellow campaigners in maintaining a skillful balance on the fence. But the Democrats sensed his opposition to a national bank and felt that they might exploit it
to the embarrassment of the Whig Party. They made, therefore, several attempts to lure him into an avowal of his
sentiments. Early in the campaign, at a meeting of Democrats in Pittsburgh, it was voted to send a query to Tyler
asking whether he would in any event sanction the incorporation of a United States bank. He was at first inclined
to accept this challenge, and accordingly wrote out a reply to
their inquiry. This was sent to his friend, Henry A. Wise,
then a member of the House of Representatives, with instructions to submit it to the Whig leaders in Washington.
They were to decide whether the answer was to be forwarded to Pittsburgh and published. Tyler's statement is
not now extant, but according to Wise's recollection of it, it
was spirited and explicit in declaring "that a bank of the
United States was unconstitutional," and that he could not

[38] *Daily Pittsburgher*, Oct. 8, 1840.

sanction "the incorporation of one without an alteration of the Constitution."

Wise submitted Tyler's reply to the leading Whigs in Congress, who decided that it would be impolitic to publish it. Mr. Tyler's opinions were already known, they argued, and, therefore, it was unnecessary to array them directly against those of many who were in favor of a bank. All who made the bank a test could ascertain his sentiments in the past, which had never been recanted, and no one could plead that they had either been concealed or that any deception was practiced.[39]

Other efforts were made to entrap the Vice-Presidential candidate. At St. Clairsville and Steubenville he was confronted with inquiries from the local Democratic clubs as to his attitude toward the bank question. In reply he expressed agreement with the position taken by General Harrison in his Dayton speech.[40]

On his return from his western trip he found awaiting him a series of questions which had been sent him (under date of October 3) by a committee of Democrats of Henrico County, Virginia. In these inquiries Tyler was asked to state his views on the Independent Treasury, a national bank, the tariff, internal improvements, and slavery in the District of Columbia. One of these queries put the bank question squarely before him. "Do you believe the Congress of the United States to be vested with power by the Constitution to incorporate a national bank? . . . Would you veto a bill chartering a national bank?"[41]

These questions were raised not to learn Tyler's position but to elicit a reply that would be embarrassing to the Whigs. For if he should take a definite stand against a national bank (as they probably expected him to do) his answer would tend to alienate the probank element of his party.

[39] Tyler, *Letters and Times*, I, 619–620; Wise, *Seven Decades*, 177.
[40] *Daily Advocate and Advertiser* (Pittsburgh), Oct. 10, 1840; St. Clairsville *Gazette*, Oct. 3, 1840.
[41] Abell, *Life of John Tyler*, 178; Richmond *Enquirer*, Oct. 9, 1840.

On the other hand, if he should pussyfoot the bank issue, he might lose the support of some of his ardent antibank admirers in the South. To sail safely between this Scylla and Charybdis required the skill of an expert and experienced political navigator. Tyler performed this difficult feat as well as it could be done under the circumstances.

Although he realized the motive that prompted this challenge, he accepted it by responding to the questionnaire. Tyler's replies were so framed as to indicate that he and Harrison were in entire accord on the principal issues of the campaign. The question as to whether internal improvements could be constructed at Federal expense was, he said, purely an academic one, as there would be no money in the Federal treasury for such a purpose. He pointed out, however, that his votes in Congress had all been against such a power. He tried to sidestep the tariff issue, but his answer gave the Democratic Richmond *Enquirer* the chance to accuse him of leaning toward the nationalist view of protection.

He admitted the constitutionality of the Subtreasury Act but was explicit in declaring against its expediency. He, therefore, favored its repeal but failed to state what he would offer as a substitute. On the bank query he replied that he and Harrison were in agreement. Both had voted for a *scire facias* in 1819 against the Second Bank of the United States. He quoted and adopted a statement made by Harrison in his Dayton address as follows: "There is not in the Constitution any express grant of power for such purpose [the creation of a national bank], and it could never be constitutional to exercise the power, save in the event the power granted to Congress could not be carried into effect without resorting to such an institution."

From the intimation that a contingency might arise in which a national bank would be constitutional it might be inferred that his old hostility to a bank had been somewhat relaxed. Other statements, however, tended to show that his position on the bank question had not been changed. In explanation of his present attitude he referred the committee to his speech in the House of Representatives in 1819 and his vote in the Senate in 1832 on the bank question. His record in both instances was decidedly against a bank. As a final profession of his faith in the doctrine of States' rights, he said, "You see I am a Jeffersonian Republican." [42]

The impression left with the editor of the *Gazette* by Tyler's speech at St. Clairsville was that he was opposed to a national bank both on constitutional and practical grounds. The position he took in favor of States' rights and Jeffersonian republicanism, said this editor, "made some old blue-lights stare." [43] On the other hand, it was afterwards charged by John Minor Botts (in a speech delivered in the House of Representatives, September 10, 1841) that Tyler in his western tour had come out squarely in favor of a national bank. But the evidence brought forward by Botts is not sufficient to sustain the accusation (see Appendix C). To deduce from this evidence proof of the charge that Tyler had given a pledge in favor of a national bank would be an arduous undertaking. This difficulty is enhanced by statements made by Tyler in a letter to Whig leaders of Norfolk and in his last speech of the campaign, which was delivered in the historic courthouse of old Williamsburg. In the letter (written February 26, 1840) he said: "If in aught I have ever departed from the principles of the old Republican Party, in word or deed, my political opponents are invited to display to the public eye the evidences of my transgression." [44] In the Williamsburg speech he maintained that he was not committed on the bank question. He intimated opposition to the bank, however, by declaring that his friends in Virginia knew his position on this issue and his strong leanings toward States' rights. [45] And yet neither assertion is a clear-

[42] Richmond *Enquirer*, Oct. 13, 1840.
Dr. Lyon G. Tyler says that Tyler's reply to the Henrico questionnaire was copied all over the Union. *Letters and Times*, I, 623.
[43] St. Clairsville *Gazette*, Oct. 3, 1840. [44] Tyler, *op. cit.*, I, 623.
[45] *John Tyler Papers* (L.C.), V, 62.

cut, positive reaffirmation of the old faith. In each is seen the attempt to straddle this important public question.

It might properly be said that this disposition to withhold from the voters his real opinions was not in keeping with that frankness and high sense of honor which Tyler so frequently professed. That he stooped to the low practices of this charlatanic campaign is a source of real regret to his admirers. And yet if he had stated his position with straightforward clarity he would have jeopardized the success of his party. He doubtless felt that a candidate for the comparatively unimportant office of Vice-President had no right to menace party harmony by thrusting forward views which could be of only academic interest to the general public. Few politicians, if any, of that or any other period would have assumed so great a responsibility. He was in a position in which the demands of candor clashed with those of group loyalty. He is to be criticized not so much for what he did in this awkward situation as for having placed himself in this dilemma. For a man of his views had no right to assume a place of leadership in a party the majority of whose members advocated measures which he had spent a life career in opposing.

Common to all the Whigs was a feeling of opposition to some of the major policies of Jackson or Van Buren and the alleged executive usurpation that was behind these policies. They were especially united in their disapproval of the financial measures of Van Buren. There was, however, no such unanimity as to the remedies that should be employed to cure the monetary evils of the day. Webster thought that while the large majority of those who opposed the financial policy of Jackson and Van Buren favored a national bank, there were many in the South and some in the North who were not bank men.[46]

[46] Tyler, *Letters and Times*, I, 344–348.
Rives said that the question of "Bank or no Bank" was not an issue in the election of 1840, though he thought that a majority of the people were opposed to a bank. *Cong. Globe*, 27 Cong., 1st sess., App., 366–368.

The editor of the *Madisonian* declared that during the campaign he heard many speeches, read many addresses, and was daily conversant with some three hundred Whig newspapers, and was willing solemnly to "aver that we cannot recollect more than one public address, one speech and two or three Whig newspapers, in which a National Bank was urged as a desirable measure, or as a question belonging to the controversy before the people." The address was the Bunker Hill declaration. The speech was the one made by a gentleman in Baltimore, which frightened the committee of arrangement and another speaker was called to the stand to deny that the issue had been truly presented.

In the address of the Whig Central Committee to the Whigs and Conservatives and in that of the Whig Central Committee of Maryland to the people (both August, 1840) no mention was made of a national bank. "At the great National Convention of Young Men, at Baltimore, in May, 1840, we heard not a word said about a National Bank." "At the great meeting of Whig merchants, addressed by Webster at New York, September, 1840, a National Bank was not called for in any of the resolutions." In reports of Whig meetings at Columbus, Ohio, Fort Meigs, Saratoga, Auburn, New York, Richmond, and Yorktown, "we find no allusion made to a National Bank." A number of instances were then cited in which statements against a bank were made at Whig meetings and by Whig newspapers.[47]

There is, therefore, no warrant for assuming that Tyler or anyone else was honor-bound to support a national bank or any other particular policy (except the repeal of the Independent Treasury Act) as a result of commitments made

[47] For these editorials, see *Madisonian*, Aug. 17, 19, 26, 1841.

On July 18, 1840, Thomas Ewing, who afterwards resigned from Tyler's Cabinet because of his vetoes of bank bills, sent a letter to a political friend in which he spoke of the *impudence* and *absurdity* of the attempt of the Democrats to make the bank the issue in the campaign. The bank, he declared, had never been considered by the Whigs "as anything more than a mere matter of conveyance—a useful article of furniture in our noble edifice." This letter was printed in the *Marietta* (O.) *Intelligencer,* July 30, 1840.

during this burlesque campaign. Indeed, if we should judge the wishes of the people in this contest by their demonstrations and by the speeches of the politicians, we should be inclined to agree with the facetious statement of Silas Wright that the only clear mandate received by the Whigs was to tear down the Capitol and erect a log cabin in its place.

But Tyler's pronouncements made during the campaign, when read in the light of his previous record, indicate that he was still holding on to his States' rights views and was, therefore, still opposed to a national bank. The intimation on his part that a situation might arise that would make a national bank necessary did not imply that in his opinion such an exigency had then arisen. And even if he conceded the constitutionality under certain circumstances of a national bank, that did not bind him to accept *any* national bank under any and all circumstances. Least of all was he pledged to the type of bank that Clay afterwards tried to force upon him.

In Virginia it seemed clear to the leaders that Tyler and Harrison were on opposite sides of the most important questions then at issue. This disagreement between the head of the ticket and his running mate was wittily summed up by John Winston as follows:\ "Tip was Bank, Ty was anti-Bank; Tip was Tariff, Ty was anti-tariff; Tip was Distribution, Ty was anti. In fact, Fellow citizens, Tip is Whig, Ty is Democrat."

When the returns had all come in, it was found that the Whigs had won, though Harrison's plurality over Van Buren was not overwhelming, being only 145,914. In the Electoral College Harrison and Tyler each received 234 votes to 60 for Van Buren. Virginia went Democratic but one elector refused to cast his vote for Johnson.[48] This vote was given to Polk.

[48] Tyler, *op. cit.*, I, 629; Edward A. Stanwood, *History of the Presidency,* 203–204; *Niles' Register*, LIX, 395.

The Whigs in accepting their victory showed unexpected moderation and good sense. They did not try to dramatize their triumph with blatant parades and public rejoicings.[49] The newspapers, however, could not entirely forego the pleasure of crowing over the defeated foe. Some of them in appraising the results of the election exhibited an intensity of feeling which showed that the taut emotions of the campaign were not yet relaxed. The *National Intelligencer* expressed its great satisfaction over the country's repudiation of Van Buren's policies in the following unmeasured terms: "It has pleased the Almighty to give to the oppressed people of this misgoverned and suffering country a victory over their weak and wicked rulers. . . . The reign of incompetency, imposture and corruption, is at length arrested, and the country redeemed." This evil administration "has fallen before the power of an abused and indignant people." [50]

For the Democrats the sting of defeat was alleviated by the feeling that they had sustained only a temporary setback and would soon be able to regain their losses. This opinion was expressed by the New York *Evening Post* in a very sane and able editorial, in which it was pointed out that the hard times were mainly responsible for the Whig victory. The Whigs "made many honest people believe that because the hard times and low prices came on under the administration of Van Buren, Van Buren was the cause of the hard times and low prices." The editor also stated that the nation in electing Harrison had not pronounced its opinion on any great public measure or course of measures, and certainly not on the question of a national bank. "The Whigs would not allow that question to be presented to the people, in the

[49] Savannah *Republican,* quoted in *Niles,* LIX, 206.
[50] *Niles,* LIX, 163.
In the newspaper comment on the results of the election very little reference was made to Tyler. Niles devotes about seven pages to a symposium of newspaper opinion and quotes from nineteen different publications. In all of this there is only one reference to Tyler. *Ibid.,* 201 ff.

election, and not only kept it out of sight, but in some instances vehemently and angrily disowned it." [51] It is doubtless true that many, perhaps most, of the leaders were for a national bank, but the people were not with them and had given them no mandate to carry out this policy.

The diverse elements of the Whig Party were not bound together with sufficient cohesion to stand the strain to which it would be subjected by the responsibilities of office. This condition was well described by Thomas Ritchie, of the Richmond *Enquirer,* who said: "We may be beaten, but we will *not stay beaten.* The victory is surprising but not overwhelming. We are defeated, but not discouraged." "This discordant combination of the odds and ends of all parties cannot long continue. Like the image of Nebuchadnezzar, which was made of clay and brass and various materials, a single stone must shatter it to pieces."

Nothing, therefore, had been decided by this election except that Van Buren would go out and Harrison would come in. The Democratic Party had been beaten only "in the organization and its candidates, it has [had] not been beaten in its doctrines or the great measures by which these doctrines are put in practice." The party had, therefore, not suffered a defeat from which it would be difficult to recover. On the other hand, the Whig administration would be confronted with obstacles that would prove insurmountable. Expectations had been raised in the various groups of the coalition which could not be met without arousing the opposition of the rank and file of the party. The later fulfillment of this prophecy was an additional proof of that political acumen which the astute Ritchie so often displayed.

[51] N. Y. *Evening Post,* quoted in *Niles,* LIX, 203–204.

CHAPTER XIV

PROMINENCE WITHOUT POWER

WILLIAMSBURG was the Mecca toward which Tyler's heart always turned. It must, therefore, have been with the most pleasing anticipations that he took up his residence there in the fall of 1837. This old historic place was now a small town with no prospect of a boom to disturb its dream of former greatness. The removal of the capital to Richmond a half-century earlier had left the town high and dry so far as political activity was concerned. No longer was its historic hotel, Raleigh Tavern, the center of be-wigged statesmen, but the town had not sunk to the level of the ordinary county-seat village. Its fifteen hundred inhabit-ants were proudly conscious of the fact that it had at one time been the political, intellectual, and social metropolis of all of the region between Philadelphia and Charleston. Besides, the mansions that had sheltered the noted patrician families in the past were in many instances now occupied by representatives of these old families, and the social life was noted for its exceptional charm. The village was also saved from intellectual stagnation by the presence of William and Mary College. This institution, though small, was still at-tracting to its venerable halls a small group of brilliant young men who were being trained for leadership in the govern-ment of the State and country.

To John Tyler and his family Williamsburg was doubt-less an ideal location for residence, and the few years spent there were probably the happiest of his life. He was bound to the place by strong sentimental ties. The close association in the past of his family and himself with the town and college had endeared both to him. Then too the simple and natural social life of the community, characterized as it was by an atmosphere of culture and dignified gayety, offered a pleasant and wholesome diversion from professional cares. The intellectual environment afforded by the town was more stimulating than would be expected from its size. The president of the college at this time was Thomas R. Dew, a writer of some note, who took a lively interest in public affairs. Prominent among the townsmen was the half-brother of John Randolph, Judge N. Beverley Tucker, a man of exceptional ability and attainments and a novelist of note.[1] Later, Judge Abel P. Upshur moved to Williamsburg, thus adding another name to this already distinguished group.[2] The association of these four intellectuals was of the most delightful character. Drawn together by similar political views and congenial tastes, there soon grew up among them a close bond of personal friendship. They would often meet of evenings to practice their skill in the fine art of conversation. Fortunately, the pleasure of these foregatherings was not marred by any presentiment of the political storm just ahead of them, which was destined to subject one of their number to such cruel lashings.[3]

We have a fine description of the Tyler residence at Williamsburg and of the home life of the family while it was dwelling there. For this account we are indebted to Mrs. Robert Tyler, who had gone to Williamsburg as a bride in 1839, at which time Robert Tyler was living with his parents. In letters to her sisters (October, 1839) she writes as follows:

The home is very large and very airy and pleasant, fronting on a large lawn and surrounded by a most beautiful garden. The parlor is comfortably furnished, and has that homelike and occupied look which is so nice. . . . The dining-room is opposite to the parlor, across a broad passage, kept too bright and shiny almost to step upon, and is also a very spacious room, with a great deal of old family silver

---

[1] Tyler, *Letters and Times,* I, 543.
[2] James City County *Tax Books* (Archives, Virginia State Library).
[3] Tyler, *op. cit.,* III, 181.

adorning the sideboard, and some good pictures upon the walls. There are two other rooms behind the parlor and the dining-room, one of which is used as a sitting and reading room, for it is a large double house flanked by offices in the yard in which the library is kept, and one of which is used for law and business purposes by Mr. Tyler's [her husband's] father and himself.

The room in the main dwelling furthest removed and most retired is the "chamber," as the bedroom of the mistress of the house is always called in Virginia. This last, to say nothing of others, or of the kitchen, storerooms and pantries, is a most quiet and comfortable retreat, with an air of repose and sanctity about it; at least I feel it so, and often seek refuge here from the company, and beaux, and laughing and talking of the other parts of the house; for here mother [Mrs. Tyler], with a smile of welcome on her sweet, calm face, is always found seated on her large arm-chair with a small stand by her side, which holds her Bible and her prayer-book—the only books she ever reads now— with her knitting usually in her hands, always ready to sympathize with me in any little homesickness which may disturb me, and to ask me questions about all you dear ones in Bristol [Pennsylvania] because she knows I want to talk about you.

Notwithstanding her very delicate health, mother attends to and regulates all the household affairs, and all so quietly that you can't tell when she does it. All the clothes for the children, and for the servants, are cut out under her immediate eye, and all the sewing is personally superintended by her. All the cake, jellies, custards, and we indulge largely in them, emanate from her, yet you see no confusion, hear no bustle, but only meet the agreeable result.[4]

From this peaceful and happy retreat Tyler was destined soon to be called to Washington to become the center of the fiercest political controversy known to American history.

Harrison, too, was living in Arcadian simplicity until aspirations for the Presidency began to disturb his serenity. His residence in the village of North Bend, about fourteen miles below Cincinnati, was a modest two-story house, sur-

[4] Mrs. Robert Tyler to her sisters, October, 1839; Mrs. Laura Carter Holloway, *The Ladies of the White House* (1870), 388–392.

rounded by productive and well-cultivated land. Here he
lived the wholesome life of a comfortable and hospitable
farmer.[5]

Late in January the President-elect left his home for the
capital. After a rather leisurely journey he reached his des-
tination (February 9) [6] on his sixty-eighth birthday. After
a brief sojourn in Washington [7] he left for a visit among his
old friends in Virginia. His ancestral home, "Berkeley," was
located on the James River in Charles City County, less than
a dozen miles from "Greenway," the birthplace of Tyler.
On his way to Charles City, Harrison stopped in Richmond,
where he was cordially received by Governor Gilmer. Tyler,
as the invited guest of the governor, also shared in these
hospitalities. After a visit of some days at "Berkeley," now
the home of his nephew, Harrison, accompanied by the Vice-
President-elect, returned to Washington, arriving there Sunday night, February 28.[8]

The inauguration took place on a beautiful day. Tyler
and Harrison marched together in the procession, the latter
being mounted on a white charger. The installation of the
Vice-President came first. At noon the Senate convened with
a full attendance. In the front semicircle were seated foreign
diplomats and the justices of the Supreme Court. Members
of the House were also present, and the floor and the galleries were crowded to the utmost capacity. The body was
called to order by the clerk and a temporary chairman was
elected. The oath of office was then administered to Tyler,
who "delivered with much grace, dignity, and self-posses-
sion" an address, which was marked by modesty, propriety,
and sound sense. In this very short speech, the printed copy

---

[5] Goebel, *William Henry Harrison*, 204–205. For picture of the Harrison
home, see opposite p. 204.

[6] *Cincinnati Republican* for Jan. 27, 1841; quoted in *Niles' Register*, LIX,
355; Nevins, Allan, ed., *The Diary of Philip Hone*, II, 519.

[7] Allan Nevins, ed., 520, 527; *Tri-Weekly Madisonian*, Feb. 11, 13, 16, 1841.

[8] Tyler, *Letters and Times*, II, 14; *National Intelligencer*, Mar. 2, 1841.

of which covered only about one-third of a column of news-paper space, Tyler reaffirmed his adherence to the doctrine of States' rights. "Here," he said, speaking of the Senate, "are to be found the immediate representatives of the States, by whose sovereign will the Government has been spoken into existence." [9]

The Vice-President's speech was followed by a short pause, after which General Harrison entered and was conducted to the seat prepared for him. A procession was formed which escorted the President-elect to the eastern portico of the Capitol. Here he delivered his inaugural address and took the oath of office as President of the United States.[10]

After the inaugural ceremonies were over the Senate re-assembled with Vice-President Tyler in the chair. Nominations for Cabinet positions were received from President Harrison and all were unanimously confirmed.[11]

During the campaign the Whig newspapers had a great deal to say about General Harrison's good health and robust constitution. His powers of endurance were doubtless overestimated and were probably not equal to the demands made on his vitality by the new responsibilities. His routine of living was disturbed by social dissipation and his peace of mind upset by the importunities of hungry office seekers. When, therefore, he was attacked by a severe pneumonia on March 24 he was unable to put up an effective resistance to the disease and thus succumbed to it on April 4, only one month after his accession. In the delirium of his last hours he addressed his physician, whom he probably took for his successor, in these words: "Sir, I wish you to understand the

[9] *National Intelligencer,* Mar. 5, 1841. For the text of Tyler's address see *Madisonian,* Mar. 6, 1841.

Even Benton, one of the most persistent of Tyler's critics, spoke of this speech as "a well-conceived, well-expressed, and well-delivered address, appropriately brief." Benton, *Thirty Years' View,* II, 209.

[10] *National Intelligencer,* Mar. 5, 1841; *Madisonian,* extra for Mar. 4; also Mar. 6, 1841; Benton, *op. cit.,* II, 209.

[11] *Madisonian,* March 6, 9, 1841; Benton, *loc. cit.,* 209.

true principles of the Government. I wish them carried out. I ask nothing more." [12]

In the meantime Tyler had returned to his home in Williamsburg with the expectation of spending the next four years in peace and quiet. As Vice-President he would be burdened with very little responsibility, for his rôle would be that of an honored moderator of a dignified legislative body. On the morning of April 5 he may have been sleeping a little later than usual or daydreaming pleasantly of the peaceful quadrennium ahead of him—a time when well-remunerated public service in Washington would alternate with delightful social diversion in Williamsburg. If such was the case, he was rudely awakened by some loud knocks on his front door at the early hour of sunrise. Going down to see who was so unmindful of the sleeping habits of the old town, he was accosted by two serious-looking messengers from the national capital. These were Daniel Webster's son Fletcher, chief clerk of the State Department, and a Mr. Beall, an officer of the Senate, who had been sent by the Cabinet to notify the Vice-President of the death of the President.[13] They had hurried to Richmond by train and from there to Jamestown by a boat chartered for the trip.

Tyler made rapid preparations for the journey, and by five-thirty [14] Monday afternoon the messengers, the new

[12] Richardson, *Messages*, IV, 22, 30, 31; Hone, *Diary*, II, 533-537; *National Intelligencer*, Mar. 31, April 5, and *Madisonian*, May 4, 1841.

[13] *Niles' Register*, LX, 84-85.

[14] An interesting account of the circumstances under which the Vice-President learned of his promotion to the Presidency is related by John S. Wise, who gives Tyler's friend Peachy as his source of information. According to this story, the Vice-President was playing marbles with his boys and had been beaten by them at the game of "knucks." He was on his knees with his knuckles on the ground to receive the penalty of defeat when he was accosted by the messenger from Washington. Rising from his humble posture, he at once donned the toga of official dignity and hastily made plans for assuming his new responsibility.

The acceptance of this tradition in its entirety involves considerable difficulty, despite the eminent authority by which it is sustained. It is hardly probable that Tyler would have been playing marbles at sunrise with his sons,

President, and his two sons were in Richmond ready to take the cars for Washington. They promptly boarded a special train for the national capital and arrived there by or before five Tuesday morning. As Harrison had died at twelve-thirty Sunday morning, only about fifty-three hours had elapsed between the demise of the President and the accession of his successor. Considering the means of travel of that day, this was a remarkable record for speed.[15]

At noon on the day of Tyler's arrival at the capital, all the heads of the departments (except the Secretary of the Navy, who was out of the city) called on him to pay their official and personal respects. "They were received with all the politeness and kindness which characterize the new President." Each member of the Cabinet was asked to remain at his post.

Tyler was then sworn into the office of President before William Cranch, chief judge of the circuit court of the District of Columbia. He felt that the oath taken as Vice-President was sufficient, but in order to forestall any doubts that might arise he took this second oath.[16] The installation took place in the parlor of Brown's "Indian Queen" hotel.

Tyler reached Washington in time to participate in the funeral ceremonies which were held in honor of General Harrison. He and the Cabinet marched in the procession immediately behind the members of the family and the relatives of the deceased President.[17] Shortly thereafter (April 13) he issued a proclamation setting aside Friday, May 14, as a day of fasting and prayer. The various religious denomi-

two of whom were grown and married and only one of whom was of marble age. See John S. Wise, *Recollections of Thirteen Presidents* (New York, 1906), 13–16.

[15] Richmond *Enquirer*, April 6, 1841; Richmond *Whig*, April 6, 1841; *Niles, loc. cit.*, 84; *John Tyler Papers* (L.C.), V, 62.

[16] *National Intelligencer*, April 7, 1841; Richardson, *Messages*, IV, 30–31; Ben: P. Poore, *Perley's Reminiscences of Sixty Years in the National Metropolis*, 2 vols. (Tecumseh, Mich.), I, 269–270.

Chief Justice Taney, who was in Baltimore, refused to administer the oath because he had not been officially requested to do so.

[17] Richardson, *op. cit.*, 29.

nations were requested on that day to observe suitable ceremonies for such an occasion, invoking the Deity "to inspire
us with proper spirit and temper of heart and mind under
these frowns of His providence and still bestow His gracious
benedictions upon our government and our country." [18]

On April 9, 1841, President Tyler issued a statement to
the American people which might be termed his Inaugural
Address. It was of moderate length and rather indefinite in
meaning. The language used was, in the main, rather commonplace and the style was not up to the standard of the
best of his speeches in Congress. His position, however, was
clearly defined on a few questions.[19] The Inaugural seems
to have made a favorable impression on the Whig Party
throughout the country. According to the Richmond *Whig*,
it was received with "a hurricane of applause" by the Whigs
and with despair by the Democrats. The *Madisonian* printed
the address side by side with Jefferson's First Inaugural
and pointed out its similarity to that great state paper.[20]

He favored the strengthening of the army and navy—
the adoption of such measures as would render both "replete
with efficiency." His foreign policy would be grounded on
the principle of "justice on our part to all, submitting to injustice from none." Allusion was made to the spoils system
and its danger in a country in which the number of Federal
employees was constantly growing. He promised to recommend to Congress such measures as would arrest the evils
of the system.

Changes should be made in the financial policy of the
government, and his sanction was promised to any Constitutional measure arising in Congress that should have for its
object the restoration of a sound circulating medium. "In

[18] Richardson, *op. cit.*, 32.
[19] This address is most accessible in Richardson, *op. cit.*, IV, 36–39.
[20] Richmond *Whig*, April 14, 15, 16, 20, 24, 1841; *Madisonian*, Apr. 12, 1841.
The Whig members of the New York legislature in a meeting April 21,
1841, adopted resolutions commending Tyler's Inaugural Address and his action in retaining Harrison's Cabinet.

deciding upon the adaptation of any such measure to the end proposed, as well as its conformity to the Constitution, I shall resort to the fathers of the great republican school for advice and instruction." This was a reassertion of his States' rights doctrine. Further on he stated that those in charge of the Federal government should be careful not to attempt any enlargement of the powers granted to them, for in so doing they would disturb the balance between the State and Federal governments.

As Harrison was the first President to die in office, there was no precedent to indicate whether the Vice-President should be accorded all the power and dignity of a regular Chief Magistrate or be regarded only as an acting chief executive. The Constitution provides that "in case of the removal of the President from office, or of his death, resignation, or inability to discharge the powers and duties of the said office, the same shall devolve on the Vice-President. . . ." Whether "the same" refers to the office or the duties is not clear from the text of the Constitution. Tyler, however, interpreted it to refer to the office and at once claimed all the rights and privileges of the Presidency. The precedent set by him has been followed in every subsequent case in which a Vice-President has succeeded to the Chief Magistracy.

But Tyler's interpretation of this clause in the Constitution was not accepted by all the leaders, either of the Whigs or the Democrats. Prominent among the Whigs who regarded him as only acting President was ex-President John Quincy Adams.[21] Some of the newspapers also took the same position, and the Cabinet, when it notified Tyler of Harri-

---

[21] J. Q. Adams, *Memoirs*, X, 463.
Clay at first was also disposed to regard Tyler as acting President. In writing to Judge N. Beverley Tucker (April 15, 1841) he spoke of him as Vice-President Tyler, and said that his administration would be in the nature of a regency. But he apparently changed his mind later for he voted in the Senate for giving him the title of President. Clay to Judge Tucker, Apr. 15, 1841; Tyler, *Letters and Times*, II, 30.

son's death, addressed him as Vice-President. The *National Intelligencer,* the leading Whig paper of Washington, argued (April 15) very sensibly against the attempt to deprive the new incumbent of any of the powers and privileges of the Presidency.[22]

When Congress met in special session (May 31, 1841) the question was raised in the House of Representatives by John McKeon, of New York, whether Tyler was entitled to the appellation "President of the United States." A resolution recognizing him as President had already been offered by Henry A. Wise, of Virginia. Tyler would claim, said he, that "he was by the Constitution, by election, and by the act of God, President of the United States." Wise's resolution was passed without a division.[23] The question of Tyler's position and title was also raised in the Senate (June 1). R. J. Walker, a Democrat from Mississippi, ably contended that the *office* of President had devolved upon the former Vice-President and not merely the duties of the office. His speech was in opposition to a measure offered that same day by Allen of Ohio. This measure provided that the Senate in its communication to the chief executive address him as "the Vice-President, on whom, by the death of the late President, the powers and duties of the office of President have devolved." This resolution was defeated by a vote of 8 yeas to 38 nays.[24]

Tyler's accession was gladly acclaimed by the States' rights wing of the Whig Party. The high opinion of him expressed by ex-Governor Gilmer of Virginia was doubtless typical of the feeling of the antibank Whigs. He spoke of Tyler's accession as follows:

"It is a source of great consolation and encouragement under these circumstances that the executive trust of the Federal government has devolved on one who is well known and justly appreciated in Virginia, and who comes up to the

[22] *Niles' Register,* LX, 98.
[23] *Cong. Globe,* 27th Cong., 1st. sess., 3–4.   [24] *Ibid.,* 5.

standard prescribed by our Jefferson in honesty, capacity, and fidelity to the Constitution. I venture to say that John Tyler will never disappoint the confidence that has been reposed in him; that he will regard his own and every other office under the government as a sacred trust, created for the public good, and not for party or for private emolument." [25] It is proper to note that this high encomium was passed by one who was in a position to know the weak as well as the strong points in the President's character.

On the other hand, those of the party who held to nationalist views must have had serious misgivings. In the opinion of an observant Democrat the Whig leaders in Washington had been thrown into the utmost confusion by the death of General Harrison.[26] One of the most unflattering opinions of the new President was the one recorded by John Quincy Adams in his Diary on the very day that Harrison died. Harrison's death, he said, made John Tyler "Acting President." "Tyler is a political sectarian, of the slave-driving, Virginian, Jeffersonian school, principled against all improvement, with all the interests and passions and vices of slavery rooted in his moral and political constitution—with talents not above mediocrity, and a spirit incapable of expansion to the dimensions of the station upon which he has been cast by the hand of Providence, unseen through the apparent agency of chance. No one ever thought of his being placed in the executive chair." [27]

Of course, this picture of Tyler is too unlike the original to be even a good caricature, but it shows the low estimate that the aged ex-President put upon the new incumbent, who, as the result of an unfortunate accident, had been able to climb up into a seat which, in his opinion, had been exalted by the ability and patriotism of himself and his father. This initial antagonism to Tyler grew into bitter opposition as the

[25] Tyler, *op. cit.,* I, 610.
[26] J. I. Hayes to Andrew Jackson, Apr. 23, 1841; *Jackson MSS.* (L.C.), CV, 22,660.
[27] J. Q. Adams, *Memoirs,* X, 456–457.

policies of the latter clashed more and more with the views of the aged misanthrope.

The first ceremonial function of the new administration was held late in April, when the ministers of foreign countries met the President for the first time. Mr. Fox, who represented the Court of Saint James, being absent on account of illness, Mr. Bodisco, the Russian minister, appeared at the head of the corps. He made a short address on behalf of himself and his colleagues, to which the President responded with an appropriate reply. In his brief remarks he said that "the people of the United States regard their own prosperity as intimately connected with that of the entire family of nations, and the cultivation of the feelings of mutual amity as the best mode of advancing that important end." As these foreign representatives were being presented to him he spoke to each of the relations past and present between the United States and his country and expressed the hope that these amicable relations would continue. In these short conversations, according to the *National Intelligencer,* Tyler "was particularly happy, and this, his first official intercourse with the representatives of other nations, was, we doubt not, exceedingly satisfactory"—and in the very best of taste.[28]

Tyler's accession to the Presidency came just six days after his fifty-first birthday. He was thus the youngest man who had up to that time been called upon to assume this high responsibility. And he was destined to face problems the proper solution of which would tax the wisdom of the fullest maturity. The accident of Harrison's death had elevated him to an awkward as well as an honored position. The anomaly of his situation was about what would have been that of W. J. Bryan had he in 1896 been nominated and elected by the Republican Party. For Tyler was at heart a Democrat, and yet he was the titular head of the Whig Party.

His first problem was that of disposing of the Cabinet be-

28 *Niles,* LX, 130.

queathed to him by Harrison. The members of this body except Webster and Granger were all partisans of Clay and were determined to use their influence in favor of his succession to the Presidency four years later. Such an attitude was not consistent with the fullest co-operation with the Chief Executive. Tyler, therefore, should have had a new Cabinet chosen on the basis of loyalty to him and his principles. But to call for the resignation of the heads of the departments would have caused a serious breach in the party. He, therefore, went along for a while with advisers who were not in entire sympathy with him. With such an official family the outlook was not bright either for harmony or efficiency.

Another serious drawback to the success of his administration was the inability of the President to take over the leadership of his party. A President cannot expect much in the way of achievement unless he is recognized as the actual as well as the nominal head of his party. In the case of John Tyler, all the circumstances were against his assumption of such control. As the Vice-Presidential candidate, he had played an inconspicuous part in the campaign, and so neither the politicians nor the people had looked upon him as an important leader. Nor had Harrison's mantle when it fell upon him endowed him with the power to control the Whigs. If the different groups that composed the Whig coalition were to be fused into a united party, the strongest faction must dominate the weaker ones. As the nationalists among the Whigs greatly outnumbered the particularists, it was hardly to be expected that the former would accept a leader from the latter group. Therefore, in the contest for party supremacy, Clay, the champion of nationalism, had every advantage over Tyler, the advocate of localism.

Nor did Clay fail to take full advantage of all the circumstances in his favor. He promptly assumed the leadership of the Whigs and determined to put through a program to his liking. It was he who had dictated the call for a special session of Congress. He had started in with his highhanded ways with Harrison. The old general resented this and on one occasion reminded Clay that he and not Clay was the President.[29]

Clay naturally thought that Tyler, a mild-mannered Virginian with a soft exterior, would not have the temerity strenuously to oppose his policies. Tyler's tactful method in dealing with his colleagues sometimes left the impression that he did not have much backbone. Clay was one of those who mistook courtesy for weakness. He failed to understand that while the President was exceptionally pleasant in his relations with others, he was unyielding when his convictions were involved. He did not realize that a gloved hand may easily be changed into a clenched fist.

Tyler and Clay, despite the divergence of their views, were on the best of terms at the beginning of the administration. Ewing, one of Clay's friends in the Cabinet, in writing to the Kentuckian (May 8, 1841), said: "No man can be better disposed [toward you] than the President. . . . He speaks of you with the utmost kindness and you may rely upon it his friendship is strong and unabated." [30] Circumstances soon took such a turn, however, as to subject this friendship to a very severe strain. A constructive program lay ahead of them, and a deadlock between their principles could be avoided only by compromise. For the clash that resulted Clay must come in for the chief blame. If he had been more conciliatory and somewhat self-effacing, important measures based on the principle of give and take could have been carried out. But Clay was imperious and determined to have his way.[31] He thus let slip a great opportunity for achievement.

His failure to grasp this opportunity would indicate that

[29] Tyler, op. cit., II, 10, note; see also N. Y. World, Aug. 31, 1880; Clay to Harrison, Mar. 15, 1841; Clay Papers, XXIII, 3908; Harrison to Clay, Mar. 13, 1841; Clay Papers, XXII, 3906.

[30] Ewing to Clay, May 8, 1841; Clay Papers, XXIII, 3913.

[31] H. W. Hilliard, Politics and Pen Pictures; quoted by Barton H. Wise, Life of Henry A. Wise (New York and London, 1899), 92. Early in the extra session Clay said to James Lyons: "Tyler dare not resist; I will drive him before me." N. Y. World, Aug. 31, 1880.

the "Great Pacificator" was greater in reputation than in character and ability. Clay's ambition to be President was a serious handicap during the greater part of his career. Especially was this the case at this time; for to his ambition was added the bitterness of disappointment, which gave his imperiousness an exceptional harshness. His defeat at Harrisburg had not caused him to give up hope of attaining the high office to which he so ardently aspired, and the Presidential bee was buzzing so loudly around his ear that he did not always hear the still, small voice of wisdom and patriotism or the loud noise of public opinion.

Harrison was committed to the one-term idea, and so it was agreed at a very early date after the election that Clay would be the next nominee.[32] The accession of Tyler injected an element of uncertainty into these plans. For if he should make a fine record and remain in the good graces of the party he would be the logical candidate for the succession. Such a danger could be averted only by Clay's assuming the leadership of the party and by discrediting Tyler in the eyes of the Whigs. Tyler felt that this was the motive that prompted Clay's opposition to him, and in this feeling he was supported by his friends.

In response to a call issued by Harrison Congress met in special session May 31, 1841. The Whigs had a comfortable majority in the lower house and a safe though narrow majority in the Senate.[33] The body was promptly organized, and next day the President's message was received and read. The message on the whole was well written. Its style was clear, though not brilliant, and the general tone of the document was prudent and dignified.

The message began with a graceful compliment to General Harrison by suggesting that Congress make some financial provision for his family owing to the fact that his estate

---

[32] Harriet W. Weed, *Autobiography of Thurlow Weed*, I, 507.

[33] According to Niles, the Whig majority in the House of Representatives was forty-nine; in the Senate, seven. *Niles' Register*, LX, 195.

had been subjected to considerable expense by his removal
to Washington.

A sensible statement was made as to what would be his
course in dealing with other powers. The conciliatory but
firm attitude in this announcement of foreign policy was particularly happy in view of the fact that the relations of the
United States with both England and Mexico were tense,
not to say menacing, at the time.

The dangerous financial question was not sidestepped.
He alluded to the fact that the estimated revenues for the
current year would be less than the disbursements, and suggested that proper measures be adopted for meeting the
deficit. In doing this no change in the Compromise Act of
1833 should be made "except under urgent necessities, which
are not believed at this time to exist." He hoped that a permanent system of revenue—one imposing discriminating
duties on imports for purposes of revenue—would be
adopted. The creation of a "suitable fiscal agent" was recommended—one "capable of adding increased facilities in the
collection and disbursement of the public revenues." "Upon
such an agent depends in an eminent degree the establishment of a currency of uniform value."

"The Subtreasury system is unsatisfactory and has been
plainly condemned by the voice of the people. No other
financial scheme has been agreed upon, and so it is incumbent upon Congress to devise a plan." "I shall be ready to
concur with you in the adoption of such system as you may
propose, reserving to myself the ultimate power of rejecting any measure which may in my view of it, conflict with the
Constitution or otherwise jeopardize the prosperity of the
country—a power which I could not part with even if I
would, but which I will not believe any act of yours will call
into requisition."

In suggesting the creation of a "fiscal agent" to manage
government funds, the President evidently did not intend to
surrender his lifelong position on States' rights. For refer-

ence was made to the "imperious necessity" of restraining
the Federal officials within the range of their respective
powers and of thus maintaining the balance between the
authority delegated to the Federal government and that retained by the States and the people. He also spoke of keeping "the States in a condition the most free and respectable
and in the full possession of all their power." [34]

Tyler might have spared himself the trouble of discussing
a proposed fiscal agent for the government, as scant attention was paid to his suggestions on that point by the group
of Whigs which controlled both branches of Congress. This
group looked to Clay as their leader, and the latter was not
disposed to share his power with the President. Accordingly,
he at once began to assert his authority in the Senate with
little or no regard for the sensibilities of the titular head of
the party. His assumption of party leadership was publicly
made when early in the session (June 7) he offered six resolutions as a plan of work for the session.[35] These resolutions
provided for the repeal of the Independent Treasury Act,
the establishment of a national bank, an increase in the im-
port duties to provide an adequate revenue for the government, the distribution of the proceeds from the sale of public lands, and other measures of minor importance. This
program was strictly in accord with the principles of the
nationalist wing of the Whig Party, and showed that Clay
had never been converted to particularism or else had back-
slidden into straightout nationalism. It also revealed his intention to override the scruples of a President whom he chose
to regard only as a sort of regent.[36]

In including a national bank in the agenda of the special

[34] For the text of this message, see Richardson, *Messages*, IV, 40–51.
This message, like the Inaugural, was well received by the Whigs. The
Richmond *Whig* said (June 5, 1841) that with a single exception (that of the
New York *American*) every Whig paper seen by the editor had highly com-
mended the message.

[35] *Congressional Globe*, 27th Cong., 1st sess., 22. See also *Niles*, LX, 238.

[36] Clay to Judge N. Beverley Tucker, Apr. 15, 1841; Tyler, *Letters and
Times*, I, 30.

session of Congress, Clay fully realized that he was running counter to the wishes of the President. For Tyler had written to him a month earlier (April 30) expressing the wish that action on the bank problem and other intricate questions would be postponed in order that he might have more time to formulate a matured plan of public policy with reference to them. If Clay should be unwilling to accept this suggestion and should insist upon the passage of a bank measure, he hoped it would be so framed as to avoid all constitutional objections.[37]

Clay was now announcing as a Whig program measures which he would not have dared to offer in the campaign of 1840 as a platform of the party. If the Whig leadership had in this campaign taken a definite stand in favor of these measures the party would in all human probability have been defeated at the polls. To make the acceptance of these policies a test of party loyalty would be, therefore, to appraise political orthodoxy by an unfair standard. To enlist the President and the other States' rights Whigs in support of this program would necessitate the use of exceptional tact and diplomacy

[37] Tyler to Clay, April 30, 1841; Tyler, *op. cit.*, III, 92–94.

In this letter Tyler stated that his mind was made up as to the need of repealing the Subtreasury Act and of the strengthening of the military defenses. "There's not a seaport town that does not hold its existence at the will of a great naval power." If nothing else is done during the extra session, great good will be accomplished. It will be for Congress to decide whether other measures shall be considered.

"As to a Bank, I design to be perfectly frank with you—I would not have it urged prematurely. The public mind is in a state of great disquietude in regard to it." The recent exposures of the Bank at Philadelphia have not been calculated to put this perturbation at rest. The "close division of votes by which, if at all, it will pass through Congress will encourage the *ultraists* in efforts to destroy it, before it can go into operation. I apprehend a strong protest from the minority and an avowed purpose to cancel it, the charter, at a future day. Should this be done, are you sure that capitalists will adventure their capital in it?" . . . "If, however, you see nothing in this of force, then I desire you to consider whether you cannot frame a Bank as to avoid all constitutional objections—which of itself would attach to it a vast host of our own party to be found all over the Union."

Tyler had also had a conversation with Clay at the opening of the special session, in the course of which he made plain his attitude on the bank question. Tyler to Tazewell, Oct. 11, 1841; *John Tyler Papers* (L.C.), II, 6408.

on the part of Clay. But Clay was not in the humor for diplomacy. His imperious mood was on, and he was resolved not to be thwarted in his plans by (as he considered) an easy-to-manage Virginian whom accident had placed in a chair that was too high for him.

Apparently, the long friendship which had existed between them for more than a score of years had terminated at the opening of the extra session of Congress. At that time Tyler presented to Clay a plan for a national bank (the one formerly offered by Judge White) which would avoid the constitutional objections raised by the States' rights advocates.[38] This measure is said to have been heartily endorsed by Webster and reluctantly accepted by the other members of the Cabinet. When it was presented to Clay, he objected to it and stubbornly refused to accept it. Thereupon, according to a very probable tradition,[39] "the President took fire and exclaimed: 'Then, sir, I wish you to understand this— that you and I were born in the same district; that we have fed upon the same food, and breathed the same natal air. Go you now, then, Mr. Clay, to your end of the avenue, where stands the Capitol, and there perform your duty to the country as you shall think proper. So help me God, I shall do mine at this end of it as I think proper.' "

The Whigs in Congress showed a willingness to obey

[38] Judge Tucker had recommended a plan for a bank which Tyler preferred to the one he proposed. But those around him considered it too new and bold and so he fell back upon the simpler plan which was framed in accordance with Judge White's suggestion. In accepting the latter plan he was apparently acting on the advice of Senator Rives. Judge Tucker to Tyler, Apr. 11, 1841; *Tucker Papers* (Williamsburg); Tyler to Judge Tucker, July 28, 1841; Tyler, *Letters and Times*, II, 54; *Tyler's Quarterly*, XXII, 85–86.

[39] I have used the word "tradition" as a designation for this story because I could find no contemporary account of it. My only authority for it is a statement, unsupported by documentary evidence, made by Dr. Lyon G. Tyler in his biography of his father. The adjective "probable" is justified by the fact that this biography is a very careful and reliable work, and it is not likely that Dr. Tyler would have related this story as a fact unless he had some basis for it. He may have had access to a paper that I have been unable to examine. Tyler, *Letters and Times*, II, 33–34. See also Fuess's *Life of Caleb Cushing*, I, 301.

Clay's orders, and on June 8 a bill passed the Senate providing for the repeal of the Independent Treasury Act. After having been passed by the House, it was sent to Tyler for his approval.[40] As the President in speeches in the campaign and in his message to Congress had expressed disapproval of the Subtreasury system, he willingly signed this bill.[41] This reversal of a major policy of the previous administration caused great rejoicing among the Whigs of Washington. In celebration of this event a large group of them marched in procession up Pennsylvania Avenue accompanied by a hearse bearing a coffin labeled "The Subtreasury Plan." [42]

The ready acquiescence of Tyler in the first of Clay's measures did not indicate that the former had willingly abdicated the leadership of the party to his brilliant rival. It only meant that so far the views of the two had been in unison. Conflict would arise as soon as the President would be asked to put aside his States' rights scruples and endorse the bank policy of the Senate leader. Whether Tyler could be persuaded into an attitude so inconsistent with his previous lifelong record was a matter of considerable uncertainty with Clay and other Whig leaders. It looked, therefore, as if a fight were impending, and the political war horses were already sniffing the air of battle.

[40] *Cong. Globe,* 27th Cong., 1st sess., 36, 313.
[41] *National Intelligencer,* Aug. 19, 1841.
[42] Poore, *Perley's Reminiscences,* I, 271–272.

CHAPTER XV

AN ILL-MATCHED TEAM

EARLY in the extra session of Congress it became clearly apparent to the initiated that a rift had developed in the Whig ranks. That the attempt to carry out Clay's program would widen this rift into an irreparable breach it took no prophetic insight to foresee. The real fight came when Clay attempted to put through his bank policy. Clay had complete control of the great majority of his party in both houses of Congress and was using his power in highhanded fashion. Silas Wright, Jr., in writing to Van Buren (June 21, 1841) said that Clay was irritable and unhappy but was in perfect control. "He is much more imperious and arrogant with his friends than I have ever known him, and that you know, is saying a great deal." [1]

It is not easy to understand Clay's ascendency over a party which had refused to name him as its standard-bearer a year and a half earlier. The Washington correspondent of the New York *Herald* declared that Clay's influence over both houses of Congress was extraordinary and illimitable. "He predominates over the Whig Party with despotic sway. Old Hickory himself never lorded it over his followers with authority more undisputed, or more supreme. With the exception of some two or three in the Senate, and fifteen or twenty in the House, Mr. Clay's wish is a paramount law to the whole party." This ascendency he attributed to his "powerful intellect, courage, bold and determined spirit,

[1] Van Buren Papers (L.C., abbreviation for Library of Congress), XLIII, 10,055–56.

The best account we have of the bitter political fight between Tyler and the Clay Whigs is given in the first half of G. R. Poage's *Henry Clay and the Whig Party* (Chapel Hill, 1936).

and a perseverance that no difficulties can thwart or discourage." [2] More important than these qualities of leadership was the fact that he represented the dominant wing of the party and thus held the party whip. With such a disciplinary weapon he could easily force would-be insurgents back into regularity.

The odds were overwhelmingly against the President in the contest he was forced to wage against his formidable opponent. His Whig following in Congress was so small that they were not improperly designated "the Corporal's Guard." The only Whig Senator who supported him loyally to the end of the bank fight was Rives, whose election Tyler had opposed most strenuously. Clay's most persevering lieutenant and the President's most persistent enemy in the House, was John Minor Botts, who, as one of the "Impracticable" Whigs, had fought with Tyler in the Virginia legislature against the election of Rives to the United States Senate. Surely politics had recently brought about some strange mutations.

Tyler's position was still further weakened by the fact that some of his adversaries were members of his own official household. Even his best weapon, that of the patronage, could not be wielded with entire effectiveness because it was dulled by the power of the Clay-controlled Senate to hold up his appointments to office. With the cards thus stacked against him, he was defeated before the game began.

Anyone who could read aright the signs of the times could see that there were only two alternatives before the President. The one was to obey the behests of conviction and adhere to his States' rights principles. Such a policy would mean a bitter fight, ending in defeat, disgrace, and expulsion from his party. The only gain that could accrue from such a sacrifice would be a feeling of self-respect and a consciousness of honesty and integrity, with the hope of an ultimate vindication by history.

[2] N. Y. *Herald,* July 30, 1841.

The other alternative was to swallow his constitutional scruples and accept the nationalist policies of his powerful opponent. By so doing he would have recognized Clay as mayor of the palace and accepted for himself the futile but honored place of *roi faineant*. In that event he would have enjoyed peace and popularity, and, to all outward seeming, his administration would have been a success. The Presidential chair in which he would have been comfortably ensconced would not have been a seat of the mighty but would have become the high chair of an infant.

It is to the everlasting credit of Tyler that in this choice he put loyalty to duty and conviction above considerations of expediency. It is not improbable, however, that there was bound up with this high motive the hope that this policy would prove the right road to the succession. If so, it only goes to show that Tyler, like any other man similarly placed, was not unmindful of personal ambition while trying honestly to promote the best interests of his country. Such a mixture of prudence and patriotism would give no warrant for the savage criticism that was hurled against him by his enemies. But there were two points on which he was open to criticism. In the first place, he should never have put himself into this situation, that is, no one with his views should have run for the Vice-Presidency on the Whig ticket. Secondly, he should have conducted his fight with more firmness, boldness, and wisdom. Had he done so he might have parried some of the blows that were aimed at him and might have inflicted heavier ones upon the head of the enemy.

The ball was started rolling when on June 3 the report of Ewing, the Secretary of the Treasury, was read in the House. This report recommended the repeal of the Independent Treasury Act and the creation of a fiscal agent of the United States.[3] A few days later the Senate adopted a resolution offered by Clay calling upon Secretary Ewing to com-

[3] *Cong. Globe,* 27th Cong., 1st sess., 18–21.

municate as soon as possible a plan for a bank or fiscal agent.[4] In response to this request Ewing promptly reported (June 12) a scheme which provided for a central bank in the District of Columbia with branches, or offices of discount and deposit, located in the several States with their consent.[5] In creating this bank Congress might be considered as acting not in its national capacity but as the legislative body of the District of Columbia. This would do away with the constitutional objection to the creation of the central bank. The provision that no branch be located in any State without its consent would remove the constitutional objection to the establishment of branches.[6]

The plan outlined by Ewing had the endorsement of Tyler, who urged Clay to support it.[7] Merchants from the principal commercial cities had been invited to Washington to discuss the proposal. While they had some doubts as to whether the stock would be subscribed, they promised to do all they could to make it a success. Webster thought it a good scheme and the only one on which an agreement could be reached. The failure of the Whigs in Congress to accept it started all the trouble. "Here," he said, "was the origin of distrust, disunion, and resentment." [8] If Clay had responded favorably to Tyler's request and accepted this measure it would have been adopted by Congress without substantial amendment.

---

[4] *Cong. Globe*, 27th Cong., 1st sess., 22–23.
A like request was made by the House of Representatives on June 21 (*ibid.*, 86). Two days later Ewing sent in his plan to the House and it was referred to a special committee headed by John Sergeant, of Pennsylvania. On July 21, Sergeant reported to the House a bank bill substantially the same as that offered by Clay in the Senate. *Ibid.*, 238; see also Cushing's "Address to His Constituents," *Niles' Register*, LXI, 109–111.

[5] *Cong. Globe*, loc. cit., 48–49; *Niles*, LX, 232–234.

[6] No definite statement in Ewing's plan indicates that Congress was to act as the legislature of the District. But there is no doubt that in the mind of the President it was this feature of the bill, together with that requiring the assent of the States for the branches, that made the proposal constitutional.

[7] Tyler to Judge Tucker; Tyler, *Letters and Times*, II, 54.

[8] Webster to Hiram Ketchum, July 16, 1841; *Writings of Daniel Webster* (Nat. Ed.), XVI, 344–348; Webster's Faneuil Hall Oration, Sept. 30, 1842; *ibid.*, III, 133.

Such a bill would have been signed by the President and the bitter fight between him and the Whig majority might have been avoided. But Clay willed otherwise.

Ewing's proposal was submitted to a select committee of the Senate, of which Clay was chairman. The report of the committee was made by Clay on June 21. In this report both the expediency and the constitutionality of a national bank were taken for granted. The plan suggested differed in some details and in a few important principles from the one proposed by the Secretary of the Treasury. It was based on the assumption that Congress in chartering the bank was acting in its capacity as the legislature of the whole country and not of the District of Columbia. The parent bank was to be located in Washington because of the alleged financial advantages that would accrue from the proximity of the bank to the government. But the consent of the States was not to be required for the establishment of the branches. That would rob the bank of its national character and give it the character of an enlarged District bank with branches in the States. Such a banking system would be inefficient and for the stock of such an institution there would be no subscribers.[9]

The adoption of this report without change would constitute a virtual revival of the Second Bank of the United States, the legality of whose charter Tyler had always denied. To expect him, therefore, to go along with such a policy was to assume that he had suddenly abandoned the principles for which he had always contended and adopted those against which he had fought during his entire career. For the plan outlined by Clay could be endorsed only on the acceptance of the extreme nationalism of Hamilton.

W. C. Rives, of Virginia, leading supporter of the Administration in the Senate, realized the inconsistency of Clay's bill with Tyler's States' rights views. Accordingly, he offered as an amendment to the measure the clause in Ewing's plan which provided for the assent of the States to the establish-

[9] *Cong. Globe, loc. cit.,* 79–81; also *Niles' Register,* LX, 237, 258–260.

ment of branches.[10] This amendment, he said, was in con-
sonance with the views of the Administration. The right of
Congress to charter a bank in the District of Columbia was
generally conceded and had been exercised from the origin
of the government up to the present time. It had been contended that if Congress were not granted power by the Constitution to establish branches throughout the country it could
not derive such power from the consent of the States. To this
objection Rives gave this reply: "The States are sovereign-
ties. Virginia has a right to permit a branch of the Bank of
England at Richmond if she pleases." [11] This amendment
was defeated, and Clay was for a time insistent upon his
proposal. There were a few Whig Senators who were unwilling to vote for a measure so antagonistic to Tyler's well-
known convictions. The bill could not pass without their
support, and so compromise was the only alternative to a
deadlock.

It was at this juncture that John Minor Botts tried to put
in an oar. He had been a strong antibank man and still
claimed to be on intimate terms with the President although
he had as early as June 2 accused him of having surrendered
himself to "backstairs influence." [12] Botts had, as he thought,
hit upon a formula which would serve as a basis for agreement between Clay and the President. Accordingly, he hurried to the White House and, as he maintained, secured
Tyler's assent to the plan. The latter afterwards strongly
denied that he had approved the proposal suggested by Botts.
On the contrary, he had spurned it as "a contemptible subter-
fuge behind which he would not skulk." [13]

As to which of these two contradictory accounts is correct
the impartial student has some hesitancy in declaring. If
Botts's version is accepted there arises the difficulty of explaining why the President endorsed in private a policy which he

[10] Cushing's "Address to his Constituents," *Niles*, LXI, 109–111; *Cong. Globe, loc. cit.,* 133.
[11] *Madisonian*, July 3, 1841.   [12] *Niles*, LXIV, 215.
[13] Tyler, *Letters and Times*, II, 56, note, and 66.

shortly afterwards repudiated in public. Furthermore, if he gave his enemies through the Botts suggestion a stick with which to break his own head, we must charge him with folly as well as mendacity.

After considerable discussion Clay was convinced that his bank measure could not pass in the form originally presented. So he offered (July 27) an amendment to his bill embodying the proposal attributed to Botts. By this amendment, which had been agreed to by the Whig caucus,[14] the assent of the States would be necessary for the establishment of branches of the bank; but such assent was to be presumed in respect to any State whose legislature at its first session after the passage of this act did not unconditionally express its assent or dissent to the establishment of a branch within its limits. The amendment was adopted by a vote of 25 yeas to 24 nays, one Senator who opposed it being absent.[15]

This amendment was a cross between Ewing's proposal and the one first submitted by Clay. As Caleb Cushing, a Representative from Massachusetts, properly showed, it had the defects of both plans without the merits of either, and was obnoxious to both the nationalists and the particularists.[16] The bill as thus amended passed the Senate on July 28 by a vote of 26 yeas to 23 nays. The measure was rushed through the House on August 6, the fifth day after it was introduced in that body. A prominent Democratic Representative complained that only four days were allowed for its discussion although it was the most important bill of the session.[17]

When the bank bill was before the President it was discussed at length by the Cabinet. "Mr. Ewing read a long and

[14] New York *Express*, July 28, 1841, cited by G. R. Poage, *Henry Clay and the Whig Party*, 64.

[15] There was also a clause providing for the establishment of branches in any of the States (without their assent) if Congress should deem it necessary and proper for the carrying out of its powers. *Cong. Globe, loc. cit.*, 254, 256.

[16] Cushing's "Address to his Constituents," *Niles' Register*, LXI, 109–111.

[17] *Cong. Globe, loc. cit.*, 260, 303; *Niles*, LX, 358; A. V. Brown to Jackson, Aug. 8, 1841, *Jackson MSS.* (L.C.).

able paper, and the rest of us delivered our opinions verbally. We all earnestly recommended the President to sign the Bill." [18] Tyler, however, was not greatly influenced by this official advice, for he was still a firm believer in States' rights and was opposed on constitutional grounds to a national bank of the old type. As has already been shown, he was not bound to support such a bank by any commitments made in the campaign of 1840. He was, therefore, as free to veto the bank bill as Clay and his supporters had been to pass it. The charge of broken pledges would have no better basis in the one case than in the other. Nor had he, either in his public utterances or private communications since the election, indicated a change in attitude toward the bank question.[19]

[18] Statement made by Webster. See *Memorandum* by Webster, manuscript in the Library of Congress.

[19] It was charged, however, by John Minor Botts that Tyler had declared in favor of a national bank just prior to his accession to the Presidency. This commitment, he said, was made on the occasion of Harrison's inauguration. At that time the hotels of Washington were so crowded that Botts had difficulty in finding a room for himself. As an accommodation to him, Tyler shared his room at Brown's Hotel with Botts. In the intimate conversation between these two political friends on this occasion, Tyler (so Botts afterwards declared) expressed himself as in favor of a national bank. To this statement we cannot attach much importance, for it was made from memory two years later at a time when the old friendship between these Virginia Whigs had been changed into bitter enmity.

Moreover, Botts after the break with Tyler seems to have had a tendency toward misunderstanding his former friend and reading into his assertions interpretations that were not intended. In support of this assumption is the fact that Waddy Thompson and Botts received directly opposite impressions as to Tyler's bank views at an interview they had with him shortly after Botts's bedroom conversation with the Vice-President-elect. Thompson came away from the conference with the feeling that Tyler would veto a bill for the establishment of a national bank and Botts with the impression that he would endorse such a measure.

Furthermore, it is very difficult to explain why Tyler should have been so free in expressing his opinions to Botts on this dangerous question, when he was so guarded in his declarations to his other friends. We are also at a loss to reconcile the attitude imputed to him by Botts with the one he took two months later in letters to Rives and Clay. For in these latter communications he clearly indicated that his States' rights principles were still holding and that any bank measure to receive his approval must be framed in accordance with his constitutional scruples (pages 214, 215). Tyler, *Letters and Times,* III, 92–94.

For Botts's account of the bedroom conversation with Tyler, see Tyler, *op.*

The President gave no hint to the public as to his intentions regarding the bill until his veto message was sent to the Senate. This uncertainty gave rise to considerable speculation and discussion in Washington as to what action he would take. "Nothing is thought of, dreamed upon, or sworn about now," said the correspondent of the New York *Herald,* "but the fate of the bank bill. . . . Politicians discuss it morning, noon and night—in the Avenue, in the House, over their lunch at the refectory, in the Capitol, over their coffee, their wine, etc." The ladies talk of it on all occasions among themselves and to the gentlemen. It is a favorite topic with the hackney coachman. "An enthusiastic bank man from Arkansas, a gallant, generous planter, who thinks with perfect independence, and acts accordingly, stands ready every day to bet any sum from one hundred to a thousand dollars, either that there will, or will not be a veto, and he has no choice in the side." [20]

Tyler's silence was not due to indecision, for the bill had hardly got through Congress before he had made up his mind to veto it.[21] He did not send in his veto message, however, until next to the last day of the ten-day period allowed him for deliberation. This delay was probably due to the fear that a prompt veto would jeopardize the bankruptcy bill, then pending in Congress, the enactment of which was favored by the President. By thus waiting he hoped that the latter measure would be passed before his veto was sent to the Senate.[22]

Despite the reticence of the President, there gradually developed the feeling that the bill would be vetoed. This

---

cit., II, 105, note. For Waddy Thompson's account of the same interview, see Tyler, *ibid.,* II, 16–17.

[20] New York *Herald,* Aug. 5, 1841.

[21] R. McClellan, writing to Van Buren on July 30, 1841, said that Tyler's friends, Governor Gilmer and others, say "confidentially but confidently" that Tyler will veto the bill. *Van Buren Papers,* XLIII, 10,077. On the day after the bank bill passed the House, Gilmer said in a letter to Franklin Minor, the *"President will veto the bank bill"* (the italics are his). He was sure of this, he said, because the President had consulted with him "freely but confidentially about measures and men." *John Tyler Papers* (L.C.), V, 175–176.

[22] New York *Herald,* Aug. 11, 1841.

opinion was based on the sentiments expressed by Tyler's friends and in articles appearing in the *Madisonian,* the Presidential organ. On Thursday, August 12, this view received strong confirmation from an indiscretion of Robert Tyler, the President's son. At that time young Tyler engaged in a discussion with a New York Representative in the lobby of the House, in the course of which he denounced the bill as unconstitutional. "To suppose," he said, "that his father could be gulled by such a humbug compromise as the bill contained, was to suppose that he was an ass." [23]

Next day a committee of Representatives from Ohio and one or two Senators waited on the President to learn his decision and to prevail upon him to sign the bill. He declared that he had never been so perplexed and exercised over any question before but felt that he would have to veto the measure. His mind, however, was still open to conviction. He would go to church on Sunday and would "pray earnestly and devoutly to be enlightened as to his duty in regard to this great measure." [24]

On August 16, John Tyler, Jr., the President's secretary, came to the Senate with the veto message. He made his way with difficulty through the crowd which surrounded the door of the Senate Chamber. At once the other business was suspended and the message was read.

The reasons for the veto as presented in the message were, in summary, as follows: The provisions of the bill conferring on the bank the power to make local discounts were unacceptable on practical grounds, but the main objection was more deep-seated. The measure rested on an interpretation of the Constitution which was entirely at variance with the States' rights views of the President. "The power of Congress," he argued, "to create a national bank to operate *per se* over the Union has been a question of dispute from the origin of the Government. . . . my own opinion has been

[23] Cincinnati *Daily Gazette,* August 18, 1841. See also Poage, *op. cit.,* 70.
[24] *Ibid.,* August 21, 1841.

uniformly proclaimed to be against the exercise of any such power by this Government."

Strong objection was made to that clause in the bill which provided that the consent of any State to the location of a branch within its limits should be assumed if its legislature at its first meeting after the passage of this law should not expressly declare against the establishment of a branch. He pointed out that in many of the States elections for the legislature had already been held without any knowledge on the part of the people that such a question would be considered. The representatives in such States might wish to submit the question to their constituents before taking such action. This could not be permitted under the act. Moreover, if the popular branch of a State legislature should vote overwhelmingly against the location of a branch and the Senate should fail to concur in that action, such nonaction on the part of the legislature would, under the provisions of the bill, be accepted as the assent of the State to the location of a branch or branches within its limits. Or if both houses should vote against the establishment of a branch, and the governor should veto the bill, the legislature would still be considered as having given its assent. "I must, therefore, regard this clause as asserting the power to be in Congress to establish offices of discount in a State not only without its assent, but against its dissent, and so regarding it I cannot sanction it." [25]

At the close of the reading there was slight applause from the gentlemen's gallery by the striking of the floor with canes. This was followed by one or two faint hisses. Several Senators arose at once loudly demanding that the galleries be cleared. Senator Benton was very much excited over the hisses from the gallery, which, he declared, were an insult to the Senate and President of the United States offered by bank ruffians. He moved that the offender be arrested and brought to the bar of the Senate. Several Senators tried to persuade him to withdraw his motion, among them Rives and Buchanan.

[25] Richardson, *Messages,* IV, 63-68.

Rives contended that Tyler would be the last person to resent
this criticism as he was in favor of allowing every American
citizen the amplest liberty of opinion and speech. Besides, the
hissing had probably come in a moment of excitement. At
Benton's insistence a man was arrested and taken into custody. He admitted his offense and expressed deep regret for
it. Benton thereupon moved that he be discharged from
custody and this was accepted by general consent.[26]

The Democrats were as jubilant as the Whigs were despondent over the veto. On the evening after the veto message was sent, a number of Democratic Senators went to the
White House to congratulate the President upon his "patriotic and courageous" action, and "the congratulations gradually degenerated into convivial hilarity." A few days later
Clay in a speech in the Senate ridiculed this meeting in most
clever fashion. "He recited the speeches he supposed to have
been delivered on that occasion by Democratic Senators
to the Whig President, imitating the style of the different
orators, especially Calhoun, Benton, and Buchanan, in so
striking and artistic a way as to win the involuntary applause even of some of the victims." [27]

A very different exhibition of feeling regarding the veto
was staged that same night. A mob of about thirty persons
got together, and after toning up their courage at a tippling
house with bad brandy, proceeded to the Presidential mansion. It was after midnight (about two o'clock in the morning, according to one account) when they appeared at the
White House with blunderbusses, drums, and trumpets.
They raised noisy shouts of "Huzza for Clay!" "A Bank!
A Bank! Down with the Veto!" which were followed by
the loud braying of the trumpets. The ladies of the mansion
were frightened by such an unusual spectacle. To Mrs. Tyler, who had been confined to her chamber for two years by

[26] *Niles,* LX, 393–394; *Madisonian,* Aug. 16, 19, 1841.
[27] Carl Schurz, *Henry Clay,* II, 207; Benton, *Thirty Years' View,* II, 328–
330.

a paralytic stroke, the experience must have been a most trying one. When a light appeared in one of the rooms a panic seized the crowd and it hastily departed. Next night the President was burnt in effigy near the White House.[28]

At the call of Mayor W. W. Seaton, a large number of the citizens of Washington met in front of the city hall to protest against the effort "made by a few worthless individuals" to insult the President and his family. Resolutions were adopted which strongly condemned the conduct of the mob and expressed respect for Tyler both as President and as a man. It was pointed out with appreciation that for many years as a Congressman he had "manifested the greatest zeal in the promotion of the best interests of the District of Columbia and the city of Washington." When these resolutions were presented to Tyler he responded to them in a sensible, conciliatory speech in which he said that he did not regard the act of the mob in a very serious light.[29]

This insult to the President doubtless called to his attention that historic occasion when a French mob assailed the ears of their king with the cry, "Down with Monsieur Veto!" In referring to the incident in a conversation with President Buchanan twenty years later, he indicated that he regarded it as a serious affair (page 447). At the time, however, he acted as if he were not in the least perturbed by it. When the rowdies who had participated in this disgraceful performance were brought up for trial, the prosecuting attorney read before the court a letter from the President asking for a *nolle prosequi* in the case. In this letter Tyler excused the rioters on the ground that the demonstration "was one of those outbreaks of popular feeling incident, in some degree, to our form of government, and entirely evanescent and harmless in character." On the basis of this request, the prosecuting attorney asked for a *nolle prosequi*, which was granted. Thereupon the counsel for the offenders

[28] *Madisonian,* August 19, 1841.
[29] *National Intelligencer,* Aug. 20, 23, 1841.

rose and expressed the deep regret of his clients for their action and their sense of the President's magnanimity in authorizing, in so graceful a manner, the abandonment of the prosecution.[30]

As was to be expected, the action of Tyler in vetoing the bank bill aroused a storm of opposition among Whig leaders. According to the *Madisonian*, the Northern Whig press had received the veto with decided expressions of dissatisfaction,[31] while the tone of the Democratic press was that of exultation. The Whig papers were, many of them, very violent in their denunciation of the veto, and continued "to pour out vials of wrath upon the head of Mr. Tyler." "The vocabulary of the language seems to have been ransacked for words to express their angry denunciation." [32]

The *National Intelligencer*, the leading Whig organ of Washington, while regretting the action of the President, was more mild and reasonable than were these other critics. It contended that the popular suffrage in 1840 had indicated a desire for a national bank as clearly as it had for the repeal of the Subtreasury or any of the other Whig measures. The writer admitted that Tyler had in both branches of Congress spoken and voted against a bank as unconstitutional, but it was hoped that the President would make a distinction "between the legislative and the executive character, which would allow of his signing an act in one capacity which he would vote against in the other." The *Intelligencer* felt, however, that the President had vetoed the bill for reasons which it was bound to respect. It was, therefore, in favor of going ahead with the rest of the Whig program and of making another effort at the bank. The fact that this editorial was either written or inspired by Tyler's Secretary of State may account for its mildness.[33]

---

[30] *Madisonian*, Nov. 25, 1841; Richmond *Enquirer*, Nov. 26, 1841.
[31] *Niles*, LX, 392.   [32] *Madisonian*, Aug. 25, 1841.
[33] The proof of this last statement is to be found in the fact that in the *Webster Papers* there is one in Webster's handwriting on which this edi-

The Baltimore *American,* while regretting the veto, took the sensible position of not questioning the honesty of the President. It advised against giving way to feeling and urged co-operation between Congress and the executive on other points of the Whig program. The New York *American* (August 17) was rather bitter in its disappointment. It declared that Tyler had violated his oath to support the Constitution in that he had ignored a decision of the Supreme Court declaring a national bank constitutional.

Some of the Democratic papers were as extravagant in their endorsement of the veto as their Whig contemporaries were in its condemnation. The Washington *Globe* (the leading Democratic paper of Washington) considered (August 16) that the veto had killed the bank for this Presidential term, and rejoiced over the fact. It lauded Tyler for his independence.[34]

It is needless to say that Jackson was greatly pleased with the action of Tyler. One of his friends in Washington hastened to congratulate him on the veto. The Democrats, he said, regarded the President's action as "a plain, straightforward, rejection of the Bill—a *real* veto." An old-time Democrat was quoted as saying, "Egad, he had found one of old Jackson's pens and it wouldn't write anyway but plain and straightforward." [35]

The advocates of the bank bill contended that inasmuch as the Supreme Court had repeatedly asserted the right of Congress to establish a national bank, the constitutionality of the question was no longer open to dispute. In answer to this contention Cushing presented the following argument:

---

torial is based. *The Writings and Speeches of Daniel Webster* (Nat. Ed.), XV, 135–136; *National Intelligencer,* August 17, 1841.

[34] For the reaction of the press toward the veto, see *Niles' Register,* LX, 390–392.

The veto did not affect the stock or money market in Wall Street. *National Intelligencer,* Aug. 19, 1841.

[35] D. S. Carr to Jackson, Aug. 18, 1841; *Jackson MSS.* (L.C.).

The Supreme Court has only decided that if the Federal legislature considers any particular fiscal agent or bank necessary and proper as a means for the execution of any of the powers granted to Congress, then it has authority to create such an institution. But the obligation of deciding whether any proposed measure is necessary or proper is imposed upon the legislative branch of the government. In determining this fact, the House, the Senate, and the President all have a responsibility. Each in acting has to follow the dictates of an enlightened conscience. The President, acting in his legislative capacity, is charged with this responsibility and cannot divest himself of it on the ground that it has already been passed upon.[36]

The attempt to pass the bill over the President's veto was made in the Senate on August 19. There was not the slightest possibility of overriding the veto and all the discussion on the bill was entirely for political effect. And yet Clay felt it worth his while to talk for an hour and a half on this dead measure, as it afforded him the opportunity of publicly arraigning his former personal and political friend. The bill was defeated by a vote of 25 yeas to 24 nays.[37]

Clay's lengthy harangue was a severe excoriation of the President. While he referred to Tyler as "the distinguished citizen, long my personal friend," there was nothing in the address except a few empty protestations to indicate that this friendship still subsisted. Clay contended that the President in his address to the people of the United States (April 10) had indicated his acceptance of the constitutionality of a national bank.

In promising to be guided in constitutional interpretation by the "fathers of the great republican school," the President was, as Clay maintained, in effect declaring his adherence to the later view of Madison, according to which the right of Congress to establish a national bank was no

[36] Cushing's "Address," *Niles*, LXI, 109.
[37] *Cong. Globe*, 27th Cong., 1st sess., 352.

longer open to question. "It was," he said, "by every man with whom I conversed on the subject at the time of its appearance, or of whom I have since inquired, construed to mean that the President intended to occupy the Madison ground and to regard the question of the power to establish a national bank as immovably settled; [and I think] that this was the contemporaneous and unanimous judgment of the public."

It is difficult to believe that Clay was sincere in this part of his speech. That Tyler in referring to the policies of "the fathers of the great republican school" had in mind Madison's early opposition to the First Bank of the United States rather than his support of the Second Bank is the only assumption that could be made in the light of his whole previous record. The fact that Tyler had voted against a recharter of the bank that Madison had favored was sufficient proof that he was referring to the early particularism of Jefferson and Madison rather than to their later nationalism.

Despite the objections of the President to the measure, so ran Clay's argument, he should have yielded to the views of a majority of Congress and the opinion (unanimous, so Clay heard) of his Cabinet. This position was especially untenable. In the first place, the narrowness of the majority by which the bill had passed the Senate showed that there was no overwhelming sentiment in that body for the measure. But even if the majorities in both houses had been large, the President was not bound to yield to the wishes of Congress. For to concede such a power to the legislature would be to deny the validity of that clause in the Constitution which confers veto power on the President.

Clay's reference to the views of the Cabinet was particularly unhappy. There is nothing in the Constitution or the traditional practice of the country which obligates a President to accept the views of his Cabinet. Both in theory and in practice the Cabinet is purely an advisory body. Moreover, Cabinet meetings were and are secret, and knowledge of the official position of this body on any public question could be obtained only in the case of an accidental "leak" or a grave indiscretion on the part of one or more of its members. Therefore, in announcing information as to the sentiments of the President's advisers the Kentucky Senator was either reflecting upon the honor or loyalty of one or more of them, or else was advertising his own meddling curiosity.

Clay went on to show that if it had been known at the Harrisburg Convention that Harrison would die in a month and Tyler would veto a bank bill passed by a Whig majority, Tyler would not have received a single vote at Harrisburg nor a single electoral vote in the election. It is doubtless true that if such foreknowledge had been available Tyler would not have been nominated at Harrisburg or elected at the polls. But it is also true that if the program which Clay was now urging before Congress had been published as the platform of the Whig Party in the campaign of 1840, the log cabin would not have triumphed over the palace.

At one place in his speech, Clay went so far as to say that if Tyler could not sign the bill he should have allowed it to become a law without his signature or have resigned, as he had done when as Senator he could not conform to the wishes of Virginia on the expunging resolution. He overlooked the important fact that Tyler had never, even in the days of his rampant particularism, claimed for Congress the same power over the President that a State legislature has over a United States Senator of its own choice. Nor did it seem to trouble Clay that in thus suggesting such subordination of the executive to the legislative branch of the government he was committing an act of the gravest inconsistency. For he was one of the advisers of Tyler who had strongly urged him to disregard the instructions of the Virginia Assembly and retain his seat in the Senate.

The general tone and character of this speech was not up

to the standard that one had a right to expect of Kentucky's most brilliant orator. This unnecessary philippic against a quondam friend did not add anything to the reputation of the "Great Pacificator." It was marred in spirit by a strain of personal rancor which added little or nothing to its effectiveness. To hazard "an intimate personal friendship of twenty years' standing" at the behest of conviction is to exhibit a sacrificial patriotism worthy of a Titus Manlius. Unfortunately, however, one has the feeling that this attack on Tyler was made more in the spirit of anger than in sorrow, and was motivated by politics rather than patriotism. There are little thrusts here and there that smack of petty spite. It was in this speech that first appeared the expression, "corporal's guard," as applied to the few supporters of Tyler in Congress.[38]

Other Whig leaders were as violent as Clay in their criticism of the President. He was accused of having violated pledges made in the campaign and in so doing of having been guilty of party perfidy. The most blatant of all these critics was John Minor Botts. This *advocatus diabolus* of the Tyler administration made a speech in the House of Representatives (September 10, 1841), in which he elaborated at great length this accusation against his former friend.[39]

Tyler's motives were seriously questioned by his critics. It was charged that he wanted to succeed himself, and felt that by vetoing the bank bill he would hold the States' rights Whigs in line and attract to himself those Democrats who believed in States' rights. Indeed, advice to this effect was given him by Edmund Ruffin, a strong States' rights leader. That Tyler wished to succeed himself goes without saying.

[38] Clay's attack on the President on this occasion was made in two speeches, the second being a reply to Rives, who had answered his first address by a defense of the President. For these speeches see C. Colton, ed., *The Works of Henry Clay* (Fed. Ed., G. P. Putnam's Sons), II, 358–374.
[39] *Cong. Globe*, 27th Cong., 1st sess., App., 385–389.

But the charge that he was actuated primarily by this motive in antagonizing Clay has little or no evidence to support it except the accusations of strongly biased enemies.

The most natural explanation of his action is that he was obeying the dictates of a States' rights conscience. That he still held to these views after his elevation to the Presidency is evidenced by a statement which he made to Edmund Ruffin June 28, before the bank act was passed. He told Ruffin that he proposed to maintain the States' rights principles, even if he had to stand alone.[40] He had also indicated to Duff Green, in a letter written before his accession to the Presidency, that he would oppose any bill for chartering an old-fashioned bank.[41]

[40] *Farmer's Register,* IX, 253; Ruffin's MS. Diary (L.C.), Nov. 14, 1857; *Tyler's Quarterly,* XXII, 85-86.
[41] Duff Green to Tyler, Paris, Apr. 28, 1842; *Duff Green Papers* in possession of Professor Fletcher M. Green, Chapel Hill, N. C.

CHAPTER XVI

POLITICAL OSTRACISM

THE veto of the first bank bill by the President had
greatly accentuated the split that had been gradually
developing in the Whig ranks. Whether this breach would
be healed or widened into a permanent division of the party
would depend upon the concessions which each side would
be willing to make in the interest of conciliation.

It is quite doubtful as to whether Clay and the Whig
leaders who were aligned with him really wanted to bridge
the chasm that had opened between themselves and the
President. There is strong ground for suspecting that they
welcomed a quarrel that would eliminate Tyler and his
premier as possible Whig nominees for the succession and
leave the field clear to the popular Kentuckian.[1] It was
thought that Tyler would be a candidate for a second term,
and this fear was confirmed by a report made by Botts of
an alleged conversation held between him and the President
early in the extra session. According to Botts, Tyler was
looking forward to a twelve-year period in office.[2]

While we cannot accept as established fact the unsup-

[1] On July 2, 1842, J. J. Crittenden, one of Clay's closest friends, wrote to
Clay as follows: "If we can only keep up the feeling that now exists, your
election will be certain. Tyler is one of your *best friends*. His last Veto has
served us all well." *The Papers of John Jordan Crittenden* (L.C.), VIII, 1495–
97.

[2] *Niles' Register,* LXIV, 215.
Botts's account of this interview presents Tyler in a very different light
from that in which he appears in his public utterances and his private correspondence. In Botts's account Tyler is represented as making a frequent
and rather awkward use of profanity and cutting a sorry figure. This por-
trayal is so unlike that of other contemporary descriptions that the fairminded
student is warranted in doubting its accuracy. He has a right to suspect that
the incident has not only been highly colored but also misstated.

ported statement of Tyler's bitterest enemy, yet it was doubtless believed at the time by Clay and his followers. Furthermore, there is reason to think that the President at this early date aspired to the Whig nomination in 1844, as he had every right to do. Nor is there any doubt that Clay had fully decided to enter the race and was resolved not to be thrown off the track by an accidental President.

Tyler's friends contended that the intention of breaking with the President on the part of the Whig majority in Congress antedated the bank issue. George H. Proffit, a Representative from Indiana, who was a member of the "Corporal's Guard," said that "from the first meeting of Congress up to this hour, there has been a determination on the part of some gentlemen to create an issue with the President." [3] Color is lent to this supposition by the fact that the bank Whigs showed dissatisfaction with Tyler almost from the beginning. As early as July 4 Clay expressed the fear that Tyler's heresies would endanger the existence of the Whig Party. [4] This suspicion of the President on the part of Clay's followers was sensed by Tyler and his friends. One of the latter, Representative Gilmer from Virginia, said in the House (July 27) that both he and the President had been proscribed by the Whigs. [5]

But whatever may have been their real purposes, the Whig leaders must *appear* willing to approach Tyler in the spirit of compromise. Good politics demanded that the blame for the failure of the bank measure should be laid at the door of the President. Accordingly, an effort was at once made to adjust the differences between the President and Congress. A. H. H. Stuart, a Whig Representative from Virginia, was induced to see the President with the view to coming to an understanding with him. Tyler received him

---

[3] *Niles,* LXI, 93.
[4] Calvin Colton, ed., *Private Correspondence of Henry Clay,* 454; quoted by H. von Holst, *Constitutional History of the United States* (Chicago, 1888–92), II, 423.
[5] Adams, *Memoirs,* X, 515.

cordially and indicated that a plan of compromise might be agreed upon. An amendment to the bank bill had been proposed (July 3) by Senator Bayard, and Stuart now offered this amendment with the clause stricken out which authorized the bank to change the agencies in the States into offices of discount and deposit. After two other changes had been made,[6] Tyler accepted the plan and asked Stuart to go to Webster and have him prepare a bill in accordance with the agreement. "As I rose to leave him," said Stuart, "after cautioning me not to expose him to the charge of dictating to Congress, he held my right hand in his left, and raising his right hand upwards, exclaimed with much feeling: 'Stuart! if you can be instrumental in passing this bill through Congress, I will esteem you the best friend I have on earth.' " [7]

It was at this point, however, that Tyler made a serious error in tactics. By showing on this occasion such enthusiasm for a bank and by stating two days later in Cabinet meeting that a bank bill could be passed in forty-eight hours, he supplied his enemies with ammunition which they were not slow in using against him. It gave them the excuse for railroading the second bill through Congress on the ground that the President wanted quick action. And as the President's enthusiasm for a national bank soon afterwards began to wane it afforded a seeming basis for the charge that either the President did not know his own mind or else his statement to Stuart was an attempt at deception.

After his interview with Tyler Stuart drove to Webster's residence, but not finding him at home returned to his boardinghouse. That evening he reported the results of his conference with the President to the joint committee, made up of eminent Whigs from both houses of Congress, "whose business it was to fix up measures for the action of the whole

---

[6] For the text of the Bayard Amendment, with the modifications suggested by Tyler, see Appendix A.

[7] For Stuart's statement see Benton, *Thirty Years' View*, II, 344.

party in Congress." At the close of an excited debate the committee decided to recommend that the Whigs in Congress accede to the President's views. This recommendation was afterwards accepted by the Whig caucus. John Sergeant, of the House, and J. M. Berrien, of the Senate, were selected to frame a bill on the basis of the Ewing proposal or some other plan that would be acceptable to the President. They were to seek an interview with Tyler, if necessary, to make certain that there was no misunderstanding of his opinions. Clay was scheduled to deliver on the seventeenth his speech against the first veto. As it was anticipated that his comments might antagonize Tyler and make him less amenable to compromise, it was decided, in agreement with Clay, that the latter's speech would not be made until the nineteenth.[8]

These efforts at compromise would indicate that the Whigs were really desirous of meeting the President's wishes and of arriving at harmony in the party. That such was the sincere intention of a number of Whigs there can be no reasonable doubt. On the other hand, the continuous hounding of the President by the Whig press, the terrible philippic pronounced against him by Clay, and the other abusive attacks on him made in both houses of Congress, culminating in the insulting Coffeehouse Letter of the boorish Botts (pages 232, 266), tend to show that the dominant leaders were trying to widen rather than close the breach in the party. There is some evidence in support of the charge that they had decided to offer a second bank bill of such a character as to embarrass the President and cause the resignation of his Cabinet.[9]

[8] Stuart's Statement; Benton, *op. cit.*, II, 347.
Senator W. C. Dawson, on Berrien's invitation, also went along, and was present when the conference was held with the President.
[9] On the day of the veto (August 16) the President received a letter from a gentleman of the "strictest veracity," who had received his information from two members of the House of Representatives (William Russell, of Ohio, and John Taliaferro, of Virginia). The contents of this letter were, in part, as follows: "The [Whig] caucus last evening, after much disagreement, came

Sergeant and Berrien had two conferences with the President [10] for the purpose of coming to an understanding with him on the bank question. Following the precedent of Madison, Tyler declined to discuss with them the details of any suggested plan, but "expressed himself in favor of a fiscal agency divested of the discounting power, and limited to dealing in bills of exchange. . . . He declared his determination to confer with his Cabinet as to whether the assent of the States ought to be required in the establishment of the agencies to be employed by the corporation. . . ." [11]

Tyler met his Cabinet on the morning of the eighteenth, soon after his second conference with Berrien and Sergeant. For an account of this Cabinet meeting and some other events in the bank controversy we are indebted to the Diary of Secretary Ewing and to a *Memorandum* drawn up by Webster (probably about that time) and written out in his own hand. This paper, which has never been published, has recently been acquired by the Library of Congress. Webster's account is, in part, as follows:

"We understood that Mr. Sergeant would introduce the Bill into the House. He [the President] then requested Mr. Ewing and myself to see Mr. Berrien and Mr. Sergeant, and, not committing or pledging him, nor professing to speak by his authority, nevertheless to state what changes, from the last Bill, would in our opinion, lead him to sign the new Bill; and he pointed out those changes. They were, in effect, to make a Bank of issues, deposit, and exchanges; without power of discounting promissory notes. And for

___

to the resolution to pass a Bank bill on Mr. Ewing's plan. The object seems to be your destruction and dissolution of the cabinet. They say that you and the cabinet stand pledged to support that scheme and that you cannot now assent to it; ergo, a veto of that would place you fully in the arms of the Locos [Democrats], and your cabinet would abandon you. This is the calculation." Tyler, *Letters and Times,* II, 81, note.

[10] One of these conferences was held on the morning of the seventeenth and the other on the morning of the eighteenth. Autograph *Memorandum* by Webster, Library of Congress; "Ewing's Diary," *Amer. Histor. Review,* XVIII, 99–100.

[11] Statement made by Senator Berrien; *Niles,* LXII, 245.

such a Bank he did not intimate that he requested the assent of the States.[12]

"I took a carriage and came immediately to the Capitol and saw Messrs B[errien] and S[ergeant]; suggested to them the provisions and modifications which I supposed would ensure the President's signature; [illegible] and appointed an hour for them to meet Mr. Ewing in the afternoon.

"It is proper to say here, that while these endeavors [were being made] to have the Bill altered to his mind, the President frequently expressed an earnest wish that the subject might be laid over till the next session."

That same afternoon Ewing and Sergeant were received by Berrien at his lodging and the details of a measure were then and there agreed upon in conformity with the views of the President as reported by Webster and repeated by Ewing. From the sketch thus outlined Sergeant prepared the bill that he afterwards introduced into the House of Representatives.[13] This measure was known as the Fiscal Corporation Bill.

Sergeant offered his bill in the House on Friday, August 20,[14] and next day a printed copy of it was placed on the desk of each member. Ten minutes later Sergeant offered a resolution providing that the debate on the bill in the committee of the whole be closed not later than four o'clock that same afternoon. Roosevelt, of New York, moved as an amendment to this proposition, that all debate be stopped at once, as the short period allowed was equivalent to cutting off debate entirely. Sergeant, shamed by this derisive

---

[12] Ewing understood the President as being willing to accept a bank with agencies in the several States having power to receive and disburse the public moneys and to deal in bills of exchange. These agencies were to be established without the consent of the States. "Ewing's Diary," *Amer. Histor. Review*, XVIII, 101.

[13] Statement by Senator Berrien (September, 1842) ; *Niles, loc. cit.*, 245.

[14] For the text of this bill, see *National Intelligencer*, Aug. 24, 1841.

criticism, changed his resolution so as to extend the time of discussion from Saturday to Monday afternoon. Several Democratic members asked to be excused from voting on the ground that they had had no opportunity to examine the bill. Their requests were refused, and the resolution was passed.[15]

On Monday, August 23, the bill was debated in the committee of the whole, each speech being limited to one hour's length. Promptly at four o'clock the bill was reported to the House by the committee of the whole and later the same day was passed without further debate. The final vote was 125 yeas to 94 nays.[16] The House bill was reported to the Senate the following day and was promptly referred to a select committee appointed by the president of the Senate.

Berrien, as chairman of the select committee, reported the House bill to the Senate without amendment (Monday, August 30). It was taken up by the committee of the whole on Wednesday, September 1. Berrien spoke for more than two hours in favor of the new bill, saying that it would be accepted by the President. The measure was opposed by Rives and the leading Democratic Senators, such as Tappan, Benton, and Buchanan. The provision for bills of exchange, they maintained, would permit the discounting of promissory notes, a power which the President was unwilling to grant to a national bank without the assent of the States. Senator Tappan declared that it was a very common practice in the western country to make loans and discounts in the form of exchanges. Most of the western States used this method rather than that of direct discounting.

Clay supported the bill though it did not go as far as he desired. He regarded it as of some value, however, as it provided for the regulation of the exchanges of the country and the supply of a currency having uniform value through-

[15] Cong. Globe, 27th Cong., 1st sess., 366–368.
[16] Ibid., 370–372; Benton, op. cit., II, 337.

out the nation. After several amendments, proposed by Democratic leaders, had been voted down, the bill passed the Senate (September 3) by a vote of 27 yeas to 22 nays.[17]

While the bank bill was resting in committee, there occurred an incident which served as a strange but pleasant interlude in the tense situation that had developed between Tyler and Clay. The occasion for this episode was a supper given at the home of Attorney General Crittenden, which was a "promiscuous party of Whigs of all shades." The President had been invited but had declined. Late in the evening, probably after inhibitions had begun to melt away under the influence of champagne and madeira, it was decided to send a deputation to the White House to constrain its occupant to join the hilarious group. The Executive Mansion had been closed for the night, but they went in and took the President by storm to the party. On arriving at the house of the Attorney General, Tyler was met at the door by Clay, who greeted him with, "Well, Mr. President, what are you for, Kentucky whisky or champagne?" "He chose champagne, and entered into the spirit of this frolicsome agony as if it was congenial to his own temper." Clay is said to have quoted to the President those lines from Shakespeare's Richard III which speak of the dangers and inconveniences of conscience.[18]

Although Tyler had decided at once to veto the second bank bill,[19] he kept it for six days before returning it with his objections. On September 9 he sent his veto message to the House of Representatives. The general tone of the message indicated that he was very reluctant to withhold his assent from this measure. In thus dashing the hopes of the bank Whigs for a second time he was, he declared, acting from an

17 *Cong. Globe, loc. cit.*, 418-419.
18 Adams, *Memoirs*, X, 544-545; N. Y. *Herald*, Sept. 11, 1841.
19 "Ewing's Diary," *Amer. Histor. Review*, XVIII, 109.

imperative sense of "constitutional duty." He was willing
to go as far as his principles would admit in the direction of
conciliation and it was with great pain that he felt "compelled to differ from Congress a second time in the same
session."

But the bill was, in his opinion, clearly unconstitutional.
It provided for the creation of a corporation by Congress
acting as the national legislature and not as the legislature
of the District of Columbia. The corporation so established
would operate "per se over the Union by virtue of the un-
aided and assumed authority of Congress as a national
legislature, as distinguishable from a bank created by Congress for the District of Columbia as the local legislature
of the District."

The provision for dealing in exchange was also objected
to. It would permit the bank "to deal in bills of exchange
drawn in one State and payable in another without any restraint. The bill of exchange may have an unlimited time to
run, and its renewability is nowhere guarded against. It may,
in fact, assume the most objectionable form of accommodation paper." Under the proposed charter the bank could
"indulge in mere local discounts under the name of bills of
exchange" and could engage in "a system of discounts of the
most objectionable character."

It was at this point that Tyler's case was strongest. He
had all along been opposed to establishing in the States,
without their assent, branches of a national bank that would
engage in a discount business. This idea was behind his
support of the Ewing bill and his opposition to the first
bank bill. The objectional practice, he contended (and
with strong reason), would be permitted under this measure, though it would masquerade under the title of dealing
in exchange. The President could have strengthened his
position considerably if he had elaborated his argument on
this point more clearly and fully.

There is nothing in the phraseology or general tone of

this message to indicate that Tyler was throwing down the gauntlet to his party. On the contrary, it urged Congress in a spirit of anxious entreaty not to push to extremes its differences with the executive. The hope was expressed that Congress, satisfied with the immense amount of work already performed, would take no further action on the bank question until the executive and Congress could come to an agreement on financial policy. The President pointed out the fact that the shortness of the time intervening between his installation and the meeting of Congress had precluded his offering a financial plan at this special session. He intimated, however, that at the opening of the regular session he would have a proposal to offer.[20]

This message was not a long one and was not as well written as were most of Tyler's state papers. The style is rather commonplace, and is not characterized by that clear simplicity which the handling of a bitterly controversial subject demanded. The phrase "bill of exchange" is difficult for a layman to understand. Therefore, the attempt to show the identity of the practice of issuing discounts with that of dealing in exchange (as provided for by the bill) should have been supported by a line of reasoning so clear as to be understood by anyone of average intelligence. Such an elucidation of the President's position was probably excluded by the limitations of space imposed upon the message. But in the light of subsequent developments, the President should not have been held within these bounds, even if breaking over had been an offense against convention and good taste. For the shortcomings of the message, Wise must bear a considerable share of the blame, as he claims the honor of having written it.[21]

The Whigs in Congress could not have been surprised at

[20] For the text of this message see Richardson, *Messages,* IV, 68–72.

[21] Wise says that this second veto message was prepared by a friend of the President, who accepted it with slight modifications. He does not say who this friend was, but intimates strongly that it was himself. Wise, *Seven Decades of the Union,* 190.

the President's veto, even though they were sorely disappointed. For whatever may have been the original understanding between Tyler's representatives (Ewing and Webster) and the emissaries of the Whig caucus (Sergeant and Berrien), it had become clear before the bill had gone through the House that the President had either been all along opposed to such a measure or else had changed his mind. The fact that Wise, Proffit, and Gilmer, his spokesmen in the House, and Rives, his only Whig supporter in the Senate, were fighting the bill so strenuously should have been notice enough of his opposition to it. Besides, Tyler sent messages to members of Congress through Wise, Webster, and other friends clearly stating his disapproval of the measure.[22]

[22] According to a statement made to Webster by two Representatives from New York, Tyler had on the morning of August 23 declared to these Congressmen that he would suffer both of his arms to be cut off before he would sign the bill then pending in the House of Representatives. On that same day and the next the President was "agitated and excited and wished me [Webster] to get the Whigs to put off the measure. I told him I could not ask one or two members to join their opponents in postponing the measure, but if he wished me, as a member of his Cabinet, to make the suggestion to the Whigs generally, I would do so. Accordingly I spoke to such Whig members of the Senate as I saw, and on the 25th addressed" a letter to Messrs. Bates and Choate, Senators from Massachusetts, representing the President as having regretted that a second bill was in progress. See *Niles*, LXI, 54–55; Webster's *Memorandum*.

If Wise's account (written from memory a third of a century after the event) can be accepted, Sergeant, on the day before the measure was offered in the House, was told by Wise that the President did not wish to be considered as being committed to the bill; "and, if he was so understood, he desired the mistake to be corrected before it [the bill] was reported; that he could not consent to sign the bill in the form in which it was last presented to him." Wise, *op. cit.*, 189.

Tyler in his defense declared that he sent a second message to Sergeant by Williams, of Connecticut, and Gregg, of New York, the night after the bill was offered in the House, expressing anxiety to see him and stating that he could not sanction the bill he had reported, without amendments. To all members of Congress who fell in his way a similar communication was made. To some he gave an amendment which, if adopted, would have removed the constitutional difficulty. Tyler said that he thought that "some fifty members of the House were fully apprised of my objections." "I hesitate not to say that every member of the Whig party thoroughly knew that it [the second bank bill] could not receive my approval." Tyler, *op. cit.*, II, 88, 98–102.

Even some of his most bitter assailants admitted that Tyler wanted Congress

From this evidence we may safely conclude that the President had definitely decided against the bank bill some time before it was passed; and that he had notified the Whig leaders in the House of Representatives of his position as early as the night after and possibly the day before the bill was presented in the House. By going ahead with the bill, without making any changes in it, after this notice had been served, the Whig leaders seemed bent on a breach with the President and desirous of using the bank measure as a means to that end.

The conciliatory tone of the President's message did not cushion it against the blows that were hurled against it. As was expected, the second veto let loose a hurricane of hostile criticism. On the day after the veto message was received in the House, Botts pronounced a severe philippic of one hour on the President, accusing him of treachery to the Whig Party. He was answered by Mr. Gilmer in a speech of equal length. Gilmer "was not less personally severe on Botts, who resented it more in temper than in words." [23] An effort to pass the bank bill over the President's veto failed.

These vetoes ended the attempt to establish a national bank. No further effort to ally the banking business with the Federal government was made for a score of years. By this exercise of his veto power the President performed a real service to his country, and despite the loud cries of disappointed politicians, the country seems to have sustained him in this action. If the bill had been accepted by him it is quite likely that the bank would not have been successfully launched. The opposition of the Democrats and their determination (openly declared in Congress) to agitate in favor of a repeal of the charter would doubtless have fright-

---

to postpone action on the bill. Ewing in a letter to Crittenden December 6, 1842, said that Tyler desired the postponement of the measure, and that he [Ewing] had interviewed Congressmen in the attempt to influence them in favor of delay.

[23] Adams, *Memoirs*, XI, 12.

ened away subscribers and prevented the sale of an adequate amount of stock.

Nor was there at the time any strong popular demand for such a financial institution. The victory of the Whigs in 1840 could not be construed as a mandate from the people to establish a national bank. The election of that year was not a plebiscite for or against such an institution, as the bank was not a clear-cut issue in the campaign. When it is remembered, moreover, that the Whigs had received only a narrow majority of the popular vote and that a considerable number of Whigs were in agreement with the Democrats in opposing a national bank, it would seem that at the accession of Tyler a majority of the people of the country were indifferent or opposed to a national bank. So little interest was manifested in it that the Whigs did not mention it in their platform of 1844. In the previous year, Webster who had been one of the most ardent champions of a national bank, referred to the bank question as if it were an issue of ancient history. "Who cares," said he, "anything now about the bank bills which were vetoed in 1841? Or who thinks now that, if there were no such thing as a veto in the world, a Bank of the United States, upon the old models, could be established?" [24]

On September 13 (the day Congress adjourned) some fifty or more of the ultra Whig members of Congress held a caucus on Capitol Square and issued an address to the people of the United States. In this pronouncement they repudiated Tyler and all his works, declaring that the alliance between the President and the Whigs was at an end. [25]

[24] This statement is found in one of Webster's private papers of the year 1843. See *The Writings and Speeches of Daniel Webster* (Nat. Ed.), XV, 187.

[25] *National Intelligencer*, Sept. 16, 1841; *Niles*, LXI, 35–36; G. T. Curtis, *Life of Daniel Webster*, II, 207–209; [J. P. Kennedy], *Defence of the Whigs* (N. Y., 1844), 122–124.

The Whig caucus met on Saturday, September 11, and appointed a committee of eight to draw up resolutions. The caucus met again on Monday and unanimously adopted the report of the committee, which was written by the

His expulsion from his party was now formal and complete. Henceforth he was a President without a party.

The cue given by the politicians in Congress was taken up by the Whig press, which throughout the country joined in the chorus of vituperation. Webster also came in for a due share of abuse for remaining in the Cabinet.[26] This attack by the Whig newspapers had begun even before the second veto, as a veto was expected. The New York *Herald* listed seven important Whig papers which were preparing to denounce the President, and had begun before the veto was sent in.[27] The *Lexington* (Ky.) *Intelligencer,* Clay's special organ, was quoted as saying: "If a God-directed thunderbolt were to strike and annihilate the traitor, all would say that 'Heaven is just.' " [28] Among the very bitterest of all his newspaper antagonists were the New York *Courier and Enquirer* and the Richmond *Whig.*[29] The attacks of the latter must have been especially galling to Tyler, for this paper was published at the capital of his own State. Imagine his chagrin when he read an editoral like the following, penned by John H. Pleasants, the retiring editor of the *Whig:* "I knew Mr. Tyler well, personally, and had known him long, and I could not believe, that a man so commonplace, so absolutely inferior to many fifteen shilling lawyers, with whom you may meet at every county court in Virginia, would seriously aspire to the first station among man-

---

novelist-politician, John P. Kennedy. Webster thought that some of the Whigs who were present did not approve of the proceedings. Kennedy, on the other hand, maintained that the meeting was attended by from sixty to eighty Whig Congressmen, being nearly all who were in Washington at the time. With few exceptions, he continued, the Manifesto issued by the caucus had received the approbation of every Whig member of the Twenty-seventh Congress.

[26] *The Writings and Speeches of Daniel Webster* (National Edition), XVIII, 117.

[27] N. Y. *Herald,* Aug. 16, 1841.

Ewing, in his Diary, said that before the second veto was sent in the "Whig papers from all the West and S. W. today [September 5] were filled with the most bitter denunciations against the President on account of the first veto." *Amer. Histor. Review,* XVIII, 111.

[28] Quoted by the *Madisonian,* Nov. 18, 1841.

[29] The *Madisonian,* Oct. 16, 1841.

kind."[30] As late as December, 1841, the *Whig* was still showering "vulgar and infamous abuse" on the President.[31]

The New York Whigs, meeting in State convention (October 7, 1841) at Syracuse, approved the action of the Cabinet in resigning and expressed strong disapproval of Tyler's policy. The gratitude of the convention was extended to Clay, who was warmly commended.[32] Millard Fillmore said (September 23, 1841), "I have heard of but two Tyler men in this city [Buffalo] and none in the country, and I need not add that both of these are applicants for office."[33]

The storm raised by his veto of the second bank bill was probably greater than Tyler had anticipated, although he expected that his act would evoke loud criticism. Threats and adjurations, he said, were addressed to him by numerous deputations to approve the second bank bill. Hundreds of letters were received threatening Tyler with assassination. "The fires of a thousand effigies lighted the streets of the various cities." "Indignation meetings were everywhere held; . . . and a universal roar of Whig vengeance was heard in every blast."[34] Even his own people in Virginia were loud in their criticisms. Meetings were held at Richmond and Charles City Courthouse at which his veto policy was strongly condemned.[35] *Et tu, Brute!*

[30] Quoted by the *Madisonian,* Nov. 13, 1841.
[31] *John Tyler Papers* (L.C.), V, 152.
[32] *Niles' Register,* LXI, 126–127.
[33] Frank H. Severance, ed., *Millard Fillmore Papers,* 2 vols. (Buffalo, 1907), II, 225.
[34] *John Tyler Papers* (L.C.), V, 95, 101.
[35] Richmond *Daily Whig,* Aug. 31, Sept. 23, 1841.

CHAPTER XVII

PERFIDY OR PATRIOTISM

IN the short period of less than six months Tyler had enjoyed the thrill of sudden elevation to the highest station in the republic and had suffered the bitterness of defeat and disgrace. To the Whigs he was indebted for both experiences. They had hailed his accession with mild hosannas, and now they were greeting his name with loud maledictions. Surely the Tarpeian Rock is close to the Capitol. During the unhappy days of September, 1841, the truth of this old adage must have been borne in upon the discredited President.

One naturally asks, What manner of man was this incumbent of the Presidential office? What were the elements in his character that evoked such a storm of criticism? If we should accept the answers of his enemies to these questions we would conclude that an emissary of Satan had once again slipped into a place of undue prominence. On the other hand, if we base our estimate on the unbiased appraisals of Tyler's contemporaries, we come to a very different decision. Fortunately, we have a number of statements from those who knew him, and from them we can form an approximately correct opinion as to his character and personality.

He was favored with exceptional physical and intellectual attractions. He was six feet tall and rather gaunt in stature. Mrs. Anne Royall, who saw him in 1829, gave this description of him: "Senator Tyler, of Virginia, is a fine-looking man. He is very fair, with a high retreating forehead, Roman nose and features of the best Grecian model." [1]

[1] Mrs. Anne Royall, *Letters from Alabama on Various Subjects* (Washington, 1830), I, 550, note.

Once two Americans who were in Naples happened to be present when a bust of Cicero was unearthed. On seeing it both exclaimed, "President Tyler!" [2] Henry A. Wise, who knew him intimately, thought that he resembled the pictures of Charles I.[3]

The attractiveness of his personality was enhanced by the naturalness, simplicity, and cordiality of his manners, and the excellence of his conversational powers.[4] He was a wide reader and was thus in possession of a good store of the kind of information that enriches conversation. When he was in the Provisional Congress of the Confederacy the members would cluster around him at odd hours, being attracted by his interesting personality.[5] Colonel J. S. Cunningham, who knew him well, said that he "was the most charming man in conversation and the most bewitching in his hospitality, and winning in his eloquence that I have ever had the good fortune to meet." [6]

Another description of his personality, given by H. W. Hilliard, one of his ardent admirers, was as follows: "His head was fine, the forehead high and well developed, the aquiline nose and brilliant eyes giving to his expression the eagle aspect, which distinguished him at all times, and especially in conversation. His frankness imparted an indescribable charm to his manners, and the rich treasure of his cultivated mind displayed itself without effort or ostentation in the Senate Chamber, and in conversation he surpassed even Mr. Calhoun." [7]

If the last-mentioned estimates were colored by personal

---

[2] *Tyler Papers* (L.D., abbreviation for "Lion's Den," the home of Mrs. Lyon G. Tyler. The papers thus referred to were in her possession when examined).

[3] Wise, *Seven Decades of the Union,* 32.

[4] *John Tyler Papers* (L.C., abbreviation for Library of Congress), V, 143–144; Tyler, *Letters and Times,* I, 356.

[5] Eulogy by William H. Macfarland; Tyler, *Letters and Times,* II, 676.

[6] Colonel J. S. Cunningham to L. G. Tyler, December 23, 1881; Tyler, *op. cit.,* I, 544, note.

[7] H. W. Hilliard, *Politics and Pen Pictures* (Putnam's, 1892), 18–19.

or political friendship, as doubtless they were, no such reason for partiality can be found in the appraisal of the President made by Charles Dickens, who was not usually inclined to exaggerate the good qualities of Americans. Visiting the White House in March, 1842, Dickens recorded his impression of the President as follows: "He looked somewhat worn and anxious, and well he might, being at war with everybody—but the expression of his face was mild and pleasant, and his manner was remarkably unaffected, gentlemanly, and agreeable. I thought that, in his whole carriage and demeanour, he became his station singularly well." [8]

Tyler was accused by his opponents, and probably with reason, of being a vain man. C. J. Ingersoll said of him in 1842: "But vanity in him, as in Mr. Adams, supplies all other wants and sustains a tottering statesman." [9] In appraising this estimate we must remember that any opinion regarding Tyler expressed by Ingersoll at this time would be strongly colored by partisan bias. A similar impression, however, was received by Edmund Ruffin, who in later years was kindly disposed toward the ex-President. He said (in 1857), "Mr. Tyler has always been a vain man." While noting this mark of littleness, Ruffin was prompt to point out another quality which is characteristic of great men only: "And one of his great merits was the absence of envy or jealousy of superior minds, which is so often seen exhibited in men of inferior ability when raised to stations far above their capacity." [10]

If Tyler were as vain as he is represented, it was not a grievous fault, for he had more reason than most men for indulging that weakness. The rapid elevation to the highest station in the land would have caused anyone to have a high regard for his own ability.

[8] Charles Dickens, *American Notes*, 145; N. Y. *Herald*, March 12, 1842.
[9] Ingersoll to Van Buren, *Van Buren Papers*, XLIV, 10,328–29.
[10] MS. *Diary of Edmund Ruffin* (L.C.), Nov. 14, 1857.

As has already been shown, Tyler was a public speaker of no mean attainments. Although he cannot be classed with Webster and Clay, there are passages in some of his addresses that deserve to rank with the productions of these brilliant orators. The contemporary estimate of his ability as a thinker and speaker which is probably as nearly accurate as any we have is the one made by Edmund Ruffin, although he was generally inclined to underestimate Tyler's intellectual gifts and force of character. He said (in 1857) : "John Tyler's intellectual powers have been more showy than solid, or deep. He is not eminent either as an organized thinker, or strong reasoner, nor has he by industrious labor much cultivated his natural quick mental powers. But though without the higher qualities of a debater, or controversialist, he is a very ready and fluent and pleasing speaker and writer—and by his smooth and flowery language, has, with most auditors, more reputation and success than many far more able and solid reasoners who have less command of words and figures of speech." [11]

A more favorable opinion of Tyler's oratory was expressed by Jefferson Davis, who regarded him as the most felicitous among the orators he had known.[12]

Tyler had no bad habits, except that at times he indulged in mild profanity.[13] It is true that he drank wine and other alcoholic beverages and was particularly fond of champagne.[14] At the time of his death he had a valuable stock of wine in his cellar, which was sold by Mrs. Tyler in 1863 for $4,000 in Confederate money.[15] He was not, however, intemperate in his use of intoxicants. The failure of his

[11] Ibid.   [12] Tyler, Letters and Times, III, 183–184.
[13] Tyler Papers (L.D.) ; N. Y. American, Mar. 14, 1842.
[14] Tyler, Letters and Times, I, 288; II, 248; John Tyler Papers (L.C.), III, 6621, 6672.
[15] Inventory of personal property belonging to Tyler at his death. This inventory is among the Tyler Papers at "Lion's Den." In that same year Mrs. Tyler sold two horses for $800. This shows that the value of his wine was equal to that of ten horses.

enemies to accuse him of drunkenness is proof positive of his sobriety.[16]

In one particular he was a bigger man than his more illustrious contemporaries. During the period in which he was active in public life spite played a large rôle in American politics. The relations of the leading statesmen of the time —Jackson, Clay, Calhoun, Benton, Webster, and Adams— were characterized by feelings of bitter antagonism. As a rule, each of these politicians regarded his opponent as a personal as well as a political enemy. Benton and Clay were on unfriendly terms; Calhoun and Benton were usually at enmity; and Webster was at outs with Benton, Calhoun, and Jackson. The ill will which Jackson showed toward Clay and Calhoun after his break with the latter was of the most savage intensity. Adams, moreover, was a sort of Ishmael, who seemed to be against almost everyone in public life—"with malice towards all, with charity for none." [17]

John Tyler was a notable exception to this rule of hate. He had better cause for holding malice against his opponents than anyone else, for he had been attacked more fiercely than any other public man of his day. Indeed, he holds a unique place in the history of misrepresentation. The faults attributed to prominent men by malice and partisanship are generally based on some quality in their personality. Usually slander has some slight foundation in fact on which to rest. But this was not the case with John Tyler. Not only were his shortcomings exaggerated into serious faults and his

[16] Sometimes, however, he brought on a sick headache by drinking two glasses of wine. Mrs. Tyler to her mother, July (?), 1844; *Tyler Papers* (L.D.).

In his *Reminiscences,* Perley Poore (a contemporary whose statements sometimes have to be taken with a grain of salt) says that President Tyler's sideboard was abundantly supplied with wine, mint-julep (in the summer), and eggnog (in the winter), and that he dispensed these refreshments lavishly to his guests. *Perley's Reminiscences,* I, 281.

[17] Van Wyck Brooks, *The Flowering of New England* (N. Y., 1936), 25.

weaknesses into imbecilities but his very virtues were trans-
muted by slander into vices. The.calumny heaped upon him
did not incite in Tyler that lasting bitterness of feeling
which is so often induced by a defamation of character. He
refused to nurse his wrath to keep it warm, but allowed it
gradually to cool. It was doubtless due to his good disposition that he never had to resort to the code to uphold his
honor during a long political career. The ability to forgive
his enemies was also a valuable political asset and was one
of the reasons for his rapid advancement in public life.

Tyler sprang from the soil of his native Virginia. The
adjective "autochthonous" applies to him as fully as it did
to the ancient Greeks, with whom originated the idea and
the word. I know of no other American statesman who more
fully epitomized in his life the political and social ideals of
the region in which he was born and reared. If Tidewater
Virginia, in the period between the war for American independence and that for Southern independence, had wished
to see the incarnation of its own social ideals it had only to
study the life of this distinguished son. In his character were
embodied nearly all of the virtues of this fine old civilization. These virtues, though they were coupled with some
of the shortcomings, were almost entirely divorced from
the faults and vices of the age.

It was to his identification with the life of Virginia that
he owed some of the finest traits in his character. His respect
for the ideals of the generation to which his father belonged caused him to accept, as a matter of course, the
high standard of public honor practiced by the leaders of
that day. Tyler's integrity in public affairs was so deeply
ingrained that he was apparently beyond the reach of temptation. Although he was in Congress at a time when so great
a man as Webster could stoop to receive a retainer from a
corporation whose interests he promoted in the Senate,
Tyler seems never to have so much as thought of getting

money in this way. The fact that during his political career he was often in financial straits is eloquent testimony of his unimpeachable honesty.

To the opportunities afforded him from childhood by the charming social life of the Old Dominion he was largely indebted for his poise and dignity, good taste, his kindliness toward men, his gentleness and gallantry toward women, and a superb self-confidence that ruled out all feeling of inferiority. No effort had to be spent in social climbing, for in his case social position was not something to be achieved but to be taken as a matter of course. His relations with his fellows were, therefore, characterized by an unaffected naturalness and nonchalance that was in no whit marred by the snobbishness so often exhibited by those who strive for a social eminence to which they were not born.

In his personality were thus to be found to an unusual degree those traits that mark the gentleman, and no finer gentleman than John Tyler ever donned the senatorial toga or sat in the seat of the Chief Magistrate of the United States. And yet this affable Virginian, whose social graces would have been an ornament to any drawing room, was the center of the most violent storm that ever raged in American politics.

As has already been shown, the main cause of this controversy was his action with reference to the second bank bill. To determine, therefore, whether he merited the condemnation that was pronounced against him, we have to know the answers to the following questions: (1) Did President Tyler at any time endorse the second bank bill either in principle or in detail? (2) Did he change his attitude on this bill? If so, why? (3) By what motives was he actuated in vetoing this second measure (the Fiscal Corporation Bill)?

(1) The charge was made at the time and widely accepted that the bill sponsored by Sergeant was shown to

the President and approved by him before it was offered to the House. This accusation was repeated by a select committee of the House of Representatives, in a report delivered August 16, 1842. The committee was composed of ten members, with ex-President John Quincy Adams as chairman and the ubiquitous Botts as a member. The report, which was a severe arraignment of Tyler's administration, declared that the bill had been presented to the President beforehand "in the very terms which he had prescribed as necessary to obtain his sanction." [18]

From a casual glance this looks like a formidable indictment. A charge brought by an ex-President of the United States cannot be treated with short shrift as if he were an inconspicuous politician. And yet this statement would not be admitted as evidence in any court of modern justice. In the first place, it is based on hearsay testimony, and no evidence is cited to support the rumor. In the second place, it emanated from men who were bitterly hostile to the President and were doing all they could to discredit him. As Tyler pointed out, some members of the House committee had been most abusive of him for the preceding twelve months—"men of such embittered feelings," that they "would not be permitted to serve on a jury to settle a two-penny matter in regard to which" he should be a litigant.[19]

Tyler answered this accusation with a most positive denial. "I declare," he said, "under all the solemnities that can attend such a declaration, that my assent to that bill was never obtained." [20]

If this were all the evidence we have that bears on this dispute, we should have to render a verdict in favor of the defendant. For an unauthenticated rumor, even when repeated by men of eminence, is not to be weighed against the solemn declaration of a President of the United States who

[18] The text of this report is given in *Niles' Register*, LXII, 395–397.
[19] Tyler, *Letters and Times*, II, 99.　　　　[20] *Ibid.*, 98.

up to that time had always enjoyed a high reputation for truthfulness. But statements made by Ewing, Berrien, Sergeant, and Webster raise other problems that are not so easy to solve.

According to a later assertion made by Ewing, he was informed by Webster on September 5, 1841, that he (Webster) had taken a copy of the bill to the President, "who examined it, and, after an amendment of the title approved it." [21] This charge was confirmed in part by Senator Berrien, who understood from Sergeant that the latter had, before introducing his bill, sent a copy of it to Webster to be submitted by him to the President. In Sergeant's statement the correctness of Berrien's account was vouched for except that part of it which covered an interview at which he (Sergeant) was not present. This was an indirect corroboration of the assertion that Sergeant had sent a copy of the bill to Webster before it was offered in the House. On its face this looks like a strong case in favor of Ewing's accusation. And yet it is difficult to reconcile this statement, made nine months after the event, with the silence of his diary, written at the time. In his diary he speaks of an interview he held with Webster on this same fifth of September. At this meeting he discussed the grounds for Tyler's alleged commitment in favor of the second bank bill, but made no mention of the President's having seen the text of the bill. [22]

Webster made no public declaration at the time, and his reticence might be construed as giving assent to the charge. While he maintained a discreet silence toward the public, he confided to his unpublished *Memorandum,* already referred to, some statements that have a significant bearing on the controversy. ". . . the President," so ran the *Memorandum,* "wished me to get him a copy [of the Sergeant Bill], before it was introduced. I did so, went with it to him, and read [it] over with him. Attention was, of course,

[21] *Niles,* LXII, 245.   [22] *Amer. Histor. Review,* XVIII, 110–111.

most particularly drawn to the provision of the 16th
Art[icle] of the 11th section of the Bill. To this he expressed no objection whatever. He made no mention of the
necessity of State assent, to a Bank for carrying on Exchanges between the States. But he wished the title of the
Bill, and the name of the Corporation altered. Using a
phrase very common with him, that names are things, he
said he did not wish it to be called a Bank. I sat down at
his table, struck out Bank and wrote the title as it finally
passed. He wished a reduction of Capital from 30 millions
to 20, or 15—pressing the latter—and he wished the corporation to be restrained from selling the U[nited] S[tates]
Stocks, except in [illegible] or by authority of Congress.
And he suggested no other alterations whatever. I went
immediately to my lodgings on Cap[i]tol Hill, sent for
Mr. S[ergeant] to the H[ouse] of R[epresentatives], and
he came over. I showed him the prepared alterations. He
copied the title, in his own handwriting, and afterwards told
me that he reduced the Capital to 21 millions instead of 20,
for more convenience and [illegible]."

We cannot conceive of any motive that would prompt Webster to make a false record of these events in a private memorandum which he kept concealed from the public eye. But
the effort to reconcile this account with the contents of a
letter written by him on August 20, 1841, raises a problem
for which no solution can here be offered. This letter was
written to Tyler at eleven o'clock on the morning of the day
on which Sergeant offered his bill in the House of Representatives. This communication was as follows:

My dear Sir: I am promised a copy of the paper (the bill) by twelve
o'clock, or a few minutes after, and have left a messenger to bring it
immediately to me. It is uncertain whether anything will be done
today, but I understand there is a strong desire for immediate action.
The alterations which I suggested were assented to at once, so far
as the gentleman himself was concerned to whom the suggestions were
made. I have done or said nothing as from you or by your authority,

or implicating you in the slightest degree. If any measure pass, you will be perfectly free to exercise your constitutional power wholly uncommitted, except so far as may be gathered from your public and official acts.

I am, most truthfully and faithfully, yours,

Daniel Webster.[23]

In the original manuscript there was appended to Webster's letter a memorandum in Tyler's handwriting in these words: "The alterations were of no moment, and affected no principle. The bill was to have been submitted for my alterations, and an opportunity to make them was not allowed."

If we assume that the account in Webster's *Memorandum* is correct and that no mistake as to date or content was made in copying Webster's letter of August 20,[24] we find it difficult

[23] Tyler, *Letters and Times*, II, 85–86. This letter was copied in *The Writings and Speeches of Daniel Webster* (Nat. Ed.), XVI, 354. The original manuscript of this letter is not in the collection of *John Tyler Papers* in the Library of Congress, and I have not been able to locate it, as Dr. Lyon G. Tyler in publishing it in his *Letters and Times* gave the Address of John Tyler, Jr., as the only reference for this important document. I could not find this letter among the papers given in this address, but the report of the speech which is now available is incomplete. Three installments of the text were printed in the *Madisonian* for May 25, 28, 29, 1841. At the end of this month the *Madisonian* went out of existence, and the Tyler address seems to have been left suspended in mid-air. This letter was afterwards published in *Tyler's Quarterly* with the notation that the original manuscript is in the archives of the New Hampshire Historical Society. Mr. Otis G. Hammond, Director, has not been able to find this letter in the society's collection of Webster papers.

[24] It may be thought that as Webster's *Memorandum* is undated and his letter of August 20 cannot now be found, neither document should be accepted as evidence on this disputed point. To take this view, however, would be to push skepticism beyond the limits prescribed by sound historical criticism. The *Memorandum* was in Webster's handwriting and was probably written in 1841. But if it were written at any time of the eleven years of his later life (he died in 1852) his recollection of the outstanding events in this heated controversy must have been substantially accurate. On the other hand, it is inconceivable that Dr. Lyon G. Tyler, a man of unimpeachable integrity and high standing as a scholar, would have sponsored a document the genuineness of which he had reason to question. Of course, this does not rule out the possibility that he may have been mistaken or that a mistake in copying might have been made. It is not probable, however, that any serious mistake has been made by the copyist, and so I see no reason to question the genuineness of this letter.

to escape the conclusion that this latter paper was not only a false but a foolish and inexplicable communication. The apparent contradictions between the two documents are hard to explain on any other supposition.[25]

Even if Tyler had not seen in advance the text of the Sergeant Bill, he had, so his enemies declared, accepted in principle the provisions of the measure before it was offered in the House of Representatives. The answer to this charge involves not only a statement but also an interpretation of facts. As Representative Stuart's report of his interview with Tyler is cited as testimony by both sides in the dispute, its substantial accuracy may be accepted as beyond question. It is well established, therefore, that Tyler was on August 16 committed to the bank policy outlined in the agreement between himself and Stuart.

The question now arises, Were the provisions of the Fiscal Corporation Bill in substantial accord with the understanding arrived at between Stuart and the President? The latter contended that they were not; his enemies maintained that they were. A comparison of the text of the bill with that of the Bayard Amendment as modified by Tyler's suggestions (see Appendix A) shows that there were differences in meaning in the two proposals. In the bill the capital stock of the bank was to be twenty-one million dollars, whereas Tyler had named ten or fifteen million as the maximum figure for

[25] There is a possible explanation of these contradictions, but it involves an appeal to that broad charity which deals indulgently with stubborn facts. It is quite likely that Webster in reporting to Sergeant the changes in the bill suggested by Tyler presented them not as suggestions from the President but as revisions which in his [Webster's] opinion would be accepted by Tyler. If this was the case, he was carrying out the President's instructions and was leaving him wholly uncommitted so far as Sergeant was concerned. There would still remain, however, the task of reconciling another contradiction between the Memorandum and the letter. In the former Webster definitely says that he showed the bill to Tyler; in the letter he leaves the impression (and this impression is confirmed by Tyler's endorsement on the letter) that he had not seen the bill. The only possible way to reconcile these apparent contradictions is to assume that in the Memorandum Webster was referring to the Sergeant bill as first framed, and that in the letter and endorsement on it both he and Tyler were referring to the bill in its final form.

the initial capitalization. Tyler had suggested the insertion of a clause to meet the objections of those States which had statutes against establishing agencies of foreign banks within their limits. This restriction was not in the bill. In the Bayard Amendment there was a provision allowing the corporation to deal or trade in bills of exchange, though nothing was said about bills or drafts drawn in one State and payable in another. The right to deal in this latter type of drafts was clearly granted in the bill. Another objection—probably the most serious of all—raised by Tyler was that Congress in chartering the bank was acting in its capacity as the national legislature rather than as the legislature for the District of Columbia. He had all along been opposed to this interpretation of the powers of Congress.

The importance that should be attached to these divergences is a matter of opinion. We have no means of refuting the claim of the President that this dissimilarity was of such significance as to warrant the exercise of the veto. If we accept Tyler's view his second veto was as consistent with his principles and general policy as was the first. For according to his statement, the second bank bill was as offensive from a constitutional point of view as the first one and was objectionable on the score of expediency. On the other hand, if we agree with the Whig interpretation, the President either practiced an intentional deception on the Whigs [26] or else changed his mind before the bill was passed. Just what motive could have prompted him to promise support for a measure which he expected to veto is very difficult to find. Such a course might have held up the storm of opposition for a short time but would have given it greater vehemence when it should burst upon him. It seems, therefore, that we can dismiss the charge of deception as the explanation of his action.

(2) There is some evidence to show that the President may

[26] Benton, *Thirty Years' View*, II, 344.

have changed his mind on the bank bill before it had been passed. Pulled away from a bank policy by the advice of his "Kitchen Cabinet," who appealed strongly to his States' rights scruples, and drawn to it by his desire to keep in line with his party, he was in a position which would have excused some vacillation in opinion. According to the statement of Bell, the ardor displayed in favor of a bank in the interview with Stuart on the evening of August 16 had considerably cooled by the next day. For the President at that time expressed doubt as to whether "he would give his assent to any bank bill." [27]

If the President had decided not to accept any bank bill and was glad of an excuse for a veto, the question next arises, Why did he change his mind?

One reason given by Tyler's enemies as an explanation of his veto was his ambition to be re-elected. Seeing that there was no hope of securing the nomination for the succession at the hands of his own party, he looked to the Democrats for support and was willing to purchase this support at the price of betraying his own party. That Tyler was anxious to succeed himself is more than likely, but that he was willing to sacrifice his honor to attain this objective is most improbable. If this had been his motive he would have welcomed a fight with the Whigs and would have negatived the bank bill with joyous alacrity. But he was undoubtedly in the opposite frame of mind when he reluctantly sent in his second veto. Both Ewing and Webster speak of Tyler's great mental perturbation during the days immediately preceding the final veto.[28] So great was his disquietude that he thought of coupling with the second veto message a statement declaring that he would not be a candidate for the succession. He was advised by his Cabinet, however, that it would not be wise to make

[27] *Niles,* LXI, 54.
[28] See Ewing's Statement. Webster in a letter to Mr. Ketchum, Aug. 22, 1841, said, "The President is agitated." *Writings and Speeches of Daniel Webster* (Nat. Ed.), XVIII, 109.

such an announcement, and so this intention was not carried out.[29] Furthermore, if Tyler had been trying to curry favor with the Democrats, he would (if he had acteu wisely) have taken a definite stand against any national bank and would not have held out to the Whigs a promise of acceptance if a proper bank measure were adopted.

Another cause of Tyler's alleged change of attitude on the bank question, as given by some of his contemporaries, was a wound to his pride inflicted by an insulting letter written by John Minor Botts. Ewing thought that the President was favorable to the bill until August 20, when he was apprised of the contents of Botts's Coffeehouse Letter.[30] Webster was of the same opinion. The President, he said, regretted that a second bank bill was in progress, but had been disposed to consider calmly and conscientiously whatever measure might be presented to him. In the meantime there had come to his notice "Mr. Botts's most extraordinary letter." [31] On that day he went to the State Department and "sat an hour, and complained very much of the ill treatment which he received from Mr. Botts and other Whigs. He ap-

[29] Tyler, op. cit., II, 102.

[30] Ewing's Statement; Tyler, op. cit., II, 112.
Botts's Coffeehouse Letter referred to above was a communication sent by him to the coffeehouse in Richmond. This coffeehouse was a sort of clubroom and news center. It was the custom of the proprietor to put on the table in the reading room for the perusal of his patrons all letters and papers received that bore on public affairs. Botts's letter was regarded as belonging to this class and so was placed on this public table. Dr. Adams, a friend of Tyler, made a copy of the letter and sent it to the *Madisonian,* which published it August 21, 1841. Botts maintained that he had not intended this letter for publication but had sent it to the proprietor as a private communication. The letter, he declared, had been stolen from the coffeehouse. Dr. Adams resented this accusation and challenged Botts to a duel, but the latter declined to accept the challenge. The Coffeehouse Letter was sent from Washington under date of August 16, 1841. The writer predicted that Tyler ("Captain" Tyler, as he called him) would veto the bill in an effort to curry favor with the Democrats. But "he'll be headed yet" and "will be an object of execration with both parties." The letter was most insulting both in tone and content. Richmond *Daily Whig,* Aug. 27, 1841.

[31] Webster to Mr. Ketchum, Aug. 22, 1841; *Writings and Speeches of Daniel Webster* (Nat. Ed.), XVIII, 109.

peared full of suspicion and resentment. I began to fear another veto." [32]

On the other hand, Henry A. Wise, who was in the best position to judge as to his motives, thought it was amusing to say that Tyler's decision had been caused by Botts's letter.[33] Of the correctness of Wise's view I am not so sure. There are a number of facts indicating that the President was opposed to the enactment of any bank legislation at the special session of Congress, and that the willingness to waive his objections was prompted by the desire to maintain harmonious relations with his party. But the unjustifiable attack on him by Clay, the insulting letter of Botts, the scurrilous articles in Whig newspapers, and the dictatorial suggestions gratuitously offered by Tallmadge,[34] all tended to show that reconciliation with his party was hopeless. To have signed the bill under such circumstances would have been to yield to threats. A proud-spirited man like Tyler did not like to be browbeaten.

(3) The prime reason for the veto was doubtless his objections to the bill; for his States' rights conscience, which was being prodded into supersensitiveness by Wise, was still troubling him.[35] But it is not at all improbable that these objections would not have loomed so large had he been treated with any semblance of courtesy and respect by the leaders of his party. If in the exercise of his veto power he was influenced by the desire to show his independence and protest against the indignities to which he had been subjected, he was, of course, acting from improper motives, but many men high in public esteem have done wrong on far less provocation.

[32] Webster's *Memorandum*.
[33] H. A. Wise to J. B. Coles and others, Nov. 5, 1841; Tyler, *op. cit.*, II, 113–114.
[34] In a letter to the President urging him to sign the second bank bill Senator Tallmadge, of New York, assumed a dictatorial attitude which was nothing short of downright effrontery. *Niles*, LXI, 108–109.
[35] Wise, *op. cit.*, 187–188.

Furthermore, it is not an unpardonable sin for a President to change his mind or even disregard a previous commitment. And Tyler in particular had an exceptional excuse for refusing to observe his pledges. Even if he had made the promises attributed to him, he was not bound by them after the Whig leaders had repudiated their part of the contract. For if he had ever shown any disposition to accept a bank it was done with the implied understanding that his yielding on this point would be received by the majority faction in the party as a peace offering. But before the second bank bill was passed he was convinced that his compliance with their wishes would not cause his Whig enemies to bury the hatchet. By continuing their savage attack on him they violated the terms of the compact. It was, therefore, unreasonable to expect the President to be bound by alleged promises to a group which showed no sign of observing its part of the agreement.

It will have to be admitted, however, that the President did not exhibit in his management of the bank question the boldness, wisdom, and firmness that should characterize the policy of a Chief Magistrate. The accusation of his enemies that he showed vacillation in his negotiations with Congressional leaders is not without foundation; but it is easier to overlook this shortcoming in the harassed President than to excuse those who maneuvered him into a position from which there was no escape except by a sacrifice of principle or dignity or both.

When this bitter contest was over, Tyler could console himself with the thought that he had not departed from his States' rights principles. He had kept the faith, even though he had not fought a good fight.

CHAPTER XVIII

CABINET CHANGES

JOHN TYLER, like John Adams before him and Andrew Johnson after him, inherited a ready-made Cabinet. This circumstance was a handicap to the incoming President in all three instances. In each case the Chief Magistrate had as his most intimate official advisers men whose loyalty to someone else was stronger than that which they felt for their chief.

Harrison's Cabinet was as follows: Daniel Webster, of Massachusetts, Secretary of State; Thomas Ewing, of Ohio, Secretary of the Treasury; John Bell, of Tennessee, Secretary of War; George C. Badger, of North Carolina, Secretary of the Navy; Francis Granger, of New York, Postmaster General; and J. J. Crittenden, of Kentucky, Attorney General.[1] Clay was offered any place in the Cabinet that he might wish, but he declined office, preferring to remain in the Senate, where, as he considered, he could "most effectually serve the new administration, and be ready to enter the field four years hence." [2]

All the members of the original Cabinet except Webster and Granger were partisans of Clay. In the controversy that would be inevitable between Tyler and Clay, should the latter endeavor to carry through Congress his nationalistic measures, a majority of the President's Cabinet would be allied with the opposition. Nor was he sure of the enthusiastic support of Webster and his friend Granger. Webster was the dean of the nationalists and in former times had been regarded by Tyler as the archenemy of sound political doc-

---

[1] *National Intelligencer*, Mar. 8, 1841.
[2] Allan Nevins, ed., *Diary of Philip Hone*, I, 514.

trine.[3] As it turned out, however, Webster gave no trouble and cordial relations grew up between the premier and his chief. In later years Tyler regarded Webster as "the first among statesmen" [4] and as "the model of a Cabinet officer." [5]

Apparently, the members of the Cabinet were not inclined to accord the President the deference which his position gave him the right to expect. According to a story related years afterwards by John Tyler, Jr., President Tyler's private secretary, Webster at the first Cabinet meeting held by Tyler expressed to the President the hope and expectation that he would carry out the ideas and customs of his predecessor. He then went on to state that under Harrison it had been the practice for *all* measures relating to the administration to be brought before the Cabinet and be decided by the opinion of the majority, the President having only one vote along with the rest. Whereupon Tyler, amazed at "this exhibition of adamantine cheek," arose and spoke substantially as follows:

"I beg your pardon, gentlemen; I am very glad to have in my Cabinet such able statesmen as you have proved yourselves to be. And I shall be pleased to avail myself of your counsel and advice. But I can never consent to being dictated to as to what I shall or shall not do. I, as President, shall be responsible for my administration. I hope to have your hearty co-operation in carrying out its measures. So long as you see fit to do this, I shall be glad to have you with me. When you think otherwise, your resignations will be accepted." [6]

Under such circumstances, only two alternatives were open to the President. One was to dismiss his Cabinet and form a new one; the other was to accept it and lean heavily upon a "Kitchen Cabinet" for advice. To choose the former alternative would be to incite a family row at the outset of his ad-

[3] *John Tyler Papers* (L.C.), I, 6283.
[4] *William and Mary College Quarterly* (first series), XIV, 195.
[5] Tyler, *Letters and Times*, III, 197.
[6] Interview given by John Tyler, Jr., in 1888; see *Lippincott's Monthly Magazine*, XLI, 417–418.

ministration. In order to avoid this he decided to retain Harrison's Cabinet and choose as his real counsellors a small group of friends who were in entire accord with his States' rights views. In this unofficial Cabinet were included Thomas R. Dew, president of William and Mary College; Judge N. Beverley Tucker, of Williamsburg; Duff Green; Representatives Wise, Gilmer, Mallory, and Cushing; and Senator William C. Rives.[7] Dr. Dew and Judge Tucker were the "Brain Trust" of the group, though they probably did not exert as much influence on the President as some of the others.[8] First in importance in this list of advisers was Henry A. Wise. Tyler afterwards said of him: "He is truly a most extraordinary man. I have never known but one man more thoroughly at home upon all subjects and that is L. W. Tazewell."[9] In his opinion Wise, more than any other one man, was entitled to the credit for the Whig victory in 1840.[10]

It is unfortunate when a high functionary is forced to seek advice outside the legally ordained channels. A liaison

[7] *Van Buren Papers* (L.C.), XLIII, 10,082, 10,102.

[8] Dew's duties at the College kept him at Williamsburg, and it was only during the extra session of Congress that he found time to go to Washington. What influence Judge Tucker exerted was confined to the early part of the term, for later on a coldness arose between him and Tyler which terminated their confidential relations. The ardor of this friendship had begun to cool as early as September 13, 1841. In a letter to Mrs. Tucker of that date Tucker indicated disapproval of Tyler's course. This estrangement had grown into a definite break by August, 1844, as is shown by the fact that when Tyler and Tucker at that time happened to be on the same steamboat on the James River neither spoke to the other. The cause of this unfortunate breach in an old friendship is not given in the sources that have been examined. A possible explanation lies in the fact that while Tyler was cordial to Tucker's suggestions he seems not to have accepted many of them. The latter's bank plan, as has been shown, was not adopted. Tucker wrote a series of long articles for the Richmond *Enquirer* making suggestions as to the policy that should be pursued at Washington. He had also given Tyler some advice when the latter passed through Richmond on the way to Washington. All this tends to show that the Judge placed a high estimate on these ideas, and, therefore, he may have felt slighted by the President's disinclination to take them as seriously as he felt that they deserved. Tucker to Mrs. Tucker, Sept. 13, 1841, Aug. 5, 1844; Wise to Tucker, June 15, 1842; Tucker Papers *National Intelligencer*, Oct. 9, 1841.

[9] Tyler to Robert Tyler, May, 1859; Tyler, *Letters and Times*, II, 550.

[10] Tyler to Wise, Nov. 25, 1840; *ibid.*, III, 84–85.

with an unofficial group generally arouses a jealousy similar to that occasioned by a love affair outside the home. This is particularly true when, as in this case, the unofficial advisers are not qualified by wisdom and experience for so great a responsibility. Tyler, therefore, did not in the beginning have the benefit of the sanest counsel. Wise especially was unequal to the rôle of mentor to a President. He was brilliant but young, and his judgment lacked the stability that comes with years and experience. Besides, too often he al-lowed emotion to usurp the place of reason.

The new administration started out with every indication of harmony, but in a little while signs of discord began to appear. There was no actual friction, however, until July, 1841, when the chief clerk in the land office dismissed thirteen of his assistants. Ten of the dismissed employees appealed to Tyler, who promptly ordered their reinstatement. As Ewing, the Secretary of the Treasury, had approved the action of the chief clerk, some hot words passed between him and Tyler. But this was not a serious quarrel, and the disagreement was passed over quietly.[11]

As has already been shown, the immediate occasion of the disruption of the Cabinet was the President's rejection of the second bank bill. The Cabinet was in favor of a national bank, and all of its members except Webster resigned in protest against the veto. In order that these resignations might weaken and embarrass Tyler as much as possible, it was arranged that they be made in unison and announced in a dramatic way. With the view to agreeing upon some plan of united action Secretary Badger invited the other members of the Cabinet to a supper at his house on Thursday, September 9. All but Granger attended, but when Webster saw that it was to be a meeting with Clay he retired. The others decided to resign as a body and make common war against the Administration. Although Clay was a member

[11] New York *Herald,* July 26, 1841; Marcy to Van Buren, July 20, 1841; *Van Buren Papers,* XLIII, 10,069.

of the supper party, he did not attend the conference at which the decision was made, but was conversing with the family at the time. These circumstances lent confirmation to the charge that the disruption of the Cabinet was the result of advice given by Clay.[12]

Webster was urged to join them (so wrote Tyler in 1845), "and it was declared to him that if he would resign, I would necessarily have to vacate the government by Saturday night, and thus Whig rule be thoroughly re-established." Webster had too much sagacity not to see that what would happen would be the establishment of *"Clay rule* only, and nothing more." [13]

All the members of the Cabinet but Webster sent in their resignations on Saturday, September 11. John Tyler, Jr., was present when these letters came in. With watch in hand he noted the exact time at which each was received. The first arrived at 12:30 P. M. and the last at 5:30 P. M. On that same afternoon Webster came in, and, "in his deep-toned voice, asked, *'Where am I to go, Mr. President?'* The President's reply was only in these words, *'You must decide that for yourself, Mr. Webster.'* At this Mr. Webster instantly caught, and said, *'If you leave it to me, Mr. President, I will stay where I am.'* Whereupon, President Tyler, rising from his seat and extending his hand to Mr. Webster warmly rejoined, *'Give me your hand on that, and now I will say to you that Henry Clay is a doomed man.'* " [14]

[12] This accusation was denied by Ewing, who maintained that while the course of the Cabinet was yet undetermined the members refrained strictly from all conversation with Clay. Ewing to Clay, Nov. 1, 1843; *Clay Papers,* XXIII, 4007; *National Intelligencer,* Sept. 18, 27, 1841; G. R. Poage, *Henry Clay and the Whig Party,* 101; F. Webster, ed., *The Private Correspondence of Daniel Webster,* 2 vols., II, 110; C. M. Fuess, *Daniel Webster,* 2 vols. (Boston, 1930), II, 98.

[13] Tyler to Alexander Gardiner, May 6, 1845; *John Tyler Papers* (L.C.), III, 6515–16.

[14] John Tyler, Jr., to Lyon G. Tyler, Jan. 29, 1883; Tyler, *Letters and Times,* II, 121–122, note.

Although the above account was written more than forty years after the event, we have reason to believe that it is substantially correct. It was corroborated, except for the dialogue between the President and Webster, by ex-

All of the members who resigned except one sent letters giving reasons for their action. Granger, the political ally of Webster, sent no letter. Indeed, he apparently had no serious grievance against the President, but resigned rather than separate from his friends in Congress and the Cabinet.[15] The letter of Crittenden was short, stating that he was not in accord with the President, especially with his veto policy and felt that he should therefore resign.[16]

In the other letters of the retiring Cabinet officers there was expressed marked disagreement with Tyler's veto policy. The most virulent of these attacks was made by Ewing. Not only did he flay the President for his attitude toward the second bank bill (see pp. 259 f.), but he also complained that the Washington correspondent of the New York *Herald*, a Tyler paper, had been very abusive of the Cabinet and had

President Tyler himself in a letter to Alexander Gardiner, May 6, 1845. Tyler, *op. cit.*, II, 97.

Ewing's account of the sending in of his resignation was as follows: His was the first of the letters of resignation to reach the Executive Office. Suspecting that it was unduly harsh, Webster secured the President's permission to see it before it was read by the latter. Thereupon Webster sent hurriedly for Ewing to come to his office. Upon his arrival there, Webster requested Ewing to soften the tone of his letter as Tyler was well disposed toward him and had authorized him (Webster) to promise his Secretary of the Treasury the choice of the foreign missions if he should depart as a friend. The irate Secretary, however, declined to make the desired changes, and so Webster handed the document to his chief. "Ewing's Diary," *American Historical Review*, XVIII, 112.

[15] Letter from Millard Fillmore, Sept. 23, 1841; F. H. Severance, ed., *Millard Fillmore Papers*, II, 226.

In a conversation with Philip Hone, Granger explained that his chief cause of dissatisfaction with the President was his refusal to turn Democrats out of office (although he had promised to do so) and put Whigs in their places. Some violent and active opponents of the Administration, he said, had been retained because the President was endeavoring by such a policy to win recruits from the opposition to the party which he was trying to form in his own interest. *Diary of Philip Hone*, II, 563-564.

Before reaching a decision Granger asked the Whig Representatives from New York whether he should resign from the Cabinet. In reply nine members of the New York delegation expressed the unanimous opinion that he should go along with his colleagues, although their spokesman, Millard Fillmore, considered the resignation of the Cabinet as an unwise policy. *Francis Granger Papers* (L.C.); *National Intelligencer*, Sept. 16, 1841.

[16] *Madisonian*, Feb. 25, 1841.

betrayed a knowledge of Cabinet secrets. This would indicate that there had been a leak. Tyler was responsible, it was intimated, for this leak and was conniving at the abuse of the Cabinet members.[17]

It is true that the Washington correspondent of the New York *Herald* had been making a series of attacks on the Cabinet and had professed a knowledge of Tyler's intentions which other newspaper correspondents did not seem to have. He made prophecies as to what action Tyler would take on both the first and the second bank bills. Some of these forecasts were clearly based on Tyler's past record and were in the nature of inferences that could be drawn without any inside information. On the other hand, the foreknowledge asserted by the *Herald* was at times proclaimed with such an air of certainty as to justify the opinion that it was speaking with authority.[18] To the enemies of Tyler it seemed that James Gordon Bennett, in the editorial office of the *Herald,* was, like the prophet of old, reading the bedchamber thoughts of the ruler at Washington.

These indiscreet reports sent in from Washington by the correspondent of the *Herald* and the editorial comments on them gave some show of reason for the suspicion that Cabinet secrets were leaking out in improper fashion. But there is no evidence that the President was in any way responsible

[17] Ewing's statement is given in Benton's *Thirty Years' View*, II, 345. A later statement by Ewing appeared in *Niles' Register,* LXII, 244–246. For the statements of Bell and Badger, see *National Intelligencer,* Sept. 21, 22, 1841.

[18] In a postscript to a dispatch from Washington there appeared (August 9, 1841) this statement: "We learn, by an intimate friend of ours, and a personal friend of Mr. Tyler's, who arrived last night from Washington, that beyond a doubt the Bank Bill will be vetoed. There will be a terrible fuss—no row—much blowing off of steam, and unquestionably a reconstruction of the Cabinet. One, and perhaps two, members of it will remain in office. There is no mistake in this." New York *Herald,* August 16, 17, 18, 19, 23, 1841.

Botts complained that James Gordon Bennett spent the greater portion of his time at "the Palace," and was on intimate terms with the President. He predicted in advance, even to the hour, all that was to happen, while Tyler's constitutional advisers were kept in ignorance of his plans. It ought to be added, however, that the events predicted did not always arrive on schedule time. *Ibid.,* August 28, 1841.

for this unwise publicity. Webster was of the opinion that it had its origin in the indiscretions of Tyler's two sons.[19] But this accusation is unfair to both Robert and John Tyler, Jr., as there is no evidence to support such a view.

The most plausible explanation is the one given by John Tyler, Jr., namely, that the exceptional insight as to what was going on exhibited by the *Herald* correspondents was explained by their energy and ability to scoop the news.[20] The editor of the *Herald* took the same position, and scoffed at the idea that his newspaper had had access to any improper sources of information. The fact that his paper outran its competitors in giving governmental news was due, he said, to the thoroughness with which his six reporters covered the situation in Washington.[21]

The unsustained accusation that Tyler or his sons had purposely or inadvertently given out Cabinet secrets and had inspired attacks on members of the Cabinet was countered with the charge that Ewing and Bell in their statements had undoubtedly made public some of the most secret deliberations of the Cabinet. The members of the Cabinet who were guilty of this offense may have felt that the exceptional circumstances with which they were confronted justified this departure from well-established usage—that in no other way could they fully explain their actions and properly defend their reputations. This is not a satisfactory defense. When men are entrusted with such great responsibility they are never to be excused for allowing private aims to outweigh considerations of public policy.

The timing of these resignations would indicate that this was a move on the part of Clay's friends to compel the resignation of the President. As they were not sent in until the afternoon of Saturday and Congress had voted to adjourn the following Monday, very little time was left for the selection of a new Cabinet. Tyler was of the opinion that vacancies

---

[19] Adams, *Memoirs*, XI, 14.   [20] Tyler, *op. cit.*, II, 123, note.
[21] New York *Herald*, Sept. 18, 1841.

of this sort occurring while the Senate is in session had to be filled before Congress adjourned [22] or else remain vacant until the next session of Congress. It looked, therefore, as if the Clay party hoped and expected that the President would be unable to make a selection on such short notice. If so he would be without a Cabinet for three months. He could not carry on for that length of time without the assistance of departmental heads and so would be forced to abdicate. In that event Samuel L. Southard, president of the Senate, a Clay adherent, would succeed to the Presidency.

Tyler, however, was not taken completely by surprise, and was more ready to meet the emergency than his enemies had anticipated. A new Cabinet was chosen at once and the names of the appointees were sent to the Senate before it adjourned. The Senate had no excuse for rejecting these nominees and they were promptly confirmed. If Tyler's enemies were actuated by the motives attributed to them, they were thwarted in their evil designs by his prompt action.

The retirement from the Cabinet of the other members left Webster in an awkward, not to say, embarrassing position. If he held on to his place he could be charged with party irregularity, as the great majority of the Whigs sided with Clay in this controversy. He would also be identified with a discredited administration. On the other hand, to follow the lead of his colleagues would be to forfeit an honored place, and one of his weaknesses was an overfondness for office.[23] It is true that he declared it to be "a matter of the most perfect indifference to him whether he retained or resigned" the

---

[22] Tyler, *op. cit.*, II, 96.

The President, it is now held, can fill such vacancies after Congress adjourns, but the appointees receive no salary until they are confirmed by the Senate. There is some doubt, however, as to the correctness of this view, as no decision covering the point has been handed down by the Supreme Court. President Roosevelt was recently (1937) advised by Attorney General Cummings that he could fill after the adjournment of Congress a vacancy on the bench of the Supreme Court occasioned by the resignation of a justice while Congress was in session. See S. P. Orth and R. E. Cushman, *American National Government* (N. Y., 1931), 276.

[23] Bancroft to Van Buren, Feb. 21, 1842; *Van Buren Papers*, XLIV, 10,265.

office; but it is the custom for politicians to talk in this fashion. Tyler, he said, had never shown him any disrespect, and he believed that the President wished him to retain his place. Moreover, to resign at that juncture would be to give up all hope of succeeding his chief in the Presidency. For a break with Tyler would mean a tie-up with the tail of Clay's kite. Then, too, he had entered upon diplomatic negotiations with the British minister which gave promise of yielding new laurels to his fame.

As the decision he was called on to make would be fraught with such important consequences to himself, he felt that he should have the advice of his closest political friends before taking any action. Accordingly, next day after the veto message was sent to Congress, he invited the Whig Representatives and Senators from Massachusetts to come to his house for a conference. That evening (September 10) the two Senators and eight of the twelve Representatives, including John Quincy Adams and Caleb Cushing, came in response to this request. He notified them of the intention of his colleagues to withdraw from the Cabinet and asked their advice as to whether he should resign with them. Adams in speaking of the decision reached at this conference, said: "We all agreed that Mr. Webster would not be justified in resigning at this time; but we all felt that the hour for the requiem of the Whig party was at hand." [24]

Webster, therefore, decided to hold on to his seat in the Cabinet. In his public statement he gave two reasons for not acting in line with his colleagues. These were: (1) He had seen no sufficient reason for the dissolution of the Cabinet. (2) If he had resigned he would have given the President sufficient notice to enable him to select a suitable person to

[24] Adams, *op. cit.*, XI, 13-14.

On that same day or the next, Webster wrote to Philip Hone the following note: "Ewing, Bell, Badger, Crittenden resign to-morrow. *Let me know whether the Whig public expect me to follow suit, or to hold on a while for the sake of or on account of the foreign relations of the country.*" *Diary of Philip Hone*, II, 560 (Sept. 11, 1841).

whom he could entrust the delicate diplomatic negotiations then pending.[25]

The promptness with which the President chose his new advisers showed that he had been giving considerable thought to the reorganization of his Cabinet. It is evident that he would have welcomed these resignations if they had come in such a way as not to reflect discredit on his administration and in time for him to have made new appointments without detriment to the public service. The lack of harmony between the President and his official advisers made it desirable that he have a new Cabinet, one that would be more in accord with his views and policies. He had, therefore, decided before the second veto,[26] and probably before the first,[27] upon a reorganization of his Cabinet. He was led to or confirmed in this decision by his advisers of the "Kitchen Cabinet." From a letter in the New York *Herald*, a paper which, it was thought, reflected Tyler's views, it would seem that the members of the Cabinet had already outstayed their welcome.[28]

There is evidence to show that Tyler at one time desired the resignation of his entire Cabinet. A. P. Upshur was of the opinion (September 7, 1841) that the President wanted to get rid of Webster and, therefore, was planning to give him the London Mission.[29] S. S. Nicholas stated that some time prior to the second veto, Tyler had decided to dismiss

---

[25] G. T. Curtis, *Life of Daniel Webster,* II, 81.

[26] Duff Green, in a letter to the President on September 10, 1841, referred to a conference held between them on the previous Tuesday (September 7). Green understood that Tyler had at that time decided upon a change in his Cabinet. Duff Green to Tyler, Sept. 10, 1841; *Duff Green Papers* (Chapel Hill, N. C.).

[27] Gilmer, one of Tyler's closest friends, in a private letter as early as August 7 said that it was then confidently anticipated by the President's friends that there would be a new Cabinet. *John Tyler Papers* (L.C.), V, 175.

[28] In this letter members of the Cabinet were accused of remaining in their places contrary to the wishes of the President "and in spite of the neglects and slights which he put upon them with a view to make them resign." Benton, *Thirty Years' View*, II, 353.

[29] A. P. Upshur to N. Beverley Tucker, Sept. 7, 1841; *John Tyler Papers* (L.C.), VII, 436–437.

his whole Cabinet. With this in view he sent to Baltimore
for Louis McLane and offered him the chief post in the new
Cabinet. McLane, however, was distrustful of the President
and declined the offer.[30] Nicholas thought that the chief
purpose behind the proposed reorganization was the removal of Webster from the Cabinet council. If Upshur and
Nicholas were correct in their views Tyler soon changed his
attitude toward Webster, for we have every reason to believe that he was pleased with Webster's refusal to resign
with his colleagues.[31]

Before he had selected his new Cabinet, the President must
have realized that the break with the Clay Whigs was final.
Any effort, therefore, to placate his party by Cabinet appointments would be hopeless. Despite this situation, however, he did not go outside the Whig ranks in choosing his
new advisers. All of them were Whigs who had originally
been Jackson men and had left the Democratic Party because
of their disagreement with some of Jackson's policies. They
were all, or nearly all, men of ability, though most of them
were not well-known nationally. The *National Intelligencer,*
which would be inclined to underrate rather than overrate
them, said: "The appointments are upon the whole better
than could have been expected. . . . They are all gentlemen
of honorable repute, of intelligence, and, we believe, of busi-

---

[30] S. S. N[icholas] to J. J. Crittenden, Jan. 22, 1842; *The Papers of John Jordan Crittenden* (L.C.), VIII, 1432.

According to Nicholas, when McLane came to Washington to confer with Tyler, he was told by the intermediary that the President was at the home of Crittenden drinking hot whisky punch. McLane felt that if he was thus partaking of the hospitality of a man whom he intended to remove, he could not be trusted.

[31] A statement made years later (1857) by Tyler to Edmund Ruffin indicates that the relations between Webster and Tyler changed for the better soon after the latter's accession to the Presidency. According to this account President Tyler had a feeling that at first Webster was inclined "to join quiescently in the general but disguised Whig conspiracy against me. But he soon saw that I would not come into their measures, or be governed by any influence— and then he yielded to my views, and ably and in good faith aided me to carry them out." The ex-President regarded Webster, he said, as among the first of American statesmen. MS. *Diary of Edmund Ruffin* (L.C.), I, 222.

ness habits." The New York *Times* considered the new Cabinet members as "men of ability and integrity; and well qualified, we doubt not, as any who could have been selected to discharge the high trusts confided to them."

Upshur, Secretary of the Navy, and Legaré, Attorney General, were able lawyers (the latter especially), though neither of them had been in a position to advertise his success. Legaré was not in the good graces of Calhoun, and his selection indicated that the Administration was asking no favors of the great Nullifier. Upshur was a judge of the General Court of Virginia, having been appointed to the place in 1826 when Tyler was governor. He had played a prominent rôle in the Virginia Constitutional Convention of 1829–30. Spencer, Secretary of War, had been associated with Tyler in the House of Representatives and was chairman of the committee (of which Tyler was a member) which made a report unfavorable to the Second Bank of the United States (1819). He was now Secretary of State for New York. Lately he had been active in his opposition to the policy of the Administration, and for this reason surprise was expressed that Tyler would offer and he would accept the place.[32]

The clamor for Webster's resignation became greater after the negotiations with Lord Ashburton had been com-

---

[32] "Before being tendered a position in Mr. Tyler's Cabinet, he [Spencer] had written an address upon his [Tyler's] treachery to the Whig party, more severe than anything that appeared from any other quarter. He fairly flayed the President, lashing him as with a whip of scorpions." Nathan Sargent, *Public Men and Events* (Philadelphia, 1875).

John McLean, of Ohio, had been offered the Secretaryship of War, but had declined it as he was unwilling to give up his place as associate justice of the Supreme Court of the United States. Walter Forward, of Pennsylvania, became Secretary of the Treasury and Charles A. Wickliffe, ex-Governor of Kentucky, Postmaster General. He was hostile to Clay. Wise was offered the post of Secretary of the Navy but declined it. *Niles,* LXI, 33; *Daniel Webster Papers* (L.C.), VI, 165,888; *William and Mary College Quarterly* (first series), XX, 7; *Tucker Papers,* Williamsburg (Wise to Tucker, Sept. 11, 1841); *John Tyler Papers* (L.C.), II, 6405.

For newspaper opinion regarding the members of the new Cabinet, see *Niles,* LXI, 98–100.

pleted.[33] He grew tired of bearing the odium that attached
to him because of his connection with an unpopular administration. Besides, when the President was ready to take up
the Texan negotiations it was embarrassing to have a Secretary of State who was opposed to annexation. As the acquisition of Texas became one of Tyler's main objectives, he
and his premier would soon have to come to the parting of
the ways. Both Tyler and Webster were anxious, however,
that the latter's retirement would be effected without disturbing the cordial personal relations that still existed between them. Tyler, therefore, wished to provide Webster
with a good comfortable berth when he should leave the
Cabinet.

At one time it was hoped that Edward Everett, American
minister to England, would be willing to exchange his place
for the China Mission. In that event, according to newspaper
reports, Webster would succeed Everett at the Court of St.
James. Webster, however, declared that he had no desire
to go to London and, so far as he was concerned, there was
no connection between the offer to Everett of the China
Mission and the possibility of his appointment as minister
to England.[34] Be that as it may, Everett was unwilling to
go to China, and so the London post did not become vacant.
Another plan was to send Webster on a special mission to
England to arrange a settlement of the Oregon dispute and
catch up other ends of diplomacy which were still hanging
loose. Tyler in a confidential letter to Representative Cushing expressed the wish that an appropriation be made to
bear the expense of this mission. The request was refused
by the House Committee of Foreign Affairs, although it was
supported by Adams, the chairman.[35]

Despite the failure of these efforts, Webster had by the
spring of 1843 made up his mind to withdraw from the

[33] Curtis, *Life of Daniel Webster,* II, 130–131.
[34] Webster to Everett, Mar. 10, 1843; *Daniel Webster Papers* (L.C.), VII,
16,865–76.
[35] Adams, *Memoirs,* XI, 327–328, 329–330.

Cabinet. In a letter to Nicholas Biddle (March 2, 1843), he stated this intention and gave his reasons. The President, he charged, was resolved to be a candidate for the succession and was using the patronage to further that aim. He was "quite disposed to throw himself into the arms of the loco foco [Democratic] party." [36] This was doubtless more of an excuse than a reason, but it afforded him a plausible pretext for disassociating himself with an unpopular administration. The withdrawal, which was announced May 8, 1843, did not arouse any ill feeling between himself and the President. The correspondence by which the resignation was accepted was of the most cordial nature,[37] and Tyler and Webster maintained uninterrupted friendly relations until the death of the latter.

On the retirement of Webster, the State Department was *ad interim* under the charge of Legaré who still held on to the office of Attorney General. Shortly afterwards, Legaré died in Boston, where he, Tyler, and Webster had gone to attend the Bunker Hill celebration.[38] The President now moved Upshur up to the State Department and chose David Henshaw, a Democrat, for the Navy Department.[39] John Nelson, of Maryland, another Democrat, was appointed Attorney General.[40]

In the meantime Forward had resigned his post as Secretary of the Treasury and Caleb Cushing was nominated as his successor. But the Whig Senate was in no mood to honor such a close friend of Tyler—one of the "Corporal's Guard"—and so he was rejected.[41] Thereupon John C.

[36] R. C. McGrane, ed., *The Correspondence of Nicholas Biddle Dealing with National Affairs* (Boston and N. Y., 1919), 345–346.

[37] *The Writings and Speeches of Daniel Webster* (Nat. Ed.), XVI, 404–405; *Daniel Webster Papers* (L.C.), VII, 16,930.
Tyler in accepting Webster's resignation said: "I do not mean to flatter you in saying that in conducting the most delicate and important negotiations you have manifested powers of intellect of the highest order and in all things a true American heart."

[38] *Niles,* LXIV, 261.   [39] *Ibid.,* 307.

[40] *John Tyler Papers* (L.C.), II, 6438.

[41] *Niles,* LXIV, 2, 30; Tyler, *Letters and Times,* III, 104–105.

Spencer was nominated and confirmed (March 3, 1843).
The transfer of Spencer from the War to the Treasury Department left the headship of the former department vacant.
To this post Tyler appointed (March 9, 1843) James Madison Porter, a Democrat from Pennsylvania.

By choosing three Democrats for these vacancies, Tyler
had made his Cabinet half Democratic and half Whig. He
had thus taken a long step toward the party to which he
had formerly belonged. These selections were all interim
appointments and had yet to run the gauntlet of the Senate.
When they came before the Senate in December, 1843, all
of them except Henshaw and Porter were promptly confirmed. The latter were voted against by the Whigs partly
because of their ill will toward the President and partly because of their determination to thwart his alleged attempt
to form an alliance with the Democrats. Quite a number of
the Democrats also voted against Porter and Henshaw because they feared that as members of Tyler's Cabinet they
would use their influence against Van Buren.[42] The President nominated William Wilkins, of Pennsylvania, and
T. W. Gilmer, of Virginia, for the posts of Secretary of
War and of the Navy respectively. These nominations were
promptly confirmed.[43]

By the explosion on the *Princeton* Gilmer and Upshur lost
their lives and two new appointments had to be made. The
place of Secretary of the Navy was offered to Judge John
Y. Mason, a Democrat from Virginia. At first he gave the
impression that he would not accept the offer, and James
K. Polk was next approached. Polk, who was a Democrat of
the strictest regularity, was too astute a politician to link
up his political fortunes with those of a President who had
no party or effective organization behind him. So after advising with Jackson he sent in a courteous reply declining the

[42] *Niles,* LXIV, 307; LXV, 353; *Marcy Papers* (L.C.), IX, 34,082; Detroit
Daily Advertiser, Mar. 28, 1843; *National Intelligencer,* Jan. 16, 31, 1844.
[43] *John Tyler Papers* (L.C.), V, 186; VI, 285.

offer. Before this reply reached Washington, Mason had reconsidered and declared his willingness to accept the post. The President was now in a very awkward position, and he had to inform Polk, through his intermediary, Mr. Theophilus Fisk, that the place was no longer vacant.[44] Mason was duly confirmed and became Tyler's last Secretary of the Navy.[45]

To find a suitable person for the vacant Secretaryship of State was a more difficult task. After John Nelson, the Attorney General, had acted in this capacity for a short time, Calhoun was offered the place. This was an unfortunate choice and Tyler realized the unwisdom of it. John Tyler, Jr., said that no other act of his administration caused his father so much regret as this appointment. If the Texan negotiations (which at that time were the chief interest of the President) were successful, Calhoun because of his prominence might receive for the achievement the laurels to which Tyler was justly entitled. The President felt that annexation could not succeed without the support of the Democratic Party, which was now dominated by the Jackson-Van Buren wing, and so he was at this time trying to conciliate this group. Jackson had been warming toward Tyler since his veto of the first bank bill, and recently by a lucky stroke the latter had won the gratitude of the Old Hero. Upon the recommendation of the President, Congress had remitted the fine of $1000.00 that had been imposed upon Jackson in connection with the New Orleans campaign. Tyler had even tried to win over Benton by appointing his son-in-law, Lieutenant John C. Frémont, commander of the Oregon exploring expedition.[46]

---

[44] For the correspondence that passed between Theophilus Fisk and Polk, see Tyler, *Letters and Times*, III, 133-134; *Polk Papers* (L.C.), LVI, 2761.

[45] *National Intelligencer*, Mar. 14, 16, 1844.

[46] Tyler, *Letters and Times*, II, 292.

Benton was not very grateful to Tyler for this honor to his son-in-law. He contended that not the President, but Frémont's superior officer, was due the credit for his appointment. Benton, *op. cit.*, II, 478.

The policy of placating Tyler's former political enemies would not be advanced by promoting Calhoun to the high place of Secretary of State. He had little influence outside of South Carolina, and was at enmity with Jackson and Van Buren. Besides, J. Q. Adams and the antislavery leaders regarded him as the "high priest of Moloch, the embodied spirit of slavery." Nor were there any personal reasons for the President's making Calhoun his premier. A coolness had sprung up between them in the campaign of 1840, and since that time they had exchanged only formal civilities.[47]

It was to the officious meddling of Henry A. Wise that Calhoun owed his appointment. After the death of Upshur, Wise felt that Calhoun could do more than anyone else toward carrying out the annexation program. Besides, he felt grateful to Calhoun and his friends because one of the latter, Senator McDuffie, of South Carolina, had ably defended him when his name was before the Senate for the French Mission in 1842–43. To pay this debt of gratitude he did not scruple at capitalizing his friendship with the President to the point of placing the latter in a most embarrassing position.

Without consulting Tyler he saw McDuffie and suggested Calhoun for the place of Secretary of State. Owing to Wise's intimacy with Tyler, McDuffie assumed (as he had every right to do) that the offer had come from the President and wrote to Calhoun accordingly. By this act of bold presumption Wise had put Tyler in a position where he either had to nominate Calhoun or else break with the oldest and dearest of the few political and personal friends that were still remaining to him.

After his interview with McDuffie, Wise went to take breakfast with the President. In the course of the conversation he discovered that Tyler was opposed to the appointment of Calhoun as Secretary of State. Thereupon, he noti-

[47] Tyler, *Letters and Times,* II, 295–296.

fied Tyler of his imprudent commitment to McDuffie.[48] A man with a fiery temper would have sent Wise away with a deserved rebuke which would have forever prevented his meddling in other people's affairs. According to John Tyler, Jr., the President was at first greatly angered and inclined to banish Wise forever from his presence. After a display of temper which was unusual for him, he decided that he could not afford to break with a friend so tried and true. Besides, to refuse to appoint Calhoun now would be to antagonize not only him but also McDuffie and his other supporters. Moreover, Wise approached him at a time when his emotions were still unsettled as a result of the terrible excitement over the *Princeton* disaster. Tyler also wanted to adjust the Oregon dispute and felt that Calhoun would be the proper person for conducting the negotiations. So he accepted the commitment that Wise had imposed upon him, though, according to his son, he never entirely forgave Wise for his presumptuous blunder.[49]

Having decided on the selection of the great Southern leader, the President after "a free and frank conversation" with Senator McDuffie and Mr. Holmes, of South Carolina, sent in to the Senate (March 6) the name of Calhoun for this important place. On that same day he wrote to Calhoun notifying him of this action and giving reasons for it. He pointed out that the "annexation of Texas to the Union, and the settlement of the Oregon question on a satisfactory basis, are the great ends to be accomplished: the first is in the act of competition and will admit of no delay. The last had but barely opened when death snatched from me my lamented friend." [50]

Calhoun's nomination was unanimously confirmed by the Senate the day on which it was presented. He replied ac-

---

[48] Wise, *Seven Decades of the Union*, 222–225.
[49] *Lippincott's Monthly Magazine*, XLI, 417–419.
[50] Tyler to Calhoun, Mar. 6, 1844; *Report Amer. Hist. Asso.*, 1899, II, 938–939.

cepting the office but, as he said, with great reluctance and on condition that he might be at liberty to retire when the negotiations were finished. "Nothing short of the magnitude of the crisis," he explained, "occasioned by the pending negotiations, could induce me to leave my retirement." [51]

After Calhoun and Mason had come into the Cabinet that body was dominated by Southern influence. It is said that Spencer, with his Northern sentiments, now fell into disfavor with Tyler, and was largely ignored by his chief.[52] At any rate, one would judge from the way in which the Secretary of the Treasury gave up his post that he was not very happy in it. The President asked him to deposit a part of the secret service funds with a confidential agent in New York for possible use in connection with the Mexican expedition. Believing the order to be illegal, he refused to obey it and promptly resigned (May, 1844).[53] George M. Bibb, of Kentucky, was chosen in his place.[54]

Whether this was a pretext for or the cause of Spencer's resignation and whether Tyler wished to be rid of him we can only conjecture. According to Dr. Lyon G. Tyler, Spencer had a more personal reason for leaving the Cabinet. His son, who had been serving in the navy, was shot for mutiny (November, 1842) by order of Captain Alexander S. Mackenzie. When Captain Mackenzie arrived at port a naval court was ordered for his trial and an investigation of the case was made. Mackenzie was acquitted, "and," said the President, "I could do nothing but approve the sentence." Spencer, who was then Secretary of War, urged the President to set aside the verdict and order a new trial for the slayer of his son. Tyler's refusal to comply with this re-

---

[51] Calhoun to Tyler, Mar. 16, 1844; *ibid.*, 577.

[52] The fact that Tyler had in the previous January nominated Spencer for a seat on the bench of the Supreme Court of the United States might indicate that the President was trying to get him out of the Cabinet. *Niles*, LXV, 353.

[53] *Ibid.*, LXVI, 209.

[54] *Ibid.*, 258; *National Intelligencer*, June 17, 1844.

quest may have given his Secretary a lasting grievance.[55]

Tyler now had a Cabinet which with the exception of Wilkins was made up entirely of Southern men. They were in agreement with the President in favor of the annexation of Texas and in opposition to a protective tariff and abolition. Harmony had been secured in his political household, but at the cost of subjecting his administration to the charge of sectionalism.

[55] *William and Mary College Historical Quarterly* (first series), XVIII, 174–175.

For an elaborate discussion, with numerous excerpts from the documents, of the alleged mutiny of young Spencer and his execution at sea and the trial of Mackenzie, see Benton, *Thirty Years' View*, II, 522–562.

CHAPTER XIX

TARIFF AND DISTRIBUTION

TYLER must have breathed a sigh of relief when the extra session of Congress finally came to an end. It had lengthened out through an unusually hot summer and was termed the "Dog Day Session." The President was delayed in Washington for more than a month awaiting the arrival of the members of his new Cabinet, and it was not until after the middle of October that he was able to leave the capital for a much needed rest.[1] The past seven months had been a time of incessant labor and constant strain. For a month or more of this period he had to act as his own Secretary of War, Secretary of Navy, and Postmaster General.

The first few days of this short vacation were devoted to visiting Norfolk, the public works at Fortress Monroe, the navy yard and dry docks at Portsmouth, and the United States warship, *Delaware,* lying in Hampton Roads. When he arrived at Williamsburg the citizens welcomed him by giving a ball in his honor.[2] Shortly afterwards, he was again honored by being invited to a public dinner given for him by some of his old constituents at "Cedar Hill," in New Kent County. In his letter declining this invitation he referred to the abuse that had been heaped upon him and said that "the light reflected from burning effigies served to render the path of duty more plain." [3] On the return to Wash-

[1] *The Papers of Daniel Webster* (L.C., abbreviation for Library of Congress), VI, 16,594; *National Intelligencer*, Oct. 22, 25, 1841.
[2] *Daily Richmond Whig*, Oct. 23, 1841; *Webster Papers*, VI, 16,592–93; *Niles' Register*, LXI, 131.
[3] Tyler, *Letters and Times*, II, 128–129.

ington he stopped at Richmond for a brief stay. According to the account of the hostile Richmond *Whig*, he was received very coolly by the Whigs of that city. Very few of them called to pay their respects, and what courtesies the President received were accorded him by the Democrats.[4]

During this period of leisure Tyler was formulating the financial scheme which had been referred to in his last message to Congress. He wrote two letters to L. W. Tazewell, setting forth his own ideas and asking for suggestions from the latter. The fact that Tazewell had gone back to the Democratic Party had not caused Tyler to abate the high opinion which he had always held of his old friend's character and judgment.[5] Just what response Tazewell made to these inquiries we do not know.

As a result of his vacation labors, the President was ready in December with a financial plan which he called the Exchequer. By it the safekeeping and disbursement of the public moneys would be under the charge of a board of control at Washington and agencies established at strategic financial centers throughout the country. This financial organization would also be authorized to buy and sell domestic bills and drafts and thus afford a means of exchange in the commerce between the States. It could receive individual deposits of gold and silver and issue certificates therefor which would be redeemable in these metals. These silver and gold certificates would have been of the same character as those that were in use prior to 1933. The volume of sound paper currency could be increased by the issuance of treasury notes in limited amounts. The plan was similar to the one proposed by President Jackson in his message of December, 1830.[6] When this scheme was submitted to the Cabinet it received its enthusiastic support, and only one modification was made at the suggestion of that body. The

[4] *Daily Richmond Whig*, Nov. 11, 1841.
[5] Tyler to Tazewell, Oct. 11, Nov. 2, 1841; Tyler, *op. cit.*, II, 127–128, 129.
[6] Richardson, *Messages and Papers of the Presidents*, II, 529; IV, 84–87; *Madisonian*, Dec. 11, 1841.

President was, therefore, entitled to full credit for the authorship of the measure.[7]

John C. Spencer, who had been one of the strongest opponents of the Second Bank of the United States, and Webster, who had always been the ardent champion of a national bank, both praised the plan in unmeasured terms. Spencer said that it had been "approved by some of the most competent financiers of this country and of England, and pronounced to be adequate to all our wants, safe in its operations, and calculated to furnish the most perfect currency that could be devised." It was, in its essential features, "far preferable to any other that has [had] been submitted" and would "accomplish all the purposes for which it was designed, without hazard to the government, without danger to the people, and without stimulating anew the reckless spirit of speculation, whose excesses we have all such cause to mourn."[8] Webster in his Faneuil Hall Speech (September 30, 1842) said that the Exchequer plan had his "hearty, sincere, and entire approval." "I am ready," he continued, "to stake my reputation, that, if this Whig Congress will take that measure and give it a fair trial, within three years it will be admitted by the whole American people to be the most beneficial measure of any sort ever adopted in this country, the Constitution only excepted."[9]

The President in his first annual message, December 7, 1841, gave in outline a plan of finance that the Secretary of the Treasury would present in detail to Congress if it were required.[10] At the request of Caleb Cushing the Secretary of the Treasury presented the President's scheme. Despite the merit of the proposal it was doomed to failure. To hope that the dominant party in Congress would endorse a measure suggested by a President whose leadership it had just

[7] *John Tyler Papers* (L.C.), II, 6433.   [8] *Niles,* LXIII, 141.
[9] *The Writings and Speeches of Daniel Webster* (National Edition), III, 133, 135.
[10] Richardson, *op. cit.,* IV, 84–87.

repudiated would be to ignore all the probabilities. Even if there had been no ill feeling between them, Clay would have been slow to sponsor an act which would strengthen his opponent's chances for the Presidency. For in the controversy between Tyler and Clay the latter acted as if he had rather be President than right.

A bill embodying Tyler's suggestions was offered in the House but never received proper consideration.[11] It was assailed from all quarters. Some said it would be a lifeless machine—would do no good and no evil. Others felt that it had a great deal too much vitality and would increase the executive power. "One party called it a ridiculous imbecility; the other, a dangerous grant, that might subvert the Constitution."[12] The Exchequer, thought the New York *Herald*, was a halfway house between a national bank and the Subtreasury. For that reason it was opposed by Benton and the other ultra-Democrats, who favored the Subtreasury, as well as by the Clay press, which advocated a national bank.[13] The bill was accordingly tabled in the session of 1841–42. In the next session it was voted down, and no further effort was made to carry out the Exchequer plan.[14]

The repeal of the Independent Treasury Act and the failure of the bank and Exchequer measures left the Federal government without a legal repository for its funds. State banks were, however, used for this purpose and the public moneys were safely cared for.

The assembling of Congress in regular session (December, 1841) was the signal for another bitter fight between

[11] *Cong. Globe*, 27th Cong., 2nd sess., 248–249; *National Intelligencer*, Dec. 22, 1841.

[12] Philip Hone characterized the Exchequer as "a machine to go without wheels, a mill without water, a steam engine without fuel, a sort of bank and no bank." Allan Nevins, ed., *The Diary of Philip Hone*, II, 577.

[13] New York *Herald*, Dec. 25, 1841; Richmond *Enquirer*, Dec. 15, 1842; *Daily Richmond Whig*, Jan. 1, 1842.

[14] *Cong. Globe*, 27th Cong., 3rd sess. (Jan. 27, 1843), 215.

the President and the Whigs. The causes of controversy this time were the tariff and the proposed distribution among the States of the sales of Federal lands.

As has already been seen, the third item on Clay's program was the raising of an adequate revenue by the imposition of tariff duties. The fourth was the prospective distribution among the States of the proceeds from the sales of public lands. A strong reason for raising the tariff duties was the need of getting an increase of revenue to balance the budget. It was estimated that the deficit in the Federal treasury would be at the end of the year 1841 more than eleven million dollars.[15] If this deficit was to be wiped away and the budget balanced, an increase in tariff duties would have to be made. The distribution of the proceeds from the public land sales would be a great boon to the States, many of which were staggering under debt burdens too heavy for them in a period of hard times.

Tyler, in his first message to the special session of Congress (June 1, 1841), had declared in favor of both of these policies.[16] He was careful, however, to suggest that no tariff bill should be framed that would violate the Compromise Tariff Act of 1833. This Compromise was dear to his heart. He had given it his ardent support when it came up in the Senate, and Clay by offering it had won his gratitude and admiration.[17] He took the position, therefore, that the compromise measure "should not be altered except under urgent necessities, which are not believed at this time to exist." [18] To steer these policies around the Compromise snag was no easy task. But inasmuch as Clay and Tyler were both favorable to them it looked as if it might be done.

With the view to attaining these objectives two bills were passed by Congress during the extra session. The first of these provided for the distribution among the States of the

[15] Richardson, op. cit., IV, 42–43.

[16] Ibid., 43, 47–48.

[17] See p. 425.

[18] Richardson, op. cit., 43.

proceeds of the sales of Federal lands. To this act was attached the condition that distribution was to be suspended whenever the tariff duties should exceed the twenty per cent level.[19] The second of these measures provided for an increase in the revenue by an extension of the tariff. This act was not inconsistent with the Compromise, as the increase in the duties was made by imposing the twenty per cent rate, the ultimate maximum, on articles then on the free list or taxed less than the maximum.[20]

One of these bills had been passed just before and the other just after the President had vetoed the Fiscal Corporation Bill. He approved these measures and thus went along with the Whig majority in Congress at a time when the newspapers and the leaders of the party were heaping abuse upon him. In so doing he exhibited a self-control and mildness of temper that is unusual in public officials.

The agreement between the President and the Whig majority in Congress was, however, more apparent than real. While both were in favor of distribution and an increase of the tariff, the reasons for this position were quite different in the two cases. Clay and his followers advocated a higher tariff primarily as a protection to American manufactures and secondarily as a means of increasing the revenue. They supported distribution largely because it would drain off one source of revenue and create a vacuum to be filled by taxes. This would necessitate the continuance of a high tariff to meet the needs of the government. Tyler, on the other hand, favored an increase of the tariff mainly for revenue purposes and only incidentally for protection. He recommended distribution solely as a relief measure for the States

[19] This act also included a provision granting pre-emption rights to settlers who had occupied and improved and erected a dwelling on public lands. The holder of such a claim could buy the land covered by it (not to exceed 160 acres) at the minimum price. Temporary laws of a like character had been passed before, but by this act the pre-emption system became a permanent policy. For the text of this law, see *U. S. Statutes at Large*, V, 453–458.

[20] *Ibid.*, 463–465.

and was unwilling for it to serve as an excuse for raising the tariff beyond the demands of the Treasury.

This initial agreement as to policy, despite the divergence of opinion behind it, was made possible by the rosy expectations as to future revenue indulged in by Tyler and his Secretary of the Treasury. Ewing in his report to Congress, submitted early in June, 1841, estimated that the tariff increases contemplated would provide more than enough revenue for the running expenses of the government. The proceeds from the sale of the public lands could, therefore, be used for other purposes.[21] Unfortunately the hoped-for prosperity on which this prophecy was based was slow in arriving, and when Congress assembled in December for the regular session the condition of the Federal finances was anything but promising.

The report of the Secretary of the Treasury at this session estimated that the total receipts for the year 1841 would be a little more than thirty million dollars, nearly one half of which had come from treasury notes and loans. Despite this large borrowing there would still be a small deficit at the end of 1841. For the year 1842 a deficit of fourteen millions was forecast. Moreover, of the loan of twelve million dollars voted by Congress at the special session, less than one half had been subscribed. The reason for this, in the opinion of the President, was the short length of time that the bonds had to run, and so he suggested an amendment to the law making the bonds not disposed of payable at a more distant date.[22]

In a special message to Congress on March 25, 1842, the President made a more definite recommendation as to the tariff. In order to meet the expenses of the government and provide for adequate national defense it would be necessary to put the tariff rates above the twenty per cent maximum on some important articles. These raises should be made primarily for the purpose of increasing the revenue

[21] Richardson, *loc. cit.*, 184–185.   [22] *Ibid.*, 81.

but they would necessarily afford incidental protection to manufactures. Regret was expressed for the necessity of departing from the principles of the Compromise of 1833, as this would cause the distribution of land-sale proceeds automatically to cease.[23]

This message proved to be an empty gesture, for the Whig majority in both branches was more inclined to disregard than to accept the recommendations of a President whom it had repudiated. Despite Tyler's insistence on prompt action, Congress was slow to take up the important revenue question. Finally two bills were passed, one providing for a provisional and the other a permanent tariff. The former (passed June 25, 1842) postponed for a month the reduction in rates that were due on July 1 under the Compromise Act. It also retained the principle of the distribution of land sales among the States, though it postponed until August 1 the distribution that would have been made on July 1.[24] There was need of a temporary tariff act, it was urged, as doubt had been raised as to the legality of collections after June 30 under the Act of 1833.

Tyler considered that Congress was morally obligated not to suspend or repeal the Act of 1833 except under imperative necessity. That the financial needs of the Federal treasury constituted such an exigency he was forced to admit. He would agree, therefore, to suspend the Compromise to secure the revenue needed by the government; but he was not willing to sacrifice it on the altar of protection or distribution. A measure of protection to manufactures should be granted, but only so much as was incidental to a tariff policy which would put the credit of the country on a solid basis. He, therefore, vetoed the bill on the ground that it violated the principle of both the Compromise and Distribution Acts.[25] Nor did he consider that this temporary measure was urgently needed, for he had been advised by the

---

[23] *Ibid.*, 108–109. [24] *Cong. Globe*, 27th Cong., 2nd sess., 615, 688.
[25] Richardson, *op. cit.*, IV, 180–183.

Attorney General that collections could still be made after June 30 under the Act of 1833.[26]

The attempt to pass the provisional tariff bill over the President's veto was unsuccessful.[27] In the meantime Congress had taken up the question of a permanent tariff. A bill was passed on August 5 [28] which was substantially the same in principle as the temporary tariff vetoed by the President. For it not only raised the tariff rate above the twenty per cent level but provided for the unconditional continuance of distribution. The measure was carried by narrow majorities in both houses.[29]

That the President would veto such a measure should have been clearly evident to anyone who had any faith in his loyalty to conviction. The acceptance of this bill after the rejection of the one of the previous June would have been the height of inconsistency. It looked (as was charged by a Democratic Representative) as if the Whig majority was mainly interested in "heading" the President. By forcing him to an unpopular veto it would place him in an unfavorable light with the public and thus make him the scapegoat.[30]

Four days after the bill was passed by Congress the President, against the urgent advice of Webster,[31] returned it to the House of Representatives with his objections. His veto message was an able state paper. In it the President expressed great reluctance to disagree with Congress on the measure and presented strong reasons for his disapproval.

[26] House Ex. Docs., 31st Cong., 2nd sess., Document 55, pp. 1505–13.
[27] Cong. Globe, loc. cit., 717–718.   [28] Ibid., 852.
[29] Ibid., 762, 852.
In the House of Representatives the vote (July 16) was 116 yeas to 112 nays; in the Senate 25 yeas to 23 nays.
[30] Ibid., 735–736.
[31] Webster strongly urged the President to accept the measure, although he admitted that Congress should not have united the tariff with distribution. The country, he said, was in such an awful state that he would almost give his right arm if the President would sign the bill. Webster's Writings (Nat. Ed.), XVI, 381.

The greatest objection was the provision for raising the tariff rates above the twenty per cent level and at the same time continuing distribution. "While the Treasury is in a state of extreme embarrassment, requiring every dollar which it can make available, and when the government has not only to lay additional taxes, but to borrow money to meet pressing demands, the bill proposes to give away a fruitful source of revenue . . . a proceeding which I must regard as highly impolitic, if not unconstitutional." This policy while it would add materially to the embarrassment of the Treasury would afford to the States no decided relief.[32]

In vetoing this unwise measure the President was acting strictly in accordance with sound financial policy. It would have been preposterous for the Federal government to alienate an important source of revenue at a time when it could not balance its budget on running expenses and could not borrow money except at high rates of interest. The veto was, to be sure, another cause of friction between the executive and legislative branches of the government and another occasion for widening the rift in the Whig Party. These were considerations, however, which should have had little or no weight in determining his action.

It was unfortunate that the President on this occasion should have weakened his impregnable position by expressions of regret for this disagreement with Congress. He now owed nothing to a party that had excommunicated him, whatever may have been his obligations at the beginning of his term. Moreover, the breach between Congress and the President was irreparable and no breath should have been wasted in deploring this situation. He should have stated the reasons for his veto boldly and without apology and left protestations of regret to those leaders who had sponsored this absurd measure. Tyler was evidently a close student of

[32] Richardson, *op. cit.*, IV, 183–189.

Shakespeare, but there was one utterance of the noted dramatist that he must have overlooked. It was: "The lady doth protest too much, methinks."

The Whig leaders in Congress proceeded to act on the assumption that Tyler had again betrayed his party and to punish him for this alleged treason. To talk of a President's disloyalty to a party from which he had been expelled would under ordinary circumstances have appealed irresistably to the sense of humor of politicians. But by this time the hatred which the Whigs had for Tyler seems to have paralyzed their risibles, and in all seriousness they undertook to flay him for his political irregularity.

The veto message was, therefore, referred in the House to a special committee of thirteen members, of which John Quincy Adams was chairman and Botts a member. If the House of Representatives had been carefully combed there could not have been found two members better qualified to vent spleen upon the President than these his two archenemies.

The report of the committee was quite in keeping with the expectations raised by its personnel. The majority report (made August 16, 1842), which was signed by Adams and nine other Whigs, did not confine itself to the tariff veto, but assailed the whole official conduct of the President and charged him with offenses of the gravest character. The report also recommended that an amendment to the Constitution be proposed which would enable Congress by a bare majority of both houses to pass a bill over the President's veto. The majority of the committee also were of the opinion that the President deserved impeachment, and they refrained from recommending this expedient only because they felt it would prove abortive.[33]

The severe arraignment of the majority report was based not on carefully sifted evidence but on facts distorted by

---

[33] *Cong. Globe, loc. cit.*, 894–896. The text of the report is also given in *Niles*, LXII, 395–397.

partisanship and rumor colored by hate. When viewed by the student of history in an attitude of cool objectivity it appears more as an indictment of the committee than of the President. For the emotional, biased statements made in the report cannot properly be admitted as evidence against the President, while they afford irrefutable proof of the bitterness and unfairness that characterized the findings of the committee.

There was a minority report signed by two Democrats, C. J. Ingersoll and James I. Roosevelt.[34] A counter report, which was in the nature of a protest, was also sent in by Thomas W. Gilmer, of Virginia, a member of the "Corporal's Guard." In both of these minority reports the President was upheld and the action of the House with reference to the veto condemned. Gilmer contended that the House of Representatives in tabling the veto and referring the President's reasons for the veto to a committee instead of reconsidering the measure was running counter to traditional practice and the spirit of the Constitution.[35]

The majority report was adopted by the House by a vote of 98 to 90.[36] The adoption of this report led the President to send a protest to the House (August 30, 1842). This was a dignified statement conveying strong arguments logically arranged and forcefully expressed. In making this accusation Congress had, he affirmed, been unjust to him as a man, had infringed his powers as Chief Magistrate of the American people, and had violated in his person the rights secured to every citizen by the laws and the Constitution. "I have been accused without evidence and condemned without a hearing. . . . I am charged with violating pledges which I never gave, . . . with usurping powers not conferred by law, and, above all, with using the powers conferred upon the President by the Constitution from corrupt motives and for unwarrantable ends. And these charges are made without any particle of evidence to sustain them, and, as I

[34] *Cong. Globe, loc. cit.,* 899–901. [35] *Ibid.,* 896–899. [36] *Ibid.,* 907–908.

solemnly affirm, without any foundation in truth." The
whole proceeding of the House of Representatives he
characterized as *ex parte* and extrajudicial. If he were guilty
of the high crimes charged, Congress should have employed
the method of impeachment and trial.[37]

Although Tyler asked that this statement be entered upon
the journal of the House of Representatives as a solemn and
formal declaration against the injustice and unconstitutionality of such a proceeding, the request was voted down. By
raking up a former act of his, Tyler's enemies were able to
attach a sharp barb to this refusal. In 1834 President Jackson was censured by the Senate for the withdrawal of government funds from the Second Bank of the United States.
Jackson sent to the Senate a formal protest against this procedure. The Senate refused to receive this protest, and both
Tyler and Webster had voted for the resolutions of refusal.
On the motion of Botts, the House now (August 30)
adopted three resolutions which were a verbatim copy of
the Senate resolutions of 1834.[38] It doubtless afforded Botts
satanic glee to mete out poetic injustice to his former friend
for a partisan sin committed by the latter while he was in
the Senate.

The Whig press joined in the chorus of abuse against
Tyler, led by the politicians, while the Democratic papers
acclaimed his veto policy. The *Daily Richmond Whig* said:
"Again has the imbecile, into whose hands accident has
placed the power, vetoed a bill passed by a majority of
those legally authorized to pass it." [39] Of all the criticisms
hurled against the President, that pronounced by the Whigs
of his own county probably cut most deeply into his feelings.
Resolutions were adopted at Charles City Courthouse (August 18) which strongly condemned his entire course and
declared that the Whigs did "most solemnly repudiate him

[37] Richardson, *op. cit.*, IV, 190–193.   [38] *Cong. Globe, loc. cit.*, 973–975.
[39] *Daily Richmond Whig*, July 2, August 17, 1842; Richmond *Enquirer*,
July 5, Aug. 16, 1842.

and his political treacheries." In the list of those who signed these resolutions was the name of Hill Carter, of "Shirley," at whose beautiful home Harrison and Tyler spent the night on the way to the inauguration in 1841. The *Whig* in commenting on these resolutions said that Tyler when he read them would doubtless exclaim, *"My native land,* good night!"[40]

After the President had vetoed the provisional tariff law the ever-ready Botts made an effort in the House of Representatives to have him impeached. He preferred a number of charges against the President and offered a resolution calling for the appointment of a committee of nine Representatives to inquire into the truth of these complaints. This resolution was defeated (January 10, 1843) by a vote of 83 yeas to 127 nays.[41] According to the Richmond *Whig,* most of the Whigs throughout the country were not in favor of this policy, though every member of the party acknowledged the justice of the articles preferred by Botts. Such a course, however, would be unwise because it might give too much importance to the insignificant incumbent; "it might invest nothingness with consequence."[42] Such an attempt was also pronounced unwise by Clay.

Despite all the noise made by the Whigs in Congress and through the press, the President had won over them in this fight. They realized that they dared not return to their constituents without having enacted a revenue measure. So they were forced to yield to Tyler and present another bill without the objectionable distribution clause. Accordingly, such a measure was passed, though it was carried by a very narrow majority in each house.[43]

This law raised the general level of duties to that of 1832,

[40] *Daily Richmond Whig,* Aug. 30, 1842.
[41] *Cong. Globe,* 27th Cong., 3rd sess., 144–146.
[42] Richmond *Enquirer,* July 5, 15, 1842; *Daily Richmond Whig,* July 20, 1842.
[43] *Cong. Globe, loc. cit.,* 912, 923–926, 960, 973; *Webster's Writings* (Nat. Ed.), III, 130.

and was quite satisfactory to the protectionists throughout the country.[44] It was objectionable, however, to the low-tariff advocates, especially those in South Carolina. The *Columbian South Carolinian* (Calhoun's organ) berated Tyler for signing the bill, which it denounced as "the most flagrantly protective, fraudulent, perfidious, oppressive, unjust, and unconstitutional tariff bill that has ever passed." [45]

When it is recalled that Tyler had been a lifelong opponent of protection and that the tariff of 1832 had caused the nullification of South Carolina, it might be thought that his endorsement of this boost in the tariff rates involved a sacrifice of his deep-rooted convictions. But this was not the case. His advocacy of an increase in duties was prompted not by a change in views but by a recognition of the necessities of the government. Like Grover Cleveland at a later time, he was confronted with a condition not a theory. And it is a credit to his statesmanship that he gave more heed to the needs of the government than to the teachings of an abstract political philosophy.

[44] For the text of this tariff law see *House Docs.*, 61st Cong., 2nd. sess., no. 671, pp. 120–139. For important tables showing by comparison the rates of the tariff acts of 1816, 1824, 1828, 1832, and 1842, see *Niles*, LXIII, 39–40. See also D. R. Dewey, *Financial History of the United States* (New York, 1912), 238–239.

[45] Quoted by *Niles*, LXIII, 140.

CHAPTER XX

SUCCESSFUL DIPLOMACY

TYLER'S success in handling the foreign affairs of the country was in marked contrast to his inability to realize his aims as to domestic policy. Few administrations, if any, in the entire history of our country can point to greater results in the settlement of important and difficult diplomatic problems. For these achievements President Tyler is entitled to a large measure of credit. He not only manifested a deep interest in these questions but also kept in close touch with the negotiations that led to their solution. It was in diplomacy that the good points in his personality appeared to the greatest advantage. His tact, courtesy, and facility for making easy contacts with others acted as a lubricant to prevent friction from becoming dangerous in certain tense situations.

When Tyler acceded to the Presidency our relations with England had assumed a threatening aspect.[1] In the unwelcome legacy left to him by his predecessor were three causes of dispute between the United States and Great Britain. These were: (1) the *Caroline* case and the McLeod incident that grew out of it;[2] (2) a disagreement as to the loca-

---

[1] As late as October, 1841, Secretary Wickliffe in an address at a dinner given to him by his neighbors, said: "At this moment we are threatened with a war by the most powerful nation of Europe." *Niles' Register*, LXI, 131.

[2] The *Caroline* was an American vessel which had been aiding the Canadian rebels in 1837. While this vessel was lying on the American side of the Niagara River, an expedition from Canada came over, cut the moorings of this ship, set her on fire, and allowed her to drift over Niagara Falls. In the attack on the *Caroline* an American citizen named Durfree was killed.

The British government justified this action of the Canadians on the ground that it was a necessary means of defense. Our State Department would not concede this point. It was not until July, 1842, that an agreement was reached. At that time Webster and Lord Ashburton, special minister from England

tion of the northeast boundary; and (3) the question of the right of visit and search in connection with the suppression of the slave trade. These issues had aroused a feeling of bitterness, which in each case had been intensified rather than alleviated by the discussions that had rotated around them. Another cause of friction was the *Creole* case,[3] which arose soon after Tyler's accession.

There were other reasons, more or less intangible, for

---

to the United States, came to an understanding which was acceptable to President Tyler. *Cong. Globe,* 29th Cong., 1st sess., 617; *The Works of Daniel Webster,* 6 vols. (Boston, 1851), VI, 259–262, 300, 302; G. T. Curtis, *Life of Daniel Webster,* II, 121, note.

Alexander McLeod, a Canadian, had come over to New York, and while in his cups boasted that he had killed Durfree when the *Caroline* was destroyed. He was arrested (November, 1840) and later brought up for trial in a New York State court. The British government strongly protested against his arrest, contending that persons engaging in a transaction of a public character could not incur private or personal responsibility. Webster agreed to this view but was unable to secure McLeod's release, as the New York authorities insisted on holding him for trial. Several letters regarding the case passed between the President and Governor Seward, of New York. These were sharper in tone than would ordinarily be expected of gentlemen in high position. The difficulty was finally solved when the prisoner was declared not guilty by the New York court.

To prevent such an embarrassing situation from arising in the future Webster, with Tyler's approval, drafted a bill to cover such eventualities, which was passed by Congress in August, 1842. By this act the Federal courts were given jurisdiction in all cases in which aliens had been charged with crimes committed under authority of a foreign government.

For an excellent account of the McLeod Case, see M. L. Bonham, Jr., "Alexander McLeod: Bone of Contention," in *New York History,* XVIII, 189–217. See also G. T. Curtis, *Life of Daniel Webster,* II, 62, 62, note, 64, 86; *Webster's Works,* VI, 247–250, 267–268; Tyler, *Letters and Times,* II, 206–207, 208 ff.; Adams, *Memoirs,* XI, 21, 26–27; George E. Baker, ed., *The Works of William H. Seward,* 5 vols. (New York, 1884), 558–559, 560–577; Richardson, *Messages,* IV, 75.

[3] The *Creole,* an American vessel, had sailed (October, 1841) from Hampton Roads, Virginia, for New Orleans, with a cargo of merchandise and slaves. When she got out to sea some of the slaves revolted, overpowered the officers and crew, and forced the mate to steer for Nassau, a British port in the Bahama Islands. Here the slaves that had participated in the mutiny were kept in custody and the others were liberated by the authorities. Secretary Webster, of course, protested against this highhanded act, but the British government was slow to make amends for it, and the dispute was not settled until 1853. J. B. Moore, *History and Digest of the International Arbitrations to Which the United States Has Been a Party,* 6 vols. (Washington, 1898), 410–411, 417.

the growth of misunderstanding between the two kindred peoples. Some of the States had repudiated their debts, and as a result English creditors had lost heavily. The rebellion against British authority which had broken out in Canada had not yet entirely subsided, and some of our citizens were in sympathy with the rebels. Webster reported (July, 1841) that there were "Hunters' Lodges" and "Patriotic Societies" all along the Canadian border from Maine to Minnesota. They were, he thought, in constant communication with the insurgents and were trying to provoke a war between Canada and the United States.[4] The President issued a proclamation (September 25, 1841) warning the members of these lodges against making incursions into Canada or collecting money for that purpose. Such offenders would be punished under the laws of the United States and if caught by the British authorities would not be reclaimed as American citizens.[5] Despite the vigilant efforts of the government to maintain a strict neutrality in this revolt, British fears exaggerated the activities of these American sympathizers with the insurgents and saw in them a feeling of hostility to England on the part of our people in general.

Webster was able finally to come to an understanding with the British foreign office as to the *Caroline* affair and the McLeod incident. Steps were also taken toward the settlement of the *Creole* case, though an agreement was not reached by the end of Tyler's administration.

The President did not take an important part in the conferences and communications regarding the *Caroline*, McLeod, and *Creole* incidents, but he co-operated with and effectively supported his Secretary of State in his efforts to adjust these differences. He was, however, entitled to a good deal of credit for the settlement of the controversy over the

[4] Webster to Tyler (about July, 1841); C. H. Van Tyne, ed., *The Letters of Daniel Webster* (N. Y., 1902), 232–233. See also the President's Proclamation of September 25, 1841; Richardson, *Messages and Papers of the Presidents*, IV, 72–73.
[5] *Niles*, LXI, 66–67.

northeast boundary. He took an active interest in the proceedings and was able to give Webster valuable assistance in the negotiations.

The dispute over the boundary between Maine and New Brunswick was as old as the nation itself and owed its origin to the vague or inaccurate wording of the treaties of Paris (1782, 1783). By 1798 the northeastern boundary of the United States had been fixed from the mouth to the source of the St. Croix River, but the rest of it was still under dispute. Before the accession of Tyler the location of the line ceased to be merely a question for academic discussion but had become the occasion of a dangerous practical controversy. The citizens of Maine and those of New Brunswick came to blows in the disputed area, the Aroostook Valley. These clashes (1838–39), sometimes called the "Aroostook War," might easily have led to international strife. General Scott was sent to the frontier and through his agency the friction was temporarily suspended.[6] Efforts at arbitration made in 1840 were futile, and so the disagreement over the northeastern boundary was one of the most pressing of the problems left to Tyler by his predecessor.

With the hope of adjusting the controversy, Lord Aberdeen (who had succeeded Lord Palmerston as Secretary of State for Foreign Affairs in the new British Cabinet) sent a special minister to the United States with power to settle all the points of difference between the two countries. "In the choice of the individual for the mission," he declared, "he had been mainly influenced by a desire to select a person who would be peculiarly acceptable to the United States as well as eminently qualified for the trust." [7]

The person selected for this important post was Alexander Baring, first Lord Ashburton. His wife was the daughter of a prominent American and he had a feeling of strong

[6] *The Works of Daniel Webster*, V, 93–94.
[7] Everett to Webster, December 31, 1841; *The Diplomatic and Official Papers of Daniel Webster, while Secretary of State* (N. Y., 1848), 33.

attachment for her country. During his entire public career of thirty-five years, both as a member of Parliament and as a member of the banking company of Baring Brothers, he had been assiduous in promoting peace and harmony between the two great English-speaking nations.[8] He was now giving up the retirement which he preferred to assume this difficult task, only because he "could not resist the temptation and the hope of being of some service to my country and to our common race." [9]

One circumstance that made the task more difficult was that Maine and Massachusetts, as well as the United States and Great Britain, were parties to the controversy and participants in the negotiations. Maine asserted jurisdiction over the disputed area, and both Maine and Massachusetts claimed equal ownership of its public lands.

Lord Ashburton arrived at Washington early in April (1842) with authority to agree upon a conventional line.[10] He was accompanied by three secretaries and five servants. He and his suite were very conciliatory and tactful in their social relations.[11] This cordiality was warmly reciprocated by social and official Washington, and a round of entertainments was given in his honor.[12]

The most elaborate of these affairs was the one given on June 12 by the President at the White House. Owing to Mrs. Tyler's illness, Mrs. Robert Tyler was then acting as mistress of the White House, and she and the President did the honors so well as to win praise even from John Quincy Adams. He admitted that the guests, about one hundred in number, including himself, Lord Ashburton, Webster, Mrs. Madison, and the ladies of the gentlemen present, were

[8] Ashburton to Webster, Jan. 2, 1842; Van Tyne, *Letters of Daniel Webster,* 253.
[9] Lord Ashburton to Webster, June 21, 1842; *Cong. Globe,* 27th Cong., 3rd sess., 5.
[10] New York *Herald,* Apr. 7, 1842; Adams, *Memoirs,* XI, 122.
[11] Benton to Van Buren, June 3, 1842; *Van Buren Papers,* XLIV, 10,305.
[12] Adams, *op. cit.,* XI, 133, 139, 150–151, 172, 174.

treated in royal fashion. "The courtesies of the President and of Mrs. R. Tyler to their guests were all that the most accomplished European court could have displayed." [13] And this from one who was quite familiar with European courts and was by no means inclined to exaggerate any merit that might attach to the President or his family.

The negotiations between Webster and Lord Ashburton were carried on in the main by informal conferences rather than by formal notes. In these conferences the "mere etiquette, the unnecessary mystery and mummeries of negotiations, were dispensed with." [14] According to a statement made by Tyler in later years, the negotiations were conducted without protocol or letter. "The letters were written after agreement, and each submitted to me and received my correction.[15] This informality was planned by Webster, because he thought that an understanding could more easily be arrived at in this way.

At one time the negotiations were in serious danger of being wrecked by the stand taken by the Maine commissioners. In a letter to Webster they showed an uncompromising attitude of opposition to the demands of Lord Ashburton and were by no means tactful in expressing their objections.[16] Ashburton was so discouraged by this flare-up that he was on the verge of ending his mission and returning home. The terrific heat of a typical Washington summer was making inroads on his comfort and strength and causing him to long for a change of climate. Writing to Webster on July 1, he said: "I contrive to crawl about in these heats by day and pass my nights in a sleepless fever. In short, I shall positively not outlive this affair, if it is to be much prolonged." [17] His anxiety to return home was increased by an unfavorable turn which the *Creole* case had taken. No wonder Webster be-

---

[13] Adams, *op. cit.*, XI, 174.   [14] *Niles*, LXIII, 37.
[15] Tyler to Robert Tyler, Aug. 29, 1858; Tyler, *Letters and Times*, II, 242.
[16] The Maine Commissioners to Webster, June 29, 1842; *Cong. Globe*, 27th Cong., 3rd sess., 14–16.
[17] Curtis, *Life of Daniel Webster*, II, 113, note.

came discouraged and felt that the negotiations had gone backward instead of forward.

It was at this juncture that the President was able to give most effective aid. He realized that if this attempt to settle the controversy failed, relations between the two powers would be more strained than before. He asked Lord Ashburton for an interview, which was granted. At this conference he impressed upon him the importance of continuing the negotiations and induced him to remain at his post. The situation was one which called into requisition the President's suavity of manner, conversational ability, and familiarity with the amenities employed in diplomacy. By the use of these qualities he was able to divest argument of disagreeable personal allusions and persuade without antagonizing. In this respect he was superior to Webster, whose nerves, frayed by ill-health and the heat, were not at all times sufficiently steady for him to maintain the poise and composure necessary for success in diplomacy. He always admitted the important part played by Tyler at this critical point in the negotiations.[18]

By a policy of give and take, Lord Ashburton and Webster were able to iron out their differences in their conferences, and in due time an agreement was reached on all the disputed points of the northeast boundary. Under the terms of this treaty the United States received about seven of the twelve thousand square miles in dispute. This compromise was quite a concession on the part of the United States; for in the light of later evidence it appears that the boundary claimed by our government was the same as the one agreed upon by the commissioners in 1782.[19] But this unconscious

[18] Webster to Everett, June 28, 1842; Curtis, *op. cit.*, II, 104–107. Tyler, *op. cit.*, 458.

[19] Old maps with the northeast boundary marked in accordance with the understanding of 1782 have come to light since this treaty was signed. One of these was discovered in the archives of Spain as late as 1933. These maps show that our government was right in its original claim as to the Maine-New Brunswick boundary. See S. F. Bemis, *A Diplomatic History of the United States* (New York, 1936), 262–264.

sacrifice of a few thousand square miles of land was in the nature of a peace offering and was a small price to pay for the adjustment of a dispute that had menaced the amicable relations of two great powers for two generations. Maine and Massachusetts were induced to accept the settlement by the promise that $125,000.00 would be paid to each of them out of the Federal treasury as compensation for the lands given up by them.[20]

After having settled the boundary dispute, the peace-makers turned their attention to the question of the slave trade. At that time slave vessels could go from the coast of Africa and deliver their cargoes at a West Indian or South American port without much fear of molestation. To put a stop to this the British government suggested that all the powers interested in the suppression of this traffic allow each other to exercise a limited right of search, or at least of visitation. Some of the leading nations of Europe had signed with England a treaty giving to each signatory a partial right of search. Lord Aberdeen expressed the hope that the great American Republic would accede to this treaty and thus align herself with the other Christian powers in the cause of mercy and peace. He did not claim for British cruisers the right to interfere with American vessels, even if they were engaged in the unholy traffic. All he asked was that British ships be allowed to stop slavers that were strongly suspected of making a fraudulent use of the American flag or American papers, "in order to take such means as were indispensably necessary for ascertaining the truth." [21]

Such a request President Tyler was unwilling to grant. In his first annual message to Congress (December, 1841), he declared that the acquiescence in such a practice would be to forfeit a right clearly recognized in international law and subject our merchant vessels to unnecessary annoyance. He

[20] *Cong. Globe, loc. cit.*, 19–21.
[21] Aberdeen to Everett, Dec. 20, 1841; Webster, *Diplomatic and Official Papers*, 145.

admitted that it was quite probable that the American flag had been "abused by the abandoned and profligate of other nations," and called the attention of Congress to this fact with the view that something be done to remedy this evil. He also recommended the strengthening of the laws for the suppression of the African slave trade.[22]

In taking this position, Tyler was acting within the rights of his country as defined by international law; but by so doing he put the United States in the unenviable position of thwarting the commendable efforts of other powers to stamp out a nefarious practice. The rigid insistence upon our technical rights at this inopportune time was doubtless due to memories of the War of 1812, which had been brought on largely by British practices connected with the assertion of the doctrine of visit and search.

The feeling in the United States against visit and search was so strong that Webster would not agree to discuss it, as Ashburton wished, but a practical plan for putting a stop to the slave trade was adopted. It was agreed that each nation will "maintain on the coast of Africa . . . a naval force . . . of not less than eighty guns to enforce, separately and respectively, the laws . . . for the suppression of the slave trade." Each squadron was to be independent of the other, but the officers of each were to receive from their respective governments such instructions as would enable them to co-operate whenever the exigencies should demand it.[23]

The treaty was signed August 9 and sent to the Senate two days later. The Committee on Foreign Relations reported it without amendment, and it was ratified by a vote of thirty-nine to nine. All the negative votes but one were cast by Democrats.[24]

[22] Richardson, IV, 77–78.
[23] For the text of this treaty see W. M. Malloy, Treaties, Conventions, International Acts . . . between the United States of America and Other Powers, 3 vols. (Washington, 1910–23), I, 650–656.
[24] Webster's Works, VI, 365–366.

Both Tyler and Webster were proud of their success in thus settling this long-standing dispute and they were justified in claiming for themselves a large measure of credit for this result. Tyler, writing to Tazewell (October 24, 1842), expressed the opinion that if the administration had nothing to its credit up to this time but the English treaty it would be "fairly entitled to some small share of praise." [25] In the opinion of the late John W. Foster, the negotiation of this treaty was Webster's greatest achievement in diplomacy. [26]

While Webster has been highly praised for this fine service to his country, due credit has never been accorded President Tyler for the part he played in these delicate and important negotiations, though there is abundant evidence to show that both Webster and Lord Ashburton recognized the value of his contribution to the final result. Webster said that "the negotiations proceeded from step to step, and from day to day" under the immediate supervision of the President. [27] "In the late negotiation with the English envoy I acted, of course, by the authority and under the direction of the President. If the immediate labor devolved on me, the constant supervision and final sanction belonged to him." [28]

In a letter to the President (August 24, 1842) Webster expressed his appreciation of the former's valuable assistance in the negotiations in the following terms:

I shall never speak of this negotiation, my dear sir, which I believe is destined to make some figure in the history of the country, without doing you justice. Your steady support and confidence, your anxious and intelligent attention to what was in progress, and your exceed-

[25] *John Tyler Papers* (L.C.), 6432–33.
In a letter to Webster, April 21, 1846, Tyler said that "if we had consummated no other act than the Treaty, we should have better deserved any other fate, than the violent and august denunciation to which we have been subjected." Van Tyne, *Letters of Daniel Webster*, 317.
[26] John Foster, *A Century of American Diplomacy* (Boston and New York, 1900), 283.
[27] Webster to Cass, Dec. 20, 1842; *Niles*, LXIV, 79.
[28] Daniel Webster to Jonathan Thompson, George Griswold, and others; *The Writings and Speeches of Daniel Webster* (Nat. Ed.), XVI, 387.

ingly obliging and pleasant intercourse, both with the British minister
and the commissioners of the States, have given every possible facility
to my agency in this important transaction. Nor ought I to forget the
cordial co-operation of my colleagues in the Cabinet, to every one of
whom I am indebted for valuable assistance.[29]

It was due to Tyler's suggestion that all the articles
agreed upon by the negotiators should be put together in
one treaty and not submitted to the Senate in the form of
separate treaties, as Webster advised.[30] If the latter course
had been pursued, some important provisions of the settlement might not have been ratified. Tyler's greatest contribution, however, lay in the tact and fine courtesy he always
exhibited in his intercourse with the British envoy. That
Lord Ashburton was strongly influenced by this friendly attitude of the President is indicated by a letter sent by him
to Webster (January 2, 1843) in which he asked that his
respectful acknowledgments be presented to the President
"for his always kind reception to me." "His conduct through
the course of my mission inspired me always with the greatest respect." [31]

The feeling of the Whigs against Tyler was still so bitter
that they were not inclined to show any appreciation for
this important service. On the contrary they were rather
disposed to insult him whenever occasion offered. Their attitude is seen in an incident that occurred at a dinner given to
Lord Ashburton in New York (September, 1842). A toast
to the Queen of England was responded to by loud applause
while one to the President was received in silence. The people of New York, however, did not approve of this act of
churlishness. As a protest against it a large mass meeting
was held and thousands of citizens marched in procession
carrying banners on which were inscribed the legend, AN IN-
SULT TO THE PRESIDENT IS AN INSULT TO THE NATION. A
meeting was also held in Philadelphia at which were adopted

[29] Quoted by Foster, *op. cit.,* 283.
[30] *Tyler's Quarterly Historical and Genealogical Magazine,* VIII, 21.
[31] Fletcher Webster, ed., *The Private Correspondence of Daniel Webster,*
II, 164.

resolutions censuring those persons who had participated in this unfortunate affair.[32]

While the Webster-Ashburton Treaty removed the actual causes of dispute on the points covered, there was still enough vagueness in the wording of it to give rise to an academic misunderstanding. The President was of the opinion that Great Britain, by accepting a plan that would supersede the practice of visit and search, had given up that right in time of peace, so far as American vessels were concerned. The British authorities did not accept this view, but made it clear that they still adhered in principle to the right of visit but not of search in time of peace. They declared, however, that the right would be used only to determine the character of the vessel. Moreover, if in the exercise of this authority any loss or injury should be sustained by an American vessel prompt reparation would be made.[33]

In this way ended one of the most important chapters in the history of American diplomacy. To John Tyler, as well as Daniel Webster and Lord Ashburton, we owe a debt of gratitude for this happy outcome. The diplomatic situation at the accession of Tyler and the achievement of himself and his premier were later correctly summarized by him as follows: "The peace of the country when I reached Washington on the 6th day of April, 1841, was suspended by a thread; but we [Webster and he] converted that thread into a chain cable of sufficient strength to render that peace secure." [34]

[32] Allan Nevins, ed., *The Diary of Philip Hone,* II, 618–619; *Madisonian,* Sept. 13, 15, 1842.

[33] For the position of Lord Aberdeen see a letter from Webster to Everett, Mar. 28, 1843; Webster's *Works,* VI, 331–342. For the views of Tyler and Webster see *ibid.* and Tyler's messages of December 6, 1842, and February 27, 1843; Richardson, IV, 195–196, 230–231. See also Tyler to John Tyler, Jr., Sept. 7, 1858; Tyler, *Letters and Times,* II, 240–242; *John Tyler Papers* (L.C.), IV, 6801–03.

[34] Tyler to Webster, Mar. 12, 1846; *Webster's Writings* (Nat. Ed.), XVI, 444, note.

CHAPTER XXI

A PRESIDENT WITHOUT A PARTY

ONE of the chief functions of a President of the United States is to suggest legislative measures and induce Congress to pass them. This service cannot be performed unless he has behind him a party that looks to him for leadership. As Tyler was "a President without a party" (to use a phrase coined by Clay [1]), he was handicapped as to his greatest responsibility. Moreover, the opposition of the Whig Party, which dominated both houses of Congress in the first part of his term and the Senate throughout his entire term, restricted his power of appointment and thwarted his aims with reference to foreign policy.

His influence was further weakened by the hostility of the Whig newspapers, which continued to chorus a hymn of hate until the end of his administration. In this way they whipped up public sentiment against him and did all they could to strip him of every shred of popularity. So successful were they in this attempt that Tyler never received the share of the public esteem which his character and achievements merited. Only for a few months in the beginning of his term did he enjoy public favor. The New York *Herald* and even the Richmond *Whig* spoke of his popularity in the early days, and Amherst College in token of its regard for the Chief Magistrate conferred upon him the degree of Doctor of Laws.[2]

The honeymoon, however, did not last long, and soon we

[1] New York *Herald*, Apr. 9, 1842.
[2] New York *Herald*, July 29, 30, 1841. The Richmond *Whig* (Aug. 3, 1841) quoted the New York *Times and Star* as saying that Tyler's position was then such as likely to result in the winning of "a popularity equal to that of any President who has ruled over this Republic in its palmiest days."

hear the highest dignitary in the land termed "His Accidency," [3] an "Executive Ass," and other unflattering designations.[4] The editorials of the Richmond *Whig* were a classic in vituperation. Some of the epithets and phrases of abuse employed by this sheet were collected and reported by its rival, the *Enquirer*, as follows: "The Richmond *Whig* calls Mr. Tyler 'the Accident of an Accident'—'a famished Charles City pettifogger, whom Nature never intended to elevate above the trial of ten dollar warrants upon plain cases, a man *destitute of intellect and integrity, whose name is the synonym of nihil'*—'if so miserable a thing can be called a man!'—'base, selfish and perfidious'—'a vast nightmare over the Republic'—and exclaims with Shakespeare

'O! for a whip in every honest hand,
To *lash the rascal* naked through the world.'" [5]

With the Whig press continually making such bitter attacks on him, it is no wonder that Tyler was hated and despised not only by political opponents but also by a considerable portion of the people. His unpopularity with the masses is attested by the fact that when an epidemic of influenza swept over the country the disease was called the "Tyler Grippe." [6]

That Tyler was deeply hurt by these onslaughts on his reputation goes without saying, but he did not react to them by undignified exhibitions of emotion. While the fires were burning within, he maintained the outward appearance of a stoic calm. "So unceasing are my engagements," he wrote to a friend, "that I rarely ever hear anything of the abuse of the malignants who are perpetually assailing me. The elements are all in motion about me, and yet I labor on in the faithful discharge of my duties, without being affected by

[3] New York *Courier and Inquirer*, quoted by the Richmond *Whig*, Apr. 13, 1842.
[4] Richmond *Whig*, Sept. 28, 1841; Apr. 15, June 11, July 8, 14, Aug. 4, Nov. 9, 1842.
[5] Richmond *Enquirer*, July 15, 1842.   [6] *Niles' Register*, LXVI, 441.

them; or, if the attacks of the malignants come to my knowledge, I only hear them to despise them. I am told that one of the madcaps talks of impeachment." [7]

The President might have lessened his unpopularity if he had traveled extensively throughout the country and thus have come in contact with the people. His magnetic personality would have served him in good stead in counteracting the bad feeling which his enemies had stirred up against him. Only once, however, during his entire term did he make a journey of any length. This was the one to Boston to attend the celebration which commemorated the completion of the Bunker Hill Monument. On this northern tour he was accompanied by members of his Cabinet and other high officials.

At noon on June 8, 1843, he and his suite left the White House for the railroad station, being escorted by a procession on foot and in carriages led by a band of music. Going by special train the party stopped for a day and night in Baltimore, where the President was cordially received by the mayor. In response to the mayor's remarks Tyler made a brief but happy speech in which he likened Baltimore to "a swan sitting beautifully upon the water." He was "evidently much affected by the manifest sincerity of the welcome" accorded him. The crowd that greeted him, however, had not, in the opinion of a hostile Clay paper, been prompted by cordial feeling, but rather by "curiosity to see the Chief Magistrate of the Union." A banquet and public reception at Barnum's City Hotel, followed by a theater party in the evening, ended the first of a series of full days for the President.[8]

Next morning Tyler and his suite left by train for Wil-

---

[7] Tyler to Robert McCandlish, July 10, 1842; Tyler, *Letters and Times,* II, 172–173; Tyler to Silas Reed, Dec. 1, 1848; MS. in the Library of the Pennsylvania Historical Society.

[8] *National Intelligencer,* June 9, 1843; *The Sun* (Baltimore), June 9, 1843; Baltimore *American and Commercial Daily Advertiser,* June 9, 1843.

mington. Here they were met by a committee from Philadelphia and escorted by steamboat to the latter city. The
events of the day and night spent in Philadelphia were much
the same as those that characterized the stay in Baltimore.
A public reception was given in Independence Hall, the
enjoyment of which was considerably marred by the exceptionally hot weather. The City Council, dominated by
Whigs, did not participate officially in the formal ceremonies. For this lack of respect shown the Chief Executive
it was taken seriously to task by the *Pennsylvanian,* a Democratic sheet, which accused the Council of exhibiting a
churlish partisanship.[9]

After spending Sunday at Princeton with his friend, Captain R. F. Stockton, of the Navy, Tyler went on to New
York.[10] He was agreeably surprised at the way in which he
was acclaimed by the people of that city. The account of his
reception was described by the *Express* as follows:

The details of the visit, speeches, processions, etc. called forth by the
visit of the President to the city of New York show that the city
poured forth in mass, without reference to party prejudices or party
preferences, and therefore there probably has been the greatest display
ever before made in honor of a public man. From 11 o'clock A. M. to
3 P. M. there was one continued stream of population from the upper
parts of the city to the Battery, and when Mr. Tyler landed at Castle
Garden there were on and in the vicinity of the Battery and the Bowling
Green, probably sixty thousand people. The military and the cavalcade,
and the procession were nearly one hour and a half in passing, but
in these processions were but a very small part of the immense multitude. Mr. Tyler belonging to no party, and no party intending to be-
long to him, there was not only a curiosity to see this novelty of a
President without a party, but an emulation among the contending
parties to turn out and swell the crowd. Thus a crowd GEN. JACKSON

---

[9] *The North American and Daily Advertiser* (Philadelphia), June 9, 10,
1843; *The United States Gazette* (Philadelphia), June 12, 1843; the *Pennsylvanian* (Philadelphia), June 10, 1843.
[10] New York *Weekly Herald,* June 17, 1843.

himself could not draw, nor GEN. HARRISON, the most popular of our late Presidents, Mr. Tyler *did* draw. . . .

. . . .

The President . . . was drawn in a barouche uncovered through the streets, and from 4 o'clock P. M. to 8½ P. M. he was exhibited to the public gaze. . . .

This unfriendly sheet was careful to point out, however, that the great concourse which greeted the President had no political significance. "Not one of the numerous speeches," it stated,

which have been addressed to him [President Tyler] [on his trip to Boston] from the time he set out from Washington until he left New York made the most distant allusion to his re-election; not a shout from the member of any crowd, nor a banner nor inscription of any kind from any quarter has been heard of, which had a tendency to convey the slightest indication to the President that there was a voter who intended to support him at the next contest.[11]

After a three days' sojourn in New York and Brooklyn, the President proceeded by boat on his journey to New England. Stopping at Stonington, Connecticut, he was received by the warden with a speech of hearty welcome, to which he replied "with neatness and propriety." A unique feature of the reception given him here was described by the correspondent of the New York *Herald* as follows:

Although it was only half past six in the morning, at least about five hundred young ladies, very beautiful, waited on the President with bouquets. The procession of young ladies was headed by a sweet girl of sixteen, who, on presenting MR. TYLER with a beautiful bouquet, said: "Allow me, Mr. President, to have the honor to present you with some of the sweetest flowers of Connecticut." The PRESIDENT stooped down and kissed her, saying: "My dear young lady, you are one of the sweetest flowers that Connecticut can possibly produce." He then

[11] *New York Morning Express,* June 12, 13, 14, 15, 17, 1843; *New York American,* June 13, 1843; *National Intelligencer,* June 12, 14, 16, 1843.

kissed all the young ladies that were introduced to him, to the amount of several hundred.[12]

At Providence, Rhode Island, the Presidential party was received in an appropriate manner by the mayor, governor, and other persons of distinction. "The reception of the President by the citizens at the depot was enthusiastic in the extreme." The address of welcome by the mayor, though cordial, was a model for pith and brevity, as it consisted of only two sentences. Tyler's reply was "happier than is usual with off-hand effusions of this sort." In alluding to a statement of the mayor regarding the smallness of Rhode Island, Tyler said:

Whether you be great or small in point of territory, is nothing, if you possess (as you have frequently shown) a pure and patriotic spirit— since it is the spirit which makes the State as it does the man. The giant in size is nothing if wanting in spirit, while on the contrary, the pigmy, if he have a giant's heart to actuate him, becomes gigantic in the effects which he produces.[13]

The President spent a part of a day and one night in Providence and then went on by rail to Boston. He arrived on Friday morning, the day before the great celebration. It was a bad time for his reception, as it rained throughout the day. Despite the unfavorable weather conditions, he was tendered the formal courtesies due the Chief Magistrate of the country. There were the usual speech of welcome, a banquet at the Tremont House given by the City Council, and a procession through the principal streets to Boston Common. The procession passed between lines of children of the public schools who had been assembled in great numbers and who stood for more than two hours in the rain to pay their respects to the President.

If we can believe the report of *The Atlas*, a pro-Clay Whig paper, the reception given Tyler in Boston was one

---

[12] New York *Herald,* quoted in *National Intelligencer,* June 19, 1843.
[13] *National Intelligencer,* June 19, 1843; *Pennsylvanian,* June 17, 1843.

of cold, formal courtesy, with no display of warmth or enthusiasm. The procession in its line of march was "surrounded by a population as silent and demure as if a funeral pageant were passing." The faint and solitary cheers, thrown out at intervals, were few and far between.[14] The coldness of the reception given the President was doubtless greatly exaggerated by this newspaper; for, according to the *Boston Courier,* he was cordially greeted by the people when he took part in the proceedings next day.

Saturday, June 17, was a perfect day. The heavy rain had cleansed and cooled the atmosphere and it was under a bright and serene sky that the noted celebration took place. The exercises included a parade, a great banquet at Faneuil Hall, and an oration by Webster, which, in the opinion of one newspaper correspondent, "will doubtless live as long as the Monument." Thousands of the sons of New England had come from far and near to witness the scene. Prominent in the list of those who participated in the event were the President and members of his Cabinet, the Governor of Massachusetts and his attendants, and one hundred and eight surviving soldiers of the Revolution. Tyler, seated with his two sons in a splendid barouche, was a conspicuous figure in the procession. When his carriage entered State Street he was hailed with loud cheers by the dense crowd there assembled. Numerous toasts were given at the banquet. One of these was THE PRESIDENT OF THE UNITED STATES. It was received with great applause and nine regular cheers.[15]

On Monday the President paid a visit to the mill town of Lowell. He returned to Boston "harassed and worn-out." He was almost prostrated by the long journey, with its excitement and unusual exertions. While thus indisposed he received early Tuesday morning the sad news of the death

[14] *Pennsylvanian,* June 19, 1843; *The Atlas* (Boston), June 14, 17, 1843.
[15] *Boston Courier,* June 19, 20, 1843; *The Atlas,* June 19, 1843; *National Intelligencer,* June 20, 22, 1843.

of the Attorney General, Hugh S. Legaré, who had come to
Boston for the celebration.[16]

Tyler is said to have received when in Boston a request
for an interview from Wendell Phillips, who wanted to present some resolutions that had been adopted by the Boston
Abolitionists. No answer was made to this communication.[17]

An invitation from the citizens of Portsmouth, New
Hampshire, to visit that city was declined by the President.
This decision may have been influenced by the fact that a
motion to invite him to Concord was made and defeated in
the New Hampshire legislature.[18]

Tyler had intended to return leisurely via Springfield,
Albany, Buffalo, Cleveland, and Cincinnati, but the death of
the Attorney General caused him to change his plans. After
attending the funeral of Legaré he hurried back to Washington.[19]

It was doubtless with mingled feelings that the President
viewed his northern tour. He could recall with satisfaction
the popular demonstrations in his honor and especially the
great reception accorded him in New York. As an offset to
these pleasing reflections there was a realization of the coldness and inhospitality shown by Whig officials and of the
vitriolic abuse which some Whig newspapers continued to
heap upon him even during this short holiday season. No
sign of disappointment, however, did he show nor did he
allow any untoward incident to disturb his equable good
nature. His manners on these occasions, as usual, were a
strong point in his favor. His fellow passengers on the
steamboat from New York to Providence were agreeably
surprised at the way he discarded official pomp and entered
informally and naturally into the social activities on board.
The ladies of his suite also made a favorable impression by
the democratic simplicity in dress exhibited by them. Espe-

[16] *The Atlas,* June 20, 21, 1843; *Boston Courier,* June 21, 1843.
[17] *Pennsylvanian,* June 23, 1843.   [18] *Boston Courier,* June 16, 1843.
[19] *Boston Courier,* June 21, 22, 1843; *National Intelligencer,* June 24, 1843;
New York *Weekly Herald,* June 10, 1843.

cially popular was Mrs. Robert Tyler, whose attractiveness was noted by more than one newspaper reporter.

In all probability Tyler did not take the abuse that was heaped upon him by the press as seriously as one would expect. For he seemed to believe that the masses, except such as had been deceived by the politicians, were behind him in his fight with his former allies. The Whigs were defeated in the mid-term Congressional election and lost control of the House of Representatives to the Democrats. The President construed this action of the people as an endorsement of his administration and a condemnation of the policies and tactics of his enemies.[20] Fortunate it was that he could lay this soothing unction to his lacerated feelings, even though he probably misjudged the significance of this plebiscite.

It was doubtless particularly gratifying to Tyler to note that in the list of Representatives who failed of election there was included the name of John Minor Botts. His defeat did not cause Botts to cease his fight on the Chief Executive. Up until the end of his term he continued to breathe out threatenings and slaughter against him. As a final gesture of hate, he offered in the "lame-duck" House a resolution for the appointment of a committee on impeachment. It was defeated by a vote of 83 yeas to 127 nays.[21]

The National Intelligencer, the leading Whig organ of Washington, had joined the other Clay papers in an attack on the Administration. Tyler was thus forced to find another spokesman. "I can no longer tolerate the Intelligencer," he said, "as the official paper. Besides assaulting me perpetually, directly and indirectly, it refuses all defensive articles, as appears by the Madisonian of Saturday. There is a point beyond which one's patience cannot en-

[20] Niles, LXV, 212–213; Richmond Whig, May 12, 1842.
[21] Allan Nevins, ed., The Diary of Philip Hone, Jan. 14, 1843; Cong. Globe, 27th Cong., 3rd sess., 134, 144.

dure." [22] He, therefore, made the *Madisonian* the official organ (September, 1841) and gave to it the executive patronage.[23] During a good part of his administration Tyler was also supported by the New York *Herald,* and his bank policy was ably defended by the brilliant pen of James Gordon Bennett. But before the end of his term the *Herald* had begun to make "violent and reckless" attacks on the President.[24]

With the Whig press and the Whig political leaders arrayed against him, the President could not be expected to carry through many measures which required the co-operation of Congress. In that sphere of activities, however, where the executive has freedom of action, Tyler showed sound judgment and achieved exceptional success. An example of the wisdom displayed by him in the performance of his executive duties in internal affairs is afforded by his handling of the outbreak in Rhode Island, which was the chief domestic disturbance of his administration.

This little State was still using as its constitution the charter granted in 1663 by King Charles II. Under this outmoded government a large proportion of the people were disfranchised by a high property qualification for voting. By 1840 intense dissatisfaction with the suffrage restrictions had grown up among the masses and they were clamoring for a voice in the government. In response to this demand a convention, irregularly called by a mass meeting, met and drew up a constitution (1841), called the "People's Constitution," which provided for white manhood suffrage. The machinery of a State government was set up with T. W. Dorr as governor. This new government prepared to defend its existence by the use of military force.

[22] Van Tyne, *Letters of Daniel Webster,* 231.
[23] Tyler to H. A. Wise, Sept. 27, 1841; the Huntington Library MSS. This letter is published in the *William and Mary College Quarterly* (first series), XX, 7.
[24] *Madisonian,* Feb. 12, 1845.

Governor King, of the old, or Charter, government, regarded these activities of the Dorrites as insurrection, and
accordingly called out the State militia to uphold the old
political regime. As both leaders were backed by troops,
civil war seemed imminent.

In the meantime both Dorr and King had applied to the
President for aid. Tyler had kept in touch with the situation
by reports from confidential agents as well as by official
communications from the Rhode Island authorities.[25] He
realized, therefore, how much dynamite there was in this
difficult problem. If he should accede to Governor King's
request and refuse that of Dorr, he would have to deny the
legality of the popular movement in Rhode Island. To do
so would subject him to the charge of opposing democratic
rule. On the other hand, to refuse the assistance asked by
Governor King would be to acquiesce in lawlessness and rebellion.

Tyler met the issue squarely and wisely. He promised that
in case an insurrection should break out in Rhode Island
he would employ force to aid the regular, or Charter, government. It was made clear that this assistance would be
given not to prevent but only to put down insurrection, and
would not be available until violence had been committed.
He expressed great reluctance to employ the military power
of the Federal government against any portion of the people, "but, however painful the duty, I have to assure your
excellency that, if resistance is made to the execution of the
laws of Rhode Island by such force as the *civil posse* shall
be unable to overcome, it will be the duty of this government to enforce the constitutional guaranty." [26]

Along with this announcement there went some very
sound advice to both parties. Governor King was admonished to call a convention upon somewhat liberal principles

---

[25] Richardson, *Messages and Papers of the Presidents*, IV, 285, 299–301.
[26] *Niles*, LXII, 116–117, 179; Richardson, *Messages*, IV, 285, 293–294.

and to hold out a promise of pardon to the insurgents on condition of their return to allegiance.[27] He also exhorted the rebels as to the unwisdom of appealing to violence for reform and advised a recourse to argument and remonstrance, as being "more likely to ensure lasting blessings than those accomplished by violence and bloodshed on one day, and liable to overthrow by similar agents on another."

Events came to a crisis in the summer of 1842. Both sides were determined to use force and civil strife seemed inevitable. Tyler now decided upon a more vigorous policy. The Secretary of War was sent to Rhode Island with instructions to use Federal troops, if necessary, in support of Governor King's effort to put down rebellion.[28] No such action was taken, however, as the rebel troops, when attacked by the State militia, fled without resistance. In this way the insurrection came to an end.[29]

The victors had the good sense to make some wise concessions to the suffrage party. The convention which had already been called met in due time and framed a constitution which considerably broadened the suffrage.[30]

Despite the wisdom and tact with which Tyler had handled this very delicate situation, his policy received a good deal of unfavorable criticism. The suffrage party in Rhode Island accused him of having thrown the weight of the

[27] "*I am well advised,*" he wrote, "if the general assembly would authorize you to announce a general amnesty and pardon for the past without making any exception, upon the condition of a return to allegiance, and follow it up by a call for a new convention upon somewhat liberal principles, that all difficulty would at once cease. And why should not this be done? A government never loses anything by mildness and forbearance to its own citizens, more especially when the consequences of an opposite course may be the shedding of blood. Why urge matters to an extremity? If you succeed by the bayonet, you succeed against your own fellow citizens and by the shedding of kindred blood, whereas by taking the opposite course you will have shown a paternal care for the lives of your people. My own opinion is that the adoption of the above measures will give you peace and insure you harmony. A resort to force, on the contrary, will engender for years to come feelings of animosity."

[28] *Niles,* LXII, 307.

[29] *Ibid.,* 276–278, 307, 385–386; Richardson, *op. cit.,* 276.

[30] *Niles,* LXIII, 101–102.

Federal executive in the scales against popular government. Dorr was quite bitter in his denunciation of the President.[31]

Tyler's Democratic opponents tried to make political capital out of his management of the case. The Democratic members of the legislature of Rhode Island sent (February 19, 1844) a memorial to the House of Representatives complaining of the interference of the Federal executive in the suffrage movement in their State. This memorial led to the adoption of a resolution by the House (March 23, 1844) which called on the President to lay before that body all the documents covering the action of the Federal government with reference to the uprising in Rhode Island.[32] In reply the President sent to the House a message of explanation and with it the documents requested.

If the mover of this resolution intended it as a means of embarrassment to the President he was sorely disappointed. For it gave the latter the opportunity of showing how wisely he had handled the difficult problem. In his dignified and able answer he presented arguments that were unanswerable, and showed that his policy with reference to Rhode Island was unassailable.[33] So complete was his defense that even the *National Intelligencer,* the organ of his Whig enemies, expressed gratification over the message and the soundness of the principles which it laid down.[34]

Tyler's course in the Rhode Island rebellion also elicited high praise from his ex-premier. Writing to the President on April 18, 1844, Webster said that while it was his misfortune to differ with him on some subjects, it gave him pleasure with respect to others to express warm approbation.

I write [he continued] now to signify to you how greatly I was pleased with your message to the House of Representatives, on the Rhode Island business. That paper has given great satisfaction in this quarter

---

[31] Providence *Journal;* quoted by *Niles,* LXV, 20.
[32] *Cong. Globe,* 28th Cong., 1st sess., 295, 426.
[33] The President's message and documents enclosed are given in Richardson, *op. cit.,* IV, 283–307.
[34] *National Intelligencer,* Apr. 12, 1844.

to sensible men of all parties. Indeed, your conduct of that affair will appear hereafter, I am sure, worthy of all praise, and one of the most fortunate incidents in your administration, for your own reputation. The case was new and was managed with equal discretion and firmness. On the one hand it was wise to be slow in directing the use of military force in the affairs of a State; and on the other, equally wise to look to the existing government of the State, as that government which the executive of the United States can alone regard, in the discharge of its high and delicate duties. . . .[35]

This statement by Webster is a correct appraisal of the part played by Tyler in the Rhode Island drama. A careful and unbiased study of the documents can lead to no other conclusion.

A wisdom similar to that displayed toward Rhode Island was employed by President Tyler in dealing with some minor problems, both domestic and foreign, that came up during his term. He urged the strengthening of the navy and the military defenses of the country. Thanks to his policy, there was, according to the New York *Herald,* an increase in the number of warships for the first time in several years. The officers were well pleased with the policy of the President and Secretary Upshur toward the navy.[36]

Tyler favored a policy of justice and fairness to the Indians. A long and troublesome war with the Seminole Indians in Florida gave him considerable concern, but was finally brought to a close before the end of the year 1842. The Federal government, he thought, should encourage the Indians to take up the habits of civilization.[37]

Like his patron saint, Jefferson, Tyler did what he could to promote literary and scientific activity. In line with this interest he sent Washington Irving as minister to Spain and appointed John Howard Payne, the author of "Home Sweet

[35] *Private Correspondence of Daniel Webster,* II, 189–190.
[36] New York *Herald,* Aug. 23, 1841, Mar. 12, 1842.
[37] Richardson, *loc. cit.,* 80, 198–199.

Home," to the consulship at Tunis.[38] He also encouraged
S. F. B. Morse in his effort to make telegraphy a practical
success. He approved of Morse's plan for securing an appropriation from Congress to construct a line from Washington to Baltimore. The connection between these two
cities was completed by May 24, 1844, at which time the
President dispatched friendly greetings from the Capitol
to Chief Justice Taney in Baltimore. This was one of the
first messages ever sent by telegraph.[39]

One of the lesser diplomatic successes of which Tyler was
quite proud was the signing of a treaty between this country
and China. As this was the first step taken toward the opening of this exclusive country to the American people, he considered it quite an achievement. It was also especially gratifying to him that the credit for these negotiations should go
to Caleb Cushing, to whom he was very grateful for his
support in Congress and for whom he had a high personal
regard.[40] This mission had come to Cushing as a consolation
prize after his nomination for Secretary of the Treasury
had failed of confirmation in the Senate (page 283).

Edward Everett had at first been selected for this important service and his nomination was confirmed unanimously by the Senate. Although Webster and John Quincy
Adams were both anxious for him to accept, he declined the
appointment (page 282).[41] Cushing was then nominated
and was confirmed on June 17, 1844.[42]

Early in August, 1843, Cushing departed in the U.S.
steam frigate *Missouri* for the Celestial Empire. With him
went a suite of ten persons, including a linguist, physician,
draughtsman, and two attachés. On arriving at his destina-

[38] J. Q. Adams, *Memoirs*, XI, 369–370.
[39] *John Tyler Papers* (L.C.), IV, 6795–96, 6836; Tyler, *Letters and Times*, II, 381–382.
[40] Tyler to Cushing, Oct. 14, 1845; Tyler, *Letters and Times*, II, 445–446. For another letter of the same character, see *ibid.*, 459–460.
[41] Webster to Edward Everett, Mar. 10, 1843; Webster's *Writings* (Nat. Ed.), XVI, 398–400.
[42] *Niles*, LXVI, 258.

tion, Cushing found that the Chinese were well disposed
toward the Americans, and he was able to negotiate a treaty
favorable to a freer intercourse between the two countries.[43]
This treaty, with accompanying documents, was received in
Washington in December, 1844. Tyler was enthusiastic over
the results of the mission. "I thought the President," said
Mrs. Tyler in a letter to her mother, "would go off in an
ecstasy a minute ago with the pleasant news." [44] A few days
later, he submitted the treaty to the Senate and it was duly
ratified.[45]

The treaty of peace, amity, and commerce was signed at
Wang Hiya, July 3. It opened five ports to American trade
and granted to American citizens the right to reside and
trade in these ports. It provided that all "citizens of the
United States in China should be wholly exempted, as well
in criminal as in civil matters, from the local jurisdiction of
the Chinese government and made amenable to the laws and
subject to the jurisdiction of the appropriate authorities of
the United States alone." [46]

Cushing was also authorized by the President to negotiate
a treaty with Japan provided an opportunity should offer.
He was obliged, however, to return home after the negotiations with China were completed, and so no treaty was made
with Japan.[47]

Another minor treaty which Tyler set his heart upon was
the one negotiated by Henry Wheaton, American minister
at Berlin, with the German Zollverein, or Customs Union.
By this agreement the duties on tobacco and lard imported
into any of the States of the Germanic Union (Zollverein)

[43] *Niles,* LXIV, 308, 353, 369; LXVI, 414; *John Tyler Papers* (L.C.),
II, 6475.

[44] Mrs. Tyler to Mrs. Gardiner, Dec. 6, 1844; Tyler, *Letters and Times,*
II, 358.

[45] Richardson, *op. cit.,* IV, 340, 352.

[46] W. M. Malloy, comp., *Treaties, Conventions, etc. between the United
States and Other Powers,* I, 196–206; Richardson, *op. cit.,* IV, 358.

[47] Tyler to Col. J. C. Cunningham, Nov. 4, 1855; *John Tyler Papers* (L.C.),
IV, 6724–25.

were to be reduced, raw cotton was to be on the free list, and rice admitted at the low rate already in effect. For this concession the United States was to reduce the tariff on certain German products. These reductions were to apply to articles not fabricated in this country, except some two or three of very little consequence to American industry. In this way the home market for American manufactures would not be curtailed, while the foreign market for certain important farm staples would be enlarged. In giving reasons for the ratification of this treaty Wheaton announced a tariff policy which sounds very reasonable to modern ears. The proper way, he thought, to reduce the tariff is by diplomatic action, for in that way we get a compensating gain for every reduction.[48]

The treaty would undoubtedly have promoted the interests of a considerable portion of our people. This advantage was observed by the London *Times,* which in commenting on the treaty said that "Mr. Wheaton has gained the march upon all the other governments who have hitherto attempted to treat with Germany in commercial matters." [49]

The President sent in the treaty to the Senate on April 29, 1844. He indicated that as the provisions were in some respects in conflict with existing laws, he would, in case the treaty was ratified by the Senate, send it to the House for such action as might be thought sufficient to give efficiency to its provisions.[50]

The Senate on the last day of the session voted to lay this treaty on the table. This was a virtual rejection, as the time within which ratifications could be exchanged would expire before the next meeting of the Senate. In this final action the Whigs were against the treaty and the Democrats, except a few stalwart enemies of Tyler, voted in favor of it.[51]

[48] Wheaton to Tyler, Mar. 27, 1844; *John Tyler Papers* (L.C.), II, 6461–63; *Niles,* LXVI, 177; Tyler, *Letters and Times,* II, 347, 392–393; *Madisonian,* June 27, 1844.

[49] Quoted by *Niles, loc. cit.,* 194.   [50] Richardson, *op. cit.,* IV, 314.

[51] *Niles, loc. cit.,* 257, 287.

A later effort made by the President to revive the treaty ended in failure.[52] The *Madisonian* charged that the Whigs had voted against the treaty to "gratify their enmity to John Tyler," and the accusation seems to be not without foundation.

There were several other minor diplomatic questions, of more or less importance, which engaged the attention of Tyler. He felt that the Monroe Doctrine should be applied to the Sandwich Islands (the Hawaiian group). These islands because of their nearness to our western coast and because of the importance of our commerce with them should never be allowed to pass under the control of a European power.[53]

The settlement of the northwest boundary dispute was also one of the aims of the President. It would have been a source of great satisfaction to him if this question could have been covered by the treaty which located the Maine-New Brunswick line; but early in the negotiations with Lord Ashburton it became evident that this could not be expected.[54] Later our minister at London, Edward Everett, was instructed to sound out the British foreign office, without making any commitments, as to whether an understanding could be reached. Tyler was willing to accept the 49th parallel as the northern boundary of Oregon, but no offer to that effect was to be made. These conversations resulted in no understanding and the negotiations were later transferred to Washington.

In his last annual message (December, 1844) the President indicated that since the previous meeting of Congress negotiations as to Oregon had been started between the American Secretary of State and the British minister at Washington. In that same message he recommended that the settlers in Oregon be given the protection of suitable laws and that military posts be established on the route to

52 Richardson, *op. cit.*, IV, 339-340.   53 *Ibid.*, 212.   54 *Ibid.*, 196.

that far-off land. These would serve as rest stations for emigrants and places of refuge against Indian attack.

Congress did not act on this suggestion. If the trail to Oregon had been thus guarded emigration from the United States would have been encouraged and in time the policy of joint occupation would have resulted in American possession of the country by peaceful penetration. No agreement as to boundary could be reached at this time, and so the dispute went over until the next administration. During the negotiations, England offered to arbitrate the dispute but this offer was declined by Tyler.[55]

The President's concern for Oregon is said to have been stimulated by the representations of Marcus Whitman, a medical missionary to the Indians of the Columbia Valley. In the winter of 1842–43, he made a journey on horseback from Oregon to the East going to Boston in the interest of his mission and to Washington for the purpose of impressing upon the authorities there the value of Oregon and the importance of saving this vast region for the Americans. The mythmakers have been so successful in coloring this story that it is hard to disentangle fact from fiction. It is quite probable, however, that this rugged pioneer, dressed in leather breeches and worn and torn furs, with hands frozen after a three-thousand-mile ride, made a deep impression on the President and his Secretary of State, who received him cordially and respectfully.[56]

[55] Richardson, loc. cit., 337–338; John Tyler to his son [Robert?], Dec. 11, 1845; Personal MSS. (L.C.).

[56] Some writers contend that Whitman's journey to the East was primarily in the interest of his mission and only secondarily in that of Oregon. Others, however, maintain that the desire to save Oregon to the United States was his main objective in making this hazardous journey. This view is upheld by Oliver W. Nixon, How Marcus Whitman Saved Oregon (Chicago, 1895) and by George Finke, Winning the Pacific Northwest (Columbus, Ohio, 1936).

The late Professor E. G. Bourne made a careful study of the evidence behind the Whitman story and published his findings under the heading, "The Legend of Marcus Whitman," in his Essays in Historical Criticism (N. Y.,

Another diplomatic problem that Tyler and Webster had to grapple with was the relations between the United States and Mexico. There were two causes of possible friction between the two countries. In the first place, the claims held by our nationals against the Mexican government had not been satisfactorily adjusted. Secondly, the Mexican government objected to the assistance which, it alleged, the government of the United States had allowed its citizens to give Texas by the failure to enforce its neutrality laws. In connection with this complaint some loud talk was indulged in by the Mexican authorities, and for a while war was represented by the newspapers as being inevitable.[57] Webster and Tyler, however, were not bluffed by these bold pronouncements, which were intended for home consumption, and nothing came of these idle threats. In the fall of 1842 the Mexican government sent General Almonte as minister to Washington, the first to hold such a position for more than five years. "When Almonte arrived at Washington, the relations between the two countries were in better condition, with less open friction, than they had been since the battle of San Jacinto." [58]

In the meantime, Waddy Thompson, American minister to Mexico, had arrived at the hopeful conclusion that Mexico would cede Texas and California in payment of the

---

1901). He took issue with the first of the above-mentioned authors as to the part played by the missionary in saving Oregon. See also the *Dictionary of American Biography*.

Whitman's journey to the East is discussed in a scholarly manner by Clifford M. Drury in his *Marcus Whitman, M.D., Pioneer and Martyr* (Caldwell, Idaho, 1937), 307–312. The author shows that the missionary stopped at Washington, and probably before he went to Boston. He also thinks that Whitman had an interview with President Tyler but cannot say to what extent the latter's policy was influenced by this meeting.

[57] Joaquin Velasquez de Leon to Webster, June 24, 1842; Webster's *Diplomatic and Official Papers*, 301; Bocanegra to Webster, May 12, 1842; *ibid.*, 302; Webster to Thompson, July 13, 1842; Webster, *The Writings and Speeches of Daniel Webster* (Nat. Ed.), XII, 133; Tyler, *Letters and Times*, II, 258.

[58] Jesse S. Reeves, *American Diplomacy under Tyler and Polk* (Baltimore, 1907), 86, 99, 100.

claims against her held by American citizens. Writing to the President and Secretary of State in this optimistic vein, he asked for instructions that would authorize him to take up the question.[59] Both Webster and Tyler were favorably disposed toward Thompson's plan. Webster wrote that owing to the value of the harbor at San Francisco, "the President strongly inclines to favor the idea of a treaty with Mexico." He suggested that the claims be connected with the negotiations for California or at least for the harbor of San Francisco.[60] Tyler and Webster wanted to know what would be the reaction of Great Britain to this plan. Accordingly, Edward Everett was instructed to sound out the attitude of that government toward the proposal. He approached Lord Aberdeen and found that "he had not the slightest objection to our making an acquisition of territory in that direction." [61]

The seizure of Monterey by Commodore Jones, an American naval commander, put an end to this pipe dream. Relying on information gleaned from belated newspapers, this overzealous officer came to the belief that Mexico and the United States were at war and that Upper California had been ceded to England. Thereupon, he promptly decided to capture Monterey before the British admiral could arrive to take possession of the new acquisition. So in the afternoon of October 19, 1842, he sent in to the commander a formal demand for the surrender of the place. As the Mexican officer had only a small force of soldiers, poorly equipped with arms, he surrendered without attempting resistance. Next day Jones discovered that the information on which he had

---

[59] Thompson to Webster, Apr. 29, 1842; Thompson to Tyler, Apr. 29, 1842; MS. Archives, State Department.

[60] Webster to Thompson, June 27, 1842; Van Tyne, C. H., ed., *Letters of Daniel Webster*, 269–270.

[61] Everett to Calhoun, Mar. 28, 1845; MS. Archives. Tyler was even willing to make concessions to England in Oregon if she would exert her influence with Mexico in favor of the acquisition of California by the United States. Tyler to his son [Robert?], Dec. 11, 1845; *Personal MSS.* (L.C.). See also two notes from Tyler to Webster; Tyler, *Letters and Times*, II, 261.

acted was incorrect, and he at once restored Monterey to its Mexican commander.[62] The United States government was prompt to disavow the act of Jones and promise reparation. He was recalled from his command and temporarily suspended from the service. After some correspondence between the two governments a satisfactory adjustment was arranged. Webster apologized for the affront to Mexico and expressed the great regret of the President and the feeling on his part that "no such unfortunate and unauthorized occurrence ought in any degree to impair the amicable relations subsisting between the two countries, so evidently to the advantage of both." [63]

During Tyler's term administrative routine was performed with exceptional honesty, economy, and efficiency. Early in 1845 there were repeated rumors afloat to the effect that Federal officials had been guilty of serious embezzlements. This led Congress to pass a resolution (January 23) authorizing an investigation of these charges. The President was asked for information as to whether any Federal officials since August 19, 1841, had been guilty of the misappropriation of public funds and if so whether they had been prosecuted. To this inquiry Tyler sent a reply and with it letters from the heads of the War, Treasury, Navy, and Post Office Departments and the chiefs of various bureaus. From these documents it was shown that only two cases of embezzlement had occurred during this period. These were of minor importance and in both cases the incumbents had been removed.[64]

[62] For Jones's official account of this incident, see *Niles*, LXIV, 170–173. (This also includes the letters and official documents.) See also *Niles*, LXIII, 337. For an account by a Mexican newspaper, the *Diario del Gobierno* of Mexico City, based on the official reports, see *Niles*, LXIII, 322. The two accounts agree perfectly in all important particulars.

[63] Almonte to Webster, Jan. 24, 1843; H. Ex. Doc., 27th Cong., 3rd sess., no. 166, pp. 3–4. Webster to Almonte, Jan. 30, 1843, *ibid.*, pp. 5–6; Webster to Thompson, *ibid.*, p. 3 (Jan. 17, 1843).

[64] *Madisonian*, Feb. 22, 1845; Tyler, *Letters and Times*, II, 373.

In proof of the economy and efficiency with which the finances had been managed under his leadership, Tyler stated that the government had been administered for four years on the expenditures of three years of the previous administration, and yet the military arm had everywhere been strengthened and a new impulse had been given to the industry of the country.[65] When he came into office the Post Office Department had a deficit of $500,000.00, which Congress discharged by an appropriation from the treasury. During his term the postal system had been run on its own resources, and on March 3, 1845, would be found free of debt.[66]

The accession of Tyler was preceded by a quadrennium of depression, and times were still hard. Recovery was on the way but had not yet peered around the corner. As late as December, 1841, Webster alluded to "the present depressed and ruinous condition" of the country.[67] With the country in such a plight, it is no wonder that the Federal government was unable to balance its budget, and the deficit inherited by Harrison and Tyler kept piling up. The select committee of the House of Representatives, which reported (August 16, 1842) on Tyler's veto of the tariff bill, declared that the deficit had increased by at least fifteen million dollars in the course of eighteen months.[68] In spite of this excess of expenditure over income, the pay of the army, the navy, and the civil list was at times suspended owing to the utter destitution of the treasury.[69]

Under such conditions the credit of the government naturally fell to a low level. The notes issued by the treasury

[65] *John Tyler Papers* (L.C.), III, 6644.
[66] Tyler's Message to Congress, Dec. 3, 1844; Richardson, *Messages*, IV, 349.
[67] Van Tyne, *Letters of Daniel Webster*, 244. See also *Diary of Philip Hone*, II, 578, 579.
[68] *Niles*, LXII, 396.
[69] Statement made by Gilmer in a minority report (August, 1842) to the House of Representatives. *Niles*, LXII, 410.

declined in value and it was with great difficulty that loans were floated.[70] In March, 1842, the New York *Herald* said that the Federal treasury was empty, the nation bankrupt, several States bankrupt, and almost every city in debt. Owing to this lack of funds, the home squadron of the navy was lying idle and the workmen in the navy yards and arsenals were grumbling because they had not been paid.[71]

In time, however, the depression passed away and commerce and industry revived. The income of the government increased and the deficit was wiped away. National credit was raised and by September, 1842, government bonds were selling at par and some were being held at a premium.[72] The President in his last annual address to Congress stated that after making considerable payments on the public debt the treasury would still have a surplus of $7,000,000.00 at the end of the fiscal year.[73]

But neither the President nor Congress was entitled to much, if any, credit for this improvement in the financial and economic condition of the country. Recovery had come as a result of the recuperative powers of a young and healthy society. Nothing of importance had been done to assist nature in her cure of the economic disorder. When bankruptcy was facing the country Congress was throwing away its opportunity by playing politics and frittering away its time in petty bickerings. The President was too conservative to probe into the foundations of a social order to locate the fundamental causes of economic disease. There was, therefore, no attempt at a "new deal"—no serious effort to alleviate the distress occasioned by the malady or to prevent its recurrence in the future. It was fortunate for Tyler, however, that prosperity had returned while he was still at the helm, for it enabled him to contrast to his advantage

---

[70] *Niles, loc. cit.,* 4, 30; *Webster's Writings* (Nat. Ed.), III, 138.
[71] New York *Herald,* Mar. 9, 11, 1842.
[72] *Niles,* LXIII, 51.   [73] Richardson, *loc. cit.,* 346.

conditions at the time of his retirement with those he found at his accession.

As has been shown, Tyler's administration was marked by a number of events of exceptional significance. In his last annual message to Congress (December 4, 1844), he pointed out the achievements of his stormy term in the following summary:

During that period questions with foreign powers of vital importance to the peace of our country have been settled and adjusted. A desolating and wasting war with savage tribes has been brought to a close. The internal tranquillity of the country, threatened by agitating questions, has been preserved. The credit of the Government, which had experienced a temporary embarrassment, has been thoroughly restored. Its coffers, which for a season were empty, have been replenished. A currency nearly uniform in its value has taken the place of one depreciated and almost worthless. Commerce and manufactures, which had suffered in common with every other interest, have once more revived, and the whole country exhibits an aspect of prosperity and happiness. Trade and barter, no longer governed by a wild and speculative mania, rest upon a solid and substantial footing, and the rapid growth of our cities in every direction bespeaks most strongly the favorable circumstances by which we are surrounded.[74]

Truly this was a remarkable record for an administration of a "President without a party."

[74] Richardson, *loc. cit.*, 351–352.

CHAPTER XXII

TYLER AND TEXAS

THE acquisition of Texas was one of the most important steps in the territorial expansion of this country, and John Tyler is entitled to a large share of the credit for having added this vast area to the American domain. He was proud of his connection with this event and regarded it as the outstanding achievement of his administration.[1] But he did not reap the reward of his labors. Those who favored the acquisition of Texas did not accord him a due meed of praise for his efforts, and the opponents of annexation misrepresented his actions and impugned his motives. Seldom in our history has a public servant been so poorly requited for an important service to his country.

At the time of Tyler's accession to the Presidency, Texas had been an independent republic for five years, having won its independence in the battle of San Jacinto (April 21, 1836).[2] The United States had in March, 1837, recognized the independence of Texas,[3] and England, France, and other European powers had followed her example. During all this period, the people of Texas, who were mainly emigrants from the United States, had been desirous of having their new republic incorporated into the union of their fellow countrymen. This wish was shown unmistakably when in the plebiscite (September, 1836) on their constitution they gave an overwhelming majority in favor of annexation to the United States. The Texan government, therefore, as

---

[1] Tyler, *Letters and Times,* II, 468.
[2] *H. Ex. Doc.,* 25th Cong., 1st sess., no. 40, p. 6.
[3] *Cong. Globe,* 24th Cong., 2nd sess., 83, 219, 268–270, 274; J. D. Richardson, *Messages and Papers of the Presidents,* III, 281.

early as December, 1836, offered annexation. This offer and one made the next year were declined by the Washington government.[4]

This repulse to her advances was disappointing and humiliating to the debutante republic. Having failed to win the desired suitor by leap-year diplomacy, she retired into maidenly reserve and resolved to await overtures from him as the next step in the courtship. Accordingly, the offer was formally withdrawn the next year by order of President Houston.[5] No other proposal for annexation was made by Texas until after Tyler's accession.

Tyler was anxious for the annexation of Texas from the beginning. As early as October, 1841, he had broached the question with Webster pointing out the great advantages to the country as a whole that would result from annexation. "I really believe," he said, "[that] it could be done. Could the North be reconciled to it, could anything throw so bright a lustre around us? It seems to me that the great interests of the North would be incalculably advanced by such an acquisition." [6] But Webster was opposed to annexation, and Tyler did not urge it while the latter was at the head of the Department of State.[7] To what extent his inaction was due to deference to Webster's wishes it is difficult to say.

He showed good judgment in not pressing the matter at the beginning of his administration. Webster was engaged in important negotiations with Great Britain first over the McLeod case and then over the northeast boundary dispute. Any disagreement at that juncture between the President and his premier would have jeopardized these important negotiations. Lamar, who was now President of

---

[4] Hunt to Forsyth, Aug. 4, 1837; *H. Ex. Doc.*, 25th Cong., 1st sess., no. 40, pp. 2–11.

[5] Statement by Houston in a speech at New Orleans May, 1845, quoted in *Niles' Register*, LXVIII, 230.

[6] Tyler to Webster, October 11, 1841; C. H. Van Tyne, ed., *Letters of Webster*, 239–240.

[7] *The Writings and Speeches of Daniel Webster* (Nat. Ed.), XVI, 417.

Texas, was opposed to annexation. Moreover, by the so-
called "Gag Resolutions," the House of Representatives
was refusing to receive antislavery petitions. This policy
was keeping the slavery dispute at white heat in Congress
and stiffening the opposition of the North to the acquisition
of any more slave territory. These obstacles were insuperable
barriers to annexation at the beginning of Tyler's administration. The President, therefore, had no option but to pursue a policy of watchful waiting with the hope that these
difficulties would in time be removed.

Late in the year of 1841 Lamar was succeeded in the
Presidency of Texas by Houston, a friend of annexation.
Twice during the year 1842 Texas was offered to the United
States and each time the offer was refused. Tyler would
gladly have accepted this proposal had he not felt that a
treaty of annexation would at that time have been rejected
by the Senate.[8] In August, the next year, the tender was
withdrawn.

Houston now took a new tack. He instructed Van Zandt,
Texan chargé d'affaires at Washington, to leave all further
action looking to annexation to the initiative of the United
States.[9] He also began to encourage closer relations with
Great Britain and apparently paraded any incidents that
pointed to an understanding between Texas and England.
Whether this was a flirtation to arouse the fears of the
United States and awaken at Washington a greater concern
for annexation or whether it was a *bona fide* effort to enlist
the aid of England in securing the independence of Texas
is a matter of dispute. Houston afterwards said in a speech
(made at New Orleans May, 1845) that he had "coquetted
a little with Great Britain" in order to make the United
States jealous. His plan was to play upon the fears of the
Senate and make it realize the danger of allowing the prize

[8] *Niles,* LXXIII, 147.
[9] H. K. Yoakum, *History of Texas,* 2 vols. (New York, 1855, 1856), II, 407.

to slip from its grasp.[10] Tyler, however, regarded Houston's "billing and cooing with England" as a real love affair, as serious "as any in the calendar." [11] If the desire to arouse in the United States a greater interest in Texas was the main purpose behind Houston's "flirtation" with England, he certainly made a correct appraisal of American sentiment and discovered the proper method of hitching this feeling to his purposes.

The retirement of Webster from the Cabinet and the transfer of Abel P. Upshur from the Department of the Navy to that of State gave Tyler a premier who could entirely match him in enthusiasm for the acquisition of Texas. "If there existed a more enthusiastic advocate of annexation [than Upshur]," said Tyler at a later date, "or one whose energies of body and mind were more unremittingly devoted to its accomplishment I must say that I do not know the man." When he was Secretary of the Navy he urged the President to seize this opportunity for enlarging the area of his country. He was told by the latter that the state of affairs at the time was such as to make it unwise and imprudent for him to propose annexation.[12]

But shortly after Webster's retirement Tyler definitely decided to take steps looking toward annexation. The final decision was precipitated by fear of the influence that England would gain over Texas if the latter were not soon annexed to the United States. Financial and social conditions in the new republic had gradually become worse, and by the end of the year 1842 it looked as if it could not continue its separate existence unless there was some strong outside power on which it could lean.[13] England, it was thought, stood ready to serve as a prop to this tottering state.

[10] Niles, LXVIII, 230; Polk Papers (L.C.), 6759.
[11] Tyler, op. cit., III, 124.   [12] John Tyler Papers (L.C.), IV, 6901–02.
[13] General Houston, in his Presidential address of December, 1842, gave a most despairing account of conditions at that time. For this address see Niles, LXIV, 18–19.

Such a connection between the two countries would be fraught with danger to the United States. Our commercial and naval supremacy over the Gulf of Mexico would be menaced if Texas were brought under the protection of Great Britain. Moreover, if this great power, already in possession of Canada to the north of us, should get a firm grip on a large area of territory on our southwestern border, our country would, in a war with England, be between the upper and the nether millstone. Such were the fears that disturbed Tyler and Upshur, and, therefore, they favored annexation on the broad ground that it was conducive to national security.

They also felt that the acquisition of Texas was necessary to protect slavery in the South, which would be seriously menaced if British antislavery influence should become dominant in Texas. For it was generally known that the British government was strongly opposed to slavery and stood ready to lend its influence in favor of abolition wherever it could be exerted properly and effectively. An alliance between England and Texas might, therefore, result in the abolition of slavery in the latter country. This would be a great blow to slavery in the South. If there should be a large area of free territory contiguous to the slave States, slave property in the border Southern States would become very insecure. Fugitives would be constantly escaping to free Texas, and efforts to regain them by their masters would cause continuous strife. The loss of their property would result in dissatisfaction among slaveowners, which would weaken their loyalty to the Union, and the friction incident to the escape and attempted return of fugitive slaves would complicate our relations with Texas and jeopardize our friendship with Great Britain, the protector of Texas.

That both Tyler and Upshur were troubled by apprehensions as to such possibilities there can be little doubt; but to what extent there was real ground for these fears is still a matter of dispute. The cause of their alarm as to the abolition menace was some communications that passed in the summer of 1843 between Ashbel Smith, Texan minister to England and France, and Lord Aberdeen, British Secretary of State for Foreign Affairs. These communications showed that the English government was anxious to encourage the abolition of slavery everywhere—Texas included—though they may not have warranted the extreme uneasiness felt by the President and his premier. Reports of this correspondence were sent to Tyler by Duff Green, his confidential agent in England, who was acting as a sort of ambassador at large. In a long letter to his chief, Green said: "I am authorized to say to you by the Texian minister that Lord Aberdeen has agreed that the British government will guarantee the payment of the interest on the loan upon condition that the Texian government will abolish slavery." [14]

Spurred on by these fears, Upshur decided to take steps looking to the acquisition of Texas. Accordingly, he offered to negotiate for a treaty of annexation.[15] This proposal was rejected by President Houston. The reason given by him for so doing was that through the friendly aid of some European governments an armistice with Mexico had been arranged with the prospect of permanent peace with that power. This intervention had been given with the expectation that Texas would remain independent if peace with

[14] Duff Green to President Tyler, London, July 3, 1843; *Duff Green Papers* (in possession of Professor Fletcher M. Green, Chapel Hill, N. C.).

There is some discrepancy between the views of Ashbel Smith and Duff Green regarding the attitude of the British government toward abolition in Texas, and later correspondence between Upshur and Everett is confirmatory of Smith's version. For this reason opponents of annexation at the time and historians of later years have charged that Tyler and Upshur had hastily acted on false information. But the disagreement between these two statements is not marked and even if it were, the President and Secretary of State would be justified in accepting as true the report of a confidential agent. Benton, *Thirty Years' View*, II, 606–608; Jesse S. Reeves, *American Diplomacy under Tyler and Polk*, 128, 132, 133; *S. Ex. Doc.*, 28th Cong., 1st sess., no. 341, pp. 27, 37, 40.

[15] Upshur to Van Zandt, Oct. 16, 1843; *S. Pub. Doc.*, 28th Cong., 1st sess., no. 341, p. 37; George P. Garrison, ed., *Diplomatic Correspondence of the Republic of Texas*, II, *An. Report of the Amer. Historical Asso.*, 1898, II (1), 221–224.

Mexico were assured. To accept the offer of annexation would, therefore, be to cause the good offices of these friendly powers to be withdrawn. He did not think it politic "to abandon the expectations which now exist of a speedy settlement of our difficulties with Mexico . . . for the very uncertain prospect of annexation to the United States." For he believed that the approval of annexation by the other branches of that government "would be, if not refused, at least of very uncertain attainment." [16]

Houston's rejection of the offer did not discourage Upshur but only prodded him on to further effort. By making a canvass of Congress he was convinced that sentiment in that body had by the first of the year become much stronger in favor of annexation than it had been when he first made the proposal. Writing to Murphy, American chargé in Texas, under date of January 16, 1844, he reported that there was a strong support for it in the North, as well as in the South, and every day the measure was growing in popularity. "I feel a degree of confidence in regard to it that is little short of absolute certainty." "Measures have been taken to ascertain the views of Senators upon the subject, and *it is found that a clear constitutional majority of two-thirds are in favor of the measure.*" [17] He instructed Murphy to make this report to Houston and to lose no time in pressing the matter on him, as the friends of annexation in Congress were impatient to move forward.

Acting on this information, which he had probably confirmed on his own account, Houston and his Cabinet decided to accept the proposal and to send a commission to Washington to negotiate a treaty. This understanding was based on the pledge made by Murphy that the United States would

---

[16] Anson Jones to Van Zandt, Dec. 13, 1843; *ibid.*, 232–233.

[17] Upshur to W. S. Murphy, Jan. 16, 1844; Tyler, *op. cit.*, II, 283–284. Henry Clay, writing to J. J. Crittenden from New Orleans, February 15, 1844, reported General F. Mercer as saying that forty-two Senators had indicated a willingness to vote for annexation. *The Papers of John Jordan Crittenden*, IX, 1664.

protect Texas against attack during the progress of the negotiations by putting a sufficient naval force in the Gulf of Mexico and by stationing troops on the southwestern border of the United States.[18] Upshur also told Van Zandt verbally that the moment the treaty was signed the President would make a precautionary disposal of troops in the neighborhood of Texas, and employ all the means placed within his power by the Constitution to protect Texas from foreign invasion.[19]

With these assurances Houston sent General J. P. Henderson to Washington to act with Van Zandt in negotiating a treaty. Before he arrived the *Princeton* disaster had occurred resulting in the death of Upshur and Gilmer, another strong advocate of annexation. In this way the negotiations were delayed; but Tyler was determined to go ahead with his plans despite the loss of two such ardent supporters of the cause.

Murphy had exceeded his authority in pledging to Houston the protection of the American army and fleet while negotiations were pending, and this promise was disavowed by Nelson, the acting Secretary of State. The President was willing to station a navy in the Gulf of Mexico and military forces on the southwestern border as a means of precaution pending negotiations. These ships and men could be used *at the proper time* but not at the period indicated by Murphy's stipulations.[20]

When Murphy, acting on these instructions, withdrew his pledge of protection, the Texan authorities again resolved to frighten the United States into action by the threat of British influence. Anson Jones, Texan Secretary of State, feeling that the United States was recovering a little from its alarm, said: "I will have to give them another scare. One or two doses of *English calomel* and *French quinine* have to

[18] Murphy to Tyler, Feb. 17, 1844; Tyler, *Letters and Times*, II, 287–288. Murphy to Jones, Feb. 14, 1844; *Niles*, LXIV, 231.

[19] *Niles, loc. cit.*, 230–231.

[20] Nelson to Murphy, Mar. 11, 1844; *ibid.*, 232.

be administered, and the case will be pretty well out of danger." [21] The plan had the desired effect, for Murphy again became alarmed over the British danger and communicated his fears to President Tyler. He reported that Houston and his Cabinet and all his confidential friends were secretly opposed to annexation. He also spoke of the number of British agents that were in communication with Houston.[22]

When Henderson arrived in Washington he and Van Zandt insisted upon a pledge of protection before they would agree to the treaty. Tyler, probably frightened by Murphy's alarming report, agreed that the naval and military forces of the United States could be used to protect Texas after the treaty was signed but before it was ratified.[23]

Calhoun had no difficulty in getting Henderson and Van Zandt to accept the treaty after the promise of protection had been given. The ease with which their consent was won lends color to the statement that Upshur and Van Zandt had agreed upon a treaty and had even committed its terms to writing. According to an interview given out by John Tyler, Jr., in 1888, the text of this treaty was copied by Upshur in his own hand the night before the explosion on the *Princeton* and left on his table to be signed next day.[24]

The treaty, written by Calhoun, was signed April 12,

[21] Anson Jones, *Memoranda and Official Correspondence Relating to the Republic of Texas; Its History and Annexation* (New York, 1859), 335–336.

[22] Murphy to Tyler, Mar. 10, 1844; MS. in Department of Archives, Washington, D. C.

[23] Calhoun to Van Zandt, Apr. 11, 1844; H. Ex. Doc., 28th Cong., 1st sess., no. 271, pp. 96–97.

Reeves represents Calhoun as having induced Tyler to "about face" on the pledge to Texas. The pledge now made, however, was the same, or about the same, as the verbal promise given by Upshur to Van Zandt. J. S. Reeves, *American Diplomacy under Tyler and Polk*, 144.

[24] It should be remembered that Vergil Maxcy, who was in confidential relations with Upshur, quoted the latter (as early as December 10, 1843) as saying that the terms of a treaty had already been agreed upon between him and the Texan minister. Maxcy to Calhoun, Dec. 10, 1843; *An. Rept. Amer. Histor. Asso.*, 1899, II, 900–904; *Lippincott's Monthly Magazine*, XLI, 417–419.

1844. By the terms of this agreement the citizens of Texas would be incorporated into the Union and admitted "to the enjoyment of all the rights, privileges, and immunities, of citizens of the United States." The public lands of Texas were also ceded to the United States and her debt, amounting to ten million dollars, was assumed. Not a word about boundaries is found in the treaty.[25]

Tyler was prompt to carry out his pledge of protection to Texas pending the negotiations for annexation. On May 15 (1844) he notified the Senate that United States warships had been sent to the Gulf of Mexico and land troops stationed at Fort Jessup on the Texan border. In this short message he made it clear that these forces were to be employed to protect Texas from an attack by Mexico while the treaty was under consideration. He declared it to be his opinon that the United States, having by the treaty of annexation acquired a title to Texas which only required the action of the Senate to be perfect, should regard any attempt by a foreign power to invade Texas as an act of hostility to the United States and one which he would be justified in resisting by the employment of the military forces at his disposal.[26]

One important objection to the acquisition of Texas was the probability that it would affect adversely the friendly relations that existed between Mexico and the United States. For Mexico had never recognized the independence of Texas, and before the negotiations for annexation had begun, the Mexican foreign office had notified our government that it would view the passage of an act by Congress for the incorporation of Texas into the United States as equivalent to a declaration of war.[27] Although the President did not

---

[25] *S. Pub. Doc.,* 28th Cong., 1st sess., no. 341, pp. 10–13.

[26] Richardson, *Messages,* IV, 316–318. For an article criticizing the President for this action, see *National Intelligencer,* May 16, 1844; *Niles, loc. cit.,* 177.

[27] De Bocanegra, Mexican Minister of Foreign Affairs, to Waddy Thompson, Aug. 23, 1843; *Niles,* LXV, 264.

consider that Mexico had any grounds of complaint against the United States for having negotiated a treaty of annexation, yet he was anxious to avoid war with our southern neighbor. A messenger was, therefore, sent to Mexico to induce that government peaceably to acquiesce in the union of Texas with the United States.[28]

Ten days after it was signed, the treaty was submitted (April 22) to the Senate for ratification.[29] With the treaty the President sent a special message, together with certain documents in support of the treaty, which had been selected by the Secretary of State.[30] This selection was made with the apparent view of sustaining the thesis that annexation was necessary for the salvation of the United States. England's efforts in Texas in behalf of abolition were a menace to the institution of slavery, and a danger to slavery was a danger to the permanence of the Union.

The President in his message gave strong arguments in favor of annexation. He contended that the incorporation of Texas into the United States would promote the interests of all sections of our country. Texas being blessed with a soil of inexhaustible fertility and a very favorable climate would, under the aegis of American protection, soon become wealthy. This would lead to an increase of commerce and especially of the coasting trade. As the Northern and Middle States enjoyed a monopoly of this business, they would receive large benefits from this stimulus to their commerce. From the West the Texans (who would devote most of their time

[28] Benton, *Thirty Years' View*, II, 608.

[29] The reasons for this delay as given by the President were as follows: (1) The Secretary of State wanted to prepare an answer to Lord Aberdeen's letter in which he had given the position of the British government with reference to Texas and abolition. (2) It required several days to copy the numerous documents which were to be transmitted with the treaty. (3) Tyler wanted Senator King's successor to be appointed and be present when the treaty came before the Senate. *Tyler's Quarterly Historical and Genealogical Magazine*, VI, 229.

[30] Sen. Ex. Doc., 28th Cong., 1st sess., no. 341, pp. 5–54.

For Calhoun's correspondence regarding Texas, see R. K. Crallé, comp., *The Works of John C. Calhoun*, 6 vols. (1851–79), V, 321–414.

to the cultivation of cotton, rice, and sugar) would buy beef, pork, grain, and other food products. The Southern and Southeastern States would gain a feeling of security against both foreign and domestic efforts to disturb their tranquility.

If this opportunity for annexation should be lost the results might be most hazardous. It would produce such an alienation of feeling on the part of the Texans as to cause them to look to other nations for aid. In order to secure this assistance Texas might enter into dangerous alliances with foreign powers or offer them discriminating duties in trade. Either alternative "would prove disastrous in the highest degree to the interests of the whole Union." It would be a very poor policy for us to permit "the carrying trade and home market of such a country to pass out of our hands into those of a commercial rival." If Texas should remain permanently outside our tariff wall, smuggling on an extensive scale would be carried on, which could not be prevented by an army of customhouse officials. This would cause not only a material loss to our revenues but would lead to interminable strife between the people of the two countries.

He very properly pointed out that "there exists no civilized government on earth having a voluntary tender made it of a domain so rich and fertile, so replete with all that can add to national greatness and wealth and so necessary to its peace and safety that would reject the offer." "Under every view which I have been able to take of the subject, I think that the interests of our common constituents, the people of all the States, and a love of the Union left the Executive no other alternative than to negotiate the treaty." [31]

It will readily be seen from this summary that the President urged annexation as a broad national policy. If he had rested his case on these unanswerable arguments he would have left his opponents little ground on which to stand. Un-

[31] Richardson, *op. cit.*, IV, 307–313.

fortunately in his effort to show how the South would be benefited by annexation he exposed himself to the charge of linking up the Texan question with the slavery issue. In a few sentences in his message he alluded to the danger to the permanence of the Union, if Texas were not admitted, which would result from Great Britain's desire to see slavery abolished everywhere (even in the United States) and from her efforts to mediate peace between Mexico and Texas on the basis of abolition in Texas.[32]

Just why Tyler allowed this lapse into sectionalism to mar an otherwise able state paper we cannot definitely explain. It may have been inserted out of deference to the wishes of his premier, who wanted to emphasize the proslavery argument. The smallness of the space devoted to it in his message would indicate that he did not intend to present as his main argument the fear of the antislavery activity of the British government in Texas. That his great aim in urging annexation was the desire to promote the interests of the country as a whole is borne out by statements made by him after his retirement from the Presidency. In a letter to his son Robert in 1850 he avowed that his view as to annexation was not sectional but national. "It embraced," he said, "the whole country and all its interests. The monopoly of the cotton plant was the great and important concern. That monopoly, now secured, places all other nations at our feet. An embargo of a single year would produce in Europe a greater amount of suffering than a fifty years' war. I doubt whether Great Britain could avoid convulsions. And yet, with these results before him, Mr. Calhoun unceasingly talked of slavery and its abolition in connection with the subject. That idea seemed to possess him and *Upshur as a single idea.*" [33] In other letters he expressed the same view.[34]

[32] Richardson, *op. cit.,* IV, 312.
[33] Tyler, *Letters and Times,* II, 483. See also *John Tyler Papers* (L.C.), IV, 6885.
[34] *Tyler's Quarterly,* XII, 236–237; *John Tyler Papers* (L.C.), III, 6557–58.

As it turned out, Calhoun's overemphasis of the abolition danger did not exert any influence to speak of in favor of the rejection of the treaty; for the vote that finally determined the fate of the treaty in the Senate was given on partisan rather than sectional grounds. The national conventions had been held and the Texan question was considered not on its merits but only as a factor in the political situation. Clay, the Whig nominee for President, had come out against annexation,[35] and so the Whigs both in the North and the South opposed it. The Democrats had nominated Polk and declared in favor of re-annexation. They could, therefore, be expected to vote for ratification; but they were in the minority in the Senate, and some of them were disgruntled over Van Buren's defeat. To bring the recalcitrant members in line, a letter from Jackson was published in which he declared that a Senator who would vote against annexation would be a traitor to his country.[36] Only seven Democrats were willing to risk the displeasure of the Old Hero and voted nay. One other Democrat, Hannegan, of Indiana, was absent. The remaining fifteen Democrats and one Whig voted yea. All the Whigs but this one voted nay. So the vote stood 16 yeas to 35 nays.[37]

This vote showed that Upshur in estimating the supporters of the treaty in the Senate at forty had badly misjudged the sentiment of that body or else politics had completely upset his calculations.[38] It must also have been a surprise as well as a disappointment to Tyler. He afterwards contended that when he signed the treaty he expected both Clay and Van Buren to favor ratification. This hope was based on the

---

[35] *National Intelligencer,* April 27, 1844.
[36] *The Daily Globe* (Washington), Mar. 20, 1844.
[37] *Niles, loc. cit.,* LVI, 241.
[38] *An. Report of Amer. Histor. Association,* 1899, II, 934.
John Tyler, Jr., said that a number of Senators who had been induced to support the treaty afterwards joined the opposition and voted against it. This change in attitude was caused, he thought, by the appointment of Calhoun to the Secretaryship of State. *Lippincott's Monthly Magazine,* XLI, 417–419.

fact that each had, on a former occasion, tried to purchase Texas and neither had made any public utterances up to that time which would indicate a change in attitude.[39]

After the Zollverein and Texas treaties had both been rejected by the Senate, Calhoun became discouraged and advised the abandonment of all further effort at negotiation on any subject. Tyler, however, had not given up hope and was displeased at the pessimism of his Secretary of State. Indeed, he resolved to call for his resignation if he did not soon rally from his despondency. Happily the President was spared a break with his premier by a return of the latter to a hopeful attitude toward Texan relations.[40]

Since annexation had failed in the Senate, the best chance for acquiring Texas was by a joint resolution of both houses of Congress. Accordingly, two days after the rejection of the treaty by the Senate, Tyler sent to the House the rejected treaty along with the documents that had been before the Senate. In the accompanying message he stated that no negotiations with Mexico had preceded the signing of the treaty, for such negotiations would have proved not only abortive but insulting to Texas, and possibly offensive to Mexico. As Texas had maintained her independence for eight years and during that time "no army has [had] invaded her with a view to reconquest," she had every right to be treated as an independent nation. Therefore, no negotiations with Mexico for Texas could be carried on "without admitting that our recognition of her independence was fraudulent, delusive, or void." He felt that if this opportunity for annexation were lost Texas would forthwith "enter into a treaty of commerce and alliance offensive and defensive [with Great Britain]."

In closing he said that while he regarded annexation by treaty as the most suitable form in which it could be effected, still he stood ready to co-operate with Congress in any plan for annexation compatible with the Constitution. "The great

[39] Tyler, *Letters and Times,* II, 348.   [40] *Ibid.,* 331.

question is not as to the manner in which it shall be done but whether it shall be accomplished or not." [41]

The action of the President in thus appealing from the decision of the Senate afforded Benton the opportunity of making a savage attack upon him. In an abusive speech of two hours' length (June 13) he contended that as the Senators are made by the Constitution the advisers and controllers of the President in case of treaties, to appeal from their decision was to insult the Senate and to merit impeachment. He pronounced the Texas project as a fraud upon the people—a base, wicked, miserable, presidential intrigue.[42]

The session of Congress was too near its end for any action to be taken on so important a question. Therefore, while a motion looking to annexation was made in each House, Congress adjourned without either of these motions coming to a vote. But Tyler was assured by prominent Democrats in the House that annexation should not be permitted to rest.[43]

The election of 1844 might properly be considered a plebiscite in favor of the annexation of Texas. The "re-annexation of Texas and the re-occupation of Oregon" was the main plank in the Democratic platform, and the victory won by this party at the polls would indicate that a majority of the American people were in favor of the acquisition of both of these regions.

When Congress assembled in December, 1844, Tyler in his annual message recommended that the provisions of the rejected treaty be accepted by Congress in a joint resolution. He took the position that the recent Presidential election had shown that "a controlling majority of the people and a large majority of the States have declared in favor of immediate annexation." There was no appeal in the message to sectionalism or proslavery sentiment. On the other hand, there was a renewal of the arguments formerly advanced in

[41] Richardson, *op. cit.*, IV, 323–327.   [42] *Niles, loc. cit.*, 241.
[43] Tyler to General Howard, June 18, 1844; *Tyler's Quarterly*, VI, 231.

favor of annexation as an advantage to the country as a whole.

The objection that Mexico had raised to annexation should be disregarded, for she had no ground of complaint. Mexico was despoiled of nothing, "since Texas was forever lost to her." Despite the threats of Mexico no apprehensions of war were entertained by the executive. On the contrary it felt that had the treaty been ratified by the Senate, a prompt settlement would have followed which would have been to the entire satisfaction of Mexico. An additional argument in favor of annexation—one not given before—was that Mexico's obstinate continuance of the war with Texas was exhausting both countries and rendering them the easy prey of outside powers. Annexation would end this sad state of affairs.[44]

As Tyler had no party to support him, it might seem that his recommendation regarding Texas would be disregarded. This was by no means the case. The endorsement of annexation by the people in the recent campaign had given the question a new importance. It could not, therefore, be ignored. Even if the Congressmen had been inclined to sidestep the issue, they would have been forced into action by pressure from their constituents. For petitions from individuals and resolutions adopted by State legislatures showed that the people considered the subject a matter of outstanding importance. The acquisition of Texas, by enlarging the area of slavery, would give the South a stronger and the North a relatively weaker voice in the government of the Union. The advocacy of annexation, therefore, came mostly from the former section and its opposition mainly from the latter.[45] Exceptions to this rule were resolutions in favor of annexation adopted by the legislatures of Maine and New Hampshire.[46]

[44] President Tyler's Fourth Annual Message, Dec. 3, 1844; Richardson, *op. cit.*, IV, 341–345.

[45] *Cong. Globe,* 28th Cong., 2nd sess., 78, 89, 133, 137, 154, 171, 178, 194, 211, 233, 237.

[46] *Ibid.*, 92, 277.

Congress, therefore, took prompt action. After several resolutions had been offered and considerable discussion carried on in each house, a bill providing for annexation by a joint resolution of both houses of Congress was passed by the House of Representatives (January 25, 1845).[47] The Senate was apparently unwilling to accept the House measure without modification. Benton, who had formerly demanded the consent of Mexico for annexation, now offered a resolution authorizing the President (he had in mind Polk, the President-elect) to negotiate a new treaty with Texas.[48] He, Tappan, and a few other Van Buren Democrats were holding out against the House resolution, but evidently would be glad of an excuse to vote for annexation if they could do so and at the same time save their faces. To aid these die-hard Van Burenites to escape from their dilemma and support annexation without apparent inconsistency, Senator R. J. Walker offered a compromise plan. By his resolutions the House measure was coupled with that of Benton as alternative plans with the proviso that the President decide as to which should be put into effect.[49] The annexation proposal as thus amended was accepted by both houses of Congress.[50]

The terms of the joint resolution were more favorable to Texas than were those of the original treaty. By the former Texas was to be admitted as a State without going through the territorial period. New States, not exceeding four in number, could with the consent of Texas be created out of her territory. Such new States if north of the 36° 30′ line were to be admitted without slavery. If south of that line they should come in with or without slavery as their citizens might desire. Texas was to pay her own debt but was to retain her public lands.[51]

Tyler had felt that if his plan of securing Texas were consummated it would be necessary to keep Texas in line as

[47] *Ibid.*, 193–194.   [48] *Ibid.*, 244.   [49] *Ibid.*, 359.
[50] *Ibid.*, 362–363, 372.   [51] *Ibid.*, 127–128.

well as to secure the assent of Congress. Despite the rejection of the treaty the people in Texas were still strong in
their desire for annexation; but there was enough uncertainty in President Houston's attitude to warrant real concern. Anson Jones was of the opinion that Houston had been
opposed to annexation ever since the treaty had been rejected by the Senate. According to Ashbel Smith, Houston
had, by the beginning of 1845, come to feel that annexation
would not promote the interests of either Texas or the
United States.[52] Tyler, therefore, had reason for feeling
nervous over the advances that Houston was making toward
the British government.

Upon the death of Howard, American chargé d'affaires
in Texas, Tyler appointed in his place Andrew J. Donelson,
the nephew of Mrs. Jackson. The object of this appointment was to bring the personal influence of Jackson to bear
upon Houston. Tyler wrote to Jackson at the time, notifying him of the appointment of Donelson and of the reasons
for so doing. He felt that this appointment would "have a
controlling influence with General Houston and incline him,
if he entertains any feelings antagonistic to the United
States and favorable to England, to pause ere he declares
against annexation." [53]

The reports sent back by Donelson emphasized the necessity of haste in consummating annexation. "Every day's delay," he said, "is adding strength to the hands of those who
are playing the game for the ascendency of British influence
in this Republic. Delay will increase the difficulties already
in our way, if it does not make them insuperable." [54]

The joint resolution for annexation reached President
Tyler on March 1, 1845, and at once received his approval.

[52] Ashbel Smith, *Reminiscences of the Texas Republic* (Galveston, 1876),
69–70.
[53] Calhoun to Donelson, Sept. 16, 1844; *An. Report of Amer. Histor. Asso.*,
1899, II, 614–615. Tyler to Jackson, Sept. 17, 1844; *Tyler's Quarterly*, VI,
233–234.
[54] Donelson to Calhoun, Nov. 23, 1844 (received Dec. 28); cited by Reeves,
op. cit., 181.

On that same day Tyler also discussed with Calhoun the advisability of immediate action. The President stated that his mind was fully made up as to the choice of the two alternatives. He considered that the Senate amendment had been tacked on solely for the purpose of appeasing the discontent of one or two Senators. If further negotiations with Texas were attempted it would defeat annexation altogether. He felt "that Texas, in consequence of the defeat of the late treaty by the Senate, would listen reluctantly to any new proposition for negotiation; that this reluctance would be greatly increased by reason of the very small majorities in Congress by which the resolutions had passed, which might well create a doubt whether a two-thirds vote could be obtained for the ratification of a treaty, and that these doubts might very wisely incline Texas to throw herself upon the good offices of Great Britain and France, with a view to obtain the recognition of her independence by Mexico, in preference to relying on the uncertain contingency of a new negotiation." Calhoun agreed to this view.

The President then said that his only hesitancy in acting promptly came from a feeling of delicacy to his successor. Calhoun advised that this feeling be waived and that immediate action be taken. Tyler had the legal authority to move and should act without delay. The necessity for prompt action was so great as to overrule all other considerations.

The President directed Calhoun to call a Cabinet meeting for the next day, which was done. The members of the Cabinet were all in favor of choosing the House resolution rather than resorting to negotiation. Tyler repeated to them his feeling about taking immediate action, and the Cabinet was unanimous in advising against delay. It was pointed out that Polk and his advisers "would necessarily have to take some time to look around after he and they had been installed in office, and that if Texas was lost by delay the censure would fall on my administration."

It was decided that to save the point of delicacy Calhoun

should see Polk, inform him of the President's decision, and give the reasons for this action. Calhoun waited on Polk after the meeting of the Cabinet and carried out these instructions. Next morning he reported to President Tyler the result of the interview, "which was, that Mr. Polk declined to express any opinion or to make any suggestion in reference to the subject." Accordingly, instructions were sent immediately to Donelson directing him to consummate the plan for annexation. These instructions were drawn up by Calhoun and approved by Tyler.[55]

Tyler showed good judgment in promptly forwarding to Texas the proposal of the joint resolution. His choice of alternatives was also a wise one. Two years of persistent effort on his part had issued in success and he had a right to harvest the fruits of his labors. To expect that he would stand aside and allow another to reap what he had not only sown but assiduously cultivated was to attribute to him a degree of self-abnegation not characteristic of human nature. Even if he had been willing to lay aside all personal considerations, he had no right to jeopardize annexation by assuming the risks of an unnecessary delay.

The action of the United States government came just in time to save the cause of annexation, for events were moving in the opposite direction in the south. Thanks to the good offices of the British and French chargés at the Texan capital, a treaty had been drawn up between Texas and Mexico providing for the recognition of the independence of Texas by Mexico on condition that the former would promise never to consent to union with another country. If this agreement were carried out all hope for annexation to the United States would be blasted. The preliminary treaty was accepted by the Mexican authorities and ratified by the Mexican Congress.[56] It was now incumbent upon the govern-

[55] Tyler, op. cit., II, 364–365; John Tyler Papers (L.C.), IV, 6901–02. The above statement is based on Tyler's account of this event made on November 27, 1848.

[56] Ashbel Smith's Reminiscences, 72.

ment and people of Texas to decide whether they preferred independence and peace with Mexico or annexation to the United States. The convention called to consider annexation declared (July 4) for it with only one dissenting vote. The Texan Congress had already voted unanimously in favor of rejecting the Mexican treaty and accepting the offer of the United States. In October the people ratified the act of the convention by an overwhelming majority.

Tyler was justly proud of the part he had played in the acquisition of Texas.[57] It was the outstanding achievement of his career, and he resented every effort to take from him his due meed of credit. When Houston in May, 1847, made a statement ascribing the success of annexation chiefly to General Jackson, Tyler replied by saying that he had initiated the negotiations before he had consulted the Old Hero. He admitted, however, that Jackson had aided greatly and had been a tower of strength to the cause.[58]

Tyler's greatest rival for the honor was his premier, Calhoun. When Benton in a speech in the Senate (February 24, 1847) charged Calhoun with being the main instigator of annexation, the latter admitted the accusation and assumed for himself an honor which was not his due. From his speech in reply to Benton it would seem that he, not Tyler, was the chief agent in bringing about annexation. He asserted that *he* had chosen the House resolution. Tyler was justly incensed at this unfair claim of his former Secretary of State, and in a letter (March 11, 1847) to his brother-in-law, Alexander Gardiner, gave vent to expressions of strong resentment. He said:

"*If he* [Calhoun] *selected,* then Texas is not legitimately a State of the Union, for Congress gave the power *to the President to select,* and not to the *Secretary of State.*" With greater bitterness of feeling than was his wont he spoke of

[57] Tyler to General Thomas J. Green, Feb. 28, 1856; *Huntington Library MSS.*
[58] Tyler, *Letters and Times,* II, 428–431.

Calhoun as "the great 'I am' " and referred to Benton as "the most raving political maniac I ever knew." [59]

Tyler was persistent in his refusal to allow the friends of Calhoun to appropriate for the great Carolinian the credit for the acquisition of Texas. Writing to a friend in 1856, he declared that if Upshur had not been killed the treaty would have been signed without Calhoun's knowledge; [60] that if Van Zandt had had full power the negotiations would have been finished in a week from their inception; and that if General Henderson (the second commissioner from Texas) had reached Washington before Calhoun's arrival, the treaty would have been signed by Mr. Nelson, Secretary of State, *ad interim*.[61] That this claim on the part of the President is in accordance with the facts we have every reason to believe.

Although Tyler was not accorded due credit for annexation by supporters of the movement, he became the chief target for the criticism of the anti-Texan forces. The storm of opposition which had raged throughout the greater portion of his term had somewhat abated just prior to the beginning of the negotiations. When, however, it was made public that there were plans for acquiring new slave territory the winds of abuse were loosed in the North and the President became the center of a cyclone of vituperation that was exceptional even for that age of virulent hate. His critics could see in this acquisition of an empire nothing but the selfish designs of the slavocracy to extend its nefarious power. That the President had succumbed to such malign influences was only an additional proof that he had bartered away his soul to the evil one. It was suggested in all serious-

[59] Tyler to Alexander Gardiner, March 11, 1847; Tyler, *op. cit.*, II, 417–419, 420; R. K. Crallé, ed., *The Works of John C. Calhoun*, 6 vols. (N. Y., 1854–61), IV, 262 ff.

[60] On this one point, however, Tyler was mistaken, for as has already been shown (page 374), Gilmer and Maxcy had, without the knowledge of the President, notified Calhoun sometime before the *Princeton* disaster that negotiations had begun.

[61] *John Tyler Papers* (L.C.), IV, 6746–47.

ness that he should be impeached and hurled from his high office for having so abused the authority of the Chief Magistracy. Even so eminent and well-placed a person as Chancellor Kent, of New York, lent his legal reputation in support of this foolish proposition.[62] Annexation, it was contended, meant war with Mexico. This contention was voiced by the New York *Tribune* (March 1, 1845) when it said (anent the joint resolution): "We have adopted a war ready made, and taken upon ourselves its prosecution to the end."[63]

His enemies were not content with charging him with the high crime of sectionalism. They accused him of having been influenced by lower and more sordid motives. The *National Intelligencer* spoke of his having been surrounded by speculators in Texas stock and land and of having been influenced by them "to that unwise measure."[64] In reply to this unfair accusation Tyler denied that he knew of any such speculations in connection with the negotiations. He had never owned, he said, a foot of Texas land or a dollar of Texas stock. Moreover, in these negotiations the strictest secrecy was observed and, therefore, the owners of Texas land or stock could not have known about them until the preliminaries were nearly all arranged.[65]

Tyler's achievement, however, did win some recognition from the friends of Texas. The Democratic leaders in the South gave lip service in appreciation of his support of their cause. Andrew Jackson was loud in his praise of the President's Texan policy. When Tyler sent a strong protest to the Mexican government against a contemplated invasion of Texas and threatened to view it as an act of war against the United States, his action was warmly approved by the Old Hero. "This is the true energetic course," wrote the

[62] See Tyler's speech accepting the nomination for the Presidency in 1844; Tyler, *Letters and Times,* II, 343.
[63] Allan Nevins, ed., *American Press Opinion* (N. Y., 1928), 162–163.
[64] *National Intelligencer,* May 25, 1847.
[65] Tyler, *Letters and Times,* II, 423–426.

latter to James K. Polk.[66] Even John Quincy Adams, who
was one of his bitterest critics, had to admit that Tyler had
acted with "intrepidity and address." [67]

The people of Texas seemed to realize the significance of
his efforts on their behalf, and on July 8, 1845, the convention at Austin adopted resolutions of thanks to Tyler and
his Cabinet for the early and resolute stand they had taken
in favor of annexation.[68] Another token of appreciation was
the naming for the President of both a county and a county
seat in Texas. The ladies of Brazoria also sent him (January 1, 1846) a silver pitcher as a New Year's gift in token
of his work for annexation.[69] Tyler had to content himself
with such mild expressions of appreciation for an achievement by which there was added to the national domain,
peaceably and honorably, without money and without price,
a region vastly greater in extent than areas which European
powers have been willing to purchase at the cost of lavish
expenditure of blood and treasure.

[66] Tyler, Letters and Times, III, 151.
[67] J. Q. Adams, Memoirs, XII, 22.
[68] William and Mary College Historical Quarterly (first series), XV, 41–42.
[69] John Tyler Papers (L.C.), III, 6610; VIII, 661; Tyler, Letters and Times,
II, 411–412, 450.

CHAPTER XXIII

POLITICS AND PATRONAGE

PATRONAGE is one of the most effective weapons that a President has at his command. It can be wielded in support of his policies and in the furtherance of his political ambitions; but it is a two-edged sword, and unless skillfully used may cut into his own popularity as well as into the strength of his antagonists. With Tyler this weapon was dulled by the power of the Senate to reject appointments, for his enemies, both Democrats and Whigs, used this authority to the limit. It was, however, the only instrument he could employ against the opposition which continually beset him.

Tyler started out with fine intentions regarding the civil service. In his Inaugural Address he said: "I will remove no incumbent from office who has faithfully and honestly acquitted himself of the duties of his office, except in such cases where such officer has been guilty of an active partisanship or by secret means . . . has given his official influence to the purposes of party, thereby bringing the patronage of the government in conflict with the freedom of elections. Numerous removals may be necessary under this rule." [1] In keeping with this policy he had instructions sent to all the heads of the departments directing them not to use the Federal offices to advance partisan purposes.[2] It is needless to say that the exigencies of practical politics did not permit of his living up to this high ideal.

The pack of office seekers that had hounded Harrison to death were in the offing when Tyler came into power. The

[1] J. D. Richardson, *Messages and Papers of the Presidents*, IV, 38.
[2] *Niles' Register*, LX, 51–52; LXI, 67.

367

attempt to find places for this hungry crowd of deserving Whigs would have overtaxed the strength and patience of the shrewdest and most callous politician. Tyler was able to handle them with less strain than was the case with his predecessor. It was his plan that all applications for office should be made to the head of the department concerned and not to the President directly. The office seekers disregarded this wish, however, and crowded into the White House at all hours. For many of them the only effective argument was a firmly closed door.[3]

In the first part of his term Tyler was accused by the Richmond *Enquirer* of wholesale removals cf Democrats from office.[4] As was to be expected, he used his power of appointment and removal in some cases to reward his friends and penalize his enemies. After his expulsion from the Whig Party, his enemies were Clay Whigs and Van Buren Democrats, and he, therefore, did not favor them in dispensing the patronage. The leaders of these two groups thereupon raised the cry of proscription and hurled maledictions upon him. Particularly severe were the excoriations of the regular Whigs, who accused him of prostituting the civil service to his own wicked purposes. If Tyler was motivated too strongly by partisanship in handling the civil service, he was only taking a leaf out of the book of his enemies; for the Clayites and Van Burenites of the Senate frequently for partisan reasons voted to reject worthy nominations made by him.[5] Furthermore, it was utterly preposterous to expect a President to employ the patronage to strengthen a po-

[3] New York *Herald,* Jan. 19, 31, 1842; Richmond *Enquirer,* May 21, 1841; *Madisonian,* Nov. 16, 1841.

[4] Richmond *Enquirer,* Apr. 20, May 7, 14, 18, 1841.

[5] Among the appointments made by the President and rejected by the Senate (in addition to those of the Cabinet already mentioned) were those of Henry A. Wise, John C. Spencer, and George H. Proffit. Wise was nominated for minister to England; Spencer for justice of the United States Supreme Court; and Proffit for minister to Brazil. *Niles,* LXIV, 2, 29–30; LXV, 305, 353; Tyler, *Letters and Times,* II, 398; N. Y. *Herald,* May 7, 1842; *National Intelligencer,* Jan. 9, 12, Feb. 1, 1844.

litical faction which was constantly trying to discredit him
and a party which had excommunicated him and invoked
upon him all the curses in the devil's prayer book.

Tyler's term of four years was one continuous political
campaign. The desire to elect Clay to the Presidency in 1844
was behind virtually all the attempts at legislation made by
Whig Congressmen. The brilliant Kentuckian, having lost
all hope of carrying out his original program, withdrew from
the Senate (March 31, 1842) and went home to look after
his private affairs and to devote his energies to the campaign
for the Presidency.[6] On taking leave of his colleagues, he delivered a farewell address that was a remarkable achievement in oratory. With the inspiration of a sympathetic audience that crowded the floor and the galleries, he made the
occasion one of unusual dramatic interest. So moved were
his hearers that the Senate, after an awed silence, voted to
adjourn in appreciation of the deep impression created by
the address.[7] When he left the Senate Clay did not, however, abate his interest in public affairs, and by a correspondence with his successor, J. J. Crittenden, he kept in close
touch with the maneuvers of the politicians at Washington.[8]
Clay and his friends were determined to consolidate the
Whig Party under his leadership and keep it dominant in
the country. This meant the sacrifice of Tyler and the defeat
of the Democracy. They were triumphantly successful in
the first objective, but this result was achieved at the cost of
the second.

Tyler was also engaged in political activity. As he had no
party of his own, he was trying to form a third party that
would support his policies and stand behind his candidacy in
1844 if he should decide to offer for re-election. At first his
aim was to win to his support the States' rights Whigs and

[6] See a letter from Clay to Mr. Brooke, of Virginia; quoted by Carl Schurz
in his *Henry Clay*, II, 222.

[7] T. H. Benton, *Thirty Years' View*, II, 398–403; *National Intelligencer*,
Apr. 2, 1842.

[8] For this correspondence, see *The Papers of John Jordan Crittenden* (L.C.).

the moderates of both parties. The patronage was used as a means to this end. In the latter part of his term, when he was making every effort to secure support for his Texan policy, he tried to win over the Van Buren-Jackson wing of the Democratic Party (page 285). It was doubtless in line with this purpose that a seat on the Supreme Court bench was offered to Van Buren [9] and later to Silas Wright [10] and a place in the Cabinet to James K. Polk (page 284).

According to his accusers, the desire to succeed himself was the motive that prompted these approaches to his former enemies. That he was using the patronage to build up his political fences with the view to succeeding himself is doubtless true. If so, he was only doing what nearly every other occupant of the White House has done, both before and after his time. There was, however, another reason for creating a pro-Tyler party. Such a party would insure the success of the measures that the President was urging before Congress. There is, therefore, every reason to think that Tyler's purpose in making his appointments was as high as that of the general run of his successors and predecessors. The ascription of low motives in the exercise of this power is but another evidence of that satanic hate with which his foes dogged his footsteps.

The President was also accused of being unjust in his removals and unwise in his appointments. No doubt there were instances in which employees were removed without just cause, and, of course, a number of improper appointments were made. The case that created the greatest stir and

---

[9] Silas Wright was asked by one of Tyler's friends whether in the opinion of the former Van Buren would accept the appointment of justice of the Supreme Court. Wright's reply was as follows: "Tell Mr. Tyler from me that, if he desires to give this whole country a broader, deeper, heartier laugh than it ever had and at his own expense, he can effect it by making that nomination." Silas Wright to Van Buren, Jan. 2, 1844; *Van Buren Papers,* XLVIII (L.C.), 11,250–51. This letter has been published in Charles Warren's *The Supreme Court in United States History,* 3 vols. (Boston, 1923), II, 382–384.
[10] New York *Tribune,* Feb. 16, 1844; New York *Journal of Commerce,* Mar. 9, 14, 1844; cited by Warren, *op. cit.,* II, 389.

aroused the most unfavorable criticism was the discharge of Jonathan Roberts from the collectorship of the port of Philadelphia. If we are to credit fully a statement of the *Madisonian,* Tyler had scarcely a friend among the more than one hundred officials in the customhouse. He, therefore, asked that a few of the employees be removed and their places filled with supporters of the President, a request with which the collector would not comply. Roberts, however, states that he was asked to dismiss thirty-one of his subordinates. The implication is that there was no ground for these removals except alleged political activity of the wrong sort. On the other hand, Tyler's son and biographer, Dr. Lyon G. Tyler, maintains that Roberts "had swept into the collector's office at Philadelphia the very scum of the city." Roberts demurred to the President's order and went to Washington to induce him to withdraw it. After considerable delay and difficulty he saw the President, who treated him coldly and even discourteously. The collector was unable to convince Tyler of the reasonableness of his request and so was removed.[11]

There is no evidence, however, of wholesale removals. The *Madisonian* stated (July 21, 1843) that nineteen twentieths of the Federal offices were at that time held by men who were opposed to the President. A few months later it was of the opinion that with few exceptions, each one admitting of the most ample justification, the great body of officeholders was unchanged. Among them were some of the bitterest enemies and most active revilers of the President. Again in May, 1844, this newspaper expressed the belief that a large majority of the offices of the country were then and had always been in the hands of Van Buren's and Clay's friends.[12] While the *Madisonian* was partial to the Ad-

[11] *United States Gazette,* quoted in *Daily Richmond Whig,* Sept. 17, 1842; Tyler, *Letters and Times,* III, 188; *Madisonian,* July 7, 1842; *Pennsylvania Magazine of History and Biography,* October, 1938, 514 ff.

[12] Tyler, *op. cit.,* II, 313-314, note.

All the prominent Whigs who were on foreign missions at Tyler's accession

ministration and may have exaggerated in the interest of its patron, there is good reason to believe that the President in the handling of the civil service showed not more, but probably less, partisanship than was the custom at that time.

The charge of nepotism was also brought against Tyler by his enemies. It is true that several of his relatives and family connections held Federal offices; but the number was too small to warrant a serious accusation on this score. Moreover, one of these appointments had been made on the recommendation of President Harrison and another by the head of the department concerned without the knowledge of the President.[13]

If Tyler had been a good politician, he would have known from the beginning that there was no probability of his being able to succeed himself. He was not, however, a shrewd politician, and it is not unlikely that at times he indulged in this fond hope. If so, these pleasing anticipations must have received a rude shock early in the year 1843. In January of

---

remained at their posts until the end of his term except a few who returned home on their own accord.

When Justice Baldwin, of the Supreme Court, died the President offered the place successively to John Sergeant and Horace Binney, who were pronounced Whigs and political opponents. He had also previously appointed Binney judge of the Eastern District of Pennsylvania and he had declined the position. These facts tend to show that Tyler was less partisan in the use of patronage than would be expected under the circumstances. Tyler, *op. cit.*, III, 189; Charles C. Binney, *The Life of Horace Binney* (Philadelphia and London, 1903), 229–232; *Nat. Intel.*, Jan. 14, 1842.

[13] Tyler was, however, responsible for giving his son Robert a place in the Land Office at an annual salary of $1500. When Robert left Washington he was succeeded by John Tyler, Jr. In selecting a member of his own family for this place, the President was following precedent; for the immediate predecessor of Robert Tyler was Martin Van Buren, Jr., and the successor of John Tyler, Jr., was James K. Walker, a nephew of President Polk.

John Quincy Adams joined in the charge of nepotism, alleging that the appointment of his son as his private secretary was a case in point. The unfairness of such an accusation is apparent when it is recalled that Tyler paid the salary of his secretary out of his own private funds. *Madisonian*, June 26, 1841; *An Account of the Receipts and Expenditures of the United States* for the years 1841–1845.

that year, M. M. Noah, of the *Weekly Register,* at the request of Tyler, went to Richmond to consult the political oracle, Thomas Ritchie, editor of the *Enquirer.*

Ritchie spoke very kindly and favorably of the President. He expressed the utmost confidence in his integrity, and admitted that he had done much to merit the confidence of the Democratic Party; but, said he, "the ground is already occupied, and there appears a determination in that party to do justice to those who were unfortunate in the conflict of 1840, and to reinstate them in power, in proof of unwavering confidence in their principles." As to patronage, it could, if discreetly employed, be used to sustain a party already in power, but "patronage alone could never build up a party for any man." Tyler seemed to appreciate the wisdom of this frank advice; for he said, in reply to Noah's report, "I assure you I entertain no hopes of an election myself, although some of my friends are sanguine." [14]

President Tyler not only had no organization but he had no followers of prominence who were putting up a vigorous fight for his re-election. Even some of his most confidential advisers were ardently, though secretly, supporting Calhoun for the succession. Upshur, and probably Gilmer, allowed their zeal for the cause of the South Carolinian to carry them to the point of disloyalty to the political aspirations of their chief. As early as December, 1843, both of these Cabinet officers had without Tyler's knowledge communicated, the former directly and the latter indirectly, with Calhoun

[14] *Niles,* LXIV, 394.
He did not at this time, however, entirely abandon the hope of becoming the standard-bearer of the Democrats. A letter written by him to George Roberts (September 28, 1843) shows that he was then encouraging his friends in the effort to secure for him the Democratic nomination. Furthermore, the *Madisonian* (organ of the Administration) persisted in its earnest advocacy of his nomination. A great deal of space was devoted to editorial comment, excerpts from other newspapers, and resolutions adopted by pro-Tyler meetings—all for the purpose of showing that the President was the most suitable man to serve as the leader of the Democratic forces. *William and Mary College Quarterly* (first series), XIX, 216.

and made known to him that negotiations with Texas were under way.[15] These communications show that one, and probably two, of the President's closest personal and political friends were inclined to use the Texan issue to promote not his but Calhoun's chances for the succession.

The question naturally arising is, Why did Tyler lend his name to the third party movement and become a candidate in 1844 if he knew that there was no chance of his election? This question was answered by Tyler himself. In a letter to Alexander Gardiner (July 11, 1846), he gave the following explanation: The Congressional elections of 1842 which were the greatest political victory ever won within his recollection, were "achieved entirely upon the vetoes of the Bank bills presented to" him at the extra session. After this victory both the Clay and Van Buren presses were violent in their attacks on him. Owing to this vindictive opposition "it was esteemed every way proper to organize a separate party, ostensibly in reference to the Presidency in my own person, but in truth for the sole purpose of controlling events, by throwing in the weight of that organization for the public good, in the then approaching election. For this

[15] Gilmer wrote to Calhoun on December 13, 1843, stating that negotiations had already begun and requesting of him an expression of opinion. *Annual Report of the American Historical Association*, 1899, II, 904–906.

Calhoun had already learned from Vergil Maxcy, later a victim of the *Princeton* disaster, of the precise state of the negotiations. Writing to Calhoun, on December 10, 1843, he said:—"Mr. Upshur informs me—in the strictest confidence however except to you—that the terms of a treaty between him and the Texan minister have already been agreed on and written out, and that the latter only waits for instructions from President Houston which are expected in two or three weeks." Upshur was of the opinion that the Texan question was the only one that could unite Southern support for a Southern candidate to the extent of weakening Clay and Van Buren and throwing the election into the House. The pro-Texan candidate would receive the unanimous vote of the South in the House and would, therefore, have a good chance of election. "The President has some hopes that he may become that Southern Candidate. But Mr. Upshur considers you as the only one that can be taken up." He explained that he was giving Calhoun this information in advance in order that he might be able at the earliest moment to place his views before the public and rally to himself the support of those who favored annexation. *Ibid.*, 900–904.

purpose, and with this view, and in order to preserve such organization until the proper time should arrive for striking a decisive blow, I accepted the nomination made of me by my friends at Baltimore." [16]

By throwing the weight of his political organization for the public good Tyler meant the defeat of Van Buren for the nomination, so declared John Tyler, Jr., in later years. The President's first announcement of his decision to enter the race was made to his family one morning at breakfast. He explained that he had no expectation of being elected and would allow the use of his name only to prevent the Democrats from naming Van Buren. [17]

Just how loud was the call to which Tyler responded when he led the third party movement it is impossible to say. He estimated his followers at about one hundred and fifty thousand. In a number of States mass meetings were held to endorse his candidacy. According to the presses that were friendly to the President, the numbers in attendance at these meetings showed a strong sentiment in his favor throughout the country. The Clay papers, however, contended that these gatherings were poorly attended, which indicated that Tyler's candidacy was not taken seriously by the people generally.

The movement in Virginia for Tyler's re-election was started by meetings at Williamsburg and Norfolk. [18] His boom for the succession was put on a national basis in April, 1844, when a "large number of republicans, who had been called to Washington from various quarters of the Union by other duties, spontaneously assembled" to advise as to the best means of averting the catastrophe that was impending. This committee sent out a letter to the "Democratic republicans" throughout the United States, recommending that a Tyler convention be called to meet at Baltimore on

---

[16] Tyler, *Letters and Times,* II, 341.

[17] *Lippincott's Monthly Magazine,* XLI, 420–421.

[18] *Niles,* LXV, 36; LXVI, 69, 87–88, 146; Tyler, *op. cit.,* II, 310; *Madisonian,* Mar. 12, 1844; *National Intelligencer,* Mar. 21, 1844.

the fourth Monday of May, 1844. The friends of Tyler
were to see to it that every county and district of the Union
would be represented at this convention. In the statement,
credit is claimed for Tyler for all the Democratic victories
in the elections of 1841, 1842, and 1843. These victories
were the result of his vetoes and the general success of his
administration.[19]

In response to this call, a Tyler convention was held on
May 27 in Baltimore. There were quite a number of delegates
present (estimated at one thousand by Tyler),[20] representing every State in the Union. The meeting was organized by electing Judge White of Connecticut as permanent chairman. In his address he referred to Tyler as the
man who had so nobly stood by the Constitution and saved
the Democratic Party "and raised it from the prostrate condition in which it was left at the close of the campaign of
1840." Over the speaker's chair were emblazoned mottoes:
"TYLER AND TEXAS," "RE-ANNEXATION OF TEXAS—POST-
PONEMENT IS REJECTION." Most of the delegates wore a
gilt button, with a single star, or a ribbon badge with the
portrait of Tyler on it.

On the way to Baltimore some of the delegates stopped
in Washington to see the President and receive instructions
from him. All of these were advised to go to the convention,
aid in making a nomination, and then go home to await developments. The convention was unanimous in its support of
Tyler, but there was a minority that was opposed to making
a nomination until after the other Democratic convention
had acted.

The meeting was opened by prayer led by the Rev. Dr.
Kreider, a delegate from Ohio, who also addressed the convention and concluded by proposing a resolution declaring

---

[19] *Niles,* LXVI, 104.

[20] Tyler, *op. cit.,* II, 317.

It is quite doubtful as to whether the number of delegates present was as
large as one thousand. In the unfriendly account given in *Niles' Register* it is
stated that the "room was not crowded and a large portion of the persons
within were spectators."

John Tyler the unanimous choice of the convention for President. After some debate, occasioned by those who were in favor of deferring the nomination, the motion was carried by acclamation.[21]

Tyler was notified of his nomination on May 28, and two days later he replied by accepting the honor. In his letter of acceptance he spoke of this nomination as coming from a Democratic convention which had been "delegated by no inconsiderable portions of the people in every State of the Union." He referred to the difficulties that his administration had had to encounter and the unjust criticisms that had been leveled against him. "Every harsh appellation was employed in connection with my name—mobs assembled at midnight at the doors of the Presidential mansion, and the light of burning effigies threw its glare along the streets of some of our cities." It was made clear that his chief reason for running was that by so doing he might further the policy of annexation. He put the cause of Texas above the Presidency. His acceptance of the nomination was with the understanding that if the treaty of annexation should be ratified or any other measure of annexation consummated by the present Congress, he was to be free "to pursue the course in regard to the nomination . . . that my sense of what is due to myself and the country may seem to require." [22]

Some of his friends at one time advised Tyler to seek the Democratic nomination. He would not give his consent to this plan. There was, he thought, a probability that Van Buren, an enemy of annexation, would be nominated by that party. In that event, if his name had been before the convention he would be under obligation to support a candidate whom his principles would impel him to oppose. On the other hand, by heading a third party he could frighten the Democrats into adopting a pro-Texan platform and selecting a pro-annexation nominee.[23] Amos Kendall, a shrewd

---

[21] *Niles*, LXVI, 218–220.   [22] *Madisonian*, May 30, 1844.
[23] Tyler to Wise, Tyler, *op. cit.*, II, 317; *Niles*, LXV, 91; LXVI, 87, 132.

Democratic politician, felt that Van Buren owed his defeat
in part to the opposition of Calhoun's and Tyler's supporters, who resented the savage criticism of these two leaders by the Van Buren press.[24]

The Tyler party proceeded to act as if it were going to
put on a vigorous campaign. On July 4 two different meetings were held in Philadelphia by the friends of the President, at which it was decided to have separate electors for
Tyler and put out a complete Tyler ticket for Congress and
State and county offices. It was recommended that this
course be adopted throughout the Union.[25] A successful
ratification meeting was also held in New York (July 23),
which avowed the intention of putting up separate candidates for electors, Congressmen, and county officials.[26] As
nearly all of Tyler's adherents would support Polk if the
former were not in the race, the Democratic press and leaders were frightened at this activity of the third party. They,
therefore, entered upon a strenuous campaign to induce
Tyler to withdraw.

The Democrats of Virginia took a leading part in this
movement for harmony. The Democratic electors promised that if the State gave Tyler a majority in the election
they would cast their vote for him in the Electoral College.
Ritchie, in his able editorials in the *Enquirer,* urged Tyler
to return to his first love—the party which he had been deceived into leaving. "Come," he said, "at the head of your
gallant and devoted friends, and render our common victory
and triumph certain and complete; come, and the grateful
and united voice of more than a million of freemen, rescued by
your vetoes from the domination of a monarch Bank, will

---

[24] Amos Kendall to Jackson, Aug. 28, 1844; *Jackson Papers* (L.C.), CXII,
24,667–68. "I verily believe, however, that had a mild course been pursued
towards the friends of Tyler and Calhoun from the beginning, the mischief-
makers would have found themselves powerless throughout, and that Mr.
Van Buren would have been re-elected."

[25] R. J. Walker to James K. Polk, July 10, 1844; *Polk Papers* (L.C.), LVIII,
3440–41.

[26] Tyler, *op. cit.,* II, 337.

proclaim your welcome—welcome—thrice welcome into the ranks of our republican brethren." [27] Ritchie was joined in this appeal by the Democratic press throughout the country.

Nor did New York lag behind the Old Dominion in the effort to reunite the two groups of Democrats. A meeting of Democrats was held at the Carleton House, in New York City (August 6, 1844), at which resolutions were adopted urging the importance of "a union of all those who profess the great and leading principles of the Democratic faith, however they may have been estranged by circumstances." A debt of gratitude was owed by the Democratic Party to Tyler "for his firmness and patriotism in vetoing the bill to re-charter a Bank of the United States, and to distribute the proceeds of the Public Lands, and also for his recommendation to Congress to remit the fine unjustly imposed by Judge Hall on General Jackson." As Tyler and Polk were committed to the same general principles, the former and his friends were urged to come to the support of the latter.[28] These resolutions had a favorable effect on Tyler and were, he says, one of the influences that induced him to withdraw from the Presidential race.[29] He was waited on by a committee from Tammany Hall, "who did not stop short of the declaration that I held the fate of the Democratic party in my hands and that upon my course depended its success or defeat." [30]

After the Tyler meetings were held in Philadelphia, the Democrats of that city and of New York and New Jersey became alarmed at the inroads into their ranks that might be made by this third party. Accordingly, they wrote to R. J. Walker, chairman of the executive committee of the Democratic Party, and urged him to take some action that would bring the Tylerites back into the fold. His own fears being confirmed by these apprehensions, he felt that something must be done to get Tyler out of the race. Accordingly,

[27] *Niles*, LXVI, 316, 416.
[29] *Ibid.*, II, 339–340.
[28] Tyler, *op. cit.*, II, 339.
[30] *John Tyler Papers* (L.C.), III, 6335–36.

he swallowed his pride, and arranged for a conference with
the President. His account of this meeting, as reported in a
letter to James K. Polk, was as follows:

Yesterday, although it was a most disagreeable duty, I called upon
Mr. Tyler, resolved if possible to ascertain his ultimate views. I had
a conversation with him of several hours in which he disclosed to me
confidentially all his views. He said he knew that he was to retire
to private life in any event on the 4th [of] March, and that he would
at once withdraw, but that were he to do so *now,* it would not aid
the Democratic cause, for that his friends were so exasperated by the
assaults of the *Globe* and other presses, that if he withdrew, they would
either remain neutral, or many of them join Mr. Clay. That they
considered themselves proscribed and invited not to join our party—
he stated his deep regret at this state of things, and his great anxiety
that Polk and Dallas should be elected.

Tyler thought that his adherents numbered about 150,000
and that "they were chiefly republicans who voted for the
Whigs in 1840." He was also of the opinion that if a

different course were pursued towards them, that if they could be
assured on reliable authority that they would be received with pleasure
and confidence by you [Polk] and your friends generally into the ranks
of the democratic party, and treated as Brethren and equals, that he
would *at once withdraw,* and that his friends with all their influence
and presses would then, he had no doubt, come in, and uniting everywhere zealously and efficiently with us, render our victory certain.
Of Genl. Jackson he spoke in terms of deep affection.

Walker promised Tyler that he would do all he could
to effect a cordial and honorable union between the Democratic Party and himself and his friends.

. . . Now I think that the importance of this union and co-operation
cannot be overrated. In my judgment it would be *decisive* in our
favour, and is right in itself. Now it is a delicate matter for you to
act, but could you not write a private letter to a friend, which could
be shown in confidence to Mr. Tyler, expressing such views as you
entertain of his services to the democratic party, and welcoming his

friends as brethren and equals back into our ranks? Could not Genl. Jackson write a letter to some friend (which might be published), expressing his views of Mr. Tyler's services to the party, and expressing the opinion that his friends, upon his withdrawal, would be welcomed back with cordiality and joy by the democratic party, and be placed on the same platform of equal rights and consideration, with any other portion of the democracy?

Walker considered this a matter of such importance as to justify a conference between Polk and General Jackson provided Polk agreed with this view.[31]

Polk was already disturbed over Tyler's candidacy. He was afraid that the vote for him in some of the close States would cause those States to go to Clay. He doubtless welcomed this effort at union, though, acting with his usual reticence and prudence, he did not exactly express approval. He complied, however, with Walker's request and forwarded his letter, accompanied by one of his own, to the Sage of the Hermitage. In this letter Polk indicated a strong wish that Tyler would withdraw and said that Jackson was the "only man in the country whose advice would be likely to influence him." These letters were sent by General Armstrong, Major Donelson, and General Pillow (who was to discuss the situation with Jackson).[32]

Jackson expressed strong disapproval of Walker's suggestion that he (Jackson) write a letter for publication stating that Tyler's friends upon his withdrawal would be received back into the Democratic fold upon the same terms and the same hopes as to offices as other Democrats. "Why my dear friend," he said in writing to Polk, "such a letter from me or any other of your conspicuous friends would be sezed [seized] upon as a bargain and intrigue for the presidency—Just as Adams and Clay's bargain." [33]

Jackson did, however, write a letter to Major Lewis and

[31] *Polk Papers* (L.C.), LVIII, 3440–41.
[32] Polk to Jackson, July 23, 1844; *Jackson Papers* (L.C.), CXII, 24,632–33.
[33] Jackson to Polk, July 26, 1844; *Polk Papers* (L.C.), LIX, 3599.

gave him permission to show it to Tyler, which was done. In this letter he urged Tyler to retire from the canvass, but he did not hold out any promise as to the offices.[34] Despite this omission, this communication had the desired effect on Tyler. ". . . your views," said the latter, "as to the proper course for me to pursue in the present emergency of public affairs has decided me to withdraw from the canvass." He also assured Jackson that he would try to influence his friends to vote for Polk. He indicated, however, that the attacks which Benton and the Washington *Globe* persisted in making on him were quite a hindrance to his accomplishment of this aim.[35]

On receiving this letter Jackson wrote to Blair (the editor of the *Globe*) asking him to cease his onslaughts on Tyler. "His [Tyler's] withdrawal," he said, "will ensure the triumphant election of Polk and Dallas, and the re-annexation of Texas, if the democratic presses withhold from abusing Tyler and those democrats that has [have] supported him, but hail them as brothers. In Ohio we want this aid to carry that State—for their [there] Mr. Tyler has many friends . . . I pray you to desist from the abuse of Tyler or his supporters, but treat them as brethren in democracy and hail them welcome to the support of the great democratic cause to aid in the defeat of Clay and Whiggery." [36]

Tyler now decided to withdraw from the contest for the Presidency. This decision was reached after consultation with prominent leaders of his own party. On August 20, he published in the *Madisonian* his letter of withdrawal addressed "to my Friends throughout the Union." In this letter he reviewed the events of his administration and defended himself against the criticisms of his enemies. He expressed warm appreciation of the high motives that actuated his friends in nominating him. Their purpose was, he

[34] Jackson to Lewis, July 26, 1844; Tyler, *Letters and Times*, III, 143–146.
[35] Tyler to Jackson, Aug. 18, 1844; *Jackson Papers*, CXII, 24,665–66.
[36] Jackson to J. P. Blair, Aug. 29, 1844; *Jackson Papers, loc. cit.*, 24,670–71.

said, a self-sacrificing one, as their only expectation was that of being able to vindicate his character and sustain his administration.[37]

Before retiring from the canvass, Tyler tried to make such terms with the Democratic leaders as would put his followers on the same footing as other Democrats with reference to the offices. No definite pledge to this effect could be secured, but the general tone of the Democratic press and the cordial attitude of prominent politicians led him to believe that in the distribution of the patronage no discrimination would be practiced against his supporters. The Richmond *Enquirer* had said in August that it was the desire of the Democratic Party that Tyler and his friends should co-operate with it "as brethren and as equals." The New York *Democrat* was also quoted by the *Enquirer* as saying (July 26) that almost every Democratic paper that came to its notice advocated a reunion on the basis of *"oblivion to the past,* energy and zeal to the future." [38]

The treatment of Tyler's friends by the triumphant Democratic Party was a sore disappointment to him. Not only did they fail to get their share of the new appointments but quite a number of them lost the places they already held. Tyler could do nothing to help them, as he had no influence with Polk. In letters to his friends he protested against this unjust proscription of men who had loyally supported the Democratic nominee. Writing to Captain Lestor (June 20, 1845), he spoke as follows: "It is obvious, however, that the guillotine is more active in executing the few friends I left in office than [illegible] any others." [39]

He considered the unfair treatment thus meted out to his

---

[37] *Madisonian,* Aug. 20, 1844.   [38] *Niles,* LXVI, 416.
[39] MS. in New York Public Library; *John Tyler Papers* (L.C.), III, 6517.
In a letter to Dr. Collins (September 17, 1845) Tyler expressed personal friendship for Polk but considered that the latter had made a mistake in removing all but about a half-dozen of some two hundred personal friends left in office by the former. All of these, he declared, were also ardent supporters of Polk. *Polk Papers,* LXXIII, 6938–39.

followers as a violation of the implied understanding that had obtained between him and the Democratic leaders.[40] Moreover, it was an exhibition of rank ingratitude, for he felt that Polk owed his election largely to the aid which his party had given him. Tyler afterwards said that from the moment that he withdrew from the contest Polk's election was rendered next to certain. The support of his friends in Pennsylvania enabled the Democrats to carry that State. Without the vote of that great State Polk could not have been elected.[41]

There is considerable ground for this claim. The fact that Polk and his advisers were so anxious for Tyler to get out of the race proves that they did not regard his following as negligible. After he had withdrawn, the Philadelphia *Spirit of the Times* said (August) that the "friends of Tyler to a man are joining the ranks of Polk and Dallas." [42] In several States the race between Polk and Clay was very close. It is more than probable that had Tyler remained in the field, Clay would have received the vote of one or more of these States and thereby have won the election.

It seems that Tyler in the campaign of 1844 was able to avenge himself of two of his main adversaries. His candidacy, as he considered, was one of the causes of Van Buren's failure to secure the Democratic nomination. By leading his followers into the camp of the Democrats he strengthened their cause and greatly aided in the defeat of Clay. John Tyler, Jr., was gleefully exultant over the fact that his father, who in the beginning had no party except a "corporal's guard," was able in the end to compass the downfall of two such redoubtable politicians.[43] When it is remembered that Clay and his friends had shorn Tyler of the locks wherein his political strength lay and that Van

[40] On September 13, 1844, he wrote to his daughter, Mrs. Waller: "My friends will be treated with regard and attention, and a rally on their part will secure the election." Tyler, *Letters and Times*, III, 155.
[41] *John Tyler Papers* (L.C.), III, 6535–36.   [42] *Niles*, LXVI, 437.
[43] *Lippincott's Monthly Magazine*, XLI, 421.

Buren and his followers had assisted at the operation, and when it is recalled that each of these leaders missed at this time his last real opportunity for the Presidency, it looked as if this blind Sampson on the occasion of his political death had been able to pull down the temple of the Philistines.

CHAPTER XXIV

SORROW AND ROMANCE AT THE
WHITE HOUSE

THE quadrennium of 1841–45 was quite an eventful epoch in the history of the social life at the White House. In the annals of this short period are recorded the death of one President and the wife of his successor, and the marriage of the President's daughter and of the President himself. This intermixture of sorrow and romance was also tinged with tragedy. For there were felt at the Executive Mansion loud reverberations of the *Princeton* disaster (page 398). These joys and sorrows in his domestic life must alternately have lightened and added weight to the burden of responsibility imposed upon President Tyler by his official duties. When it is recalled that his nerves were at times frayed by illness, it seems remarkable that he could have withstood without any apparent impairment of his vigor the drain on his emotions which was occasioned by these domestic experiences and the savage criticism of his public policy.

The ability of the Chief Executive to meet the demands made on his strength was doubtless aided greatly by the regularity of his habits and by a routine of duties which left no time for brooding and introspection. His daily schedule, as described by himself, was as follows:

My course of life is to rise with the sun, and work from that time until three o'clock. The order of despatching business pretty much is, first, all diplomatic matters; second, all matters connected with the action of Congress; third, matters of general concern falling under the executive control; then the reception of visitors, and despatch of private petitions. I dine at three-and-a-half o'clock, and in the evening my employments are miscellaneous—directions to secretaries and endorsements of numerous papers. I take some short time for exercise, and after candlelight again receive visitors, apart from all business, until ten at night, when I retire to bed. Such is the life led by an American President. What say you?—would you exchange the peace and quiet of your homestead for such an office? [1]

He also did a good deal of work before breakfast, which he took regularly at nine with his family. Often he would be at his desk by three in the morning working by the light of a candle. Just how he spent his leisure is largely a matter of conjecture. Very few personal letters to or from him have come down to us from this period, and consequently we have rather meager information concerning his private life. He was quite fond of the theater, and often went to see Junius Brutus Booth, especially in his renderings of Shakespearean characters. Tyler was a good horseman and doubtless often resorted to horseback riding as a means of recreation and exercise. [2]

One way in which he escaped the worries of his official duties was to go for visits (usually short ones) to his summer cottage near Hampton or to his farm on the James River. Once at least he was for a week or more at White Sulphur Springs, near Winchester, Virginia. In the late summer of 1843 he went to this resort for the benefit of his granddaughter's health, who had been seriously ill. Many people who met him here for the first time were surprised at his unassuming manners, as they had been expecting a sort of ogre. He and his youthful daughter Alice entered wholeheartedly into the amusements of the place. Both were good at bowling and Alice was an enthusiastic dancer. In his relations with his associates here he displayed his usual fine tact. On one occasion when he was introduced as "Captain Tyler" a laugh was caused by the *faux pas*. The President

[1] Tyler to Robert McCandlish, July 10, 1842; Tyler, *Letters and Times*, II, 172.
[2] *Lippincott's Monthly Magazine*, XLI, 417; Ben: Poore, *Perley's Reminiscences*, I, 281.

quickly gave the conversation such a clever turn as to relieve from embarrassment the one who made the mistake.[3] When Tyler left this watering place there were doubtless a number of new-formed acquaintances who were wondering how Whig malice could caricature such a fine gentleman into a villain.

Tyler did not continue at the White House the ceremonious etiquette restored by his predecessor, and his method of living was characterized by an unpretentiousness that was truly Jeffersonian. G. P. A. Healy, the artist, who was his guest while copying Stuart's portrait of Washington, was astonished at the informality of the President in his home life. Attended by his old family slaves, the Chief Magistrate lived in the Executive Mansion precisely as he had in his Virginia home. He and his family were driven around in a secondhand carriage that had formerly belonged to Secretary Paulding. At state dinners some of the colored waiters wore used suits of livery which had been bought at the sale of the effects of a foreign minister.

He was not as economical, however, as these facts would indicate, for he spent a great deal on an informal but cordial hospitality. He always invited his visitors to the dining-room to regale themselves "from a side-board well garnished with decanters of ardent spirits and wines, with a bowl of juleps in the summer and of egg-nog in the winter." [4]

The social functions of the White House constitute an important part of the activities of the President and his family. The manner in which these duties are performed has a marked bearing on the success of any administration. In the discharge of this responsibility Tyler and his family were exceptionally happy. During his entire term social life at the White House elicited favorable comment even from his bitter enemies. This was due to the good taste, sound common

[3] *Madisonian,* Oct. 8, 1842; Aug. 21, 31, Sept. 7, Nov. 9, 20, 1843.
[4] Poore, *op. cit.,* I, 303–304; R. R. Wilson, *The Capital City,* 2 vols. (Philadelphia, 1901), I, 383–384.

sense, and fine breeding of the President and the members of his household.

Tyler realized the importance of his family's measuring up to this responsibility and doubtless aided them with wise counsel. According to a story that soon began to go the rounds, when he was notified of Harrison's death he called his sons and daughters together, including his son Robert's wife, and spoke to them in substance as follows:

My children, by a deplored event I am unexpectedly elevated to the Presidency of the United States. You, as my children, of course, rise with me. You have seen little of the world, and it may be proper to beg you ever to bear in mind that this promotion is only temporary and if, at any moment, you should forget to sustain it with humility and meekness, the error of such a moment will be visited upon you bitterly. . . . True nobleness in soul is only evinced in never suffering station to tempt us into a forgetfulness of ourselves and of what we owe to others. In short, my sons and daughters, in whatever you say or do, act with reference to the day which is so close at hand, when I must return to plain John Tyler again; and may you never, as the President's family, either in thought, or word or deed, do aught which you will regret to be told of hereafter, when you shall be nothing higher than plain John Tyler's children.[5]

At the time of Tyler's accession, Washington was a small city with a population of about twenty-five thousand. The "magnificent distances" were still a marked characteristic of the place. One contemporary described it as being (in 1843) "a great village with houses scattered here and there." [6] A still more unfavorable impression of the town was received by the French minister, who wrote of it in 1840 as follows: "As for Washington, it is neither a city, nor a village, nor

[5] Washington correspondent of the New York *Herald,* Aug. 24, 1841.
This story has the ring of probability, as it accords so well with Tyler's ideas, though there is not sufficient evidence to accept it as a fact.
[6] Mrs. Sarah E. Vedder, *Reminiscences of the District of Columbia,* 67, 73.
The population, as given by the census reports, was 23,364 in 1840, and 40,001 in 1850. *Fifteenth Census of the United States,* 1930. I. Population. Number and Distribution of Inhabitants.

the country; it is a building-yard placed in a desolate spot wherein living is unbearable." [7]

The plans for its future beauty, made by L'Enfant, had as yet shown little signs of realization. The groups of houses were widely scattered and were separated by numerous unoccupied areas covered over by coarse grass, the remains of former brickyards, or other unsightly materials. Charles Dickens spoke of this "City of Magnificent Intentions," as he said it should be called, as consisting of "spacious avenues that begin in nothing, and lead nowhere; streets, mile long, that only want houses, roads, and inhabitants; public buildings that need but a public to be complete; and ornaments of great thoroughfares, which only lack great thoroughfares, to ornament." [8] Pennsylvania Avenue was macadamized between the Capitol and the White House, but none of the other streets were so paved. At Tyler's accession there was no provision for lighting the streets at public expense. The next year, however, Pennsylvania Avenue was provided with street lamps, a luxury that was denied the rest of the city until some years later.[9]

The Capitol was an imposing structure standing on a commanding eminence, but the number of mean buildings that were located near the square afforded a very unattractive setting for so fine a building. Besides, nearby there was a large unoccupied space, consisting of a cow pasture, a mosquito-breeding swamp, densely populated with croaking frogs, and vacant lots "decorated with a stone-cutter's yard, a slaughterhouse, and pigpens." [10]

Owing to her illness, Mrs. Tyler was not able to perform her social duties as mistress of the White House. The President had two attractive single daughters, Elizabeth and Alice, each of whom was well qualified for any social respon-

[7] J. W. Moore, *Picturesque Washington* (Providence, 1887), 46.

[8] Charles Dickens, *American Notes* (Illustrated Cabinet Edition, Boston), 165.

[9] John C. Proctor, *Washington, Past and Present* (New York, 1930), 117.

[10] Vedder, *op. cit.*, 67; Proctor, *op. cit.*, 119.

sibility that might devolve upon her. But Alice was too young to serve as mistress of the White House, and Elizabeth married and left Washington before the end of the first year of her father's term.[11] Tyler's son Robert had a position in the Land Office [12] and so was in Washington until the spring of 1844. During that time his wife Priscilla was First Lady. When her husband went to Philadelphia to take up the practice of the law she was succeeded by the President's second daughter, Letitia, who had married Robert Semple. Mr. Semple now had a position as purser in the navy and Mrs. Semple was free to be with her father. She acted as mistress of the White House until his second marriage.[13]

It was with considerable reluctance that Mrs. Robert Tyler gave up her pleasant duties at the Executive Mansion. In an undated letter to Julia Gardiner (the future Mrs. Tyler) and her sister, written about the time of her departure from Washington, she expressed her regrets as follows:

I find that my spirits sink lower and lower at the idea of leaving Father [the President]. I am, in fact, as devotedly attached to him as though he were indeed my own dear parent. . . . During nearly five years that I have lived with him his lips have never opened but to speak words of love to me and mine . . . and every action of his life towards me has been dictated by affection and kindness. You will not wonder, then, that I mourn to leave him.[14]

Such a high tribute could not have been inspired except by a personality of extraordinary fineness. It was very much to the credit of both Tyler and his brilliant daughter-in-law that the latter for three years maintained such harmonious

[11] N. Y. *Herald,* Mar. 20, 1842; *Nat. Intel.,* Feb. 10, 1841.

[12] N. Y. *Herald,* Feb. 12, 1842.

[13] John Tyler, Jr., to Mrs. Holloway; Holloway's *Ladies of the White House,* (New York, 1870), 397–408; *Madisonian,* Apr. 2, 11, 1844; *An Account of the Receipts and Expenditures of the United States* for the years 1841–1845.

[14] E. P. Tyler (Mrs. Robert Tyler) to Misses Julia and Margaret Gardiner; *Tyler Papers* belonging to Mrs. Lyon G. Tyler, whose home is at "Lion's Den," Charles City County, Virginia. Hereafter these papers will be referred to as *Tyler Papers* (L.D.).

relations with him in a position fraught with possibilities of serious friction.

That these young women performed the duties of their high station in proper fashion is attested by the unanimous opinion of those who attended the social functions at the White House. One of the competent observers who spoke in the highest terms of them was Mrs. Jessie Benton Frémont, the wife of Lieutenant John C. Frémont and the daughter of Thomas H. Benton, one of Tyler's most bitter opponents. In her book of recollections, she said: "Mrs. Robert Tyler, the wife of the eldest son, was every way fitted to be the lady of the White House. From both her parents, especially her witty and beautiful mother,[15] she had society qualifications and tact, while the President's youngest daughter was beautiful, as well as gentle and pleasant." [16] Young Mrs. Tyler was also fortunate in having as her social adviser the experienced and accomplished Mrs. Madison, who resided near the White House and was on friendly terms with the Tylers.[17]

Up to the first of the year 1842 it was the practice to throw the drawing room of the White House open every evening for the reception of all the acquaintances of the family and others having entree to the Executive Mansion. The house was thronged every night and the burden of entertaining these crowds became too great for the endurance of the family. Accordingly, these evening receptions were limited thereafter to two a week, being held on Thursdays and Saturdays.[18]

In addition to the twice-a-week evening parties Tyler also gave numerous formal dinners. Two of these functions were held every week during the "fashionable season" and while Congress was in session. At the first of these the guests consisted of about twenty gentlemen, usually visitors in Wash-

---

[15] Mrs. Robert Tyler was the daughter of Thomas A. Cooper, the tragedian.
[16] Mrs. Jessie B. Frémont, *Souvenirs of My Time* (Boston, 1887), 69, 98–99.
[17] It was on the advice of Mrs. Madison that she punctiliously returned all calls. *Dolly Madison Papers* (L.C.), V, Oct. 2, 1841.
[18] N. Y. *Herald*, Jan. 5, 1842.

ington from a distance. To the second were invited forty persons "usually embracing both ladies and gentlemen from among the dignitaries of the different departments of the Federal and State governments, and the diplomatic corps of the foreign governments."

A public levee was held once a month, and general receptions were given on January 1 and July 4 of each year.[19] The first of the Congressional dinners of the regular session was given on December 10, 1841. There were forty or fifty guests present, including Cabinet members and Congressmen. Prominent among the latter was the aged ex-President, John Quincy Adams. In extending these hospitalities Tyler seems to have ignored the political opposition to him except in those cases in which personal animosity had been shown or in which a divergence of opinion had run into violent abuse. On this occasion the "entertainment was magnificent, the wines superb, and whatever diversity of sentiment might exist respecting a bank and other questions of public policy, there was a concurrence of opinion as to the grace and dignity with which the President presided, and the genuine benevolence and simplicity of his character." [20]

The Washington correspondent of the New York *Herald,* who was a frequent visitor at the White House, was very favorably impressed with Tyler's skill in handling public and private social functions. The President had, he said, a natural courtesy, unmarred by any self-conscious effort, which was characteristic of the Virginia gentleman. "These qualities put his guests at ease, and throw a charm over the hospitalities of the White House, such as has never been seen and felt since the days when Mr. Madison and his accomplished lady adorned the Executive Mansion and gave tone and polish to American society." [21] As an illustration of the ease and informality that characterized the Tyler family this

[19] John Tyler, Jr., to Mrs. Holloway; Holloway, *op. cit.,* 421–424; *Madisonian,* July 8, 1841; N. Y. *Express,* July 8, 1844; Richmond *Enquirer,* Jan. 6, 1842; *National Intelligencer,* July 6, 1841, Jan. 3, 1842.

[20] N. Y. *Herald,* Dec. 18, 1841.   [21] *Ibid.,* Dec. 18, 1841.

correspondent related the story of a butcher who felt perfectly at home while dining with the President.[22]

The Tylers were hampered in the performance of their social duties by the parsimony, not to say niggardliness, of Congress in making provision for the White House. The appropriations for furniture were far below the usual amounts, and the costs for fuel and lights on state occasions had to be paid by the President out of his own funds.[23] It was a spirit of spite rather than of economy that prompted Tyler's Whig enemies in Congress to withhold the appropriations necessary for the proper upkeep of the Executive Mansion. It is no wonder, therefore, that the second Mrs. Tyler found on her arrival that the White House was, as she termed it, a "dirty establishment." [24] But despite these drawbacks, the social life at the White House was carried on in a manner well worthy of the Chief Magistrate of a great republic.

The visit to Washington of the Prince de Joinville, son of the French King, was the cause of a noted social event at the Executive Mansion. The President gave a dinner in honor of the young Prince, to which were invited members of the Cabinet, foreign ministers, and high naval and military officers. The dinner was followed by an evening party at which a large and brilliant company was assembled.[25]

An interesting event, though of no political significance, was the marriage of the President's daughter Elizabeth to William Waller on January thirty-first, 1842. Mrs. Robert Tyler, writing shortly afterwards, gave the following brief description of it: "Lizzie had a grand wedding. The guests consisted of Mrs. Madison, the members of the Cabinet with

---

[22] N. Y. *Herald*, Feb. 28, 1842.

[23] The total amount appropriated by Congress for furniture for the White House during Tyler's term was less than $4300.00. The amount spent during the years 1837–40 inclusive was $20,000.00; the amount for the quadrennium of July 1, 1845–June 30, 1849 was $18,057.17. *An Account of the Receipts and Expenditures of the United States* for the years 1837–49; *Lippincott's Monthly Magazine*, XLI, 417.

[24] Mrs. Tyler to her mother, July 14, 1844; *Tyler Papers* (L.D.).

[25] *National Intelligencer*, Oct. 2, 4, 1841.

their wives and daughters, the foreign ministers near the government, and some few personal friends outside of the family and their relatives." Mother Tyler was downstairs for the first time since she had been in Washington.[26]

Prominent in the list of notable social occasions was a reception given (March 15, 1842) in honor of Washington Irving, then ambassador to Spain, and Charles Dickens, who had come to America in the interest of an international copyright law. The fame of Dickens as the champion of the poor was at its height at that time, and the desire to see him drew an immense crowd to the reception. The number of people in the East Room alone was estimated at three thousand. The police had difficulty in keeping the passages open. The circle usually kept around the President was narrowed down almost to nothing. Mrs. Robert Tyler presided "with surpassing courteousness and grace." [27]

The most important of all the functions given at the White House—the one that had most bearing on public affairs—was the reception held in honor of Lord Ashburton (see pp. 309–310).

The gayeties at the White House were interrupted by the death of Mrs. Tyler, which occurred on September 10, 1842. Her illness, which dated from a stroke of paralysis nearly four years before, had become serious some months prior to her death.[28] During this time there was a furious outcry against the President because of his refusal to go along with the Whigs on the tariff and distribution questions. When the death of Mrs. Tyler was announced the hostile press suspended its loud baying long enough to express a high appreciation of the beautiful character of the deceased. The *National Intelligencer,* which was a bitter critic of the President's policies, paid her the following tribute: "This most

---

[26] N. Y. *American,* Feb. 7, 1842; Holloway, *op. cit.,* 419–421.

[27] N. Y. *Herald,* Mar. 20, 1842; Dickens, *op. cit.,* 182–183.
Dickens spoke of Mrs. Robert Tyler as "a very interesting, graceful, and accomplished lady."

[28] Richmond *Enquirer,* Sept. 16, 1842; Tyler, *Letters and Times,* II, 172.

estimable lady was, in life, more truly than we can represent
her in words, a Wife, a Mother, and a Christian—loving
and confiding to her husband—gentle and affectionate to her
children—kind and charitable to the needy and the afflicted.
Deeply impressed in her early life by her highly respected and
pious parents with the truthful and heavenly doctrines of the
meek Jesus, in all her actions, with whatever sphere in life
connected, self was forgotten by her and the good alone of
others remembered, which won for her wherever she was
known the love and esteem of all." [29]

Funeral services were held at the Presidential mansion at
four o'clock in the afternoon of Monday, September 12.
A sermon was preached by the Rev. Dr. Hawley, rector of
St. John's Episcopal Church, in the presence of an immense
concourse of citizens, including Cabinet members and Senators and Representatives without distinction of party.[30]
Next day the remains were taken by train to Richmond, accompanied by President Tyler, his sons, Judge Christian,
Secretary Upshur, and other gentlemen from Washington.
The funeral cortege was met at the station by a number of
ladies and gentlemen, including the acting governor, who
followed the hearse to the Powhatan House. The bells at the
Capitol and at the First Presbyterian Church tolled during
the entire afternoon. On the following morning at four, while
the Capitol bell was tolling, the sad procession started for
the eighteen-mile journey to "Cedar Grove," in New Kent
County. Here in the burying ground near the home of her
childhood the remains of Mrs. Tyler found a final resting
place.[31]

As the third year of Tyler's "tempest-tossed administration" approached its end it "found itself comparatively
tranquil and at ease." [32] The President was still anathema

[29] Quoted by the Richmond *Whig,* Sept. 13, 1842.
[30] *Madisonian,* Sept. 13, 1842.
[31] Richmond *Whig,* Sept. 14, 1842; Richmond *Enquirer,* Sept. 14, 1842.
[32] Tyler, *op. cit.,* II, 390.

to the Whigs, but since his vetoes of the tariff and distribution acts no issue more serious than that of the patronage
had risen between him and them. He was, therefore, not
being abused so roundly as formerly. While Tyler was feeling that a happier and more peaceful future was in prospect,
an accident occurred which suddenly upset his official family
and caused him to mourn the loss of dear personal friends.
This catastrophe was the explosion on the warship *Princeton.*

The *Princeton* was the invention of John Ericsson, who
afterwards made the *Monitor,* of Civil War fame. It had
been built on an improved plan and many new features had
been embodied in its construction. On Wednesday, February
22, 1844, Captain Stockton, who had command of the vessel,
invited a number of prominent people with their families for
a pleasure trip on the *Princeton,* then lying off Alexandria.
It was a beautiful day and a large number accepted the invitation—probably about four hundred in number. Included in
the group were President Tyler and several members of his
family, Cabinet members, attachés and secretaries of lega-
tions, and other public dignitaries.

Another vessel took the gay party down the river to Alexandria, stopping on the way to take on a boatload of
musicians. When this boat approached the *Princeton,* gaily
bedecked with the flags of every nation, the band struck up
"Hail Columbia" and the excursionists raised lusty cheers,
which were answered in kind by the crew of the latter vessel.
After the guests had been transferred to the *Princeton* she
proceeded down stream as far as Mount Vernon. The President and others expressed admiration for her speed and the
power of her guns, which had been fired several times. The
return trip was then begun, and again the guns were fired.

A very elaborate collation had been prepared on board for
the guests. This had been partaken of first by the ladies and
then the gentlemen. At about four-thirty the men had finished
dinner and some had gone up on deck, where the "Peace-

maker," the great gun of the boat, was stationed in the bow. Captain Stockton, at the request of Secretary Gilmer, agreed to fire a final shot. This caused an explosion that instantly killed Secretaries Gilmer and Upshur, Commodore Kennon, Vergil Maxcy, lately returned from a diplomatic residence at the Hague, and David Gardiner, a former member of the New York Senate. A number of sailors were wounded and one of them and a young colored servant of the President's died of their wounds. Several men were stunned, among them Senator Benton and Captain Stockton.

The President was by a lucky accident detained below. Just as he and a large number of ladies and gentlemen were leaving the table for the gun deck a gentleman announced that one of the ladies would give a toast. This detained them until after the explosion. Most of the ladies were below the gun deck and so escaped harm. Mrs. Gilmer, however, was near her husband when he was killed.

The bodies of the dead, terribly mangled, were left on board that night, and next day by special request of the President were taken to the White House. They lay in state in the East Room for one day. Funeral ceremonies were conducted there, with burial in the Congressional cemetery.[33] In the funeral procession of more than a mile in length, the hearses were accompanied by the Marine Band and other bands, which played funeral dirges. Each hearse was drawn by four white horses, and each horse was held and led by a colored groom dressed in white.[34]

The tragedy of the *Princeton* was a harrowing experience for the President. The loss of two Cabinet members bound to him by warm personal and political ties was a blow to his administration and a shock to his feelings. Moreover, the

---

[33] There are a number of contemporary accounts of this disaster. For two of these, see *Niles*, LXVI, 1-2, 20-21. A brief statement regarding it by Tyler can be found in Tyler, *op. cit.*, II, 390-391. For Mrs. Tyler's account, see *ibid.*, III, 226-c–226-d. See also *National Intelligencer*, Feb. 29, Mar. 4, 1844.

[34] Mrs. Sarah E. Vedder, *Reminiscences of the District of Columbia*, 72-73.

suffering experienced by the relatives of the victims made a strong appeal to his sympathies. But there came out of this trouble a solace which proved a permanent blessing to the bereaved Chief Magistrate.

Among those on board the fated vessel were two beautiful young women, daughters of one of the victims, the Hon. David Gardiner, of New York. The elder of these, Julia, had been attracting the admiring notice of the President, and he had already begun to press an ardent suit for her hand. She was hesitant about reciprocating his feelings at first and would not agree to a marriage which he was urging during the winter of 1843–44.[35] For some reason her interest in Tyler increased after the sudden death of her father.[36] It may be that something of the strong affection which she had felt for her father had been transferred to her kind, elderly lover. At any rate, it was not long before she yielded to his entreaties and agreed to become the mistress of the White House.

Our information regarding Tyler's second courtship is very meager. We have a great number of letters written at later periods by Mrs. Tyler, but there is not in the collections examined a single one that passed between her and her future husband. Just when acquaintanceship ripened into a close friendship we cannot say. Evidently she was receiving attentions from her would-be lover as early as May, 1843, for there was at that time an unfounded rumor to the effect that they were engaged.[37] In later years Mrs. Tyler made a statement regarding the President's first attempts at wooing and her reaction to them. It would seem from this account that she did not take as seriously as they deserved the initial addresses of the oldish but attractive Chief Magistrate, and for a while the courtship gave little promise of success.

But his ardor was not chilled by one discouraging incident,

---

[35] Mrs. Tyler to her mother, July, 1844; *Tyler Papers* (L.D.).
[36] Tyler, *Letters and Times*, III, 226-d–226-e.
[37] J. J. Dailey to Julia Gardiner; May 13, 1843; *ibid.*

and his persistence was rewarded when in the spring of 1844 she plighted her troth to him. In April of that year Tyler wrote to Mrs. Gardiner asking her consent to his engagement with her daughter. In her reply Mrs. Gardiner made no objection to the arrangement and at the same time expressed a very high regard for Tyler's personal character. She indicated some concern, however, as to whether he could supply her with those luxuries to which she had been accustomed.[38]

The marriage was a quiet, dignified affair, as became the second nuptials of a man of the age and position of the President. On June 25, 1844, he left Washington accompanied by his son and private secretary, John Tyler, Jr., and his friend, Captain Stockton, and arrived at New York the same day. Next day the wedding ceremony was quietly performed in the Church of the Ascension by the Right Rev. Bishop Onderdonk.[39] So secretly had their plans been made that the marriage was a great surprise even to the neighbors and friends of the Gardiner family,[40] and none of the President's acquaintances in Washington knew of it until the happy couple arrived at the White House.

The bride came from an old New York family, the American founder of which was Lion Gardiner, a contemporary of John Winthrop. He emigrated to New England in 1635 and later settled on Gardiner's Island, New York, which he purchased from the Indians. His descendants were still in possession of this island at the time one of them (seventh in direct line) became the First Lady of the Land.[41] Mrs. Tyler's mother was Juliana McLachlin, daughter of Michael McLachlin, a rich merchant of New York, whose father was killed at the battle of Culloden.[42]

[38] Mrs. Juliana Gardiner to John Tyler, April 22, 1844; *Tyler Papers* (L.D.).

[39] *Niles,* LXVI, 274; Allan Nevins, ed., *The Diary of Philip Hone,* II, 708.

[40] Alexander Gardiner to Mrs. Tyler, June 28, 1844; *Tyler Papers* (L.D.).

[41] Tyler, *Letters and Times,* III, 225. See also Curtiss C. Gardiner, *Lion Gardiner and His Descendants* (St. Louis, 1890), 3, 149.

[42] Tyler, *op. cit.,* III, 225; *John Tyler Papers* (L.C.), IV, 6829.

David Gardiner was a man of wealth and leisure and was able to devote considerable time and money toward giving his family opportunities for enjoyment. Julia had a very high admiration for her father. In writing to her mother (August, 1845) she said: "Papa was the only handsome man (*except the President*) I have ever seen." [43]

Miss Gardiner had made her bow to society at Saratoga Springs, the most fashionable summer resort in the country. Henry Clay was among the distinguished men who on this occasion reminded her of her attractiveness in most complimentary fashion.[44] In the fall of 1840 she, along with her sister and parents, entered upon a year's tour of Europe. While in Naples they received the news that General Harrison had died and John Tyler had succeeded to the Presidency.

After returning to America, her father suggested that inasmuch as they had already visited many of the European capitals they should go to Washington to spend a season at the American seat of government. So in due time the Gardiner family was domiciled on Pennsylvania Avenue in a house much frequented by politicians and statesmen. Miss Gardiner was delighted with her new surroundings and derived keen enjoyment from the intellectual society in which she was now moving. Her interest in public affairs and public men was exceptional for a young woman of her class,[45] and the fine compliments paid her by fluent politicians added greatly to this interest.

A young lady of the charm and influential connections possessed by Miss Gardiner would naturally have gravitated toward the social circle that centered at the White House. It was not long, therefore, before she was introduced to the President. Her first impression of Tyler was quite favorable. In speaking of this meeting she says:

[43] Mrs. Tyler to her mother, Aug. 16, 1845; *John Tyler Papers* (L.C.), VIII, 654.
[44] Tyler, *Letters and Times*, III, 197.
[45] See statement made later in life by Mrs. Tyler; *ibid.*, III, 194–196.

I remember my first visit to the White House, where we went a few evenings after our arrival in Washington with a Congressional party. . . . The President's break with the Whigs had been the occasion of unprecedented political excitement, and his name was on all lips. When I look back on this day and see him as he stood in the "Green Room," the room between the "East" and the "Blue," at the moment of our introduction, it appears to me no marvel, acquainted as I am with his high-toned nature, that the wild phrensy of political misrepresentation left no impression of bitterness, either upon his countenance or his voice or demeanor. He welcomed us with an urbanity which made the deepest impression upon my father, and we could not help commenting, as we left the room, upon the silvery sweetness of his voice, that seemed in just attune with the incomparable grace of his bearing and the elegant ease of his conversation.[46]

It is quite likely that Julia Gardiner in entering into a union with a man who was older than her mother was actuated by a platonic regard rather than a romantic feeling. And yet the affection which she lavished upon her husband seemed at times to be tinged with romance. Soon after her marriage she was so expressive of her feeling for him as to call forth a mild rebuke from her mother, who advised her not to caress the President too much and thus interfere, as he complained, with the proper performance of his duties.[47] Even her younger sister Margaret chided her for kissing her husband before others, and quoted an opinion once given by Mrs. DeWitt Clinton on such a lack of good taste.[48] Mrs. Tyler always spoke of her husband in the most admiring terms.[49] She adopted his Southern sentiments, and

[46] Tyler, op. cit., III, 196–197.
[47] Mrs. Gardiner to Mrs. Tyler, July, 1844; Tyler Papers (L.D.).
There have come down to us a number of letters from the second Mrs. Tyler to her relatives, which afford a good insight into her interesting personality. From these papers we are able to learn a good deal about her opinions, feelings, and mode of living. Some of these letters are among the John Tyler Papers in the Manuscripts Division of the Library of Congress. But a larger and more valuable collection is or was at "Lion's Den," in Charles City County, Virginia, the home of Mrs. Lyon G. Tyler. References to this collection are indicated by the abbreviation L.D. in parentheses.
[48] Margaret Gardiner to Mrs. Tyler, July 8, 1844; Tyler Papers (L.D.).
[49] John Tyler Papers (L.C.), VIII, 676, 692.

when the break between the North and the South came, it found her an ardent supporter of his section. Indeed, in her criticism of the North and defense of the South she was more unrestrained than the ex-President.[50] So completely did she identify herself with the South that she even learned to speak and write the Southern idiom correctly.[51]

The good opinion that she held of her husband was fully reciprocated. In writing to his daughter, Mrs. W. N. Jones, immediately after his marriage, he says: "Well, what has been talked of for so long a time is consummated and Julia Gardiner, the most lovely of her sex, is my own wedded wife. . . . She is all that I could wish her to be . . . the most beautiful woman of the age and at the same time the most accomplished." [52] Of course, this fulsome compliment is to be accepted as expressing the heated feeling of an enthusiastic groom rather than the cool opinion of a judicially-minded Chief Magistrate. But other statements made by him in later years show that he always had a high regard for her intellectual ability, tact, and charm. In May of the next year, he quoted Governor Branch as saying of Mrs. Tyler that no one knew better than she how to maintain her position. It is needless to say that Tyler concurred in this opinion and made the statement that "he never saw anyone in his life so fitted to a court." [53]

Mrs. Tyler was pre-eminently successful in the discharge of her duties as mistress of ceremonies at the White House. Her youth, beauty, enthusiasm, and intellectual brilliancy made her a most attractive figure at dinner parties and public receptions. She was, therefore, the recipient of numerous compliments on her social success. She was not, however, entirely free from criticism. There were some who accused her of hauteur and pride [54] and others of a desire to appear at public functions like a queen on her throne. As to this

[50] *Ibid.*, VIII, 278, 728; Tyler, *Letters and Times*, II, 646–653.
[51] *John Tyler Papers* (L.C.), VIII, 748.
[52] *Ibid.*, II, 6471 (June 28, 1844).   [53] *Ibid.*, VIII, 645 (May 15, 1845).
[54] Margaret Gardiner to Mrs. Tyler, Feb. 25, 1845; *Tyler Papers* (L.D.).

criticism, Mrs. Jessie Benton Frémont made the following comment: "Miss Gardiner was very handsome and has retained great health and youthfulness of appearance. There was a little laughing at her for driving four horses (finer horses than those of the Russian minister), and because she received seated—her large armchair on a slightly raised platform in front of the windows opening to the circular piazza looking on the river. Also three feathers in her hair, and a long-trained purple velvet dress were much commented on by the elders who had seen other Presidents' wives take their state more easily." [55]

That Tyler in winning a beautiful and attractive young bride was having far better luck in his matrimonial than in his political ventures was clearly observable by all. Even Buchanan, whose sensitiveness to feminine charms had been dulled by confirmed bachelorhood, appreciated what a prize the President had secured. In referring to this marriage he spoke of Tyler as being a very lucky man with both "a belle and a fortune to crown and to close his Presidential career." [56]

At the urgent insistence of Mrs. Tyler, her sister Margaret accompanied the bride and groom to Washington and remained for a short time as a guest at the White House. Mrs. Gardiner was anxious for her youthful daughters to observe the proper decorum and was prompt in giving them some sensible advice. Writing to them two days after the marriage she said: "I hope you will be as quiet as possible consistent with the President's situation: avoid public display for the present." She also admonished Margaret to be "conciliating and agreeable and not *too smart*." [57] Maternal solicitude prompted other advice from time to time, which was generally not out of place. For Mrs. Tyler in her youth and inexperience needed wise counsel in meeting the serious

[55] Jessie B. Frémont, *Souvenirs of My Time,* 99–100.
[56] Curtis, *Life of James Buchanan,* 2 vols. (N. Y., 1883), I, 529.
[57] Mrs. Gardiner to her daughters, June 28, 1844; *Tyler Papers* (L.D.).

responsibilities of her high position. The young mistress of
the White House took this advice in good part, and in reply
said: "I very well know every eye is upon me, my dear
mother, and *I will behave accordingly.*" [58]

A public reception was given by President and Mrs. Tyler
on the second day after their return to Washington (June
29). Though no announcement was made in the papers, it
was generally known that the White House would be open
to those who wished to pay their respects to the Chief Magistrate and his bride. Accordingly, the rooms were thronged
during the hours of reception. This first appearance in her
official capacity was a thrilling experience for the young
First Lady, who performed her part in a manner well
worthy of her high station.[59]

The President and his bride remained in Washington long
enough to give the usual Fourth of July reception.[60] Soon
afterwards they went to Virginia for a month on a honeymoon trip.[61] Tyler had a summer residence at Hampton,
near Point Comfort, and it was here that they spent most of
their vacation. Mrs. Tyler was surprised to find this four-
roomed one-story cottage so comfortable and well appointed
—an ideal place (she thought) for "true love in a cottage."
The building was new and everything was in happy contrast
to the "dirty establishment in Washington."

From Hampton they took short excursions to the President's estate in Charles City County and to Portsmouth and
Norfolk. Everywhere they were received with the greatest
respect. Especially pleasing to the bride were the courtesies
showered upon them by the officers at Point Comfort,[62]
where they were given a grand reception.[63] The enjoyment
of the occasion was enhanced for Mrs. Tyler by the fulsome

[58] Mrs. Tyler to her mother, July, 1844; *ibid.*
[59] *National Intelligencer,* July 3, 1844; *Niles,* LXVI, 290.
[60] New York *Express,* July 8, 1844; Philadelphia *Mercury,* July 8, 1844.
[61] *Niles' Register,* LXVI, 290.
[62] Mrs. Tyler to her mother, July 13, 14, 29, 1844; *Tyler Papers* (L.D.).
[63] *Niles,* LXVI, 322, 397.

compliments which were neatly turned in her favor. Nor was
this enjoyment marred by the knowledge that Southern gentlemen in their efforts to be affable to attractive ladies frequently temper veracity with gallantry.

With the return to Washington there began for Mrs. Tyler a strenuous social season. The numerous calls she received
kept her so busy during the day that when night came she
was fatigued and usually fell asleep as soon as her head
touched the pillow. "And yet," so she confided to her mother,
"not to have all the company and the very way I do would
disappoint me very much."

Not only did she take pleasure in associating with the
ladies of social and official Washington, but she also greatly
enjoyed those semipublic functions at which men were present. Her interest in public affairs and her anxiety for the success of all measures sponsored by her husband provided her
with a relish for political conversation that was unusual even
for the wives of statesmen and politicians. She seems to have
been especially fond of state dinners. One such was given at
the White House soon after their return from Virginia. On
this occasion she was often toasted as "Mrs. Presidentess."
To each of these compliments Tyler replied and gave such "a
finished touch to its gallantry" as to show that he was an
adept in this social game.[64]

She also speaks of a banquet given at the home of Secretary Mason which afforded her considerable enjoyment.
Those present were Sir Richard Pakenham, the British minister at Washington, and members of the Cabinet and their
wives. She was seated next to Calhoun and enjoyed his conversation most of all. He was quite complimentary and actually repeated verses to her. "We had altogether a pleasant
flirtation." These effusions of Calhoun were interspersed
with sallies of wit that now and then came across the table

[64] Mrs. Tyler to her mother, August 29, 1844; *John Tyler Papers* (L.C.),
VIII, 625, 626.

from Sir Richard, who made a favorable impression on her.[65]

The last grand function was given on February 22, 1845, as a sort of farewell party. More than two thousand invitations were sent out to select guests. Everybody in the *beau monde* wanted an invitation. "The high and spacious halls, usually cold and somber, wore a warm and cheerful aspect and no longer returned an empty echo. From the anterooms to the reception room poured a constant stream of beauty and elegance." The East Room was illuminated with a thousand candles.[66] When someone congratulated Tyler on this gathering of beauty and fashion, he replied: "Yes, they cannot say now that I am *a President without a party.*" [67]

On March 1 a dinner party was given at the Executive Mansion in honor of the President-elect and his lady. Two days later the President and Mrs. Tyler left the White House and went to Fuller's Hotel.

Just before the departure of the President and his family a crowd assembled at the White House to say goodbye to them and express regret at their leaving Washington. General Van Ness acted as spokesman for the group and in a short and appropriate talk expressed the deep appreciation of those present of the private courtesies shown and the public service rendered by the President and Mrs. Tyler. In response to this eulogy Tyler made a brief, well-worded speech, which though charged with emotion was in eminently good taste and was, in the opinion of Mrs. Tyler, a literary gem of rare excellence. "Never had I an idea," said she, "of the power of true eloquence until then." [68]

[65] *John Tyler Papers* (L.C.), VIII, 632; also Tyler, *Letters and Times,* III, 199.
[66] A long detailed account of this ball was given by Alexander Gardiner. See *Tyler Papers* (L.D.).
[67] Tyler, *Letters and Times,* II, 361; III, 199–200.
[68] Mrs. Tyler to Miss Mary Gardiner, March 21, 1845; MS. in Pennsylvania Historical Society. See also *Madisonian,* Mar. 6, 1845.

CHAPTER XXV

"SHERWOOD FOREST"

PRESIDENT TYLER played the usual part in the ceremonies that installed his successor in office. He and
Polk rode in the same carriage in the inaugural parade.[1]

Tyler's enemies, however—true to form to the bitter end
—circulated a story regarding his departure from Washington which would hold him up to ridicule. Although he
was on friendly terms with Polk and could have had no reasonable motive for refusing to participate in the inaugural
ceremonies, it was reported that he had attempted to leave
the capital on the morning of March 4. At this time, so goes
the story, he drove to the landing to take the boat for Virginia. When his carriage, accompanied by a dray crowded
with luggage and colored servants, pulled hurriedly up to the
wharf, the steamer was just leaving. Someone called and
asked that the boat wait for the President, but the surly captain (who welcomed the opportunity to parade his unwilling-
ness to accommodate the retiring Chief Magistrate) paid
no heed to the request and left him and his belongings
stranded on the wharf. A picture purporting to portray the
incident was made, and, we are told, a copy of it was hung
in every barroom in Washington. This story was, however,
manufactured out of the whole cloth, for a careful search
reveals no reliable evidence to substantiate it but much to
disprove it.[2]

In the afternoon of March 5 the Tylers left Washington
for Richmond. They were in the latter city for only a short

[1] *National Intelligencer,* March 5, 1845.
[2] This story, with a reproduction of the picture referred to above, is given
in *Perley's Reminiscences* (by Perley Poore), I, 324–325.

time, but long enough to receive numerous calls from the leading citizens. Among those who came to pay their respects were Thomas Ritchie, editor of the *Enquirer,* and the ladies of his family.[3] Next morning (March 7) they proceeded by steamboat to Tyler's estate on the James and arrived there about noon.[4] There was at the time no pier for the landing and they were sent ashore in a small boat. When the boat touched the shore three loud cheers went up from the passengers of the steamer standing on deck with hats off. This expression of esteem was the closing ritual in Tyler's long national career.

A three-mile drive from the James River landing over an indifferent country road brought the distinguished couple to their new home. On alighting the young wife crossed the threshold with a feeling of pleasurable excitement and agreeable surprise. The house had been opened by the slaves, and everything appeared neat and beautiful. A boatload of furniture and other things were on the way from the White House and a new carriage had been ordered from New York.[5] Other purchases had been and were shortly to be made in New York, including rugs, a chandelier, French mirrors, and other expensive furnishings.[6] Soon, therefore, they would be supplied not only with the conveniences but also with the luxuries of plantation life.

The estate to which the ex-President and his lady retired was a large one of about eleven hundred and fifty acres and had lately (November, 1842) been purchased at the price of twelve thousand dollars or more.[7] It was located on the

[3] Mrs. Tyler to her mother, March 6, 1845; Tyler, *Letters and Times,* II, 369–370.
[4] Mrs. Tyler to her brother, Alexander, March 6, 1845; *Tyler Papers* (L.D.).
[5] *Ibid.*
[6] Margaret Gardiner to Mrs. Tyler, 1845; *ibid.;* Tyler to Alexander Gardiner, Dec. 8, 1844; *John Tyler Papers* (L.C.), II, 6490.
[7] In the original deed 900 is given as the number of acres. See *Deed Book of Charles City County* at Charles City Courthouse, no. 9, 261–262. Other lands must, however, have been purchased by Tyler at this time or a little later, for the Land Books of Charles City County show that he was assessed for the year 1845 on two tracts of land on James River (apparently adjoining

James River in Charles City County, about thirty-five miles
from Richmond. Less than three miles away stood "Greenway," the old homestead of the family. The dwelling was
in the midst of a beautiful grove of large oaks, covering
twenty-five acres. For this reason the place had been known
as "the Grove," but Tyler changed it to that of "Sherwood
Forest." This name was chosen, it is said, because Tyler considered that his ostracism by the Whigs was like the out-
lawry of Robin Hood in the olden time. There may have
been some similarity between the dense woods of this "Sherwood Forest" and the one that served as the lair of the
English outlaw, but there was certainly the widest of con-
trasts between the personalities of the occupants of those
two places. To find in the polished, conventional, and mild-
mannered ex-President a likeness to the bold, untutored, and
law-defying English bandit would tax the ingenuity of the
most skillful sophist.

The dwelling on the estate at the time of its purchase by
Tyler consisted of a large two-and-a-half story house, with
a laundry on one side and a kitchen on the other, each of
which was twenty-seven feet from the main building.[8] Tyler
covered over these intervening spaces and thus connected
the kitchen and laundry with the central building.[9] It took
some time for these alterations and they were not completed
until after the Tylers had settled at "Sherwood Forest." In
July, 1844, while the President and Mrs. Tyler were at Old
Point Comfort for a brief vacation, they ran up to "Sherwood Forest" for a few days. The carpenters were at work
remodeling the house, and Tyler wanted his bride to offer
suggestions as to the changes that were to be made.

Mrs. Tyler was quite pleased with the appearance of the

lots), one of 1142½ acres and the other of 10 acres. See *Land Book of Charles
City County* for 1845 (Archives Department, Virginia State Library). In 1860
Tyler paid taxes on two parcels of land, one of 1089 acres and the other of
10 acres. *Ibid.*, 1860.

[8] Mrs. Tyler to her mother, July 14, 1844; *Tyler Papers* (L.D.).
[9] Mrs. Tyler to her brother, Alexander (?), April, 1845; *ibid.*

place. "I found the situation," she said, "to be a very beautiful one and though now in its partial wildness very fine in appearance, capable of being made truly magnificent. The house is very unfinished and the workmen will be engaged upon it till Christmas next. Time will make it a very handsome residence. . . . There are between 60 and 70 slaves on the estate.[10] They were all brought to the house this morning to recognize their new 'Missus.' " [11]

"Sherwood Forest" stands out from Mrs. Tyler's enthusiastic and colorful letters as a realm of peace, prosperity, and beauty—a sort of rural paradise. The grounds about the mansion house were adorned with ornamental shrubs and roses, while other flowers of numerous varieties grew in profusion. The following picture of the soothing quiet of the place was sketched a few months after she had turned her back on the thrilling social life of Washington:

I am writing to you seated in the door of the south piazza with my paper and inkstand resting on a book in my lap. The President in a large arm chair, near me on the piazza, with feet raised upon the railing, is enjoying *The Wandering Jew* received last night with your two letters and papers. The reapers have come to their labors in the fields about 500 yards from us, and their loud merry songs almost drown the President's voice as he talks with me. Once in a while a scream from all hands, dogs and servants, cause[s] us to raise our eyes to see a full chase after a poor little hare. . . .

We are removed about a mile, in a direct line, from the river, that is to say, the mansion—the estate runs down to it—and the trees on the bank that intercept the view have already been nearly cut away. Since I have been seated here I have noticed some five or six vessels pass up and down.[12]

---

[10] Mrs. Tyler probably overestimated the number of slaves on the estate at that time. The assessors' lists show that Tyler was taxed in 1845 on thirty and in 1846 on thirty-two slaves above twelve years of age. By 1860 the number had increased to forty-nine. *Property Book of Charles City County* (Archives of Va. State Library).

[11] Mrs. Tyler to her mother, July 14, 1844; *Tyler Papers* (L.D.).

[12] Mrs. Tyler to her sister, June 19, 1845; *ibid.*

The ex-President and his consort were in Eden. Only one other thing was needed to supply all the outward circumstances of happiness. This was pleasurable social contacts. For both of them were too fond of society to be content with solitude even in Arcadia. This latter condition would be abundantly met if they should be cordially accepted by the aristocracy of the community. But there was the rub. A good deal of thick ice would have to be broken.

When Tyler left the White House for his plantation on the James River he probably felt that Cincinnatus was returning to his plow. It is more than likely, however, that his Whig enemies—who regarded him as the cause of all their misfortunes—considered that Coriolanus was going into deserved exile. In this latter opinion the Whigs of Charles City undoubtedly concurred. For in August, 1842, they had held a meeting at which the policies of the President were loudly condemned and he was branded as a traitor to his party.[13] As the Whigs dominated the social and political life of the county, the Tylers had ground for apprehension regarding the attitude of the leading families toward them.

The ex-President had not been long in his new home before he was convinced that the political feeling against him was still nursed by his old neighbors. One of Tyler's favorite characters in history was Epaminondas, the great warrior and statesman of ancient Thebes.[14] He now had an opportunity to follow the example of the noted Theban, and he met the occasion in a manner worthy of his great exemplar. Epaminondas, it will be remembered, after having saved his country and received the highest honors at her disposal, suffered a temporary lapse in popularity. His enemies took advantage of this and tried to humiliate him by electing him public scavenger. He accepted the position declaring that if the office could not reflect honor on him he would reflect honor on the office.

---

[13] *Daily Richmond Whig,* August 30, 1842.
[14] Tyler, *Letters and Times,* I, 560.

Soon after Tyler retired from the highest office in the gift
of the Republic his Whig enemies in Charles City County,
without any conscious effort at imitating the ancient Thebans,
had him appointed to the lowly position of overseer of the
road on which he lived. Behind this choice was the desire
on their part to belittle him in the eyes of the public. The
opportunity for gloating over his humiliation was so good
that the county clerk notified him of his appointment in person. Tyler accepted the office and discharged its duties in an
efficient manner.[15] He was able, however, to turn the tables
on his persecutors. For a road overseer had authority to
summon for repair work all the men who dwelt on his section of the road whenever he deemed it necessary. Now
Tyler summoned his neighbors so frequently to this work at
harvest time and on other unseasonable occasions that soon
they repented of having chosen so active an overseer. While
he was not blessed with a strong sense of humor, it is more
than likely that he kept his tongue in his cheek whenever
these road-working occasions occurred.[16] When his neighbors expostulated with him and finally asked him to resign
he replied that *"offices were hard to obtain in these times,
and having no assurance that he would ever get another, he
could not think, under the circumstances, of resigning."* [17]

This hostility toward Tyler on the part of his neighbors
did not last long. In a few years it had broken down and its
place had been taken by a feeling of cordiality. The change
had resulted not from a reversal of political affiliations on
the part of the people of Charles City, but was brought
about by the dignified and good-natured demeanor exhibited
by the ex-President. He showed no malice toward his former
enemies, and never gave utterance to any abusive statements
regarding them. A tactful speech made by him on the occasion of a political dinner at Charles City Courthouse soon

[15] Diary of Edmund Ruffin; *William and Mary College Quarterly* (first series), XXIII, 198.
[16] Tyler, *Letters and Times*, II, 465.
[17] *William and Mary College Quarterly* (first series), XXIII, 199.

after his return to the county did much toward winning over his old enemies.[18]

For a decade and a half after his retirement from the Presidency, Tyler remained quietly at "Sherwood Forest," devoting his time to the pursuits and interests of a prosperous planter. He never resumed the practice of the law and was thus free to enjoy the life of a gentleman farmer. For some years he had a supervisor, who relieved him of much responsibility and worry, but during a part of the time he had to act as his own manager.[19]

While small fruits, such as raspberries, blackberries, and strawberries, were grown in abundance,[20] and large crops of potatoes and turnips are mentioned in Mrs. Tyler's letters,[21] the main dependence was wheat and corn. Tyler took a great deal of interest in the cultivation of wheat. In his correspondence and in that of Mrs. Tyler there are frequent references to the wheat crop. He sometimes spoke of his prospects for a good harvest in optimistic terms, but, like all farmers, gave vent to discouragement when weather conditions were unfavorable. His interest in the cultivation of the soil was not that of a theoretical agriculturalist who plays with a hobby, but rather that of a practical farmer who depends upon his crop for a living. His success in growing grain is attested by the fact that by it he procured the means of supporting a large family which lived up to the high standards of the Virginia aristocracy.[22]

The first harvest (June, 1845) seems to have been an ex-

[18] Tyler, *Letters and Times*, II, 466.

[19] *Ibid.*, 237; *John Tyler Papers* (L.C.), IV, 6790; VIII, 700; *William and Mary College Quarterly, loc. cit.*, 225.

[20] John Tyler to Mrs. Tyler's sister, May 6, 1847, summer, 1852; *Tyler Papers* (L.D.).

[21] Mrs. Tyler to her mother, Mar. 12, 1854, Nov. 4, 1861; *ibid.*

[22] In the late spring of 1847 two Northern gentlemen who had stopped at "Sherwood Forest" were taken over the plantation to view the crops. They were extravagant in their praise of the fertility of the soil and the fine appearance of the wheat. They had never before seen so large an acreage in wheat. Mrs. Tyler to her mother, June 1, 1847; *ibid.*

ceptionally good one. Mrs. Tyler thought that there would probably be fifty acres that would yield from twenty-five to thirty bushels of wheat per acre and that the entire crop would total 2000 bushels. "We are now [June 17, 1845]," she said, "in the midst of harvesting. . . . The President is out on horseback three or four hours every day in the fields among the slaves, encouraging them on by his presence. I often take the pony and when the sun declines join him. In the evening we sit upon the piazza and listen to the *corn song* of the work people as they come winding home from the distant fields." [23]

So encouraged was the ex-President at this high yield that in the following autumn he sowed 350 bushels of wheat.[24] He also raised large crops of corn, as a great deal of this grain was consumed on the estate by the stock and the slaves. In 1847 he planted 170 acres in corn.[25] At a later time (1849) he had such a large crop of corn that he was able to sell 2500 bushels after supplying all the needs of the plantation.[26] This harvest was spoken of in a Richmond paper as the most abundant one on James River. In 1850 Tyler began an experiment with a new guano. He used it on some of his poor land and the wheat grew as if it were on the richest of soils. His "guano wheat" was the talk of the community. The experiment was evidently a success, for two years later he had another large yield.[27]

Although Tyler had to maintain a rapidly increasing family in accordance with a high standard of living, he seems in these later years not to have been hampered by a lack of funds to the extent that had generally been the case before his elevation to the Presidency. It is true that crop failures and the discharging of security obligations at times put him

[23] Mrs. Tyler to Alexander Gardiner, June 17, 1845; Mrs. Tyler to her sister, June 19, 1845; *ibid.*
[24] Tyler, *Letters and Times,* II, 447.
[25] Mrs. Tyler to her sister, May 6, 1847; *Tyler Papers* (L.D.).
[26] Tyler, *op. cit.,* II, 482. [27] *Tyler Papers* (L.D.).

to his wits to make ends meet, but he was never reduced to
dire financial straits.[28] Indeed, he spoke on one occasion of
the prospect of leaving at his decease an estate that would
well provide for the needs of his family.

The sources now available do not fully account for this
altered condition in his finances. A partial explanation is
found in the supposition that he saved a neat little sum out
of his salary of $25,000 during the first three years of his
incumbency of the Presidential office. Confirmatory of this
theory is the fact that in the second year of his term he
purchased "Sherwood Forest," a business venture which
argued improvement in his financial status. Moreover, the
social demands usually made upon the occupants of the
White House, the costs of which cut so heavily into the income of the President, were probably not so great during
this time as they were in the latter part of his term. For the
semi-invalidism of his first wife, culminating in a serious illness and death, and the long season of mourning that followed gave excuse for the omission of some of the social
functions which under ordinary circumstances would have
been expected. If this supposition is correct the period of
economy ended with the advent of the second First Lady,
whose fondness for society led her to perform with alacrity
all the social duties imposed upon her by her high position.
It is no wonder, therefore, that the President saved no
money out of his salary during the latter part of his term.

The second Mrs. Tyler had also received a legacy from
her father's estate.[29] No figures as to the amount of this

---

[28] *John Tyler Papers* (L.C.), III, 6537, 6589, 6688, 6690; Tyler, *Letters and
Times,* II, 460, 554, 557, 563.

[29] According to a tradition in the family, the children of David Gardiner,
Sr., soon after his decease signed an agreement turning over to their mother
all of their interests in their father's estate. But there are references in Mrs.
Tyler's letters which can be understood only on the assumption that she had
some money of her own. Mrs. Tyler to her mother (date not given), 1845?;
Mrs. Tyler to her brother, Alexander Gardiner, Jan. 20, 1847; *Tyler Papers*
(L.D.).

heritage are now available, but she was reputed at the time of her marriage to be wealthy as well as beautiful.[30] Tyler had inherited from his father a large tract of land in Kentucky, which proved valuable both for agricultural and mining purposes. He sold to his brother-in-law, Alexander Gardiner, a half interest in this property for $6000.00. By the will of the latter (1851) this moiety of the Kentucky estate was left to Mrs. Tyler. Soon thereafter (1853) Tyler sold the Kentucky land for $20,000.00. These transactions made quite an addition to his funds.[31]

When the Tylers moved to "Sherwood" there were living within visiting distance a number of families that were socially prominent. As a rule each of these owned broad acres of land and numerous slaves with which to sustain family pretensions derived from a long line of ancestors. Every plantation had a name, and often the mansion house, supplied with costly furnishings, was surrounded by beautiful lawns and gardens. Along the shores of the James there were a number of fine estates each with a beautiful mansion located on an eminence overlooking the river.

On the south bank were "Lower Brandon," diagonally, and "Upper Brandon," directly across from "Sherwood Forest." Both of these estates, as well as "Berkeley" on the northern side of the James, had belonged to the Harrisons since colonial times and were still held by representatives of that historic family. "Berkeley," it will be recalled, had been the home of Governor Benjamin Harrison, a signer of the Declaration of Independence, and the birthplace of his son, President William Henry Harrison. Two other noted historic mansions on the northern, or Charles City, side of the river were "Westover" and "Shirley." "Westover," built by Colonel William Byrd, the founder of Richmond, was now

---

[30] J. T. Curtis, *Life of James Buchanan*, I, 529.
[31] *Charles City Record Deed Book*, no. 10, 516–517; Mrs. Tyler to her mother, Feb. 14, 1851; *Tyler Papers* (L.D.); Tyler to Duff Green, Mar. 29, 1852; *Duff Green Papers* (L.C.).

the home of the Seldens. "Shirley," then owned by Hill Carter, had belonged to the Hills and Carters since the land was patented in the early eighteenth century.

In time, the Tylers developed friendly social relations with these and other prominent families in their neighborhood,[32] and with some of them they were on rather intimate terms. There were numerous interchanges of visits, teas, and dinner parties with their neighbors, and life assumed an aspect of gayety that was exceptional for a rural community.

For visits to friends who did not live on the river the family carriage was called into requisition. These short journeys were made in a style befitting the station of an ex-President. The carriage was a fine one, bought in New York, and coachman and footman were always dressed in livery. But despite all these pretentious arrangements, an accident would sometimes occur to upset the dignity of the occupants of the vehicle and turn them out to walk along a dusty or muddy road. For example, on one occasion a locked wheel caused the horses to balk, and Mrs. Tyler, accompanied by her husband, had to walk in satin shoes for three miles along a rough dirt road.[33]

In making visits to "Upper" and "Lower Brandon" across the river Mr. and Mrs. Tyler always used their beautiful rowboat. This had been given to Tyler by Commodore Kennon. Mrs. Tyler's description of this boat and of the liveried slaves who rowed it was as follows:

She has been christened "Pocahontas." The cushions of the boat are very rich, of drab damask satin trimmed with blue. The color of the boat is bright blue and I have had the following costume or uniform made for the four oarsmen—bright blue and white check calico shirts— white linen pants—black patent leather belts—straw hats painted blue, with "Pocahontas" upon them in white—and in one corner of the shirtcollar (which is turned down) is worked with braid a bow and

[32] Other families with whom pleasant social contacts were maintained were the Cloptons, the Douthats, and the Wilcoxes, all of Charles City County. Mrs. Tyler to her mother, Mar. 26, April 10, 1845; *Tyler Papers* (L.D.).

[33] Mrs. Tyler to her mother, April 13, 1847; *ibid.*

arrow (to signify from the Forest) and in the other corner the President's and my initials combined.[34]

A part of each year was spent at their summer home ("Villa Margaret") at Hampton, Virginia, where sea breezes cooled the parched days of July and August. The house here was at first a modest cottage of only four rooms.[35] Improvements were later made, and in time it must have been quite a good-sized and well-appointed house; for Mrs. Tyler invested in it the $10,000.00 received by her as a legacy from her brother, Alexander.[36] In 1860 Tyler sent down from "Sherwood Forest" to the villa a ready-cut house which was set up for the servants.[37]

The social life of the Tylers was not confined to the pleasant relations with their neighbors. "It is but reasonable," said the ex-President, "that Julia should like to look out on the great world once a year." [38] "Sherwood Forest," though deep in the country and miles from any town or city, was not entirely isolated from the important centers of commercial, social, and political activity. Steamboats on the James River afforded the plantation an easy means of communication with other parts of the State and country. Seldom was communication with the outside world broken by the freezing of the river. On one occasion, however, the ice in the James kept out the steamboats, and no mail was received for six weeks (from January 8 to February 20, 1856). During that time they "knew no more of what was going on at Richmond or Washington than one frozen up in the Northern seas." [39]

The difficulties and expense of travel did, however, prove a real obstacle to Mrs. Tyler's full participation in the social life of which she was so fond and for which she was so

[34] Mrs. Tyler to her brother, Alexander, April, 1845; *ibid.*
[35] Mrs. Tyler to her mother, July 14, 1844; *Tyler Papers* (L.D.).
[36] *Deed Book of Charles City County.*
[37] Mrs. Tyler to her mother, May 15, 1860; *Tyler Papers* (L.D.).
[38] Tyler to Robert Tyler, July 17, 1854; Tyler, *Letters and Times,* II, 513.
[39] John Tyler to Henry A. Wise, March ?, 1856; *Personal MSS.* (L.C.).

well fitted. A greater restraint on her social activities was imposed by the frequent illnesses of her husband and by the limitations on her freedom caused by the rearing of a family rapidly growing into one of seven children. For several winters Tyler was afflicted for weeks and sometimes for months with colds or his old stomach trouble. During these long periods he was confined to his room or at best to his home. At such times Mrs. Tyler was not only tied down at "Sherwood Forest," but was burdened with additional responsibilities; for her husband's complaints and the sundry ailments that afflict small children added to her other numerous duties those of nurse or superintendent of a hospital.

Mr. and Mrs. Tyler sometimes went to the Sweet Springs and to the White Sulphur Springs. The latter was a very fashionable resort, and was frequented by representatives of prominent families from all parts of the South. Their first visit was in August, 1845. Although it was a "Whiggish place," Tyler had a warmer reception than he had anticipated.[40] When they were at this resort in the summer of 1853, President Pierce was also there as a guest. He was on very friendly terms with Tyler and extolled his conduct of affairs when President.[41] Twice, at least, the ex-President was at Saratoga Springs (in the summers of 1847 and 1854). On the former occasion he also made an extensive trip through central New York as far as Buffalo.[42]

Mrs. Tyler's mother and her sister Margaret paid long visits to "Sherwood Forest," and as a rule, the Tylers went every year to visit Mrs. Gardiner, who still resided in or near New York.[43] Margaret was the means of stimulating a

[40] *John Tyler Papers* (L.C.), VIII, 653; Mrs. Tyler to her mother, Aug. 10, Sept. 3, 1845, Sept. 4, 1855; *Tyler Papers* (L.D.).

[41] Tyler, *Letters and Times,* II, 505.

According to his biographer, President Pierce when at the White Sulphur Springs was met by a delegation and an address of welcome was made by ex-President Tyler. Roy F. Nichols, *Franklin Pierce* (Philadelphia, 1931), 421.

[42] David Gardiner to his mother, Sept. 12, 1847; Margaret Beeckman to her mother, Aug. 15, 24, 1854; *Tyler Papers* (L.D.).

[43] Numerous references to these interchanges of visits are found in the collections of letters at "Lion's Den" and at the Library of Congress.

lively social activity when she visited in Charles City. Her portrait, painted when she was about twenty-one,[44] shows that she was blessed with unusual physical attractions, and her letters reveal a mind of exceptional brilliance. Tyler was very fond of her, and in his letters made use of compliments that would have been considered improperly extravagant in a married man other than a Southern gentleman and a brother-in-law who was devotedly attached to an attractive wife. His summer residence at Hampton, Virginia, was called "Villa Margaret" in honor of the beautiful sister-in-law.[45]

She spent a good deal of time at "Sherwood Forest," first as a young lady in her early twenties and later as an attractive widow [46] in her early thirties. At both times she created quite a flurry in the hearts of the men, young and old. Her popularity was especially marked during the second period after her beauty had been ripened by the years and her personality enriched by experience and suffering. The desire to win her favor aroused sharp competition among the bachelors and widowers. They would ride in fox chases and contend for the privilege of presenting the brush to her. Numerous dancing and dinner parties were also given in her honor. During the winter of 1854–55 she attended eight balls, eleven dinner parties, and a countless number of "tea drinkings." All but two of these functions were given in compliment to her.[47]

[44] The original of this portrait, as well as an original of Mrs. Tyler painted at the same time, is now in possession of Mrs. Pearl Tyler Ellis, of Shawsville, Va., the only surviving daughter of President John Tyler.

[45] Mrs. Tyler to her mother, July 1, 14, 1859; *Tyler Papers* (L.D.).

[46] Margaret Gardiner was married in January, 1848, to a Mr. Beeckman. The wedding took place at "Sherwood Forest" and the ex-President gave the bride away. Next year, Beeckman was seized with the gold fever and went to California to make his fortune. While there he was accidentally shot (April, 1850). After a three-year period of mourning, Mrs. Beeckman resumed her former place in society. Margaret Gardiner to her mother, Jan. 26, 1848; David Gardiner to John Tyler, July 3, 1850, San Diego, California; *ibid.*

[47] Mrs. Tyler to her mother, Jan. 17, Feb. 8, 1855; Margaret Beeckman to her mother, Feb. 16, 1855; Margaret Beeckman to Mrs. Beeckman (her mother-in-law), Mar. 2, 1855; *ibid.*

One of the dancing parties was described by Margaret as follows:

. . . Wednesday night we all attended the party at Dr. Wilcox's. . . . We had a most merry time of it— I led off the first dance with the *Doctor*—who danced for the first time in *twenty years*. He is considerably *rotund*—and the way he perspired in the effort was a caution. The doorway was a perfect jam of old and young, curious to witness the performance. We danced incessantly till one o'clock, when the first supper was announced,—the Doctor leading me in first. The table was beautiful—he had spared no expense and I daresay laid out $150. There were three large pyramids of iced cake surmounted by three corresponding designs. . . . The mottoes and confectionery were of the most expensive kind—candied fruits and liqueur drops of every description, with the fruits, ices, etc. etc. in abundance. This over we danced again until three, when the second supper was announced, the Doctor leading me in as before. Here was profusion indeed. Such turkeys and such saddles of mutton! the fat on the former *three inches* thick—then there were venison, wild ducks etc. etc. Champagne flowed unceasingly—of the nicest kind.

Immediately after there was a motion to break up, when it was announced that the stream between the Doctor's and the Court House was so swollen by the rain that it was impossible to cross. There could be no movement until daylight with safety. The married ladies immediately made for the beds—each of them having drunk champagne enough to bring on severe headaches. I with my usual prudence had not touched a drop. After they were provided [for] all the young folks turned in pell-mell except Mary Clopton and myself, who sat the night through playing whist and watching the day-dawn. . . . With all the jollification not a gentleman shewed evidence of having drunk too much except one . . . , who perhaps looked a little funny. . . . The windows of the dancing rooms (four in number) shewed piles upon piles of negro heads. . . .[48]

Now and then personal and political friends of the ex-President would come from a distance to visit him at "Sherwood Forest." To these he extended a cordial welcome and made them feel at home with a simple and unaffected cour-

[48] Margaret Beeckman to her mother, Feb. 16, 1855; *ibid.*

tesy. Among those who so honored him were Caleb Cushing
(1845) and Governor and Mrs. Floyd. Cushing made a fine
impression on Mrs. Tyler because of the very complimentary
manner in which he spoke of her husband.[49] Former political
opponents were also included in the list of those who were
cordially received by the Tylers. Prominent among those
who belonged to this class was Edmund Ruffin, who in 1857
was a guest for several days at "Sherwood Forest." Ruffin
was then noted for his experiments in scientific agriculture
and was esteemed by Tyler on that account. Later he won
notoriety as a leader in the cause of secession and as the firer
of the first shot at Fort Sumter.[50]

It was only occasionally, however, that Tyler received
visits from his former associates in public life, and "Sherwood Forest" never became a Mecca for politicians. The
reason for this is perfectly obvious. Tyler's public career
had, according to a widespread belief, ended in failure, and
he had no political organization back of him. Consequently,
he was not sought out as a mentor by aspiring politicians. It
was fortunate for his finances and his peace of mind that such
was the case.

Only once during the first decade and a half of his retirement was the ex-President summoned to the national capital.
In May, 1846, he went to Washington to testify in behalf
of his former premier. The latter had been accused of a
misuse of the contingent fund while he held the portfolio of
State, and a hostile Democratic Congress had ordered an investigation of the charge. With the hope of doing justice to
Webster, Tyler appeared before both the House and the
Senate investigating committees. His memory had been re-
freshed by reference to some written data which he had, and
he made a favorable impression on the committees and a
good witness for Webster. Webster was cleared of the
charge, and he felt deeply grateful to his old chief for his

[49] Mrs. Tyler to her mother, June 5, 1845, May 23, 28, 1851; *ibid.*
[50] Ruffin's *Diary;* MS. in Library of Congress, November 11, 12, 13, 14, 1857.

help in bringing about this happy result. Incidentally, the ex-President was able to show a very careful management of this fund while President.[51]

Tyler was cordially received by the leading men of Washington. There was a constant stream of callers from the time of his arrival until that of his departure. He accepted invitations to dinner from Webster and President Polk. "The attentions I have received," he wrote to his son Robert, "have been of a marked character, and the politicians had much preferred that I had not come." [52]

Tyler received a number of invitations to speak or take part in public functions, some of which were accepted. Addresses were made by him at Baltimore, Richmond, Petersburg, the University of Virginia, Jamestown, and other places.[53] Mrs. Tyler sometimes accompanied him on his speaking trips, even if she had to take a baby along. On one occasion she took two babies and two nurses.[54] The oration at Jamestown, delivered on the 250th anniversary of the first settlement in Virginia (May 13, 1857), was pronounced by Governor Wise, who heard it, as "far the best composition I have ever heard or seen from him." The crowd in attendance on that occasion was estimated by Wise at about eight thousand.[55]

Another outstanding address of this period of retirement was the one delivered at Richmond (April 12, 1860) at the unveiling of the monument to Henry Clay. Speaking at the banquet given on that occasion Tyler showed that he had

---

[51] On Tyler's accession there was a balance of $16,000 in the secret service fund, all of which was consumed in meeting financial obligations incurred by Van Buren. Tyler left a balance of $28,000 in this fund. *Tyler's Quarterly Historical and Genealogical Magazine*, VIII, 29.

[52] Tyler, *Letters and Times*, II, 443–444, 455–457.

[53] *Ibid.*, 484, 534, 535, 538, 539.

[54] Mrs. Tyler, with a young baby, was with him when he made the commencement address at the University of Virginia in the summer of 1859. This trip proved quite an ordeal. The exercises were protracted into an unmerciful length. Tyler was preceded by one of the professors who read to the alumni an essay of three hours' length. *John Tyler Papers* (L.C.), VIII, 718–719.

[55] Tyler, *Letters and Times*, I, 1–34 (text of the address, 538).

forgiven, although he had not forgotten, his grievances against the great Kentuckian. After referring to the heavy blows that had been dealt him by Clay when they were at enmity ("and doubtless some of the bruises and scars which they inflicted remain to the present day"), he quickly passed to and dwelt at some length on the pleasant side of their relations. Much was made over Clay's great service in favor of the Compromise Tariff of 1833, by which civil war had been averted. It was this service, he said, that entitled the "Great Pacificator" to this monument.[56]

One useful public service performed by the ex-President, and one which doubtless afforded him great pleasure, was that of acting as a member of the Board of Visitors of William and Mary College. He held this honored position for more than thirty-five years.[57] During a good part of this time he was rector, or president, of the Board. Old William and Mary can boast of exceptional loyalty on the part of her alumni, but from none of her sons has she ever received a longer, more useful and devoted service than that rendered by John Tyler. He witnessed her successes with joy and her calamities with sorrow but not despair. This loyalty was deeply appreciated by his *alma mater,* who bestowed upon him every honor at her disposal—"added to his chaplet of fame every garland that was in her gift." [58]

[56] For the text of this speech and letters relating to it, see Tyler, *Letters and Times,* I, 464–468.

[57] Owing to the gaps in the records of William and Mary College, we cannot say definitely when he was first given a seat on the Board. A reference in his speech in the legislature in 1825 shows that he was a member at that time. Once he resigned from the Board, probably in 1846, as in October of that year he said that he was not then one of the Visitors. It seems, however, that either his resignation was not accepted or he was afterwards prevailed upon to resume his old duties; for it was not long until we find him again serving on the Board, a position which apparently he continued to hold until his death. Tyler to George Frederick Holmes, Oct. 20, 1846; *The Correspondence of George Frederick Holmes* (MS. in Library of Congress), II, no. 50; Tyler, *Letters and Times,* I, 564.

[58] Oration of Bishop Jones at the funeral of John Tyler, January 23, 1862. Richmond *Semiweekly Examiner,* Jan. 24, 1862.

In 1854 the college conferred upon him the degree of Doctor of Laws, an honor with which he was greatly pleased. Tyler, *Letters and Times,* II, 514.

On February 19, 1859, Tyler and other prominent alumni had met in Richmond to arrange for the coming celebration of the 166th anniversary of the founding of the college. Their anticipations were chilled by the news that the main building, apparatus, and library of the institution had just been swallowed up in flames.[59] But undeterred by this calamity, John Tyler and others celebrated this anniversary over the "smoking ashes" of the once venerable structure. Eight months later he participated in a most delightful ceremony —the dedication of the new college building, which, phenix-like, had risen from the ashes of the old. At the end of his address the office of Chancellor of the college was bestowed upon him by the Board.[60] Washington had been the last incumbent of this office and Tyler was very proud of this distinction. He referred to his appointment as "an honor of which I am quite as proud as of any other ever conferred upon me by my fellowmen." [61]

[59] W. A. Christian, *Richmond, Her Past and Present* (Richmond, 1912), 198, 199.

[60] For the text of this address, see Tyler, *Letters and Times,* II, 547–548. See also *John Tyler Papers* (L.C.), IV, 6836; *Minutes of the Board of Visitors of the College of William and Mary,* July 4, 1860; *Minutes of the Faculty of the College of William and Mary,* Jan. 20, 1862.

[61] *John Tyler Papers* (L.C.), VIII, 779; Tyler, *Letters and Times,* II, 382–383; Mrs. Tyler to her mother, July 6, 1854; *Tyler Papers* (L.D.).

CHAPTER XXVI

EFFORTS AT PEACEMAKING

EX-PRESIDENT TYLER kept in touch with public affairs during the entire period of his retirement at "Sherwood Forest." He was closely observant of and deeply concerned in the events that were gradually pushing the country over the precipice into the abyss of fratricidal strife. It was only as a private citizen, however, that he took part in politics, as he held no governmental position prior to the commencement of secession. He had thus no opportunity to take a public stand on the questions of the day except occasionally in an address or newspaper article. But in letters to his friends he manifested a keen interest in what was going on in governmental circles.

His interest in the events of the day was not confined to the happenings on this side of the Atlantic, but also extended to those that were disturbing the peace and quiet of Europe. He was a great admirer of Kossuth and expressed strong sympathy for the revolution in Hungary which he was leading against Austria. In a letter of July, 1849, he flayed the ruthless methods employed by the Austrians in the effort to put down this revolution. Our government should, he thought, protest against these barbarities, and if the protest were not heeded it ought to suspend diplomatic relations with Austria. The United States should not participate in the war, but it should refuse to associate with nations that fight against civilization.[1] This letter was the occasion of a eulogy on the services of Tyler pronounced by H. S. Foote in the United States Senate.[2]

[1] Tyler to Robert Tyler, July 16, 1849; Tyler, *Letters and Times*, II, 491.
[2] *Cong. Globe*, 31st Cong., 1st sess., App., 46–47.

At the time of the Crimean War, Tyler felt that it might be well for the United States government to offer mediation to the warring powers. "I see no objection," he wrote, "to tendering through an envoy *extraordinaire* the olive branch to Europe." If such a mission were offered him he might, he said, take its acceptance under serious advisement, though he did not anticipate anything of the sort.[3]

After having come back into the Democratic Party in 1844, Tyler remained in its ranks to the end of his career. Although he had been somewhat disgruntled because Polk had removed so many of his personal friends from office (pp. 383 f.), he did not allow this grievance to disturb his loyalty to the party. He voted for Cass in 1848, though Mrs. Tyler was for General Taylor, much to the amusement of her husband.[4] In 1852 he supported Pierce [5] and four years later preferred him to Buchanan, although his son Robert was active in his advocacy of the latter.[6] He felt that if the South did not favor the nomination of Pierce without first declaring definitely against the two-term idea, it would be showing great ingratitude to the President, for on the major issues Pierce had proved himself as true as steel.[7]

Tyler advocated a vigorous prosecution of the war against Mexico,[8] although he felt that this conflict could and should have been avoided.[9] When the Wilmot Proviso came up (1846), which was a proposal for the exclusion of slavery in all the territory to be acquired from Mexico, he took a decided stand against it. In an anonymous letter to the Portsmouth *Pilot* and a private letter to Alexander Gardiner,[10] he argued ably against this measure as a gross injustice to

---

[3] Tyler to Robert Tyler, Jan. 6, 1855; Tyler, *op. cit.*, II, 515.

[4] *John Tyler Papers* (L.C.), III, 6573; VIII, 686.   [5] *Ibid.*, III, 6653.

[6] Robert Tyler to Buchanan, Jan. 23, 1856; P. G. Auchampaugh, *Robert Tyler* (Duluth, 1934), 74–75.

[7] *John Tyler Papers* (L.C.), IV, 6749.

Tyler would have preferred Wise in 1856 to any other candidate, if there had been any chance of his selection. Tyler, *Letters and Times*, II, 522.

[8] *John Tyler Papers* (L.C.), III, 6543.

[9] *Ibid.*   [10] Tyler, *Letters and Times*, II, 477–479.

the South. His line of reasoning was as follows: The territories are lands owned in partnership by the States and to exclude some States and their labor system and admit others is
clearly a violation of the terms of the partnership. Furthermore, "the Wilmot Proviso is at this moment nothing less
than a gratuitous insult on the slave States. It seeks to stamp
upon the records of the country an anathema and an edict
which is unnecessary and wanton." No one doubts but that
California and New Mexico will be free States whenever the
time comes for them to form State constitutions. The Wilmot Proviso is, therefore, "to the free States an abstraction,
while to the South it is a reproach and an insult of the deepest dye."

Tyler was in favor of the group of measures offered in the
Senate by Clay which were known as the Compromise of
1850, for he considered that concessions on the slavery question would have to be made by both the North and the South
if the Union were to be preserved. While Clay's proposals
were before Congress he was asked by Senator Foote, of
Mississippi, to state his views regarding them. He answered
this inquiry in a letter by suggesting amendments, but in the
main approving the Compromise on the ground that nothing
better could be done.[11] It was very much to the credit of the
ex-President that he could so far overcome his personal enmity as to support with all the influence at his command a
policy sponsored by the man who had done more than anyone else to injure his reputation and mar his happiness. Such
a victory of reason over emotion and patriotism over pique
was rare in a day when even the ablest of statesmen often
mistook personal rancor for righteous indignation.

Tyler favored the Kansas-Nebraska Act, a measure which
provided for the organization of the territories of Kansas
and Nebraska. The people living in these territories were

[11] Tyler, *op. cit.*, II, 485–489.
In a letter to Alexander Gardiner about the same time he expressed like
views; *John Tyler Papers* (L.C.), III, 6591–92.

to decide through the action of their territorial legislatures whether they would or would not have slavery. Tyler thought that the right of the people of the territories to regulate their own domestic concerns lay at the foundation of all our institutions and was in harmony with the principles of the Revolution. He favored it not only as a proper policy for Kansas and Nebraska, but also for the government of all the territories. If such a policy were adopted it would prevent the intermeddling of Congress and give the country some freedom from eternal agitation.[12]

Tyler denied the right of Congress to restrict slavery in the territories, and did not think that free Negroes were citizens. This view had been expressed more than thirty years before the same doctrine was enunciated by the United States Supreme Court in the Dred Scott Decision. He was, therefore, very much pleased with the opinion handed down by the Chief Justice in this famous case.[13]

The ex-President was quite exercised over John Brown's Raid. He strongly commended the activity and promptitude of Governor Wise in this crisis and thought that his action would be an influence in his favor at the Charleston Convention.[14] As a protection against the danger to white security occasioned by the raid, Charles City County raised a company of cavalry for active service and planned the formation of a company of home guards for local defense. Tyler was selected as the captain of this latter company.[15]

Tyler did not relinquish his political aspirations during the quiet years at "Sherwood Forest." At times he was hopeful that he would be called back into public life. This expectation, however, was for a long time based on undue self-confidence and an unwarranted optimism rather than upon a real demand on the part of the people for his services.

[12] John Tyler Papers (L.C.), III, 6679.
[13] Annals of Congress, 16th Cong., 1st sess., 1391; Tyler, Letters and Times, I, 319, note, 497–498 and note; John Tyler Papers (L.C.), I, 626.
[14] Tyler to James Lyons, Oct. 28, 1859; Huntington Library MSS.
[15] Mrs. Tyler to her mother, Dec. 6, 1859; Tyler Papers (L.D.).

In less than a year after his return home his old political ambition began to stir mildly. It seems that J. C. Wise, of the Richmond *Examiner,* had suggested that he again aspire to high public office. In response to this suggestion, Tyler declared that "an election to the governorship would be acceptable in one point only, and that as an offset to the numerous attacks which had been made upon me, and as evidence that my native State still retained its confidence in me." [16] Nothing came of these aspirations, however, as they were not supported by any political group.

Prior to the campaign of 1856 he had some slight hope that he would be considered for the Presidency,[17] and four years later a still greater expectation. It was anticipated that at Charleston the Democratic convention would be deadlocked and none of the leading candidates would be chosen. In that event Tyler, who had been growing in popularity in recent years, would be a possibility as a compromise candidate. This plan was supported by some of his friends, among them Commodore Stockton, A. Dudley Mann, of Washington, J. D. B. De Bow, editor of the *Southern Review,* and Dr. Ryder, president of Georgetown College, who had influence among the Catholics. Tyler fell in with the idea and suggested that Stockton, De Bow, and Mann go to Charleston as delegates and be ready to present his name at the psychological moment—but only in case the impossibility of nominating any of the leading candidates should become apparent.

The ex-President had in the fall of 1859 been at Williamsburg to attend the Masonic consecration of the restored buildings of the college. He presided at the dinner and was very happy in his speech on that occasion. The applause with which this address was greeted and the cordiality with which he was received by everyone caused him to exaggerate in his

[16] Tyler to Robert Tyler, Nov. 20, 1845; Tyler, *Letters and Times,* II, 446–447.
[17] *John Tyler Papers* (L.C.), IV, 6749.

own mind his availability for the Presidential nomination. "Never have I witnessed more enthusiasm than on my being toasted. The cheering was immense. I never spoke better. Every sentence was followed by loud applause." He seemed to think that if his name were presented to the convention "the whole South would rally with a shout." [18] But he was not considered at Charleston and this expectation proved to be only a pleasant dream.

Tyler was of the opinion that the Southern delegates had acted unwisely in seceding from the Charleston Convention in 1860. For while he was opposed to Douglas, he thought the differences between the two factions of the party were a mere abstraction.[19] The Southern Democrats should have urged the nomination of some man whose name alone would have been a platform or have seceded *"universally"* and at once proceeded to adopt a platform and choose a candidate.[20]

When the division in the party became final and each faction was supporting a different candidate for the Presidency, Tyler, of course, was in favor of Breckenridge. But so anxious was he to save the country from the radicalism of the Republicans that he endorsed the fusion in New York of the Bell and Douglas following and hoped that the Breckenridge ticket there would withdraw and all Democrats would support the fusion ticket.[21] He also advised that some arrangement be made in Virginia whereby only one set of electors would be named, with the understanding that it would vote for Douglas or Breckenridge, as the popular vote should indicate. He feared that Lincoln's election would be followed by the secession of South Carolina and the other cotton States. Any effort to coerce these States back into the Union would be resisted by all the South. "When such an issue comes,

[18] Tyler, *Letters and Times,* II, 546–547, 553; III, 549; *John Tyler Papers* (L.C.), VIII, 722.
[19] Tyler, *Letters and Times,* II, 549.
[20] *Ibid.,* 559.   [21] *Ibid.,* 560–562.

then [he said] comes also the end of the Confederacy." [22]

The ex-President seems also to have acquired in his old age a farsightedness that was lacking in his prime. On the eve of the great conflict between the North and the South he showed an insight into future events that proved prophetic. Thomas Dunn English was at William and Mary on July 4, 1860, as the speaker before the Phi Beta Kappa Society. On this occasion, he and Tyler "had a lengthy talk on existing affairs." The ex-President "was in a gloomy mood over the prospects of the country. He felt convinced that the South would go to war, and equally convinced that in the end the money, resources, and numerical strength of the North would win. He had a very clear prescience, and told me that he knew the Negro character well, that there was no fear of a servile war, but that slavery would fall with the South." [23]

His gloom arose over the feeling that the disagreement between the North and the South over the slavery issue had grown into an irrepressible conflict which would result in the disruption of the Union. The rise of the Republican Party was, of course, to him a bad omen, but he seems not to have been unduly alarmed at the candidacy of Frémont, the first Republican nominee for the Presidency. In writing to his son Robert (September 27, 1856) regarding the prospects of the campaign then in progress, he expressed the belief that Frémont would not be elected. If he should be elected, however, he would hardly know what course the South should pursue. "To await the inauguration is to find ourselves under the guns of every fortification and our trade at the mercy of our enemies." Prudence would, therefore, dictate that the Southern States should prepare for a mutual understanding and co-operative action. [24]

[22] *Ibid.*, 559.
[23] Thomas Dunn English to Lyon G. Tyler, May, 1886; *John Tyler Papers* (L.C.), V, 144.
[24] Tyler, *Letters and Times*, II, 532.

The victory of the Republicans in the election of 1860 was a great blow to Tyler. Soon after it was known that Lincoln was elected he wrote (November 16, 1860) quite a despondent letter to one of his correspondents. In it he said: "I fear that we have fallen on evil times and that the day of doom for the great model republic is at hand." He could not say what course Virginia would adopt but was positively sure that she would never consent to have her slaves "confined within prescribed and specified limits and thus be involved in consequences of a war of the races in twenty or thirty years. She must have expansion and if she cannot obtain it for herself and sisters—in the Union, she may sooner or later be driven out of it." [25]

During the time of his retirement Tyler's character had mellowed and ripened into the poise and serenity that often come with age. Any bitterness of feeling that he may have had in earlier days toward his political enemies was fading away. On the other hand, that kindliness and courtesy that had always characterized his relations with others had grown into a cordial fatherliness which inspired respect and affection in the younger generation.

Religion doubtless played a part in this ripening of his character. We have very little information regarding his inner spiritual life prior to his retirement from the Presidency. We know, however, that reverence was an important trait in his character.[26] He was a member of the Protestant Episcopal Church and when President kept a family pew in St. John's Church. His theological opinions seem not to have been in any way at variance with the orthodoxy of his day. In letters to his daughter Mary, written while he was in the Senate, he expressed a firm belief in a personal God and in the value of solitude and suffering in human development. "Solitude," he said, "brings with it real pleasure, if its hours be properly improved by reflection, meditation and study. . . . The per-

[25] Tyler, *Letters and Times,* II, 574–575.
[26] Wise, *Seven Decades of the Union,* 321.

son who is a stranger to sickness is equally a stranger to the highest enjoyments of health. So that I have brought myself to believe that the variableness in the things of the world are [is] designed by the Creator for the happiness of His creatures." [27] This belief in the personality of God and the beneficence of suffering he seemed to have held until the end of his life, and it was a real solace to him when in old age disease and pain got hold upon him.

After he had retired from the arena of political strife and had settled down at "Sherwood Forest," he seems to have given serious attention to the things of the spirit. Here in the cool of the day he had a fine opportunity to meditate on the problem of eternity. Then, too, his physical suffering may have prodded him into a realization of the supreme importance of spiritual health. Whatever may be the psychological explanation of the change, there is evidence to indicate that in his declining years he was blessed with an experiential knowledge of real religion. His cheerful acquiescence in the sufferings he endured showed a spirit of resignation that was truly Christian. In June, 1855, he spoke of his many aches and pains, but was "convinced that all is wisely ordered by Providence." Again (in the spring of 1858) in alluding to the prolonged illness through which he had passed during the previous winter, he said that he could hardly understand how he had survived it. "Nothing but the kind providence of our heavenly father could have saved me." [28] After one of these long illnesses, probably the one just mentioned, he held an intimate conversation with his pastor in which he revealed a "bright faith in the Christian religion." [29]

Tyler's fears as to the results of the Republican victory in 1860 proved prophetic. Shortly after the election of Lincoln

[27] Tyler, *Letters and Times*, II, 561–562.
[28] *John Tyler Papers* (L.C.), III, 6705.
[29] Funeral oration of Bishop Johns; Tyler, *Letters and Times*, II, 683.

South Carolina withdrew from the Union and her example was soon followed by the other cotton States. President Buchanan, in his last annual message to Congress (December 3, 1860), took the position that secession was revolution, but that the grievances which the South had against the North would justify revolution if they were not righted. A State could not, he thought, legally secede; but if it did so the Federal government had no power under the Constitution to force it back into the Union.[30] Tyler approved of the President's message and considered that Buchanan was pursuing "a wise and statesmanlike course. A blow struck would be the signal for united action with all the slave States."[31]

Fort Sumter, which commanded the city of Charleston in South Carolina, was the danger point. A reinforcement of the garrison of this fort by the Federal government or an attack on it by South Carolina would be the signal for a war between North and South. Each side was anxious to avoid this responsibility, and for a while both President Buchanan and Governor Pickens of South Carolina pursued a policy of watchful waiting.

At this juncture the Old Dominion, true to her traditional policy of taking the initiative in times of crisis, assumed the rôle of peacemaker. The legislature passed joint resolutions on January 19 calling a peace convention to be held in Washington. An invitation was extended to the other States to appoint commissioners to meet in Washington on February 4 "to consider and, if practical, agree upon some suitable adjustment." The opinion was expressed that the Crittenden Compromise,[32] then pending in the Senate, would with

[30] Richardson, J. D., *Messages and Papers of the Presidents*, V, 626–639.

In the preparation of Chapters XXVI and XXVII, I have received helpful guidance from a monograph written by Mr. Meredith Parry, the subject of which is *John Tyler and Secession*. This work (which has never been published) was offered as a dissertation for the degree of Master of Arts at West Virginia University.

[31] Tyler to Col. D. L. Gardiner, Jan. 1, 1861; Tyler, *Letters and Times*, II, 578.

[32] This compromise had been offered in the Senate on December 18, 1860, by J. J. Crittenden, of Kentucky. It provided for the proposal of a constitu-

some modification serve as a basis for adjustment. The resolutions also named five commissioners to the peace convention. Prominent in this list were John Tyler and William C.
Rives.

These resolutions provided for the appointment of John
Tyler as commissioner to the President of the United States
and Judge John Robertson commissioner to the seceded
States. They were instructed respectively to request the
President of the United States and the authorities of the
seceded States to agree to abstain, pending the action of
the proposed peace convention, from "all acts calculated to
produce a collision of arms between the States and the Government of the United States." [33]

Tyler now had, as he thought, a chance to perform a real
service to his country. That he gladly welcomed this long-
deferred opportunity is clearly shown by the alacrity with
which he seized it. Although he was quite unwell at the
time,[34] he accepted the mission and proceeded at once to
Washington. He had a long conference with President Buchanan and presented to him the resolutions of the Virginia
Assembly. The ex-President was cordially received by the
President, who regarded the resolutions as of great importance and promised to recommend them in a special message to Congress.

Buchanan declared, however, that he had in no measure
changed his views as expressed in his annual message; that it
was his duty to enforce the laws; and that he would give no
pledges. He complained that the South had not dealt with
him fairly, in that the people there had made unnecessary
demonstrations by seizing unprotected arsenals and forts,
"thus perpetrating acts of useless bravado which had quite
as well be let alone." In answer to this complaint Tyler tried

---

tional amendment which would exclude slavery from all territory north of
the parallel of 36° 30′ and would establish it with Federal protection in all
the territory south of that line. *Cong. Globe,* 36th Cong., 2nd sess., 114.

[33] Richmond *Daily Examiner,* Apr. 5, 1861.

[34] Mrs. Tyler to her mother, Jan. 22, 1861; *Tyler Papers* (L.D.).

to excuse these acts on the ground that they were in response to popular excitement. If harmony were restored the property so taken would all be returned to the Federal government and so no real harm would result.

At a second meeting on the following morning Tyler was shown the portion of the President's message which recommended to Congress the avoidance of any hostile legislation pending the mediatory action of Virginia. He was quite satisfied with the message and with Buchanan's attitude. He went away, therefore, feeling that the *status quo* would for the time being be maintained.

The President's message recommending that Congress abstain from hostile measures was read in the Senate Monday morning, January 28. Ex-President Tyler listened to the reading with earnest attention and much pleasure. Congress, however, paid no attention to the Virginia resolutions. In neither House were they printed or referred to a committee. They were soon allowed to lie on the table unnoticed.

Tyler left Washington on January 29 with the expectation of returning for the Peace Convention, which was to assemble on February 4. On the day before leaving, he sent another letter to President Buchanan, in lieu of a call which other engagements prevented. In this letter he expressed appreciation of the courtesies that had been shown him and pleasure at hearing the President's message read in the Senate. He spoke of a rumor to the effect that at Fortress Monroe the cannon had been put on the land side and pointed inland. His comment on this report was "that when Virginia is making every possible effort to redeem and save the Union, it is seemingly ungenerous to have cannon leveled at her bosom." To this letter Buchanan sent a very courteous reply, stating that he would inquire into the rumors with reference to Fortress Monroe.[35]

---

[35] The above account is a summary of the report made by Tyler to Governor Letcher on his return from Washington. The text of this report, with the letters that passed between Tyler and Buchanan, was published in the Richmond *Daily Dispatch*, Feb. 2, 1861.

After a few days' rest at "Sherwood Forest," Tyler returned to Washington in time to be present at the opening session of the Peace Convention. He was anxious, he said, to win the honor of a peacemaker and a healer of the breach in the Union. It was this motive that prompted him to accept membership in the Peace Convention. He had worn all the honors of office through each grade to the highest and he now wanted to crown his career with the distinction of having restored the "Union in all its plenitude, perfect as it was before the severance." [36]

He was, however, not at all sanguine as to the results of this attempt at peace. He was troubled with the fear that the time for a convention of all the States had passed. If one had been called the preceding summer, soon after Governor Letcher, of Virginia, had recommended it, some good might have been accomplished. At that time sectional feeling had not been lashed into fury by the election of 1860 and the fire had not broken out into a flame.[37] He also regretted that the Virginia Assembly in its call had included all the States. As the seceded States would not send delegates, the convention would be dominated by the Northern States.

His plan was to have a convention of the border States— six slave and six free. To this convention two delegates each should be sent from the Northern States of New Jersey, Pennsylvania, Ohio, Indiana, Illinois, and Michigan, and the Southern States of Delaware, Maryland, Virginia, Kentucky, Tennessee, and Missouri. These twelve States were in a better position than any others to act as arbiters of the dispute, and their recommendations would probably be accepted by both sides. If an agreement could not be reached, peaceable separation might be agreed upon. This would be far preferable to a fratricidal war. For if one section should

The original letters sent by Tyler to President Buchanan are in the collection of *Buchanan Papers* in the library of the Pennsylvania Historical Society.

[36] Speech of Tyler before the Virginia Convention of 1861; Tyler, *Letters and Times*, II, 600.

[37] *John Tyler Papers* (L.C.), IV, 6903–04.

conquer the other in that war it would not gain anything. "The conqueror will walk at every step over smouldering ashes and beneath crumbling columns. States once proud and independent will no longer exist and the glory of the Union will have departed forever. Ruin and desolation will everywhere prevail, and the victor's brow, instead of a wreath of glorious evergreen such as a patriot [illegible] wear[s], will be encircled with withered and faded leaves bedewed with the blood of the child and its mother and the father and the son. The picture is too horrible and revolting to be dwelt upon."

If the recommendations of this smaller convention were not accepted by both sides, this would prove that the restoration of peace and concord was impossible. In that event the Southern States should hold a convention *as a last resort*. This convention should take the Constitution of the United States and incorporate into it such changes as would be necessary to safeguard the rights of the South. These guaranties, however, should not go "one iota beyond what strict justice and the security of the South require." The Constitution so amended should be adopted by the convention and then an invitation issued to the other States to join them under the old Constitution and flag.[38]

Tyler was accompanied to the capital by Mrs. Tyler and two of the younger children. They took up their abode at Brown's Hotel and at once became the recipients of numerous courtesies from the people of Washington. As the Peace Convention gave the ex-President his last opportunity to act in a national rôle, so it afforded the final occasion for Mrs. Tyler to experience the thrills of Washington society. Accustomed as she was to the quiet of the country, to her the life in the capital city by contrast seemed clothed with all of its

[38] These views were expressed in private letters to Caleb Cushing and David Gardiner (December 14, 1860, January 1, 1861) and in a long article published in the Richmond *Enquirer*. Tyler, *Letters and Times*, II, 577, 578; *John Tyler Papers* (L.C.), 6903–06; Richmond *Enquirer*, Jan. 17, 1861.

old charm and glamour. What with entertaining an incessant stream of callers, returning their visits, going to the Capitol, etc., she was kept engaged all the time.

A limited purse was one drawback to the enjoyment of the occasion, as the compensation allowed her husband by Virginia was not enough to cover his own expenses. Despite this handicap she had a wonderful time. Great attention was paid her and she was surrounded and flattered by the most distinguished gentlemen in the whole nation. "Wherever I went the first position was accorded me." "At [Senator] Douglas's ball it was as much our own reception as theirs; we were bowing and courtesying and shaking hands incessantly." The pleasure of their visit was increased by the kindness of Mrs. Brown, of Brown's Hotel, who placed her carriage at Mrs. Tyler's disposal during her entire stay in the city. Every day the coachman presented himself to her ready to take her out in this elegant and luxurious landau, drawn by the handsomest horses in Washington.[39]

The fact that these politicians and their ladies were dancing on a volcano which was momentarily threatening eruption did not temper their apparent hilarity. Mrs. Tyler's enjoyment of the admiration accorded her by political leaders seems to have been as keen as when she was the First Lady of the Land. The compliments paid her were as neatly turned as in the former time. The son of Henry Clay, a delegate to the Peace Convention, was as lavish in his courtly flattery of the middle-aged matron as his father had been in his compliments to the blooming debutante at Saratoga Springs a score of years earlier. This interlude of gayety, coming between the quiet years of the 'fifties and the tragic half-decade of the early 'sixties, must have been a bright spot in her memory. It was a renascence of her former glory as a social leader—a

[39] An interesting account of her experiences in Washington on this occasion is given by Mrs. Tyler in letters written to her mother at the time. See *John Tyler Papers* (L.C.), VIII, 732–733, 736–738, 808–809.

sort of Indian summer coming as a mild recurrence of the bright summer of her career at the White House just before the gloomy winter of strife and bloodshed.

Tyler was shown great respect and esteem by the delegates to the Convention and other prominent men in Washington. He was surrounded with visitors from the time he arrived. "They are all looking to him," said Mrs. Tyler, "in the settlement of the vexed question. His superiority over everybody else is felt and admitted by all." Especially gratifying to Mrs. Tyler was a statement by Rives to the effect that the influence of her husband in the country at that time was in advance of that of all others. "Mr. Barringer, of North Carolina, said to me today in the cars: 'President Tyler has had the great happiness accorded him of living to see himself fully appreciated. All party feelings have faded away, and his old enemies are among his warmest friends.' " This was indeed a high encomium on a maligned statesman.

Mrs. Tyler doubtless exaggerated in her own mind the importance of her husband's anticipated rôle in the peace negotiations. Statements quoted by her as made by members of the Convention were doubtless colored with the desire to be pleasant to an attractive woman and respectful to an aged ex-President. But after all proper deductions are made, there remains enough evidence to show that Tyler was looked to by conservative members of the Convention and peace lovers throughout the country as the leader in a movement which, it was hoped, would bring peace and harmony between the sections.

The Convention opened on scheduled time, when on February 4 commissioners from eleven States met at Willard's Hall. The meeting was called to order by ex-Governor Morehead, of Kentucky, and a temporary organization was effected. Other delegates arrived later and the total number of States represented was twenty-one. The permanent organization was effected next day, with John Tyler as presi-

dent and Crafts J. Wright, of Ohio, as secretary. Both were
unanimously chosen.[40]

On accepting the presidency of the Convention Tyler
made a sensible speech of moderate length. He extolled the
virtues of the States represented and especially praised Virginia for her part in calling the Convention. Undying fame
was predicted for those who were there to "snatch from
ruin a great and glorious confederation." The address was in
no sense remarkable, though quite appropriate to the occasion.[41]

The work of the Convention consisted in the adoption of
a series of measures which were to be presented to Congress
as clauses of a proposed amendment to the Constitution. The
first of these clauses provided: (1) that slavery be prohibited in all the territory north of the parallel of 36 degrees
and 30 minutes; (2) that slavery be continued in the territory south of that line, and that questions involving slave
property in said territory be decided by the Federal courts
according to the common law; (3) that new States carved
out of the territory either north or south of this dividing
line be admitted with or without slavery as their constitutions may prescribe at the time of their admission into the
Union.[42]

These proposals were quite different from the Crittenden
Compromise. "In substance, it excluded the slaveholder from
four-fifths of the common territories and subjected his rights
in the remainder to the decisions of Federal judges to be appointed by a Republican President." These judges could be
expected to base their decisions upon the principles of the
Republican Party, which was hostile to slavery and considered that it had no basis in common law.[43] The amendment

[40] L. E. Chittenden, *Report of the Debates and Proceedings in the Secret
Sessions of the Conference Convention* (N. Y., 1864), 9–14, 465–466.
[41] For the text of this speech see *ibid.*, 14–17.   [42] Chittenden, *op. cit.*, 43–44.
[43] D. L. Dumond, *The Secession Movement, 1860–1861* (The Macmillan
Company, New York, 1931), 248.

was adopted by a vote of nine to eight, with Virginia and North Carolina voting no.[44]

Tyler did not mingle to any great extent in the debates of the Convention, but he exerted himself in private intercourse to bring about an agreement among the members. Through James A. Seddon, one of the Virginia representatives, he offered an amendment to this first group of proposals. This amendment provided that all appointments to office in the territories lying north of the 36–30 line should be made on the recommendation of a majority of the Senators from the free States; all such appointments in the territories south of the line, on the recommendations of a majority of the Senators from the slaveholding States; and that the net proceeds from the sale of the public lands should be distributed among the States according to the combined ratio of representation and taxation.[45]

Tyler left the chair to speak in favor of this measure. The ten-minute rule was suspended in his favor, and he was given all the time he wanted for defending his proposal.[46]

In a speech afterwards made before the Virginia Convention Tyler gave his reasons for supporting the amendment. One object of the measure, he said, was to restrain Lincoln from an improper use of the patronage, for he felt that if not so restricted he would appoint to these places only Republicans, who would be hostile to Southern interests. Besides, as four fifths of the public lands had gone to the North, he thought that the distribution feature would tend to give to the South some of the benefits in the public lands.[47] Despite Tyler's earnest plea, the amendment was defeated by a vote of 5 yeas to 14 nays.[48]

Six other measures were passed.[49] These proposals, if accepted as amendments to the Constitution, would remove, it

[44] Chittenden, op. cit., Appendix, 590.
[45] For text of Tyler's amendment see Chittenden, op. cit., 328–329.
[46] Ibid., 330–334.   [47] Tyler, Letters and Times, II, 607.
[48] Chittenden, op. cit., 334.   [49] Ibid., 589–591.

was hoped, quite a number of the causes of the disputes that had arisen between the North and the South.

Of the Virginia commissioners, Tyler, Seddon, and Judge Brockenbrough voted against the chief propositions of the committee as they came up, and only Rives and Summers could be induced to approve them.

On the last day of the session the Convention passed a resolution, offered by Ewing, thanking Tyler for the dignified and impartial manner in which he had presided. This was followed by a short farewell address by Tyler. Although he was sorely disappointed over the results attained, he veiled his dissatisfaction with politeness. He declared that while he did not approve of all the resolutions—he would have preferred those of the Virginia legislature-—yet he felt it his duty to give them his official approval and support. Accordingly, he promised to recommend their adoption as strongly as he could.[50]

Tyler presented the resolutions of the Convention to Congress on February 27. They were received by the Senate and were referred to a special committee of five, of which J. J. Crittenden was chairman.[51] The majority of this committee agreed upon a recommendation that these articles be submitted to the States without change as proposed amendments to the Constitution.[52] This recommendation was rejected in the Senate by a vote of 7 to 28.[53]

This overwhelming defeat indicates that there was general dissatisfaction with the work of the Convention. The opposition included not only the Northern antislavery Senators but also many Southern Senators. In the latter group were the two Senators from Virginia, who denounced it. Senator Green, of Missouri, pronounced the resolutions as "the merest twaddle." [54]

The resolutions could not be considered in the House of

[50] *Ibid.,* 451–452.
[52] *Ibid.,* 1269–70.
[51] *Cong. Globe,* 36th Cong., 2nd sess., 1254–55.
[53] *Ibid.,* 1405.
[54] Chittenden, *op. cit.,* 533.

Representatives without displacing the regular order of business. To do this required a two-thirds vote, which could not be obtained. The proposals, therefore, failed of a hearing in the House. Tyler's opposition to the articles was by this time known, and Stevens, of Pennsylvania, in objecting to the presentation of the resolutions, facetiously declared, "I object on behalf of John Tyler who does not want them in." [55]

On returning home the Virginia delegates reported the results of the Peace Convention to the State Convention then in session at Richmond.[56] Tyler had now given up all hope of saving the Union, and felt that Virginia should act promptly. He believed that if the South would present a solid front, that is, if all the Southern States would secede, no war of great magnitude would ensue.[57] In a letter written the latter part of the year he referred sadly to the failure of his earnest efforts at the Peace Convention. He had, he said, to "address 'stocks and stones' who had neither ears nor hearts to understand." [58]

Nor did he confine his criticism of the work of the Convention to private correspondence. In a public speech made on the steps of the Exchange Hotel in Richmond, he told the people of his efforts at peacemaking and expressed his belief that nothing would come of these endeavors. He, therefore, urged the Virginians to act promptly and boldly in the exercise of State sovereignty.[59] He had now become an avowed secessionist.

Tyler's work for peace in the Convention was paralleled by a continuance of the negotiations with Buchanan which he

[55] *Cong. Globe,* 36th Cong., 2nd sess., 1331; Chittenden, *op. cit.,* 580.

[56] For the text of this report see Document no. 11, *Virginia Convention of 1861;* also Chittenden, *op. cit.,* 584–585; Richmond *Daily Enquirer,* Mar. 6, 1861.

[57] J. B. Jones, *A Rebel War Clerk's Diary,* ed. by H. Swiggett, 2 vols. (New York, 1935), 1–17.

[58] Tyler to Talbot Sweeney, Nov. 30, 1861; Tyler, *Letters and Times,* III, 173–174.

[59] Tyler, *op. cit.,* II, 616.

had been carrying on in January. A tense situation had arisen between Charleston and Washington. Governor Pickens, of South Carolina, had demanded that Fort Sumter be evacuated. Buchanan's refusal to do so was causing a good deal of friction between the President and the governor. Tyler was afraid that this friction might lead to hasty action which would bring on war.

Tyler urged Buchanan to withdraw the troops from Fort Sumter leaving only an orderly sergeant and a guard to represent the government and he (Tyler) would undertake to say that the fort would not be fired on. In this way time would be given for peaceful negotiations.[60] To this Buchanan replied that if he did this he would be burnt in effigy all over the North. To which Tyler replied, "What of that, Sir? In times as trying as these,—have I not been burnt in effigy all over the land; and have I not seen through this window these grounds illuminated by the fires? But the light of those fires enabled me only the more clearly to pursue the path of duty." [61]

[60] *John Tyler Papers* (L.C.), VI, 313.

[61] Our authority for the above story is a letter written by Dr. John R. Page to Dr. Lyon G. Tyler, Jan. 2, 1883. Dr. Page saw Tyler at the Exchange Hotel and talked with him, as he remembered, January, 1861, immediately after the latter's return from his mission to Washington. This account of the interview with Buchanan was given to him by Tyler. *John Tyler Papers* (L.C.), IV, 336.

As Dr. Page's account was written more than a score of years after the event, his recollection was doubtless inaccurate on some minor details. For example, it is hardly probable that Tyler made this statement in January; it must have been later. For the interview in which he advised the evacuation of Fort Sumter was held in February. It is possible that he may have also urged it in one of his interviews on his first mission. But if so he did not mention it in his report to Governor Letcher.

CHAPTER XXVII

"THE OLD ORDER CHANGETH"

EARLY in the session (February 7) the Peace Convention paid its respects to President Buchanan in a body. The members were received in the East Room of the White House and were presented to the Chief Magistrate by ex-President Tyler. The meeting was purely social in character and no reference was made to the troublesome questions that were then facing the country.[1]

A similar courtesy was extended to Lincoln when he arrived in Washington (February 23). On the evening of that day Tyler called on him, and introduced several members of the Convention. As these delegates were being presented individually the President-elect made brief comments, some of which were of a jocular character. His humor, however, was not particularly happy and hardly in keeping with the occasion. It may be that Lincoln was using this method to ward off any embarrassing questions that might be asked. If this were his object, he was successful, as no commitments were made. Later he returned Tyler's call.

These meetings were the only occasions on which Tyler and Lincoln ever came in contact with each other. They were of no historic significance, as they had no bearing on the questions that were disturbing the country at that time. But they serve as an important turning point in the careers of these two statesmen and in the history of the nation. The strained amenities and the simulated courtesies exchanged between the ex-President and the President-elect were in the nature of a little drama typifying the end of one era and the beginning of another. Or it might be regarded as a pleasing,

[1] Richmond *Daily Enquirer*, Feb. 9, 1861.

trivial curtain raiser to that awful tragedy that marked the transition from the Second to the Third Republic.[2] For the Second Republic was soon to undergo the pangs of death and the Third Republic experience the throes of birth.

Tyler was ending a long record in the service of the old confederacy; Lincoln was entering upon a short but important career devoted to the ushering in of a new nation. Tyler was to end his life quietly while harnessed to a cause destined to lose; Lincoln was to be cut short by assassination after giving his life for a cause that had won. There was also a striking contrast in the personalities of the two statesmen. One was of humble, plebeian origin; the other of proud, patrician birth. One was reared in the direst poverty; the other cradled in comfort if not in luxury; the one was the heir of a family of influence and affluence; the other the son of a roving ne'er-do-well, who never rose above the humblest obscurity. Lincoln was self-educated in front of a fire of pine knots; Tyler was trained in the best college of the Southland. Lincoln was awkward and ungainly; Tyler was dignified and conventional and careful as to the observance of the proprieties. Lincoln was simple, natural, and skeptical as to the importance of outward show.

Tyler's youth was spent in the aristocratic East, where society was stratified by birth; Lincoln's youth was passed on the untamed frontier of the West, where birth was of little or no consequence. Both were, in a sense, disciples of Jefferson, though neither accepted all the implications of his political philosophy. Tyler adhered to Jefferson's particularism but not entirely to his democratic leanings. Lincoln accepted his democracy but not his particularism.

Both men suffered in reputation from an incorrect popular estimate of their qualities. Tyler's suavity of manner concealed a firmness of character for which he did not always

[2] Our political development has passed through three stages since independence was declared. These three stages might properly be characterized as those of the First Republic (1776–89), the Second Republic (1789–1861), and the Third Republic (since 1861).

receive credit. On the other hand, Lincoln's ineptitude as to
the amenities covered up an inner fineness that is characteristic of high type gentlemen. For this reason Tyler's polish was
often mistaken for softness, and Lincoln's awkwardness for
boorishness. Both of these statesmen are today semimythical
rather than historical characters. In the case of Lincoln tradition has so exaggerated his virtues and covered up his faults
that one of the most human characters in history has been
idealized into a demigod. With Tyler, on the other hand, virtues have been so minimized and defects so magnified that
the reputation of a refined and well-meaning gentleman has
been handed down to us as that of a wicked renegade.

Before the Peace Convention at Washington had ended
its session, a State Convention had assembled at Richmond
(February 13) to determine what policy Virginia should
pursue in this crisis.[3] Tyler had been chosen as a member of
the Convention by his old constituents of the central Peninsula legislative district (composed of the counties of Charles
City, James City, and New Kent and the city of Williamsburg). His election had been made at a district convention
held on January 22, 1861, at Windsor Shades, in New Kent
County. He received the vote of all but eleven of the seventy-
six delegates present, although he was opposed by a prominent Whig of Charles City.

In presenting his name speeches were made in which the
delegates were asked to forget party ties and take advantage
of the opportunity of securing for this important place a
man of such outstanding reputation and character. Isaac H.
Christian, the secretary, also read before the meeting a published statement in which the ex-President had expressed his
views. In this card he had advised that Virginia do all she
could to effect a reconciliation and establish the government
on such a basis as would ensure its future peace and pros-

[3] Richmond *Enquirer*, Feb. 15, 1861.

perity. If this could not be done she should take prompt action looking to secession.[4]

As a large majority of the members of this body and of the people of the district were Old Line Whigs—who had strongly opposed Tyler's policies as President—his election was quite a compliment to his ability, integrity, and soundness of judgment. He was doubtless very much pleased with this token of esteem from his old neighbors and he welcomed the opportunity to serve his beloved State in her time of need, although with seeming modesty he expressed a preference for the comforts of his fireside.[5]

On March 1 the ex-President took his seat in the State Convention.[6] Shortly afterwards he was brought into prominence by a speech in reply to one that had been made by George W. Summers. The latter, who represented a trans-Alleghany constituency and had been a member of the Peace Convention, was opposed to secession and in favor of awaiting the outcome of peace efforts at Washington. Tyler was still quite weak from a recent illness and could not speak long at a time. His reply, therefore, consumed a part of two days (March 13 and 14). He referred to himself as "an old man wearied overmuch with a long course of public service, surrounded by all the comforts that make home attractive, with prattlers on his knee, and a glad light illuminating his household, [who] had been startled by a voice admonishing him of danger to the country, and calling for all the services he could render her. It was the voice of Virginia appealing to a son whom she had nurtured ever since he had assumed the *toga virilis*. . . ."

He pointed out the objections and shortcomings of the amendments proposed by the Peace Convention and contended that there was no prospect of securing their ratifica-

---

[4] Tyler, *Letters and Times*, II, 619–621.   [5] *Ibid.*, II, 579, 621.
[6] *Journal of the Acts and Proceedings of a General Convention of the State of Virginia* (cited hereafter as *Jour. Conven.*), 70.

tion. There was now no hope of a settlement without a dissolution of the old Union. He therefore advocated immediate secession or the adoption of a resolution insisting upon the maintenance of the *status quo* by the Federal government. Virginia was at the crossroads and had no alternative but to choose between the North and the South. "Whither are you going?" he said. "You have to choose your association. Will you find it among the icebergs of the North or the cotton fields of the South?" The material interests of the State are bound up with the South. Her association with that section is worth $300,000,000. "Decide upon association with the North, and you reduce it to two-thirds in value." Our liberties are also in jeopardy. "Brennus may not yet be in the capital, but he will soon be there, and the sword will be thrown into the scale to weigh against our liberties, and there will be no Camillus to expel him." [7] While delivering this speech his voice was so weak that he had difficulty in making himself heard. It was the substance of the address, therefore, that made such an impression on the Convention and the public generally. The editor of the *Examiner* in commenting on it said: "Who would have thought that 'the old man has so much blood in him?'"

The refusal of the Convention to approve the recommendations of the Peace Convention was a tribute to the forensic ability displayed by Tyler on this occasion. This earnest plea won recognition for him as one of the outstanding leaders of the movement for secession. The fine impression created by it was quite pleasing to him. In a letter to Mrs. Tyler he said that his speech and the one delivered by Summers were called "the great speeches of the session." [8]

Tyler did not do a great deal of speaking in the Convention, though he took a deep interest in its proceedings. His votes were cast consistently in favor of secession and for such

[7] The text of this speech is given in the Richmond *Semiweekly Examiner,* Mar. 15, 19, 1861.
[8] Tyler, *op. cit.,* 629.

measures as would aid the Southern cause. Resolutions urging the United States government to recognize the independence of the seceded States and to evacuate the forts within their limits received his support.[9] He also voted for a resolution (passed March 11) commending the Hon. J. J. Crittenden for his able and patriotic efforts in the United States Senate in behalf of a peaceable "adjustment of our national difficulties." [10]

For some time the Union party was able to defeat every proposal for an ordinance of secession that was made in the Convention. Sentiment in favor of secession became predominant, however, when Lincoln issued his call for 75,000 volunteers and asked Virginia to send her quota of these to assist in an invasion of the South. On April 17 an ordinance of secession was passed, to take effect as an act of that day when ratified by a vote of the people on the fourth Thursday of May. It is needless to say that Tyler voted for this ordinance.[11]

After the Ordinance was passed a dramatic incident was enacted by Wise and the venerable ex-President. The account of this event, as given by a young man who witnessed the scene, was as follows:

After the Convention had voted in favor of secession ex-President Tyler and Governor Wise were conducted arm-in-arm, and bareheaded, down the center aisle amid a din of cheers, while every member rose to his feet. They were led to the platform, and called upon to address the Convention. The venerable ex-President of the United States first rose responsive to the call, but remarked that the exhaustion incident to his recent incessant labors, and the nature of his emotions at such a momentous crisis, superadded to the feebleness of age, rendered him physically unable to utter what he felt and thought on such an occasion. Nevertheless, he seemed to acquire supernatural

---

[9] *Journal of the Committee of the Whole* (*Virginia Convention of 1861*), 41–42, 86 ff., 94 ff.

[10] *Jour. Conven.*, 94–97.

[11] *Ibid.*, 155, 158 ff., 164; *Journal of Secret Session* (*Virginia Convention of 1861*), 3–14.

strength as he proceeded, and he spoke most effectively for the space of fifteen minutes.

He gave a brief history of all the struggles of our race for freedom, from *Magna Charta* to the present day; and he concluded with a solemn declaration that at no period of our history were we engaged in a more just and holy effort for the maintenance of liberty and independence than at the present moment. . . . He said that he might not survive to witness the consummation of the work begun that day; but generations yet unborn would bless those who had the high privilege of being participators in it.

Tyler was followed by ex-Governor Wise, who for a quarter of an hour electrified the Convention with a burst of eloquence.[12]

Tyler did not lightly assume the responsibility of urging his State to take this fateful step. In a letter written to Mrs. Tyler on the day before the Ordinance was passed, he said that Virginia was taking a serious risk. But events had pressed so rapidly on each other's heels that submission or resistance was the only alternative left to her. He hoped, too, that the Border States would join Virginia. "If so all will be safe." "These are dark times, dearest, and I think only of you and our little ones. But I trust in that same Providence that protected our fathers. These rascals who hold power leave us no alternative. I shall vote secession, and prefer to encounter any hazard to degrading Virginia." [13]

It was in this same strain of sorrow—but not of regret—that he wrote to Mrs. Tyler next day after secession had been voted. "The die is cast and her [Virginia's] future is in the hands of the god of battle." The contest will be one full of peril, but "there is a spirit abroad in Virginia which cannot be crushed until the life of the last man is trampled out. The numbers opposed to us are immense; but twelve thousand Grecians conquered the whole power of Xerxes [Darius] at Marathon, and our fathers, a mere handful, over-

[12] Jones, *A Rebel War Clerk's Diary*, I, 22–23.
[13] John Tyler to Mrs. Tyler, Apr. 16, 1861; Tyler, *Letters and Times*, II, 640.

came the enormous power of Great Britain." "Do, dearest, live as frugally as possible in the household,—trying times are before us." [14]

Tyler regarded the conflict between the North and the South as a great blunder the chief blame for which must be laid at the door of Lincoln. For by reinforcing Fort Sumter he had brought on a clash which could have been avoided. Lincoln had made the terrible mistake of "having weighed in the scales the value of a mere local fort against the value of the Union itself." He even accused the President of acting not from patriotic motives but from the desire to consolidate behind him his faction of the Republican Party.[15] The South, he implied, was justified in its attack on Fort Sumter. "If the Confederate States have their own flag is anyone so stupid as to suppose that they will suffer the flag of England or France or of the Northern States to float over their ramparts in place of their own?" [16]

In passing judgment on these opinions, one should bear in mind Tyler's theory as to the nature of the Union. As he believed in the sovereignty of the States, he considered that under existing circumstances secession was legal and coercion revolutionary. The breakup of the Union was not caused by the secession of the South but by the nullification practiced by the North. The North by its disregard of the Fugitive Slave Law, its rejection of a decision of the Supreme Court, and the commission of other unconstitutional acts had really destroyed the Union. The secession of the South was only the withdrawal by one party from a partnership the terms of which had already been disregarded by the other. If there was any rebellion involved in this dissolution of the partnership, the rebels were not the Southerners but the Northerners. For the former had been true to the principles of the

[14] *Ibid.,* April 17 [18], 1861; *ibid.,* 641–642; also *John Tyler Papers* (L.C.), IV, 6854–55.
[15] Tyler to —— Patton?, May 7, 1861; *John Tyler Papers* (L.C.), IV, 6862–63.
[16] *The Journal of American History,* V, 628.

Constitution and the latter had violated them. The North
had thus pulled down the house and the South had only left
its ruins.[17]

In keeping with these views he felt that there should be no
war between the two republics. In the Tyler manuscripts in
the Library of Congress is a long paper in Tyler's hand in
which he argues in favor of peace. The document is addressed "to the people of the Northern States" and purports
to come from "the people of Virginia in convention assembled." It is in part as follows: "Before the sword is un-
sheathed, while we yet stand face to face to each other, both
encased in hostile armor, Virginia calls a parley and demands
to know the causes which have impelled you through your
government, to lay aside your former feelings of fraternity
and good will towards herself and her southern confeder-
ates." A feeling of the bitterest hatred toward the South
has been aroused in the masses by ambitious and reckless
demagogues, who have out-Catilined Catiline. A reconstruction of the Union would seem to be impossible, for a union
without the fellowship of good feeling is not desirable. "No,
sir, a confederacy not cemented by affection and confidence
between its members is in the nature of things destined to an
early grave."

Though reconstruction is not feasible, pacification is possible. There might be a treaty or agreement between the
two confederacies providing for favorable commercial intercourse and a satisfactory postal adjustment. This agreement
might be extended into a defensive and offensive alliance
with an understanding as to the quotas of troops to be furnished by both in case of war. After a few years under this
arrangement a feeling of brotherhood might develop and
then modifications of the arrangement could be effected in the
direction of closer association if it were desired.

[17] For Tyler's views as to the nature of the Union, see *John Tyler Papers*
(L.C.), IV, 6881–91.

How much better this would be than the shedding of each other's blood in a senseless and inhuman contest. What man can contemplate with indifference the consequences of such a war as we are now threatened with? The ties which bind families together all severed. Hatred elevated to the endeared place of love and respect. Society upturned from its foundations. Commerce annihilated. Cities sacked and pillaged—a funeral pire [sic] raised high almost as the heavens of the noble, the chivalrous and the brave—families driven out houseless and homeless—this is a faint picture, one not only to be realized in the South but in the North also. . . . But who are they that desire to preside over such a scene? [18]

No better plan than this was offered at the time for settling the difficulties that had arisen between the North and the South. If the principles underlying it had been followed in the attempt to adjust the quarrel, the country would have been spared the terrible suffering that resulted from its greatest national sin. Such an arrangement would have prevented an unnatural and unnecessary fratricidal war and would have offered possibilities for such future co-operation of the sections as economic progress would have demanded. Unfortunately, however, no heed was given to this wise suggestion. The tragedy of the situation was that at a time when Tyler's insight into the future was clearest his sane advice, owing to his lack of influence with Northern leaders, fell on their closed ears with the impressionless impact of Cassandraic prophecies.

While the Ordinance of Secession was before the people, twenty-three citizens of Alexandria sent an open letter to Tyler asking his opinion as to the propriety of voting for the Ordinance in the coming election. He replied at once giving arguments in favor of sustaining the Ordinance. To

[18] *John Tyler Papers* (L.C.), IV, 6897–99.

In the *Journal of American History* (V, 611–632; VI, 73–86) there were published some papers which a Union soldier took from "Sherwood Forest" in 1864. In this list of documents is an article in Tyler's handwriting in which the views given above are elaborated at considerable length.

vote against it would, he contended, be to affirm that the
powers at Washington had a right to invade Virginia. "It is
a fallacy to suppose that the question to be voted on is 'Union
or no Union.' The Union is gone forever, and the Constitution which ordained the Union has been torn up and trampled in the dust, and the real question is, shall we form
another Union in which our liberties and our rights will be
respected and secured, or shall we tamely submit to arbitrary
power?" [19]

After the Ordinance of Secession had been accepted by the
vote of the people (May 23) the Convention ratified the
permanent constitution of the Confederacy, and Virginia
thus became a part of the Southern republic. Before this
(April 25) a temporary alliance had been made between the
State and the Confederacy. Tyler was chairman of the committee that negotiated the agreement of temporary union and
a member of the committee that framed the ordinance of
permanent union.[20]

The Convention met for the third and last time on November 13 and remained in session until December 16, when
it adjourned *sine die*. Tyler was frequently absent during this
last term. This was due to the fact that he was also at the
same time serving as a member of the Provisional Congress
of the Confederacy. The membership of the Convention had
now been considerably reduced, owing to the refusal of most
of the trans-Alleghany delegates to return after the Ordinance of Secession had been adopted. A number of these
representatives of western Virginia were expelled late in
June on account of their Union sentiments and Tyler voted
for the resolutions of expulsion.[21]

An important resolution offered by Tyler (November 18)

[19] Richmond *Daily Examiner,* May 23, 1861.
[20] *Jour. Conven.,* 165, 186–188, 193, 195, 196; Richmond *Daily Examiner,*
Apr. 25, 1861; Richmond *Semiweekly Examiner,* May 10, 1861; *Jour. Conven., Secret Session,* 44 ff., 242, 252.
[21] *Jour. Conven., Secret Session,* 306–307, 310–315.

was one providing for the appointment of a committee to suggest measures for rescuing the waters of Virginia from the enemy. The motion was carried and he was appointed chairman of the committee. The plans as worked out by the committee were adopted by the Convention and sent to the Secretary of War and Commander Maury.[22]

From this brief summary of Tyler's record in the Virginia Convention it is clear that on his return from the Peace Convention he was strongly in favor of Virginia's withdrawing promptly from the Union. If his ideas had prevailed the Ordinance of Secession would have been passed at an earlier date than was the case and would have become effective without waiting for a vote of the people. His son and biographer was of the opinion that the South would have fared much better if this policy had been followed. For if Virginia had passed her Ordinance on March 1 instead of April 17, Maryland, Missouri, and Kentucky (so he contended) would have fallen in line and the pressure on Lincoln would have been so strong that he would not have resorted to war. But Virginia waited so long before acting that this opportunity was lost.[23]

Tyler had reason to be proud of the record he had made in the Virginia Convention. He had won the affection and esteem of his fellow members and had enhanced his reputation as a statesman. John Goode, a prominent member of this body, put him at the head of a list of eleven of the ablest debaters of the Convention.[24] Lewis E. Harvie, who served with Tyler on the committee that arranged the alliance between Virginia and the Confederacy, in a letter to Dr. Lyon G. Tyler, spoke of him in the following laudatory terms: "I esteemed your father as highly as any man I ever knew. . . . He had the entire trust and confidence of every member of the Virginia Convention, and exercised and wielded more

---

[22] *Ibid.,* 44 ff.   [23] Tyler, *Letters and Times,* II, 655.
[25] John Goode, *Recollections of a Life Time* (1906), 51.

influence and control over its deliberations and acts than any man in it." [25]

Tyler's high standing in the Convention is evidenced by the fact that he was nominated for its presidency at the beginning of the third session. He declined this honor, however, as he could not perform the duties of president of the Convention and those of a member of the Provisional Congress without neglecting one or the other.[26]

In June, 1861, Tyler was unanimously chosen by the Convention to a seat in the Provisional Congress of the Confederacy. He was nominated by Scott, of Fauquier County, who referred to him as "one to whose fame no place could add brilliancy; to whose title to popular confidence no place could give strength." [27]

As a member of the Provisional Congress he favored by his votes a vigorous prosecution of the war, but apparently did not offer many bills or resolutions of importance. When he appeared on the floor it was usually to present petitions, memorials, and claims sent to him by his constituents. A few important measures, however, were sponsored by him. One of these was a resolution instructing the Committee on Commerce to inquire into the expediency of a new system of weights and measures.[28] In voting he usually, though not always, cast his yeas in favor of sensible measures and his nays against foolish ones. His opposition to the bill providing for the sequestration of the private property of enemy aliens affords a good example of the wise use of his negative vote.[29]

When the military contest warmed up, Tyler's enthusiasm caught fire and flashed out in a manner that betokened a

[25] L. E. Harvie to L. G. Tyler, May 15, 1885; Tyler, *op. cit.*, II, 668–669.
[26] Richmond *Enquirer*, Nov. 18, 1861.
[27] Richmond *Daily Examiner*, June 22, 1861.
[28] *Journal of the Congress of the Confederate States of America*, I, 492.
[29] *Ibid.*, I, 403. According to his biographer, Tyler urged that a body of cavalry be sent immediately to seize Washington. Tyler, *Letters and Times*, II, 660–661.

more youthful spirit than would be expected from his years. After the Confederate victory at Bethel he offered in the Convention resolutions commending the conduct of the leaders and men in that battle.[30] He was also thrilled and exhilarated by the serious defeat of the Northern invaders at Bull Run. Although he was in bed convalescing from an illness, he called for champagne and made his family and friends drink the health of the Confederate generals.[31] In a speech to the volunteers made at Jamestown on July 4, he declared that he was still young enough for military service and would shoulder his musket whenever Virginia had need of him.[32]

He also shared in that groundless optimism as to the outcome of the conflict which in the beginning was characteristic of too many Southerners. This overconfidence in the military prowess of the South crops out in a letter he wrote to Mrs. Gardiner, his mother-in-law, May 2, 1861. Mrs. Gardiner had expressed concern for the safety of Mrs. Tyler and the children and suggested that they come to her home on Staten Island. In reply he said that Virginia was ready for the Northern forces. She had more troops under arms than the North could arm, provision, and support for a campaign. "The whole State is clad in steel under the command of the most accomplished leaders." [He spoke in the highest terms of General Robert E. Lee] . . . "In a week from this time, James River will bustle with fortifications, and Charles City will be far safer than Staten Island." [33]

Under the permanent constitution of the Confederacy (which went into effect February, 1862) the Congress consisted of two chambers, the Senate and the House of Representatives. At the solicitation of a number of prominent men in his district, Tyler announced his candidacy for a seat

[30] Richmond *Daily Examiner,* June 18, 1861.
[31] Frank Moore, *The Rebellion Record,* 12 vols. (1861–73), III, 11.
[32] Richmond *Dispatch,* July 9, 1861.
[33] *John Tyler Papers* (L.C.), IV, 6860–61.

in the House of Representatives.[34] As early as October 5 he
published a statement in the Richmond *Daily Examiner* indicating a willingness to serve in Congress provided the people of the district should draft him.[35]

Later in this same month the citizens of Charles City
County held a meeting and adopted resolutions endorsing
him for Representative. In response to this action he published an address "to the people of Charles City and the
other counties and cities composing the Third Congressional
District." In this paper he upheld the right of Virginia and
the other Southern States to withdraw from the Union. He
spoke of the tyranny to which the people of the North had
been subjected by a government that had trampled upon the
Constitution and mocked at a decision of the Supreme Court.
"Those very people," he continued, "who basely submit to
a despotism so unrelenting and cruel invade our soil without
a shadow of right, and declare it to be their purpose to force
us back into a Union which they have destroyed under a
Constitution which they have rendered a mockery and made
a nullity." "Surrounded thus and threatened thus, I hold it
as an axiom that no man is at liberty to decline any position
which the State or its people may, by their unsolicited suf-
frages, confer upon him. For myself, while I seek nothing
and aspire to nothing, I will decline no service which Virginia, or any portion of her people, may require me to render." [36]

Except for the insertion of brief notices of his candidacy
in the Richmond papers, he made no further effort to advance his claims to the position. His friends, however, were
active in his support. A number of letters were written to the
Enquirer and *Examiner* advocating his election. Prominent
among these was one contributed by ex-Governor Rutherford [37] and another signed "Vox Populi." [38] These news-

---

[34] Tyler, *Letters and Times,* II, 665.
[35] Richmond *Daily Examiner,* Oct. 5, 1861.
[36] For the text of this address see Richmond *Dispatch,* Oct. 29, 1861.
[37] Richmond *Enquirer,* Oct. 29, 1861.   [38] *Ibid.,* Nov. 5, 1861.

papers also strongly supported him in their editorial columns.

There were four other candidates in the race, the strongest of whom were James Lyons and William H. Macfarland. Both of the latter were Whigs and Macfarland had been an ardent Union man. Owing to this fact, he was strongly opposed by those who had been in favor of secession from the beginning. Tyler, on the other hand, was warmly advocated by this same group. The race was thus, in a sense, a continuation of the contest that had been carried on in the Convention between the Secessionists and the Unionists.

The friends of Tyler contended that his defeat would encourage the North and discourage the South. It would virtually be an announcement to the world that Virginia had snubbed her most distinguished citizen because of his intense activity in favor of secession. This would indicate that the Old Dominion was not loyal to the Southern cause. "It would go abroad to England, and there be trumpeted by our enemies that an ex-President of the United States, who had given the weight of his name and influence to the cause of Southern secession, had not strength enough to be returned to the lower house of the Confederate Congress." [39]

On the eve of the election the adherents of Lyons hit upon a rather clever electioneering idea. Tyler, it was held, should on account of his prominence be reserved for the Senate and, therefore, should not be elected to the House. In answer to this contention "Vox Populi" replied that the venerable ex-President might not, on account of his age, be willing to accept a six-year period of service in the Senate, while he was willing to serve for two years in the House. Besides, his defeat in this election would preclude the probability of his being chosen for the higher position.

The election, despite the activity of the candidates, was an exceptionally quiet one, as the chief interest of the people was in military affairs. In Richmond, the voting was carried on without ill feeling or "any of those promiscuous knock-

[39] Richmond *Daily Examiner,* Nov. 2, 1861.

downs that are sometimes incidental to a political contest." [40]
By the end of the campaign one of the candidates had with-
drawn, and Tyler had an easy victory over the other three.
He received a majority of 215 over all his opponents and
outnumbered his nearest competitor more than two to one.[41]
This plebiscite in his favor showed that the former Chief
Magistrate had finally been restored to his old and rightful
place in the hearts of his fellow Virginians.

Tyler never took his seat in the Confederate House of
Representatives, as he was claimed by death about a month
before the opening of the first session of that body. Early in
January, 1862, he was in Richmond attending punctiliously
the meetings of the Provisional Congress. On the tenth he
was joined by Mrs. Tyler, who had come to Richmond a
week earlier than she had planned. The occasion of this
haste was an unpleasant dream, which left her with a strong
feeling that her husband needed her. Arriving at the Exchange Hotel on Friday night, she found the ex-President
quite well and disposed to laugh at her premonition.

Next day to the numerous callers who came to see them
he appeared unusually healthy and cheerful. On the following morning he felt somewhat indisposed, but went down to
the breakfast room for a cup of hot tea. When he arose
from the table he had a fainting spell and was taken into the
parlor in an unconscious condition. He soon resumed consciousness, however, and walked back to his room. The
physician who attended him pronounced his ailment bilious-
ness combined with bronchitis. As he had frequently suffered
from attacks of vertigo, his friends did not consider his illness serious.

He was now confined to his room, but for several days
was able to receive callers. As late as Thursday he had a
business conference with William C. Rives. The next night

---

[40] Richmond *Daily Dispatch*, Nov. 7, 1861.
[41] Richmond *Enquirer*, Nov. 8, 1861.

he became seriously ill, and passed away shortly after midnight (Saturday morning, January 18). He was conscious up to the very last and realized his end was approaching. His last words were, "Doctor, I am going." When his physician answered, "I hope not, sir," he added, "Perhaps, it is best." [42]

The honors paid to the deceased ex-President were all that his most ardent admirers could have expected or wished. In the Virginia legislature appropriate resolutions were adopted and his character and career were highly eulogized.[43] The Confederate Congress on hearing of Tyler's death adjourned on Saturday, and on Monday devoted the whole day to tributes to his virtues and services.[44]

From Sunday afternoon (January 19) until Tuesday noon the remains lay in state in the hall of the House of Delegates. The funeral services were held at Saint Paul's Church, and were conducted by Doctor Minnegerode and Bishop Johns, of the Protestant Episcopal Church. The casket was escorted to the church and cemetery by a procession of prominent citizens and officials, including the Governor of Virginia, members of the Confederate Congress, and the President, Vice-President, and Cabinet of the Confederacy. In a drizzling rain the cortege marched to Hollywood Cemetery, where on a beautiful knoll by the side of those of President Monroe the mortal remains of John Tyler found a final resting-place.[45]

That the Southern Confederacy had sustained a serious loss in the death of Tyler was the general consensus of opinion among those who knew of his devoted service to the

[42] Mrs. Tyler's account of the illness and death of her husband is given in Tyler, *Letters and Times*, II, 670–672. See also Richmond *Whig and Public Advertiser*, Jan. 21, 1862.

[43] Richmond *Whig and Public Advertiser*, Jan. 21, 1862.

[44] *Ibid.*, Jan. 21, 24.

[45] A good account of the funeral is given in the Richmond *Semiweekly Examiner*, Jan. 24, 1862. For an excellent collection of contemporary accounts of Tyler's illness and death, the funeral, and the eulogies pronounced on him, see Tyler, *Letters and Times*, II, 670–684.

Southern cause. Commander Maury felt that the going of
the ex-President was the greatest calamity that had befallen
the Confederacy.[46] A like opinion was expressed by the Richmond *Examiner*. This newspaper not only had high words
of praise for his recent activities but also commended his
record as President. Few of those who opposed Tyler's administration, it said, could "now be found who will not
frankly admit that John Tyler's Administration was eminently patriotic, statesmanlike, and successful, both in its foreign and domestic policy." [47]

Mrs. Tyler was not able to escape the horrors of war
from which death had saved her husband. Soon after returning to "Sherwood Forest" after the funeral of the ex-
President she and all of her seven children were stricken
with illness, which continued for a long period.[48] In this same
year the Northern forces, advancing up the Peninsula toward Richmond, brought "Sherwood Forest" within the Federal lines. General McClellan, however, stationed a guard
on the plantation to see that no harm befell her.[49] The
withdrawal of the Union troops left her home free for
a while, but later it again fell into the hands of the enemy.
The officer now in charge was not so considerate as General
McClellan had been, and the estate became the prey of a
band of unrestrained soldiers, who, in the absence of Mrs.
Tyler, displayed their vandalism by destroying the pictures
and breaking up the furniture.[50] In the summer of 1864 a
neighbor passed "Sherwood Forest" and was shocked at
the signs of deterioration that were so plainly discernible.
Plowed fields had taken the place of flower garden and
lawn; most of the trees of the beautiful grove had been de-

---

[46] *Official Records of the Union and Confederate Navies,* series I, vol. VI,
633.
[47] Richmond *Weekly Examiner,* Jan. 28, 1862.
[48] Mrs. Tyler to her mother, Apr. 28, 1862; *Tyler Papers* (L.D.).
[49] Interview with Dr. Lyon G. Tyler, summer, 1934.
[50] Interview (August, 1934) with Mrs. Pearl Tyler Ellis, only living daughter of President John Tyler.

stroyed; and the mansion house had been converted into a school for white and colored children.[51]

During the war Mrs. Tyler made two or more trips north to visit her mother. On one occasion she ran the blockade to Nassau and took five bales of cotton with her.[52] Four of her younger children were taken to New York, probably in 1863, where they remained with their grandmother until the end of the war. The oldest son, Gardiner, was placed in Washington College, and so only the two youngest children were left with her.[53]

Throughout this trying period, Mrs. Tyler continued to cherish an interest in William and Mary, which had recently been burned by the Northern soldiers and whose blackened walls were still standing as a grim monument to the former greatness of the old college. Just before going North in 1863, in a letter to the former bursar, she expressed her concern for the future of the college in these words: "Alas! for the institution so beloved by my husband—I trust it will yet arise from its ashes for the benefit of some of our children." [54] It is a pleasure to note that she lived to see this hope realized and William and Mary start on a new career of usefulness with her son (Dr. Lyon G. Tyler) as president.

It was a kind Providence that fixed the date of Tyler's demise. His death came none too soon. Indeed, if he could have been removed from the scene of action a year and a half earlier he would have been spared much in the way of disappointment and suffering. For when the final summons came he was being troubled with grave apprehensions as to the fate of his beloved Southland. He was, however, rejoicing over the restoration of his popularity in Virginia. Thanks to his patriotic efforts of the preceding year, his reputation,

[51] W. H. Clopton to Mrs. Tyler, July 1, 1864; *Tyler Papers* (L.D.).
[52] *Tyler Papers* (L.D.); J. B. Jones, *A Rebel War Clerk's Diary*, II, 9; *Official Records of the Union and Confederate Navies in the War of the Rebellion*, series I, Vol. IX, 270.
[53] *Tyler Papers* (L.D.).
[54] Mrs. Tyler to Tazewell Taylor, Sept. 23, 1863; *ibid.*

which had been so besmirched in the 'forties, had been redeemed, if not cleared. Then too the invasion of Virginia
had been repelled, and the hope of ultimate victory for the
South had placed a rainbow of hope in his evening sky. On
the other hand, the prolongation of his life for a few years
would have brought to his view scenes more harrowing to his
soul than had been the terrible experiences of his Presidential
term. He would have seen thrown into discard the political
and social ideals which had been to him a religion. He would
have witnessed the devastation of large portions of the South
and the seizure of his own estate by the enemy. He would
have had to stand by in utter helplessness when "Sherwood
Forest" was shorn of its beauty, the furnishings of his dwelling broken up, and the mansion house devoted to a use which
he would have greatly deprecated.

APPENDIX A

The Bayard Amendment and the portions of the Fiscal Corporation Bill that paralleled it were as follows:

THE BAYARD AMENDMENT

That the said corporation may establish agencies to consist of three or more persons, or to employ any bank or banks, at any places they may deem proper, to perform the duties hereinafter required of the said corporation as the fiscal agent of the Government, and to manage and transact the business of the said corporation *other than the ordinary business of discounting the promissory notes* (the italics are mine). That is to say, the said corporation shall have the right at such agencies to receive deposites, to deal or trade in bills of exchange, gold or silver coin, or bullion, or goods or lands, purchased on execution, or taken *bona fide* in payment of debts, or goods which shall be the proceeds of its lands, and to circulate its notes. [And moreover, it shall be lawful for the said Board of Directors to convert such agencies into offices of discount and deposites unless the Legislature of any

THE FISCAL CORPORATION BILL

11th Section, 9th Clause. The said corporation shall not, directly or indirectly, deal or trade in anything except foreign bills of exchange, including bills or drafts drawn in one State or Territory and payable in another, or gold or silver coin, or bullion, or goods, or lands purchased on execution, sued out on judgments, or decrees obtained for the benefit of said bank, or taken *bona fide* in the payment of debts due to it, or goods which shall be the proceeds of its lands.

. . . . .

11th Section, 16th Clause. . . . it shall be lawful for the directors of the said corporation, from time to time, to establish agencies in any State or Territory of the United States, at any place or places they may deem safe and proper, and to employ any agent or agents, or, with the approbation of the Secretary of the Treasury, any bank or banks, under such agreements, and subject to such

particular State in which such agency shall be established, shall, at its next session after such agency is established, express its dissent thereto.]

The revisions suggested by Tyler and accepted by Stuart were as follows: The President thought that the capital provided for in the original bill was too large and that ten or fifteen million dollars would be enough. Stuart felt that later a larger amount might be necessary. Accordingly, they agreed upon this formula and it was written down on the margin by Stuart: "Capital to be 15 millions of dollars—to be increased at the option of Congress when public interests require." Tyler also called Stuart's attention to a statute in Virginia against establishing agencies of foreign banks in the State. To provide for this, the President insisted on inserting in the second line, after "or" and before "to employ," this condition: "in case such agencies are forbidden by the laws of the State." The last clause, enclosed in brackets, was to be stricken out. *Cong. Globe,* 27th Cong., 1st sess., 145; Benton, *Thirty Years' View,* II, 344.

regulations, as they may deem just and proper, not being contrary to law or to this charter; . . . Provided, always, That neither the said corporation, nor any agent or agents thereof, nor any bank or banks employed by the same, shall be authorized to discount promissory notes with the moneys or means of the said corporation, but shall employ the same in the business and dealing in foreign bills of exchange, including bills and drafts drawn in one State or Territory, and payable in another.

For the text of the bill, see *Bills and Resolutions of the House of Representatives,* 27th Cong., 1st sess., supplemental volume, Bill no. 14. (This is not to be confused with a bill of the same number printed in the regular volume of bills for that session.)

APPENDIX B

John Minor Botts, of Virginia, a former political ally of Tyler's but now his bitter enemy, made a fierce attack on the President in a speech delivered in the House of Representatives (September 10, 1841). In this harangue he said that in the summer of 1839 he and Tyler had traveled together in the western country for several weeks. Tyler made a visit to Kentucky this same summer to look after his landed interests in that State,[1] and it was doubtless this trip to which Botts referred. In the course of this journey, so he declared, he heard Tyler say in steamboat conversations at least twenty times, "that he was satisfied a bank of the United States was not only necessary, but *indispensable;* that the country could never get along without one, and that we should be compelled to resort to it."[2]

It is not easy to explain this statement without either accepting its truthfulness or else charging Botts with downright misrepresentation. The choice of any other alternative involves the exercise of a broad charity and considerable skill in the art of excuse-making. The fact that Botts was at the time one of the very bitterest of Tyler's enemies weakens but does not destroy the credibility of this assertion. A possible explanation lies in the theory that the impression received by Botts on this occasion as to Tyler's sentiments may have been the result of a misunderstanding. For if Tyler expressed himself on the bank question as cryptically in private conversation as he did on public occasions, there was good reason for a wrong interpretation of his attitude. Besides, Botts seems to have had difficulty on other occasions in understanding Tyler on this point (page 224, note).

While we cannot speak with positive assurance as to what opinions Tyler expressed to Botts in private conversation, we know that no such sentiments as those attributed to him were affirmed in the only public utterance on record made by him on this journey. While en route he received (July, 1839) an invitation from a group of Whigs to attend a public dinner in Louisville. He could not accept the invitation and

[1] Tyler, *Letters and Times,* I, 617–618.
[2] Botts's speech, *Cong. Globe* (Sept. 10, 1841).

471

so wrote a long letter declining it. In this communication he expressed his appreciation of the cordial hospitality that haɑ everywhere been accorded him, and then gave in a general way the principles for which the Whigs were contending. In this statement no mention whatever is made of a national bank.[3]

But even if it be granted that Botts's report of the steamboat conversations was correct and that Tyler had declared in favor of a national bank, it does not follow that the financial institution he had in mind was of the same character as the one afterwards advocated by Clay and his allies in Congress. Nor was any commitment as to future public policy involved in these informal private discussions. Tyler had not then been nominated for the Vice-Presidency, and his off-the-record views as a private citizen expressed informally to a friend could not bind his official course two years later. Neither did this alleged airing of his opinions have any bearing on Tyler's elevation to second place on the Whig ticket. For his enemies have never contended that any of the delegates to the Harrisburg Convention had any knowledge of these conversations before the nomination was made.

A more serious accusation against Tyler was the one charging him with having deceived the Harrisburg Convention by declaring to some of the delegates that he had been converted to the belief in the constitutionality and expediency of a national bank. Such an accusation was made (1842) by Dr. Frederick J. Hill, one of the delegates from North Carolina to the Convention. He asserted that in a conversation with him in Governor Owen's room at Harrisburg, Tyler had declared that his views on the bank question had changed; that he believed the establishment of a national bank to be indispensable as a fiscal agent; and that all constitutional questions ought to yield "to the various executive, legislative, and judicial decisions on the question." Two other men signed a statement (which was published in the New York *American*) to the effect that they had heard the late Governor Owen in 1840 make a similar declaration.[4]

This charge is supported by a long statement (under date of September 10, 1842) signed by eight of the ten men who represented Maryland in the Harrisburg Convention. First on the list of signatories is Reverdy Johnson, whose later prominence would tend to add weight to this accusation. This declaration, they affirmed, rested on evidence that

[3] Tyler, *op. cit.*, I, 617–618.
[4] New York *American*, July 25, 1842.

could not be shaken.[5] Just what this unshakable evidence was the statement did not disclose.

At first glance, this looks like a well-founded indictment. A careful examination of it, however, reveals flaws that tend to invalidate it in the opinion of an impartial judge. The declarations which appeared in the New York *American* under the signatures of two men about whom we know nothing may, I think, in all fairness, be ruled out as evidence. In a controversy as bitter as this one no importance should be attached to the testimony of two obscure witnesses, whose only source of information was an alleged statement of a man not living at the time.

Nor can the assertion of the Maryland delegates to the Harrisburg Convention, despite their respectability, be accepted as unchallenged evidence. In the first place, there breathes from it a spirit of bitter personal and partisan antagonism to Tyler and of the most ardent loyalty to Clay. Besides, it is based on hearsay evidence. Indeed, the wording of this statement is so similar to that of Hill's, especially in the last sentence of each, as to warrant the inference that the former was copied from the latter.

This reduces the real evidence to the affirmation made by Hill. To dispose of it is not such an easy matter. To set aside his declaration on the ground of a misunderstanding would be to ascribe exceptional stupidity to him; and to reject it on any other basis would be to charge him with willful misrepresentation or downright mendacity. And yet the acceptance of this indictment involves the hurdling of a series of difficulties that the impartial student of history finds it hard to surmount. At the outset he wonders why a weapon which could have been used with such telling effect in the controversy between Tyler and Congress should have been kept hidden away for nearly a year after the time when it could have been employed to the greatest advantage. When Botts and his confreres were raking up all the evidence they could find to bind Tyler to a bank commitment it seems inconceivable that they should have overlooked this, their strongest argument. Skepticism also arises from the fact that the one man, Governor Owen, who could have satisfied our curiosity on this point, was not living at the time the accusation was brought in his name, and did not leave any documents (so far as we know) to substantiate the charge.

Furthermore, if Tyler had thus surrendered his States' rights prin-

[5] *Niles' Register*, LXIII, 77–79.

ciples, his nomination to the Vice-Presidency is almost impossible to explain. The theory that he was put up partly to placate the Clay faction but mainly to satisfy the States' rights element of the Whig Party is the explanation usually accepted. Indeed, it seems to me that on no other assumption could his nomination be accounted for. If Tyler had announced at Harrisburg his conversion to nationalism on the bank question, he would have forfeited his only real claim to the high honor to which he aspired. In view of these circumstances, it seems highly improbable that Tyler made the announcement at Harrisburg which was imputed to him.

APPENDIX C

In his speech in the House of Representatives against Tyler (September 10, 1841), John Minor Botts tried to prove that the former had committed himself in the campaign in favor of a national bank. In support of this accusation he quoted from the public prints (though he did not give the names of the newspapers) to the effect that Tyler in a speech at Elizabethtown, Marshall County, Virginia (now West Virginia), was particularly severe on Jackson for vetoing the bank bill. He also displayed a letter from a citizen of West Alexander, Pennsylvania (dated September 2, 1841) which stated that Tyler in speeches at Wheeling and Grave Creek had denounced Jackson in the strongest terms for vetoing the United States bank bill. The correctness of this statement, declared the writer of the letter, could be vouched for by hundreds of witnesses. Botts also read an extract from the Wheeling *Gazette* (August 21, 1841) which represented Tyler as having advocated a national bank in his Wheeling address. According to this clipping, Tyler, while making his speech, "pulled from his pocket an empty purse, and, shaking it at the multitude ridiculed the idea of a metallic currency, abused the Subtreasury, and avowed a preference for 'good United States bank notes.' " [1]

This indictment is too serious to be brushed aside on the assumption that Botts was guilty of willful misrepresentation. It merits a strict examination and a careful comparison with such circumstantial evidence as is available. In appraising this testimony, it should be borne in mind that this attack was made at a time when the fight against Tyler was at its height and that Botts was doubtless the most bitter of all his enemies. It would, therefore, be utterly preposterous to expect a judicial presentation of the case by him under these circumstances.

The indictment brought by Botts rests entirely on indirect testimony, none of which can be checked. The letter used by him and the public prints referred to in a general way cannot be located. The credibility of these unknown witnesses would be difficult to establish. Such hearsay evidence cannot be accepted in the court of history unless it is sup-

[1] For the text of Botts's speech in Congress, see *Niles' Register*, LXI, 74–79.

ported by confirmatory circumstantial evidence. But what circumstantial evidence we have is against the probability of these charges.

If we accept the statement that Tyler excoriated Jackson for vetoing the bill for renewing the charter of the Second Bank of the United States, we are confronted with the great difficulty of reconciling this attitude with the known facts in his career. For Tyler voted in the Senate against the very bill that Jackson vetoed and again voted to sustain the veto. A criticism of Jackson's veto would, therefore, imply a repudiation of his own record on the Bank—a record to which he pointed with approval in a statement made and widely circulated in the last part of the campaign (see page 191 and note).

The issue of the Wheeling newspaper referred to cannot now be found, but we have a newspaper report of the speech made at Grave Creek. In this report Tyler is represented as having dramatically waved an empty purse before the audience and ridiculed the hard money policy of the Democrats. But nowhere in this account is it asserted that he favored or even so much as referred to a national bank.[2]

If Tyler advocated a national bank on the Virginia side of the Ohio he seems to have reversed his position after he crossed the river. For his invitation to Ohio was to attend a convention to be held at Columbus by Whigs who had originally been supporters of Jackson. It was hoped that Tyler's influence would win over to the Whig cause "numbers of those who are withholding their support in order to be fully satisfied that the success of the Whig candidate will secure the triumph of the principles which brought General Jackson into power."[3]

After having accepted such an invitation it is inconceivable that Tyler would have advocated a policy that was anathema to "original Jackson men," the former disciples of the archenemy of a national bank. It would have been in wretched taste, and poor taste was certainly not one of Tyler's shortcomings.

This supposition is borne out by contemporary accounts of two of his speeches on the Ohio side of the river. In the report we have of the two-hour speech he made at Columbus no mention is made of his having discussed the bank question. At St. Clairsville he stated his position with reference to a national bank in answer to questions pro-

[2] The account of this speech was published in the *Marshall Beacon* and reproduced in *The Old Confederate and Old School Republican* for Oct. 22, 1840.

[3] Tyler, *Letters and Times*, I, 624; see also the *Madisonian*, Apr. 25, 1845.

pounded by the local Democratic committee. His reply to the bank query gave the Democratic editor of the *Gazette* the impression that he regarded a national bank as both unconstitutional and inexpedient (see page 191).[4]

[4] St. Clairsville (Ohio) *Gazette,* Oct. 3, 1840.

APPENDIX D [1]

Children of John and Letitia (Christian) Tyler.

1. MARY (April 15, 1815–June 17, 1848) married December 14, 1835, Henry L. Jones, a farmer.
2. ROBERT (September 9, 1816–December 3, 1877) held position in the Land Office at Washington during a part of his father's term as President; in 1844 went to Philadelphia to practice law; later took a prominent part in Pennsylvania politics; was register of the Confederate Treasury; editor of the Montgomery (Ala.) *Mail and Advertiser;* married September 12, 1839, Elizabeth Priscilla Cooper (1819–1896), daughter of Thomas A. Cooper, the tragedian.
3. JOHN (April 29, 1819–January 26, 1896) was private secretary to his father while the latter was President; succeeded Robert in the Land Office; served as assistant Secretary of War of the Southern Confederacy; married December, 1838, Martha Rochelle, of Southampton County, Virginia.
4. LETITIA (May 11, 1821–December 28, 1907) married February 21, 1839, James A. Semple, who served as paymaster in the United States and Confederate navies.
5. ELIZABETH (July 11, 1823–June 1, 1850) married January 31, 1842, William Waller.
6. ANNE CONTESSE (b. April, 1825; lived three months). There was another child that died in infancy.
7. ALICE (March 23, 1827–June 8, 1854) married Rev. H. M. Dennison.
8. TAZEWELL (December 6, 1830–January 8, 1874), a physician, married Nannie Bridges, December, 1857.

[1] For the data on which Appendix D and Appendix E are based I am indebted to Mrs. Lyon G. Tyler, of "Lion's Den," Charles City County, Virginia. A brief statement regarding the children of President Tyler can also be found in L. G. Tyler's *Letters and Times of the Tylers,* III, 216–217.

APPENDIX E

Children of John and Julia (Gardiner) Tyler.

1. DAVID GARDINER (July 12, 1846–September 5, 1927) was a member of the United States House of Representatives (1893–97); judge of the fourteenth judicial circuit of Virginia (1904–20); married Mary Morris Jones, June 6, 1894.

2. JOHN ALEXANDER (April 7, 1848–September 1, 1883) married Sarah G. Gardiner, of New York.

3. JULIA (December 25, 1849–May 8, 1871) married William H. Spencer, of New York, June 26, 1869.

4. LACHLAN (December 2, 1851–January 26, 1902), a physician, married Georgia Powell.

5. LYON GARDINER (August, 1853–February 12, 1935), educator and author; was president of William and Mary College (1888–1919); editor of the *William and Mary Quarterly Historical Magazine* and *Tyler's Quarterly Historical and Genealogical Magazine;* author of a number of historical works, among them the *Letters and Times of the Tylers,* 3 vols.; married first, November 14, 1878, Annie Baker Tucker, daughter of St. George Tucker, of Albemarle County, Virginia; second, September 12, 1923, Sue Ruffin, granddaughter of Edmund Ruffin, noted as a writer on agricultural subjects and as a leader in the secession movement.

6. ROBERT FITZWALTER (March 12, 1856–December 30, 1927) married Fannie Glinn.

7. PEARL (June 20, 1860–   ) married Major William Munford Ellis, a farmer, who was for a time a member of the Virginia Senate. Mrs. Ellis is now living near Shawsville, Virginia.

INDEX

481